THE BIBLICAL RESOURCE SERIES

THE BIBLICAL RESOURCE SERIES

Available

John J. Collins, *The Apocalyptic Imagination,* Second Edition

John J. Collins, *Between Athens and Jerusalem: Jewish Identity in the Hellenistic Diaspora,* Second Edition

Joseph A. Fitzmyer, S.J., *To Advance the Gospel,* Second Edition

Richard B. Hays, *The Faith of Jesus Christ: The Narrative Substructure of Galatians 3:1–4:11,* Second Edition

Colin J. Hemer, *The Letters to the Seven Churches of Asia in Their Local Setting*

Anthony J. Saldarini, *Pharisees, Scribes, and Sadducees in Palestinian Society*

Mark S. Smith, *The Early History of God: Yahweh and the Other Deities in Ancient Israel,* Second Edition

Roland de Vaux, *Ancient Israel: Its Life and Institutions*

The Early History of God

Yahweh and the Other Deities in Ancient Israel

• •

SECOND EDITION

MARK S. SMITH

With a foreword by

Patrick D. Miller

William B. Eerdmans Publishing Company
Grand Rapids, Michigan / Cambridge, U.K.

Dove Booksellers
Dearborn, Michigan

First published 1990 by HarperSanFrancisco,
a division of HarperCollins Publishers

Second edition published 2002
by Wm. B. Eerdmans Publishing Co.
255 Jefferson Ave. S.E., Grand Rapids, Michigan 49503 /
P.O. Box 163, Cambridge CB3 9PU U.K.
www.eerdmans.com
and by
Dove Booksellers
13904 Michigan Avenue, Dearborn, Michigan 48126
www.dovebook.com

Printed in the United States of America

07 06 05 04 03 02 7 6 5 4 3 2 1

Library of Congress Cataloging-in-Publication Data

The early history of God: Yahweh and the other deities in ancient Israel /
Mark S. Smith; with a foreword by Patrick D. Miller. — 2nd ed.

p. cm.

Includes bibliographical references and index.

ISBN 0-8028-3972-X (paper: alk. paper)

1. God — Biblical teaching. 2. Bible. O.T. — Criticism, interpretation, etc.
3. Gods, Semitic. 4. Israel — Religion. I. Title.

BS1192.6.S55 2002
291.2′11′0933 — dc21

2002024467

For my father,
Donald Eugene Smith,
with love

Everything God has made beautiful in its own time;
also eternity God has given into their heart.

(cf. Ecclesiastes 3:11)

Contents

Foreword to the Second Edition

The last quarter century has witnessed a burgeoning of interest in Israelite religion, arising from significant new discoveries, both epigraphic and iconographic, as well as from renewed attention to the roots of monotheism in the Bible. No consensus has been reached on the origins of monotheism in ancient Israel. On the contrary, the distance between perspectives on this question may be farther than it has ever been. There are some who speak with ease of an early polytheism in Israelite religion, while others insist on the priority and generally exclusive worship of the god Yahweh from very early stages in Israelite religion.

No single study of Israelite religion during this period of time has contributed more informatively and constructively to the discussion of the issues than Mark Smith's volume, *The Early History of God: Yahweh and the Other Deities in Ancient Israel.* Its subtitle identifies not only the primary subject matter but the two perspectives that make this book so valuable. It is in a sense a study of the beginning of "God," at least insofar as the contemporary understanding of deity in western traditions reaches back to the God of Israel. Smith's effort is not to write a history of Israelite religion but a history of God, with particular attention to the way in which the understanding of deity that has so shaped Judaism, Christianity, and Islam — with influences far beyond those circles — took shape at the earliest stages. The reference to "the other deities" is appropriate because Yahweh clearly came out of the world of the gods of the ancient Near East, so that kinship relations to these other deities are there from the beginning. Smith is particularly interested in the "other deities" as they found their way into Israelite religion as objects of worship alongside the national deity, Yahweh. But on the way to that analysis, he uncovers the roots of Yahweh and Yahwism and the ways in which the other deities found their way into the profile and character of Israel's god. So the place of the other deities is not simply alongside Israel's deity but within the god Yahweh as well as in differentiation and, at times, conflict with him. The development of a typology of *convergence* and *differentiation,* sketched in the introduction and then worked out in the rest of the chapters, is a major contribution to the possibility of a complex but coherent understanding of the origins of Yahweh and the place that deity had in the extended history of Israel up to the exile. Along the way, Smith is attentive to social context and typologies within Israelite religion, particularly with regard to family and popular religion in distinction from royal and state religion.

The further groundwork laid by this book is to be found in its focus on two aspects of deity that have come to be seen in much larger ways than previously. Already before Smith's work appeared, much discussion — and some heat — had been stirred up over the discovery of texts from two different areas in eighth-century Judah alluding to an "asherah" in relation to Yahweh. The clear connection of that term to the equivalent term in the Bible — with its pejorative disdain — as well as to a goddess well known from second-millennium West Semitic texts has raised the possibility of Israel's god having had a recognized consort in pre-exilic Israelite religion. Smith takes this question up with perspicuity and careful attention to the various views on the topic, including now the most recent studies of the issue. The further dimension of Yahweh's profile that has grown in our awareness, in part because of Smith's own original research on the topic, is his solar character, an issue to which a chapter is devoted in this study.

While this major study of Israel's god has not become outdated, the second edition is a welcome contribution to the further study of Israelite religion and the roots of monotheism. Characteristically attentive to the latest research, Smith has brought his study up to date at many points. Most important is the Preface to the Second Edition, itself a small monograph looking afresh at all the issues discussed in the book from the perspective of the most recent investigations. Even within the main text, however, especially in the notes, Smith has revised without shifting position — an unnecessary move in his case because of the wisdom and judiciousness of his constructive and persuasive view of the origin and nature of Yahweh among the gods of Israel's world. By a careful reading of this book, historians and theologians alike will learn much that they need to know in order to understand the biblical God and the religious world that brought forth the Jewish and Christian scriptures.

PATRICK D. MILLER

Preface to the Second Edition

1. Recent Research on Deities

It has been over a decade since *The Early History of God* first appeared, and many new developments have taken place that have altered the landscape of research on deities. Many new inscriptional, iconographic, and archaeological discoveries pertinent to research have been made. Important new epigraphic finds bearing on deities include several inscriptions from Tel Miqneh (Ekron),[1] and the yet to be published Phoenician inscription from the southwestern Turkish village of Injirli.[2] Some of the more dramatic discoveries of iconography would be the Bethsaida stele depicting the horned bull-deity, the Tel Dan plaques representing a seated-god figure and a standing deity depicted in an unusual fashion, and the Ishtar medallion from Miqneh.[3] Finally, archaeology has further furnished students of Israelite religion with a new arsenal of data to ponder and integrate. As a result of more recent inscriptional, iconographic, and archaeological discoveries, many standard hypotheses are fading and new syntheses are emerging in their wake.

The rate of new discoveries has been more than matched by the pace of secondary literature. Over the last decade the subject of deities in ancient Israel has enjoyed a high profile in the academic world of biblical studies. Many new articles and books have appeared, treating all of the deities discussed in *The Early History of God.* Indeed, hardly a year has passed by

1. For references, see below pp. xxv, xxx.

2. For references, see below pp. 172-73.

3. For the Bethsaida stele, see below p. 84 n. 64; for the medallion, see T. Ornan, "Ištar as Depicted on Finds from Israel," in *Studies in the Archaeology of the Iron Age in Israel and Jordan,* ed. A. Mazar with G. Mathias, JSOTSup 331 (Sheffield: Sheffield Academic Press, 2001), 235-52.

without the appearance of a new volume on the goddess Asherah,[4] and many other deities have received substantial treatments in their own right. Offering broad coverage specifically on deities in ancient Israel are works by well-known European scholars (listed in order by year): O. Loretz, *Ugarit und die Bibel: Kanaanäische Götter und Religion im Alten Testament;*[5] the iconographically oriented synthesis of O. Keel and C. Uehlinger, *Göttinen, Götter und Gottessymbole,*[6] which appeared in English in 1998 under the title *Gods, Goddesses and Images of God in Ancient Israel;*[7] W. Herrmann, *Von Gott und den Göttern: Gesammelte Aufsätze zum Alten Testament;*[8] N. Wyatt, *Serving the Gods;*[9] and J. Day, *Yahweh and the Gods and Goddesses of Canaan.*[10] The apex of this line of research is the landmark volume, *Dictionary of Deities and Demons in the Bible (DDD),*[11] which appeared in a revised, expanded edition in 1999.

Complementing these works are studies devoted to West Semitic religion. These include G. del Olmo Lete, *La Religión Cananea según la liturgia de Ugarit: Estudio textuel,*[12] which was published in English as *Canaanite Religion according to the Liturgical Texts of Ugarit;*[13] a volume edited also by del Olmo Lete, *Semitas Occidentales (Emar, Ugarit, Hebreaos, Fenicios, Arameos, Arabes preislamicos)* with contributions by D. Arnaud, G. del Olmo Lete, J. Teixidor, and F. Bron;[14] and H. Niehr, *Religionen in Israels Umwelt:*

4. For references, see the section 3 below entitled "Asherah/asherah Revisited" and chapter 3.

5. Loretz, *Ugarit und die Bibel: Kanaanäische Götter und Religion im Alten Testament* (Darmstadt: Wissenschaftliche Buchgesellschaft, 1990).

6. Keel and Uehlinger, *Göttinen, Götter und Gottessymbole,* Questiones disputatae 134 (Freiburg: Herder, 1992).

7. Keel and Uehlinger, *Gods, Goddesses and Images of God in Ancient Israel,* trans. T. Trapp (Minneapolis: Fortress, 1998).

8. Herrmann, *Von Gott und den Göttern: Gesammelte Aufsätze zum Alten Testament,* BZAW 259 (Berlin/New York: de Gruyter, 1999).

9. Wyatt, *Serving the Gods* (Sheffield: Sheffield Academic Press, 2000).

10. Day, *Yahweh and the Gods and Goddesses of Canaan,* JSOTSup 265 (Sheffield: Sheffield Academic Press, 2001).

11. *Dictionary of Deities and Demons in the Bible (DDD),* ed. K. van der Toorn, B. Becking, and P. W. van der Horst (Leiden/Boston/Köln: Brill, 1995).

12. Del Olmo Lete, *La Religión Cananea según la liturgia de Ugarit: Estudio textuel,* Aula Orientalis Supplementa 3 (Barcelona: Editorial AUSA, 1992).

13. Del Olmo Lete, *Canaanite Religion according to the Liturgical Texts of Ugarit,* trans. W. G. E. Watson (Bethesda, MD: CDL, 1999).

14. Del Olmo Lete, ed., *Semitas Occidentales (Emar, Ugarit, Hebreaos, Fenicios, Arameos, Arabes preislamicos),* with contributions by D. Arnaud, G. del Olmo Lete, J. Teixidor, and F. Bron, Mitología y Religión del Oriente Antiguo II/2 (Barcelona: Editorial AUSA, 1995).

Einführung in die nordwestsemitischen Religionen Syrien-Palästinas.[15] F. Pomponio and P. Xella have produced *Les dieux d'Ebla,* a resource treating deities not only in texts from Ebla, but also in later corpora.[16] Wide coverage for Phoenician sources has been nicely provided by E. Lipiński in his volume, *Dieux et déesses de l'univers phénicien et punique.*[17]

Some histories of Israelite religion have also appeared, including R. Albertz's 1992 work, *Religionsgeschichte Israels in alttestamentlicher Zeit*[18] (which was published two years later in English as *A History of Israelite Religion in the Old Testament Period*).[19] A more recent entry in this venerable genre is the 2000 volume of P. D. Miller, *The Religion of Ancient Israel.*[20] The 2001 volume by Z. Zevit, *The Religions of Ancient Israel: A Synthesis of Parallactic Approaches,* embodies history of religion research, but this work vastly extends the traditional genre by the depth of its textual, iconographic, and archaeological treatment as well as its theoretical discussion.[21] By the time this second edition of *The Early History of God* appears in print, the field may be benefiting from the survey of Israelite religion by T. J. Lewis published in the Anchor Bible Reference Library (Doubleday).[22] Conference volumes and other collections on Israelite religion in its West Semitic milieu also have made their impact.[23]

15. Niehr, *Religionen in Israels Umwelt: Einführung in die nordwestsemitischen Religionen Syrien-Palästinas,* Ergänzungsband 5 zum Alten Testament, Die Neue Echter Bibel (Würzburg: Echter, 1998). Other important works include: J.-L. Cunchillos, *Manual de Estudios Ugaríticos* (Madrid: CSIC, 1992); W. G. E. Watson and N. Wyatt, eds., *Handbook for Ugaritic Studies,* HdO 1/39 (Leiden/Boston/Köln: Brill, 1999). See also M. Dijkstra, "Semitic Worship at Serabit el-Khadem (Sinai)," *ZAH* 10 (1997): 89-97, which announces I. D. G. Biggs and M. Dijkstra, *Corpus of Proto-Sinaitic Inscriptions (CPSI)* (AOAT 41; in preparation).

16. Pomponio and Xella, *Les dieux d'Ebla: Étude analytique des divinités éblaïtes à l'époque des archives royales du IIIe millénaire,* AOAT 245 (Münster: Ugarit-Verlag, 1997).

17. Lipiński, *Dieux et déesses de l'univers phénicien et punique,* Orientalia Lovaniensia Analecta 64, Studia Phoenicia 14 (Leuven: Uitgeverij Peeters & Departement Oosterse Studies, 1995).

18. Albertz, *Religionsgeschichte Israels in alttestamentlicher Zeit,* Das Alte Testament Deutsch (Göttingen: Vandenhoeck & Ruprecht, 1992).

19. Albertz, *A History of Israelite Religion in the Old Testament Period,* trans. J. Bowden, OTL (Louisville, KY: Westminster/John Knox, 1994).

20. Miller, *The Religion of Ancient Israel* (London: SPCK; Louisville, KY: Westminster/John Knox, 2000).

21. Zevit, *The Religions of Ancient Israel: A Synthesis of Parallactic Approaches* (London/New York: Continuum, 2001).

22. See also F. M. Cross, *From Epic to Canon: History and Literature in Ancient Israel* (Baltimore/London: Johns Hopkins Univ. Press, 1998).

23. These include, by year: *Ein Gott allein? JHWH-Verehrung und biblischer Monotheismus im Kontext der israelitischen und altorientalischen Religionsgeschichte,* ed. W. Dietrich and M. A. Klopfenstein, OBO 139 (Fribourg, Switzerland: Universitätsverlag; Göttingen: Van-

New investigations of polytheism and monotheism include H. Niehr's *Der höchste Gott;*[24] J. C. de Moor's substantial yet controversial volume, *The Rise of Yahwism: Roots of Israelite Monotheism;*[25] N. Wyatt's *Myths of Power: A Study of Royal Power and Ideology in Ugaritic and Biblical Tradition;*[26] R. K. Gnuse's combination of ancient religion and modern theology, *No Other Gods: Emergent Monotheism in Israel;*[27] and my study, *The Origins of Biblical Monotheism: Israel's Polytheistic Background and the Ugaritic Texts.*[28] There has also appeared a popular work on the subject, with essays by D. B. Redford, W. G. Dever, P. K. McCarter, and J. J. Collins.[29] A number of substantial essays have also addressed this topic.[30]

---

denhoeck & Ruprecht, 1994); *Ugarit and the Bible: Proceedings of the International Symposium on Ugarit and the Bible. Manchester, September 1992,* ed. G. J. Brooke, A. H. W. Curtis, and J. F. Healey, UBL 11 (Münster: Ugarit-Verlag, 1994); *The Triumph of Elohim: From Yahwisms to Judaisms,* ed. D. V. Edelman (Grand Rapids, MI: Eerdmans, 1996); *Ugarit, Religion and Culture: Proceedings of the International Colloquium on Ugarit, Religion and Culture. Edinburgh, July 1994. Essays Presented in Honour of Professor John C. L. Gibson,* ed. N. Wyatt, W. G. E. Watson, and J. B. Lloyd, UBL 12 (Münster: Ugarit-Verlag, 1996); *"Und Mose schrieb dieses Lied auf": Studien zum Alten Testament und zum Alten Orient. Festschrift für Oswald Loretz zur Vollendung seines 70. Lebenjahres mit Beiträgen von Freunden, Schülern und Kollegen,* ed. M. Dietrich and I. Kottsieper, AOAT 250 (Münster: Ugarit-Verlag, 1998); *The Crisis of Israelite Religion: Transformation of Religious Tradition in Exilic and Post-Exilic Times,* ed. B. Becking and M. C. A. Korpel, OTS XLII (Leiden/Boston/Köln: Brill, 1999); and B. Becking et al., *Only One God? Monotheism in Ancient Israel and the Veneration of the Goddess Asherah,* The Biblical Seminar (Sheffield: Sheffield Academic Press, 2001).

24. Niehr, *Der höchste Gott: Alttestamenticher JHWH-Glaube im Kontext syrisch-kannanäischer Religion des 1. Jahrtausends v. Chr.,* BZAW 190 (Berlin/New York: de Gruyter, 1990). Cf. the response of K. Engelkern, "BA'AL ŠAMEM: Eine Auseinandersetzung mit der monographie von H. Niehr," *ZAW* 108 (1996): 233-48, 391-407. An English summary of Niehr's work can be found in his essay, "The Rise of YHWH in Judahite and Israelite Religion: Methodological and Religio-Historical Aspects," in *The Triumph of Elohim,* ed. D. V. Edelman, 45-72.

25. De Moor, *The Rise of Yahwism: Roots of Israelite Monotheism,* Bibliotheca Ephemeridum Theologicarum Lovaniensium 91 (Leuven: Peeters/University Press, 1990; 2d ed., 1997).

26. Wyatt, *Myths of Power: A Study of Royal Power and Ideology in Ugaritic and Biblical Tradition,* UBL 13 (Münster: Ugarit-Verlag, 1996).

27. Gnuse, *No Other Gods: Emergent Monotheism in Israel,* JSOTSup 241 (Sheffield: Sheffield Academic Press, 1997).

28. Smith, *The Origins of Biblical Monotheism: Israel's Polytheistic Background and the Ugaritic Texts* (Oxford/New York: Oxford Univ. Press, 2001). For further discussion of how this book relates to *The Early History of God,* see the end of this preface.

29. *Aspects of Monotheism: How God Is One,* ed. H. Shanks and J. Meinhardt (Washington, DC: Biblical Archaeology Society, 1997).

30. For example, by year: W. H. Schmidt, "'Jahwe und . . .': Anmerkungen zur sog. Monotheismus-Debatte," in *Die Hebräische Bibel und ihre zweifache Nachgeschichte: Festschrift*

As all of the new discoveries and research indicates,[31] it is impossible to do justice to the progress of the past decade or so on the topic of deities in ancient Israel. In what follows, I would like to offer an idea of some of the main trends and ongoing problems bearing on research on deities in ancient Israel.

2. Important Trends since 1990

Looking beyond specific works on deities to the wider disciplines informing the study of Israelite religion, several new trends have emerged over the last decade. Apart from new discoveries, I would mention three trends in the study of Israelite religion.

First, the study of iconography and its relevance for Israelite religion has come to the fore with particular force. Already mentioned above is the tremendously important synthetic work by the team of O. Keel and C. Uehlinger, *Göttinen, Götter und Gottessymbole* (English translation: *Gods, Goddesses and Images of God in Ancient Israel*). The field has also benefited from the many important studies on iconography by many figures, including (the late lamented) P. Beck, I. Cornelius, E. Gubel, T. Ornan, B. Sass, and S. Timm.[32] A major "event" on the specific question of Israelite iconography

---

für Rolf Rendtorff zum 65. Geburstag, ed. E. Blum, C. Macholz, and E. W. Stegemann (Neukirchen-Vluyn: Neukirchener Verlag, 1990), 435-47; M. Weippert, "Synkretismus und Monotheismus," in *Kultur und Konflikt,* ed. J. Assman and D. Harth, Edition Suhrkamp N.S. 612 (Frankfurt am Main: Suhrkamp, 1990), 143-79; G. Ahn, "'Monotheismus' — 'Polytheismus': Grenzen und Möglichkeiten einer Klassifikation von Gottesvorstellungen," in *Mesopotamica — Ugaritica — Biblica: Festschrift für Kurt Bergerhof zur Vollendung seines 70. Lebensjahres am 7. Mai 1992,* ed. M. Dietrich and O. Loretz, AOAT (Kevelaer: Butzon & Bercker; Neukirchen-Vluyn: Neukirchener Verlag, 1993), 1-24; T. L. Thompson, "The Intellectual Matrix of Early Biblical Narrative: Inclusive Monotheism in Persian Period Palestine," in *The Triumph of Elohim,* ed. D. V. Edelman, 107-24; A. Schenker, "Le monothéisme israelite: un dieu qui transcende le monde et les dieux," *Biblica* 78 (1997): 436-48; W. H. C. Propp, "Monotheism and 'Moses': The Problem of Early Israelite Religion," *UF* 31 (1999): 537-75.

31. For further listings and discussion, see the review article of O. Loretz, "Religionsgeschichte(n) Altsyrien-Kanaans und Israel-Judas," *UF* 30 (1998): 889-907.

32. See among others, P. Amiet, *Corpus des cylindres de Ras Shamra — Ougarit II: Sceaux-cylindres en hématitie et pierres diverses,* RSO IX (Paris: Éditions Recherche sur les Civilisations, 1992); B. Sass and C. Uehlinger, eds., *Studies in the Iconography of Northwest Semitic Inscribed Seals,* OBO 125 (Fribourg: Universitätsverlag; Göttingen: Vandenhoeck & Ruprecht, 1993); I. Cornelius, *The Iconography of the Canaanite Gods Reshef and Baʿal: Late Bronze Age I Periods (c. 1500-1000 BCE),* OBO 140 (Fribourg: Universitätsverlag; Göttingen: Vandenhoeck & Ruprecht, 1994); and C. Uehlinger, ed., *Images as Media: Sources for the Cultural History of the*

and aniconism was T. N. D. Mettinger's 1995 book, *No Graven Image? Israelite Aniconism in Its Ancient Near Eastern Context.*[33] This work spawned a tremendous amount of discussion, epitomized by the essays in *The Image and the Book; Iconic Cults, Aniconism, and the Rise of Book Religion in Israel and the Ancient Near East,*[34] and an important review article by T. J. Lewis[35] as well as the overview by N. Na'aman.[36] As a result of this work, iconography has emerged as a third major set of data in addition to texts and archaeological realia in the study of Israelite religion.

Second, synthetic archaeological research has reached a new level of sophistication. Examples of important work by archaeologists interested in situating biblical texts in their larger cultural contexts include studies by L. E. Stager[37] as well as J. D. Schloen,[38] D. M. Master,[39] and E. M. Bloch-Smith, including her monograph, *Judahite Burials Practices and Beliefs about the Dead.*[40] In addition, three prominent accessible syntheses produced by senior

---

Near East and the Eastern Mediterranean (1st millennium BCE*),* OBO 175 (Fribourg, Switzerland: Universitätsverlag; Göttingen: Vandenhoeck & Ruprecht, 2000). See also the monumental volume by the late N. Avigad, *Corpus of West Semitic Stamp Seals,* revised and completed by B. Sass (Jerusalem: The Israel Academy of Sciences and Humanities/The Israel Exploration Society/The Institute of Archaeology, the Hebrew University of Jerusalem, 1997).

33. Mettinger, *No Graven Image? Israelite Aniconism in Its Ancient Near Eastern Context,* ConBOT 42 (Stockholm: Almqvist & Wiksell, 1995).

34. *The Image and the Book: Iconic Cults, Aniconism, and the Rise of Book Religion in Israel and the Ancient Near East,* ed. K. van der Toorn, Contributions to Biblical Exegesis and Theology 21 (Leuven: Peeters, 1997).

35. Lewis, "Divine Images: Aniconism in Ancient Israel," *JAOS* 118 (1998): 36-53. See also the essay of B. B. Schmidt, "The Aniconic Tradition: On Reading Images and Viewing Texts," in *The Triumph of Elohim,* ed. D. V. Edelman, 75-105.

36. Na'aman, "No Anthropomorphic Graven Image: Notes on the Assumed Anthropomorphic Cult Statues in the Temples of YHWH in the Pre-exilic Period," *UF* 31 (1999): 391-415.

37. Two particularly seminal studies by Stager are: "The Archaeology of the Family in Ancient Israel," *BASOR* 260 (1985): 1-35; and "Archaeology, Ecology and Social History: Background Themes to the Song of Deborah," *Congress Volume: Jerusalem 1986,* ed. J. A. Emerton, VTSup 40 (Leiden: Brill, 1988), 221-34.

38. Schloen, "Caravans, Kenites, and *Casus Belli:* Enmity and Alliance in the Song of Deborah," *CBQ* 55 (1993): 18-38; and *The House of the Father as Fact and Symbol: Patrimonialism in Ugarit and the Ancient Near East,* Studies in the Archaeology and History of the Levant 2 (Winona Lake, IN: Eisenbrauns, 2001). Another entry in the field is L. K. Handy, *Among the Host of Heaven: The Syro-Palestinian Pantheon as Bureaucracy* (Winona Lake, IN: Eisenbrauns, 1994). See the comments on Handy's book made by Schloen (*The House of the Father,* 356-57) and myself (*The Origins of Biblical Monotheism,* 52-53).

39. Master, "State Formation Theory and the Kingdom of Ancient Israel," *JNES* 60 (2001): 117-31.

40. Bloch-Smith, *Judahite Burial Practices and Beliefs about the Dead,* JSOTSup 123,

members of the archaeological field appeared in 2001: a beautiful volume by P. J. King and L. E. Stager, *Life in Biblical Israel*;[41] W. G. Dever's all too often venomous book, *What Did the Biblical Writers Know and When Did They Know It? What Archaeology Can Tell Us about the Reality of Ancient Israel*;[42] and the somewhat one-sided work of I. Finkelstein and N. Silberman, *The Bible Unearthed*.[43] Already cited above is the monumental 2001 volume by Z. Zevit, *The Religions of Ancient Israel: A Synthesis of Parallactic Approaches*,[44] which deserves to be mentioned in this context because of its massive synthesis of archaeological sources. Another recent entry among archaeological investigation of Israelite religion is B. Alpert Nakhai's *Archaeology and the Religions of Canaan and Israel*.[45]

Underlying the efforts at synthesis is the theoretical discussion about the relationships between primary texts and other remains in the interpretation of ancient cultures. Over fifteen years ago, F. Brandfon wrote a probing piece in which he addressed some of the theoretical difficulties.[46] Yet until relatively re-

---

JSOT/ASOR Monograph Series 7 (Sheffield: Sheffield Academic Press, 1992). See also her essay, "The Cult of the Dead in Judah: Interpreting the Material Remains," *JBL* 111 (1992): 213-24. Bloch-Smith's study of the Jerusalem temple remains the most advanced study available on the subject: "'Who Is the King of Glory?' Solomon's Temple and Its Symbolism," in *Scripture and Other Artifacts: Essays on the Bible and Archaeology in Honor of Philip J. King*, ed. M. D. Coogan, J. C. Exum, and L. E. Stager (Louisville, KY: Westminster/John Knox, 1994), 18-31, which was republished and modified in M. S. Smith, *The Pilgrimage Pattern in Exodus*, with contributions by Elizabeth M. Bloch-Smith, JSOTSup 239 (Sheffield: Sheffield Academic Press, 1997), 85-100. Similarly, her forthcoming study, "Israelite Ethnicity in Iron I" (submitted for publication; my thanks to the author for prepublication access to the article and permission to cite it), advances the current discussion of Israelite identity in the Iron I period. Truth in advertising: see the end of this preface.

41. King and Stager, *Life in Biblical Israel*, Library of Ancient Israel (Louisville, KY: Westminster/John Knox, 2001).

42. Dever, *What Did the Biblical Writers Know and When Did They Know It? What Archaeology Can Tell Us about the Reality of Ancient Israel* (Grand Rapids, MI: Eerdmans, 2001). See below for further discussion of one point in this book.

43. Finkelstein and Silberman, *The Bible Unearthed: Archaeology's New Vision of Ancient Israel and the Origin of Its Sacred Texts* (New York: The Free Press, 2001). See the review of Dever, "Excavating the Hebrew Bible, or Burying It Again?" *BASOR* 322 (2001): 67-77.

44. Zevit, *The Religions of Ancient Israel: A Synthesis of Parallactic Approaches* (London/New York: Continuum, 2001).

45. Alpert Nakhai, *Archaeology and the Religions of Canaan and Israel*, ASOR Books 7 (Boston: The American Schools of Oriental Research, 2001). See also Marit Skjeggestad, *Facts in the Ground: Biblical History in Archaeological Interpretation of the Iron Age in Palestine* (Oslo: Unipub forlag, 2001) (reference courtesy of Tryggve Mettinger).

46. Brandfon, "The Limits of Evidence: Archaeology and Objectivity," *Maarav* 4/1 (1987): 5-43.

cently this critical reflection has not informed the mainstream of the discussion. For example, W. G. Dever has long been known for his important archaeological research and sustained interest in the social sciences.[47] However, in his theoretical stance toward the historically pertinent material embodied in the Bible and archaeological record, Dever shrinks back to an entrenched position of what he himself characterizes as "common sense."[48] Why is this? I would only offer my suspicion that Dever's difficulties stem from a pragmatism (he characterizes his model as one of "neopragmatism"[49]), which evidently eshews philosophy and more specifically philosophy of history. In contrast, in 2001 two well-known figures moved this discussion to center stage. Zevit devotes the first eighty pages of *The Religions of Ancient Israel* to the subject. J. D. Schloen has offered his philosophical prolegomenon on archaeology and historical research in his book, *The House of the Father as Fact and Symbol.*[50] Schloen senses a great theoretical need where Dever assumes a posture of "common sense." Schloen comments: "Tempting as it may be to avoid explicit theorizing, the fact remains that contestable choices are embedded in even the most 'obvious' and innocent-looking of 'common sense' interpretations in archaeology and socio-economic history."[51]

Third, and related, the impact of social sciences has been felt in a stronger way over the past decade. Anthropology and sociology have informed the work of archaeologists and other scholars working in religion. Following older studies by R. Albertz on personal religion and drawing on the classic work of the sociologist Emile Durkheim, K. van der Toorn has emphasized the basic structure of the family for understanding Israelite culture and religion as a whole. His work on domestic and gender issues in religion deserves special note here, especially his impressive 1996 book, *Family Religion in Babylonia, Syria and Israel*[52] and his simpler yet useful 1994 monograph, *From Her Cradle to Her Grave.*[53] Van der Toorn is continuing the analysis of religion from the vantage point of social location. At present, he is preparing a study of intellectual reli-

47. Dever, *What Did the Biblical Writers Know?* 53-95.

48. Dever, *What Did the Biblical Writers Know?* 15, 106.

49. Dever, *What Did the Biblical Writers Know?* 266.

50. Schloen, *The House of the Father as Fact and Symbol,* 7-62.

51. Schloen, *The House of the Father as Fact and Symbol,* 8.

52. Van der Toorn, *Family Religion in Babylonia, Syria and Israel: Continuity and Change in the Forms of Religious Life,* Studies in the History and Culture of the Ancient Near East VII (Leiden: Brill, 1996).

53. Van der Toorn, *From Her Cradle to Her Grave: The Role of Religion in the Life of the Israelite and the Babylonian Woman,* The Bible Seminar 23 (Sheffield: JSOT Press, 1994). See also M. I. Gruber, *The Motherhood of God and Other Studies,* South Florida Studies in the History of Judaism 57 (Atlanta, GA: Scholars, 1992).

gion which examines the understanding of divinity and the world in scribal circles in Israel and ancient Mesopotamia. Influenced by Max Weber, J. D. Schloen offers some initial suggestions about applying the concept of the patrimonial household to the pantheon.[54] I have applied this line of inquiry in order to explore conceptual monisms within Ugaritic and early Israelite polytheisms, and in turn to understand better the background for the emergence of Judean monotheism in the seventh–sixth centuries B.C.E.[55] Similarly, studies of Anat by P. L. Day[56] and N. H. Walls[57] have looked at family structure in order to enhance the understanding of one specific deity, namely the goddess Anat. Another area where social sciences has been influential in the study of religion of Israel and Ugarit involves ritual studies (developed by figures such as Catherine Bell). As only three works informed strongly by this area, I would mention G. A. Anderson's *A Time to Mourn, A Time to Dance*, S. M. Olyan's *Rites and Rank*, and D. P. Wright's *Ritual in Narrative*.[58] Finally, studies of Israelite ethnicity have been applied to both archaeological data[59] and biblical texts.[60]

As a result of studies drawing on social sciences, texts whether biblical or extrabiblical have been situated more within the different segments of societies which produce them. This agenda is hardly new,[61] but the research

54. Schloen, *The House of the Father as Fact and Symbol*, 349-57. See also his article, "The Exile of Disinherited Kin in KTU 112 and KTU 1.23," *JNES* 52 (1993): 209-20.

55. Smith, *The Origins of Biblical Monotheism*, 54-66, 77-80, 163-66.

56. See Day's three articles: "Why Is Anat a Warrior and Hunter?" in *The Bible and the Politics of Exegesis: Essays in Honor of Norman K. Gottwald on His Sixty-Fifth Birthday*, ed. D. Jobling, P. L. Day, and G. T. Sheppard (Cleveland, OH: Pilgrim Press, 1991), 141-46, 329-32; "Anat: Ugarit's 'Mistress of Animals,' " *JNES* 51 (1992): 181-90; and "Anat," *DDD*, 36-43.

57. Walls, *The Goddess Anat in Ugaritic Myth*, SBLDS 135 (Atlanta: Scholars, 1992).

58. Anderson, *A Time to Mourn, A Time to Dance: The Expression of Grief and Joy in Israelite Religion* (University Park, PA: Pennsylvania State Univ. Press, 1991); Olyan, *Rites and Rank: Hierarchy in Biblical Representations of Cult* (Princeton: Princeton Univ. Press, 2000); and Wright, *Ritual in Narrative: The Dynamics of Feasting, Mourning and Retaliation Rites in the Ugaritic Tale of Aqhat* (Winona Lake, IN: Eisenbrauns, 2000).

59. See the discussions of Dever and Finkelstein in the mid-1990s: Dever, "Ceramics, Ethnicity, and the Question of Israel's Origins," *BA* 58 (1995): 206-10; "'Will the Real Israel Please Stand Up?' Part I: Archaeology and Israelite Historiography," *BASOR* 297 (1995): 61-80, and "'Will the Real Israel Please Stand Up?' Part II: Archaeology and the Religions of Ancient Israel," *BASOR* 298 (1995): 37-58; Finkelstein, "Ethnicity and the Origins of the Iron I Settlers in the Highlands of Canaan: Can the Real Israel Stand Up?" *BA* 59 (1996): 198-212. See further Bloch-Smith, "Israelite Ethnicity in Iron I" (submitted for publication).

60. For example, see the essays in M. Brett, ed., *Ethnicity in the Bible* (Leiden/New York/Köln: Brill, 1996); and B. McKay, "Ethnicity and Israelite Religion: The Anthropology of Social Boundaries in Judges" (Ph.D. diss., University of Toronto, 1997).

61. For example, R. R. Wilson, *Prophecy and Society in Ancient Israel* (Philadelphia: Fortress, 1980). See the review of this book by G. W. Ahlström in *JNES* 44 (1985): 217-20.

has become more influential. Accordingly, the perspectives offered in the texts may not represent the cultures as wholes (as presupposed by the long-used constructs "Israelite" and/or/versus "Canaanite"). Instead, texts have been taken as representations of the overlapping perspectives of various social factions, strata, and segments: so-called official versus popular; domestic versus public; elite versus peasant; male versus female. J. Berlinerblau has discussed sociological refinements in these categories.[62] He has also criticized the use of the long-used categories, "popular" and "official" religion.[63] How research uses and nuances these categories and their dynamic interrelationship remains to be seen. Scholars in biblical studies will continue to compare and contrast as well as critique the construction of these categories in other academic fields.[64] As a corollary of these refinements, syntheses in archaeological and textual research have further attempted to situate religious practices or notions known from texts within specific architectural locations as attested in the archaeological record. In addition to Z. Zevit's massive study cited above, I would mention in this vein T. H. Blomquist's 1999 book, *Gates and Gods,*[65] and a recent article by A. Faust on doorway orientation and Israelite cosmology.[66]

62. Berlinerblau, *The Vow and the 'Popular Religious Groups' of Ancient Israel: A Philological and Sociological Inquiry,* JSOTSup 210 (Sheffield Academic Press, 1996); and "Preliminary Remarks for the Sociological Study of Israelite 'Official Religion,'" in *Ki Baruch Hu: Ancient Near Eastern, Biblical, and Judaic Studies in Honor of Baruch A. Levine,* ed. R. Chazan, W. W. Hallo, and L. H. Schiffman (Winona Lake, IN: Eisenbrauns, 1999), 153-70. For a consideration of Berlinerblau's book, see my review in *JSS* 43 (1998): 148-51. See also Berlinerblau, "The 'Popular Religion' Paradigm in Old Testament Research: A Sociological Critique," *JSOT* 60 (1993): 3-26.

63. See the works by Berlinerblau cited in the preceding note. See also N. K. Gottwald, "Social Class as an Analytic and Hermeneutical Category in Biblical Studies," *JBL* 112 (1993): 3-22.

64. For some studies of popular religion in European studies (by year), see N. Z. Davis, "Some Tasks and Themes in the Study of Popular Religion," in *In the Pursuit of Holiness in Late Medieval and Renaissance Religion,* ed. C. Trinkaus and H. A. Oberman (Leiden: Brill, 1974), 307-36; P. M. Vovelle, "La religion populaire: Problèmes et méthodes," *Le monde alpin et rhodanien* 5 (1977): 7-32; H. Vrijhof and J. Waardenburg, eds., *Official and Popular Religion: Analysis of a Theme for Religious Studies,* Religion and Society 19 (The Hague: Mouton, 1979); and K. L. Jolly, *Popular Religion in Late Saxon England: Elf Charms in Context* (Chapel Hill, NC/London: Univ. of North Carolina Press, 1996).

65. Blomquist, *Gates and Gods: Cults in the City Gates of Iron Age Palestine, An Investigation of the Archaeological and Biblical Sources,* ConBOT 46 (Stockholm: Almqvist & Wiksell, 1999).

66. Faust, "Doorway Orientation, Settlement Planning and Cosmology in Ancient Israel during Iron Age II," *Oxford Journal of Archaeology* 20/2 (2001): 129-55.

On the whole, news vistas offered by iconographic and archaeological data have been accompanied by advances in theoretical considerations. Inclusion of a wider range of primary data has been matched by an increase in theoretical considerations and efforts at synthesis. With these changes have come several serious challenges.

3. Theoretical Challenges

While the turn of the millennium has witnessed strong research on Israelite deities and religion,[67] several older difficulties remain. Despite many gains, the basic task remains largely a matter of interpreting and integrating small pieces of evidence drawn from rather disparate sources. In studying biblical texts in particular, scholars are often dealing with literary vestiges of religious practices and worldviews. The larger works in which these older vestiges appear have so refracted the earlier religious history that their recovery requires disembedding them from their literary contexts. This may seem counter-intuitive to many readers of the Bible because such an operation often runs against the grain of the Bible's claims. In my opinion, what vestiges we have provide barely enough material to write a proper history of religion for ancient Israel. In general, it is very difficult to garner little more than a broad picture of Israel prior to the eighth century, and at times the theses offered seem conjectural. Readers missing a clear societal context (or, set of contexts) for the wider developments discussed in this book will be largely disappointed. More specifically, the vestiges of early Israelite religion point to a development which I labelled "convergence" in this book, but these vestiges all too often do not, in my opinion, provide sufficient information to illuminate their social and political background, apart from a circumstantial case made for royal impact. As for the phenomenon which I called "differentiation," I did note some of the ancient players (specifically, priestly lines as well as the writers and tradents behind the book of Deuteronomy and the Deuteronomistic History) in this development, but here too the vestiges offer only a partial view of their larger historical context.

The fundamental difficulty lies in the nature of textual evidence. Because mythic images (and little mythic narrative) have been incorporated and refracted through the textual lens of the various genres, these genres offer only a

67. For further discussion and bibliography, see M. S. Smith, *Untold Stories: The Bible and Ugaritic Studies in the Twentieth Century* (Peabody, MA: Hendrickson Publishers, 2001), 192-93.

glimpse of the larger understanding. Furthermore, the texts have been written so much after the fact or have undergone such long redactional histories that the situation with the various deities is very difficult to gauge. This situation is particularly acute with the Iron I period, but it also affects our understanding of Iron II. Archaeology and iconography, while central to the enterprise, can alleviate only some of the difficulty. Both require interpretation all too often in the face of little or no aid from roughly contemporary textual sources (apart from Judges 5 and perhaps some other small number of texts). As a result, it is generally not possible to recover how premonarchic Israel fashioned its own narrative about its religious identity (reflected in the early archaeological and iconographic evidence).[68] Instead, scholars combine a number of approaches into their syntheses: they rely heavily on the small number of early texts, they add interpretations drawn from the contemporary archaeological or iconographic sources, and they work from later texts that seem (at least, to them) to reflect the earlier situation (Zevit's work is a good example of this situation). The work remains highly inferential. This shortcoming may be overcome in the future by new discoveries, more extensive examinations of the data, and their incorporation into more theoretically sophisticated frameworks.

Recent developments have complicated the task as well. First, newer research has altered long-standing axioms of biblical studies. For example, the older source theory of the Pentateuch (often called the "Documentary Hypothesis") had already come under serious fire when *The Early History of God* first appeared (this is the reason why the conventional sigla for the Pentateuchal sources were given quotation marks). The newer redactional model developed by E. Blum[69] and extended by D. M. Carr[70] on the biblical side, and the studies of redaction in Gilgamesh by J. H. Tigay on the ancient Near Eastern side,[71] have complicated source theory without abolishing it.[72] While the death knell for source theory was sounded often over the course of the 1980s and 1990s, it has not been supplanted by a more persuasive model. Tigay's

68. For this perspective, I am indebted to E. M. Bloch-Smith, "Israelite Ethnicity in Iron I," which draws on the work of S. Cornell, "That's the Story of Our Life," in *We Are a People: Narrative and Multiplicity in Constructing Ethnic Identity*, ed. P. Spickard and W. J. Burroughs (Philadelphia: Temple Univ. Press, 2000), 43-44. Cf. the emphasis placed on traditional narrative in Schloen, *The House of the Father as Fact and Symbol*, 29-48.

69. Blum, *Studien zur Komposition des Pentateuch*, BZAW 189 (Berlin: de Gruyter, 1990).

70. Carr, *Reading the Fractures of Genesis: Historical and Literary Approaches* (Louisville, KY: Westminster/John Knox, 1996).

71. J. H. Tigay, ed., *Empirical Models for Biblical Criticism* (Philadelphia: Univ. of Pennsylvania Press, 1985), 1-20, 21-52, 149-73.

72. See further R. K. Gnuse, "Redefining the Elohist?" *JBL* 119 (2000): 201-20.

work in particular suggests that source criticism comports with what is known for the composition and transmission of ancient texts outside the Bible. Moreover, old-fashioned source criticism and redaction criticism could be combined and modified to order to provide a satisfactory range of models of textual composition that would attend to the interrelated processes of memorization and reading, writing and interpretation (addressing among other questions, Israelite practices of commemoration and memorization, both by scribes and in the wider culture).

These processes were addressed in an incipient way in the first edition of *The Early History of God* (chapter 6), but several further points about orality and scribalism have been made recently, for example by S. A. Niditch and by R. F. Person, Jr.[73] Studies also stress literacy, for example the otherwise widely varying treatments by M. D. Coogan, J. L. Crenshaw, and M. Haran.[74] M. Fishbane has nicely noted the role of interpretation in scribal practice.[75] It is the intersection of literacy, orality, interpretation, collective memory, and modes of memorization that underlay scribal praxis. Indeed, the ingredients insufficiently represented in the discussion of the praxis of ancient Israelite textual composition are, to my mind, cultural memory and memorization. The former has been addressed increasingly in recent years,[76] while the latter continues to be largely neglected. In contrast, memory and memorization are nicely noted in C. Hezser's work, *Jewish Literacy in Roman Palestine*[77] and beautifully emphasized by M. Carruthers in her two studies of medieval culture.[78] The constellation of scribal practices, including memorization, are attested for Israel in the Lachish letters.[79] As only one working model, it might

73. Niditch, *Oral World and Written Word: Ancient Israelite Literature* (Louisville, KY: Westminster/John Knox, 1996); Person, Jr., "The Ancient Israelite Scribe as Performer," *JBL* 117 (1998): 601-9.

74. Coogan, "Literacy and the Formation of Biblical Literature," in *Realia Dei: Essays in Archaeology and Biblical Interpretation in Honor of Edward F. Campbell, Jr., at His Retirement,* ed. P. H. Williams, Jr., and T. Hiebert, Scholars Press Homage Series 23 (Atlanta, GA: Scholars, 1999), 47-61; Crenshaw, *Education in Ancient Israel: Across the Deadening Silence,* The Anchor Bible Reference Library (New York: Doubleday, 1998); Haran, "On the Diffusion of Literacy and Schools in Ancient Israel," in *Congress Volume: Jerusalem 1986,* ed. J. A. Emerton, 81-95.

75. Fishbane, *Biblical Interpretation in Ancient Israel* (Oxford: Clarendon, 1985).

76. See the works cited in n. 93 below.

77. Hezser, *Jewish Literacy in Roman Palestine,* Texts and Studies in Ancient Judaism 81 (Tübingen: Mohr Siebeck, 1998), 99-100, 427-29.

78. Carruthers, *The Book of Memory: A Study of Memory in Medieval Culture,* Cambridge Studies in Medieval Literature 10 (Cambridge/New York: Cambridge Univ. Press, 1990); and *The Craft of Thought: Meditation, Rhetoric, and the Making of Images, 400-1200,* Cambridge Studies in Medieval Literature 14 (Cambridge/New York: Cambridge Univ. Press, 1998).

79. Lachish 3, 4, 5, 6, conveniently transliterated, translated, and discussed by D. Pardee,

be assumed that such a scribal praxis informed late monarchic Judean (and perhaps later) textual production that underlies those narrative works regarded later as biblical (Pentateuch and Deuteronomistic History). From the eighth century (Isaiah) through the sixth century (Jeremiah), prophetic accounts suggest a further range of models combining reading, writing, and interpretation,[80] while some sixth-century prophecy (Second Isaiah) shows an orientation around reading, interpretation, and writing.[81] Liturgical models combining memory and writing perhaps in yet other modes can be discerned in the diachronic reuse of texts, such as Psalm 29:1-2.[82] An example of priestly reading, writing, and interpretation of prior tradition and texts may be found in Genesis 1:1–2:3.[83] In addition to these models, multiple editions of biblical works proposed through text-critical analysis offer further perspective on the practices underlying some aspects of scribal compositions and transmission.[84] Well beyond the scope of this discussion, ultimately a successful history of religion will have to include working out a history of models of textual production in ancient Israel (along with criteria for assessing them), locate the witnesses to those models within their social settings, interrelate those witnesses and settings, and synthesize what information they provide about Israelite religion.

Second, literary study with little or no interest in diachronic development (coupled with a de-emphasis on ancient langages apart from Hebrew) has tended to minimize the significance of ancient Near Eastern contexts of Israelite culture, not to mention Israelite history in general and the history of Is-

---

in D. Pardee et al., *Handbook of Ancient Hebrew Letters: A Study Edition,* SBL Sources for Biblical Study 15 (Chico, CA: Scholars, 1982), 81-103.

80. The complexity of the interrelated features of orality, reading, writing, and interpretation has been underscored for prophecy in the book, *Writings and Speech in Israelite and Ancient Near Eastern Prophecy,* ed. E. Ben-Zvi and M. H. Floyd, SBL Symposium 10 (Atlanta, GA: Society of Biblical Literature, 2000). See also A. Schart, "Combining Prophetic Oracles in Mari Letters and Jeremiah 36," *JANES* 23 (1995): 75-93; and K. van der Toorn, "Old Babylonian Prophecy between the Oral and the Written," *JNWSL* 24 (1988): 55-70.

81. For some initial comments about Second Isaiah as a written composition, see below chapter 6, section 4. For reading, writing, and interpretation in Second Isaiah, see the important study of B. D. Sommer, *A Prophet Reads Scripture: Allusion in Isaiah 40–66,* Contraversions. Jews and Other Differences (Stanford: Stanford Univ. Press, 1998). Daniel 9 is a written representation of the model of inspired interpretation of the explicitly named prophetic figure of Jeremiah.

82. See the important article of H. L. Ginsberg, "A Strand in the Cord of Hebraic Psalmody," *EI* 9 (1969 = W. F. Albright Volume): 45-50.

83. I have discussed this idea in an essay entitled "Reading, Writing and Interpretation: Thoughts on Genesis 1 as Commentary" (unpublished paper).

84. See the survey in E. Tov, *Textual Criticism of the Hebrew Bible* (Minneapolis: Fortress; Assen/Maastricht: Van Gorcum, 1992), 313-50.

raelite religion specifically. To name only a handful of subdisciplines applied to the Hebrew Bible, structuralism, reader-response theory, ideological criticism, and postmodern readings have contributed to a devaluation of diachronic research, including the history of the religion of Israel.[85] While each wave of atomism within the biblical field seems to be met by an opposing wave of interdisciplinary research (which often reintegrates what has been become atomized), the sustained disassociation of the study of biblical literature from Israelite history complicates the situation. However, the neglect has cut in the other direction at the same time. The full impact of literary study, which has all too often been neglected in history of religion research (including my own),[86] has yet to be felt in syntheses of Israelite religion.

Third, and related, the study of Israelite history in particular has become more problematic over the last decade. Refined analyses reveal data which do not fit into traditional large-scale syntheses. The common models for the origins of Israel in the land (conquest, infiltration, and peasant-revolt) have all been inundated by evidence derived from surveys and excavations. Regional variations call into question the viability of a single master thesis to explain the situation on the ground. The discussions of the Late Bronze–Iron I and the Iron I–Iron II transitions have grown in complexity.[87] Serious doubts as to the historicity of the biblical descriptions of the United Monarchy have been increasingly voiced by I. Finkelstein and others; and despite strong efforts by archaeologists such as Stager and Dever in the United States and A. Mazar and A. Ben-Tor in Israel, defending the historicity of biblical events purporting to date to the tenth century has become a more difficult proposition. Pertinent studies largely from the textual side include two recent books bearing on the figure of David, produced by B. Halpern and S. L. McKenzie.[88] These attempt to sift the myth from the life of the historical Da-

85. For surveys, see D. Jasper, "Literary Readings of the Bible," in *The Cambridge Campanion to Biblical Interpretation,* ed. J. Barton (Cambridge: Cambridge Univ. Press, 1998), 21-34; and in the same volume R. P. Carroll, "Poststructuralist Approaches: New Historicism and Postmodernism," 50-66.

86. Exceptions are the works of S. B. Parker, *The Pre-Biblical Narrative Tradition,* SBL Resources for Biblical Study 24 (Atlanta, GA: Scholars, 1989); and *Stories in Scripture and Inscriptions: Comparative Studies on Narratives in Northwest Semitic Inscriptions and the Hebrew Bible* (New York/Oxford: Oxford Univ. Press, 1997).

87. For the Late Bronze–Iron I transition, see the references on p. 21 n. 9. For the Iron I–Iron II transition, see p. 15 n. 24.

88. Halpern, *David's Secret Demons: Messiah, Murderer, Traitor, King* (Grand Rapids, MI: Eerdmans, 2001); and McKenzie, *King David: A Biography* (Oxford/New York: Oxford Univ. Press, 2000). See also W. Schniedewind, *Society and the Promise to David: The Reception History of 2 Samuel 7:1-17* (New York/Oxford: Oxford Univ. Press, 1999).

vid; no simple task. Despite the challenges, these works are remarkably sane, and they would suggest the plausibility of historical recontruction based on critical analyses of biblical texts.

The historical questions remain problematic, even without introducing the further issues involved in responding to the challenges posed by figures such as P. Davies, N. P. Lemche, and T. Thompson.[89] Their efforts to locate biblical texts generally in the Persian or even the Hellenistic period pass over many linguistic and historical difficulties of their own. A recent entry in the discussion of the Iron Age is the dissertation of K. Wilson directed by P. K. McCarter.[90] Wilson disputes the historical value of the Shishak list which he argues does not provide evidence for a specific campaign by Shishak; instead, the list represents a compilation of sites designed to represent Shishak as a world-conqueror. Wilson's argument does not undermine the biblical evidence concerning Shishak's campaign, which could well have taken place as 1 Kings 14:25 claims, but his argument would preclude using the Shishak list in the discussion of correlating destruction levels at archaeological sites with the Shishak list itself. As a result, a major linchpin in tenth-century chronology falls.

More fundamental questions surrounding the definition of "history" and the Bible underlie these discussions. Biblical historians agree that the biblical narratives of the past constitute history, but their disagreement over the definition of history raises serious problems. For example, both B. Halpern and M. Brettler treat the Deuteronomistic History and Chronicles as history,[91] but they strongly differ in their understanding as to how these biblical works constitute history. Brettler rejects Halpern's view of the biblical historians as having an antiquarian interest in using sources to recover a past that they believed was the case. Instead, Brettler prefers a broader definition of history as a narrative about the past. Brettler further notes the didactic function of these works, not to mention the literary tropes that help to advance

89. A convenient listing of their works can be found in Dever, *What Did the Biblical Writers Know?* However, I do not condone the rhetoric in this work; indeed, it is the very sort of rhetoric which he deplores in their publications. See also Dever, "Histories and Nonhistories of Ancient Israel," *BASOR* 316 (1999): 89-105.

90. Wilson, "The Campaign of Pharaoh Shoshenq I into Palestine" (Ph.D. diss., The Johns Hopkins Univ. Press, 2001).

91. For example, see Brettler, *The Creation of History in Ancient Israel* (London/New York: Routledge, 1995); and Halpern, *The First Historians: The Hebrew Bible and History* (San Francisco: Harper & Row, 1988). See also F. A. J. Nielsen, *The Tragedy in History: Herodotus and the Deuteronomistic History,* JSOTSup 251, Copenhagen International Seminar 4 (Sheffield: Sheffield Academic Press, 1997).

their teaching goals. Given the difference between Halpern and Brettler over what constitutes history, one may ask if a basic problem afflicts their operating assumption that biblical narratives about the past are history. Without exhausting the considerations that go into whether these works are history, it seems worthwhile to examine the degree to which biblical presentations of the past shape the past to conform to present concerns, or in other words, how cultural memory is expressive of present vicissitudes. Brettler nicely explores this function of collective memory, and his definition does not distinguish between history and a narrative about the past produced by the collective memory of a tradition.

Where biblical scholars such as Halpern and Brettler maintain that biblical works such as the Deuteronomistic History (Joshua through Kings) and the books of Chronicles constitute history, I have my doubts about the scope of this characterization. Even in the case of the books of Chronicles, where the use of sources is clear, their author(s) may have inherited such source material from religious tradition and used that source material not simply to create a narration presenting the past, but one whose primary function was to celebrate the past as an antecedent to the present. The historical-looking work of Chronicles seems to lack some assessment of sources, and it shows a deeply commemorative function in its narrative of the past, specifically in structuring the past in terms of the present.[92] Unlike Brettler, I would probably put history and collective memory in narrative forms on a spectrum, perhaps with the crucial distinction lying not simply in using prior sources or an author's interest in the past as such (*pace* Halpern), but in an author's work being informed by some sense of what goes into the representation of the past as past.[93] In any case, this discussion indicates that these theoretical questions impinging on the Bible and its representations of the past necessarily involve a number of critical issues which

92. See Brettler, *The Creation of History in Ancient Israel,* 20-47, esp. 46.

93. On memory in the Bible, see (by year): B. S. Childs, *Memory and Tradition in Israel* (London: SCM, 1962); W. Schottroff, *"Gedenken" im Alten Orient und im Alten Testament,* 2d ed., WMANT 15 (Neukirchen-Vluyn: Neukirchener Verlag, 1967); D. Fleming, "Mari and the Possibilities of Biblical Memory," *RA* 92 (1998): 41-78. For two recent studies on collective memory, see M. Brettler, "Memory in Ancient Israel," in *Memory and History in Christianity and Judaism,* ed. M. Signer (Notre Dame, IN: Univ. of Notre Dame Press, 2001), 1-17; and R. S. Hendel, "The Exodus in Biblical Memory," *JBL* 120 (2001): 601-22. Brettler and Hendel are influenced by Y. H. Yerushalmi, *Zakhor: Jewish History and Jewish Memory* (Seattle/London: Univ. of Washington Press, 1982; rev. ed., 1989). Informed more by *Annales* figures writing on cultural memory, I am presently preparing a book-length study of memory and ancient Israelite culture and religion. The praxes of orality and scribalism mentioned above play a highly significant role in receiving, transmitting, and generating collective memory.

have yet to be assimilated into the discussion (with the partial exception of Zevit's *The Religions of Ancient Israel*).

Fourth and finally, use of the Ugaritic texts for the study of Israelite religion has evolved since the first edition of *The Early History of God.* Since 1990, comparison of Ugaritic and biblical texts has come to be viewed in more complex terms. Scholars are well beyond the situation of "pan-Ugariticism" in biblical studies derided in earlier decades. The high-water mark of Ugaritic-biblical parallels was reached with the three volumes of *Ras Shamra Parallels*[94] and the trend ebbed around 1985. Simplistic drawing of Ugaritic and biblical parallels has passed from fashion. Morever, a certain disjunction has taken place between Ugaritic and biblical studies, while more attention has been paid to locating Ugarit within its larger societal and ecological context. The French archaeological team has produced a whole new awareness of ancient Ugaritic culture. Wider interests of industry and society have been treated by the French team, and by other scholars.[95] A related development involves situating Ugaritic and Ugarit within their larger ancient Syrian context, as known at other sites, some known for decades (Mari), others more recently (Emar, Munbaqa/Tel Ekalte, ʿAin Dara, Suhu).[96] The field will also continue to be aided by Amorite material.[97]

The field of Ugaritic studies no longer holds, nor should it hold, to an unilinear focus aimed toward ancient Israel or the Bible. All these discoveries have forced scholars interested in situating the Bible in its wider West Semitic context to take a longer (perhaps more scenic) route in traveling the historical and cultural distances between Ugarit and ancient Israel.[98] Such an intellec-

94. *Ras Shamra Parallels I-II,* ed. L. Fisher, AnOr 49-50 (Rome: Pontifical Biblical Institute, 1972, 1975); *Ras Shamra Parallels III,* ed. S. Rummel, AnOr 51 (Rome: Pontifical Biblical Institute, 1981).

95. For example, S. Ribichini and P. Xella, *La terminologia dei tessili nei testi di Ugarit,* Collezione di Studi Fenici 20 (Rome: Consiglio Nazionale delle Ricerche, 1985).

96. See R. S. Hess, "A Comparison of the Ugarit, Emar and Alalakh Archives," in *Ugarit: Religion and Culture; Proceedings of the International Colloquium. Edinburgh July 1994,* ed. N. Wyatt, UBL 12 (Münster: Ugarit-Verlag, 1996), 75-84. See also in the same volume M. Dietrich, "Aspects of the Babylonian Impact on Ugaritic Literature and Religion," 33-48.

97. See H. Huffmon, *Amorite Personal Names in the Mari Texts* (Baltimore: Johns Hopkins Univ. Press, 1965); I. J. Gelb, *A Computer-Aided Analysis of Amorite,* Assyriological Studies 21 (Chicago/London: Univ. of Chicago Press, 1980); and R. Zadok, "On the Amorite Material from Mesopotamia," in *The Tablet and the Scroll: Near Eastern Studies in Honor of William H. Hallo,* ed. M. E. Cohen, D. C. Snell, and D. B. Weisberg (Bethesda, MD: CDL Press, 1993), 315-33.

98. The issues are put nicely by D. Pardee, "Background to the Bible: Ugarit," in *Ebla to Damascus: Art and Archaeology of Ancient Syria* (Washington, DC: Smithsonian Institution, 1985), 253-58.

tual situation will in no way diminish the important and deep cultural and linguistic relations between the Ugaritic and biblical texts; instead, such relations are now understood more richly. Commenting on the comparison of the Ugaritic texts and the Bible, Keel and Uehlinger are, technically speaking, right to state that the Ugaritic texts "are not primary sources for the religious history of Canaan and Israel,"[99] but such a view hardly precludes seeing the Ugaritic texts as providing some of the larger background behind the development of Israelite religion. Although it is quite correct to note the temporal, geographical, and cultural distance between the Ugaritic and biblical texts,[100] it is precisely the differences within their larger similarities that sharpen scholarly understanding of Israelite religion, in particular its differentiation from the larger West Semitic culture of which the Ugaritic texts constitute the single greatest extra-biblical textual witness. Again this issue, like the others mentioned above in this section, stands in need of further investigation and refinement.

It is clear from consideration of these challenges that the field is moving forward on several fronts that include both the collection and assessment of new data as well as the consideration of theory from various quarters. History of religion work for ancient Israel remains largely in the stage of assembling and examining pertinent data, with steps having been taken toward satisfactory theoretical frameworks for specific topics within the larger enterprise. At this point, a more overarching theoretical framework for the larger enterprise still has yet to appear. Perhaps because of its historical roots in theology, the field of Israelite religion (not to mention biblical studies generally) remains one that does not generate its own general theoretical contribution to the humanities or social sciences. Yet the successes of the recent decade should not be minimized. Increasing complexity in the patterns of religous concepts and their development has clearly marked more recent research. The factors that go into the conceptualization of Israelite religion as an intellectual project have grown enormously.

4. Asherah/asherah Revisited

I would like to take this opportunity to revisit briefly this area of the first edition of *The Early History of God,* first because the chapter on this subject received substantial criticism and because the field has maintained strong inter-

99. Keel and Uehlinger, *Gods, Goddesses and Images of God,* 396.

100. Keel and Uehlinger, *Gods, Goddesses and Images of God,* 395-96.

est in Asherah studies.[101] In the meantime, the main base of data has changed in two respects. The first is the addition of the newer inscriptional material from Tel Miqneh (Ekron).[102] The second is the increase in iconographic evidence brought to bear on the discussion. At the forefront of this effort has been O. Keel and C. Uehlinger's important iconographic work in their book, *Gods, Goddesses and Images of God,* and in Keel's 1998 *Goddesses and Trees, New Moon and Yahweh.*[103]

At this point the range of viewpoints about Asherah as a goddess in Israel is perhaps best represented on one side by S. M. Olyan's acceptance of the goddess in his important 1988 monograph, *Asherah and the Cult of Yahweh in Israel,* and on the other by C. Frevel's considerably circumscribed and extensive 1995 study, *Aschera und der Ausschliesslichkeitanspruch YHWHs.*[104] (Keel and Uehlinger's *Gods, Goddesses and Images of God*[105] combines the two views, namely that the symbol of the asherah lost its associations to the goddess by the eighth century, only to regain them by the second half of the seventh century.) Since the first edition of *The Early History of God,* several other studies have appeared. S. Ackerman has also situated the issues against the larger issue of popular religion in ancient Israel.[106] She has made a further case for a royal ideology paralleling Asherah and the queen mother in ancient Judah.[107] S. A. Wiggins has surveyed the comparative evidence, and his work

101. See the books mentioned below. For partial surveys (by year), see S. A. Wiggins, "Asherah Again: Binger's Asherah and the State of Asherah Studies," *JNWSL* 24 (1998): 231-40; J. A. Emerton, "'Yahweh and his Asherah': the Goddess or Her Symbol," *VT* 49 (1999): 315-37; and J. M. Hadley, *The Cult of Asherah in Ancient Israel and Judah: Evidence for a Hebrew Goddess,* University of Cambridge Oriental Publications 57 (Cambridge: Cambridge Univ. Press, 2001), 11-37. See also W. G. E. Watson, "The Goddesses of Ugarit: A Survey," *Studi epigrafici e linguistici* 10 (1993): 47-59.

102. Gitin, "Seventh Century BCE cultic elements at Ekron," in *Biblical Archaeology Today, 1990: Proceedings of the Second International Congress on Biblical Archaeology* (Jerusalem: Israel Exploration Society/The Israel Academy of Sciences and Humanities, 1993), 248-58. See further the discussion below.

103. Keel and Uehlinger, *Gods, Goddesses and Images of God,* 228-48, 332, 369-70; Keel, *Goddesses and Trees, New Moon and Yahweh: Ancient Near Eastern Art and the Hebrew Bible,* JSOTSup 262 (Sheffield: Sheffield Academic Press, 1998). See also U. Hübner, "Der Tanz um die Ascheren," *UF* 24 (1992): 121-32.

104. Olyan, *Asherah and the Cult of Yahweh in Israel,* SBLMS 34 (Atlanta, GA: Scholars, 1988); Frevel, *Aschera und der Ausschliesslichkeitanspruch YHWHs,* BBB 94, two vols. (Weinheim: Beltz Athenäum, 1995).

105. Keel and Uehlinger, *Gods, Goddesses and Images of God,* 228-48, 332, 369-70.

106. Ackerman, *Under Every Green Tree: Popular Religion in Sixth-Century Judah,* HSM 46 (Atlanta: Scholars, 1992).

107. Ackerman, "The Queen Mother and the Cult in Ancient Israel," *JBL* 112 (1993):

offers a critique of what he regards as the excessive claims made about the evidence for Asherah.[108] There is also John Day's treatment of the issues in his book, *Yahweh and the Gods and Goddesses of Canaan.* Additional Mesopotamian material has been supplied by P. Merlo's 1998 work, *La dea Ašratum — Aṯiratu — Ašera.*[109] The field now enjoys the benefit of having J. M. Hadley's fine study, entitled *The Cult of Asherah in Ancient Israel and Judah: Evidence for a Hebrew Goddess.* M. Dijkstra and M. C. A. Korpel have addressed the question pro and con in a recent volume of essays.[110]

At this point most commentators believe that Asherah was a goddess in monarchic Israel (e.g., Ackerman, Binger, Day, Dever, Dijkstra, Edelman, Hadley, Handy, Keel and Uehlinger, Loretz, Merlo, Niehr, Olyan, Petty, Wyatt, Xella, Zevit, as well as NJPS at 1 Kings 15:13). Some do not (e.g., Cross,[111] Frevel, Korpel, Tigay; cf. Emerton's very cautious formulation, McCarter's asherah as Yahweh's hypostasis, Miller's nuanced position of secondary divinization of the symbol). The first edition of *The Early History of God*[112] concluded that the evidence was insufficient to demonstrate that Asherah was a goddess in Israel during the monarchy and asked whether the symbol of the asherah lost its original association with the goddess at that point. I would not state categorically that there was no goddess in monarchic Israel, but would stress that the data marshalled in support of the goddess in this period are more problematic than advocates have suggested. *The Early History of God* offers arguments why Asherah may not have enjoyed cultic devotion in the period of the monarchy despite the apparently strong evidence from Kuntillet ʿAjrud and in 1 Kings 15 and 18, 2 Kings 21 and 23. Advocates for

---

385-401. The reasoning has been criticized by B. Halpern, "The New Names of Isaiah 62:4: Jeremiah's Reception in the Restoration and the Politics of 'Third Isaiah,'" *JBL* 117 (1998): 640 n. 46.

108. Wiggins, "The Myth of Asherah: Lion Lady and Serpent Goddess," *UF* 23 (1991): 383-94; *A Reassessment of 'Asherah': A Study According to the Textual Sources of the First Two Millennia* B.C.E., AOAT 235 (Kevelaer: Butzon & Bercker; Neukirchen-Vluyn: Neukirchener Verlag, 1993); "Of Asherahs and Trees: Some Methodological Questions," *Journal of Ancient Near Eastern Religions* 1/1 (2001): 158-87.

109. Merlo, *La dea Ašratum — Aṯiratu — Ašera: Un contributo alla storia della religione semitica del Nord* (Mursia: Pontificia Università Lateranese, 1998).

110. Dijkstra, "'I Have Blessed You by YHWH of Samaria and His Asherah': Texts with Religious Elements from the Soil Archive of Ancient Israel," in *Only One God?* 17-44; and Korpel, "Asherah Outside Israel," in *Only One God?* 127-50.

111. Cross (letter to me, dated 7 December 1998) comments in reference to this debate: "If you want syncretism in the Hebrew Bible, there is plenty of material to be found without manufacturing it."

112. Smith, *The Early History of God*, 1st ed., 80-97.

Asherah as a monarchic period goddess in Israel did not address sufficiently the idea that a cultic symbol may have been rendered in the likeness of an *'ăšērâ* tree or pole, a view hardly impossible for passages such as 1 Kings 15:13 and 2 Kings 21:7 (so, too, 2 Kings 23:6). What could be involved is a more elaborate royal version of the *'ăšērâ.*

Some new objections to this view have been raised since the first edition of *The Early History of God.* It has been considered implausible that cultic devotion could be paid to the cultic item of the *'ăšērâ* (as in 2 Kings 23).[113] However, J. Tigay notes an example in a discussion that many commentators have overlooked.[114] It is to be noted further that if the Jerusalemite temple tradition was aniconic or at least non-anthropomorphic for Yahweh (as many scholars argue),[115] then it would be reasonable to entertain the possibility that the image of the asherah might be at least non-anthropomorphic as well. It has also been suggested that the attestation of *'ăšērôt* as a generic word for "goddesses" demonstrates that its ancient users knew that the word *'ăšērâ* stood for a divine name.[116] However, this logic suffers from the etymological fallacy.

It is dubious to argue that the reference to the prophets of Asherah in 1 Kings 18:19 demonstrates an earlier awareness of the goddess Asherah, if this knowledge was the product of a polemical misidentification with Astarte. In other words, the symbol may have been misconstrued to pertain to some goddess because later tradents who added the reference to a putative Phoenician Asherah to 1 Kings 18:19 conflated the Phoenician Astarte (there is no Phoenician Asherah attested) with the name of the symbol and assumed that it represented a goddess named Asherah (this explanation would comport with the textual variations between Asherah and Astarte[117] and between *'ăšērôt* and *'aštārôt*).[118] Accordingly, a misconstrual informs a claim made that my "explanation of *'ăšērâ* surely still implies an awareness of the goddess Asherah in Israel."[119] Later literary usage of *'ăšērâ* implies only that at some

113. D. V. Edelman's criticism that if *'ăšērâ* is not the goddess but only a symbol, then 1 Kings 15:13 would attest to an image made for an image; see Edelman, "Introduction," in *The Triumph of Elohim,* 18.

114. J. H. Tigay, "A Second Temple Parallel to the Blessings from Kuntillet ʿAjrud," *IEJ* 40 (1990): 218.

115. See the discussions of Mettinger, Na'aman, and others noted in section 1 above.

116. J. Day, *Yahweh and the Gods and Goddesses of Canaan,* 45.

117. See 2 Chron. 15:16, discussed by Hadley, *The Cult of Asherah in Ancient Israel and Judah,* 66.

118. See Judges 3:7, discussed by Hadley, *The Cult of Asherah in Ancient Israel and Judah,* 63-64.

119. J. Day, *Yahweh and the Gods and Goddesses of Canaan,* 46 n. 12.

time in the history of Israelite religion there was an awareness of Asherah as a goddess, not necessarily still in the time when the literary usage is attested.[120]

The polemical nature of the Deuteronomistic History has been raised as a powerful argument in favor of *'ăšērâ* as a goddess. The history's handling of references (including the most crucial biblical attestation to *hā'ăšērâ* with "the baal" in 2 Kings 23:4 suggesting a deity), but it is unclear whether this is historical observation or polemic. There is an important, broader consideration in the discussion. Curiously, advocates such O. Loretz sometimes claim that those scholars who do not accept *'ăšērâ* in the passages mentioned above as a goddess have been deceived by the ideological perspective of the Deuteronomistic History or are somehow psychologically unprepared to deal with its outlook.[121] However, if it were true that the Deuteronomistic authors understand *'ăšērâ* in the passages involved as a goddess (as the advocates maintain) and if their work is an ideologically charged polemic (as the advocates also claim, rightly in my view), why should its viewpoint regarding the nature of *'ăšērâ* as a goddess during the monarchy be accepted as historically reliable? In short, the appeal to the ideological character of the Deuteronomistic History cuts as readily against those who accept *'ăšērâ* as a goddess; it might be argued that advocates are the scholars taken in by the ideological perspective of the Deuteronomistic History. On the whole, I find this particular line of discussion unproductive. Furthermore, if one were inclined to draw psychological inferences about scholars (*pace* Loretz), one might make the counterclaim that the *Zeitgeist* of our age psychologically preconditions advocates to desire to discover a goddess in ancient Israel. In short, psychological arguments are tendentious, and barring clear evidence, implicitly *ad hominem* (or, *ad feminam*).

Finally with respect to the biblical discussion, *The Early History of God* proposed that the demise of the goddess's cult would have begun by the end of the pre-monarchic period. However, this position too needs to be revisited

120. As noted by Hadley (*The Cult of Asherah in Ancient Israel and Judah*, 7, 67), a later article of mine characterizes Asherah as a goddess in Israel in the Iron Age. See Smith, "Yahweh and the Other Deities of Ancient Israel: Observations on Old Problems and Recent Trends," in *Ein Gotte allein? JHWH-Verehrung und biblischer Monotheismus im Kontext der israelitischen und altorientalischen Religionsgeshichte*, ed. W. Dietrich and M. A. Klopfenstein, OBO 139 (Fribourg: Universitätsverlag; Göttingen: Vandenhoeck & Ruprecht, 1994), 206. Hadley's discussion of my position may give the impression that it is contradictory, that sometimes I claim Asherah was a goddess in the Iron Age, elsewhere that she was not. In fact, there is no contradiction in my writing on this point, since the article speaks of the Iron Age (in a summary statement on p. 206), whereas the book distinguishes matters between Iron I and Iron II.

121. See O. Loretz, Review of *The Early History of God*, *UF* 22 (1990): 514: "The author thus exposes himself . . . as unwilling to view the new evidence without the deuteronomistic filter."

and qualified. So much relies on an argument from silence especially where the tenth and ninth centuries are involved. Accordingly, one might see the duration of the goddess's cult later and situate the beginning of the symbol's career apart from the goddess by the end of the ninth century. It is hard to be precise on this point. Different rates of change may apply in different areas or social segments or movements, and so it is possible that the transition took place in some quarters even later. The discussion warrants considerably greater circumspection in the matter of the biblical evidence.

The discussion of main inscriptional evidence from Kuntillet ʿAjrud has continued to revolve around the grammatical interpretation of *lʾšrth.* Scholars continue to debate whether the name of the goddess can take a pronominal suffix.[122] There seems to be a deadlock over this issue. For scholars wishing to obviate this difficulty and to see Asherah as a monarchic period Israelite goddess, they take refuge in the view that the word involved is instead the symbol of the *ʾăšērâ* which represents the goddess. In addition to the important grammatical question, there are semantic issues affecting the interpretation of the noun as either the goddess's name or the symbol in its putative capacity of referring to the goddess. If *lʾšrth* in the inscriptions from Kuntillet ʿAjrud refers to the goddess ("and by/to his Asherah"), then it is unclear what "his Asherah" means. Only by assuming an ellipsis of "his consort, Asherah" or the like does the word as a reference to the goddess's name make reasonable sense. If *lʾšrth* means "his asherah" referring to the symbol (surely the most reasonable view grammatically, as advocates generally hold), then "his asherah" should denote something that is not hers, but "his." On this point, Zevit correctly asks: "What would it have meant to say that the goddess *belonged to* or was *possessed by* Yahweh?"[123] I would therefore remain partial to the answer proposed in the first edition of this book, namely that a symbol had earlier referred to the goddess by the same name, but it came to function by the time of the Kuntillet ʿAjrud inscriptions as part of Yahweh's symbolic repertoire, possibly with older connotations associated with the goddess; in other words, the asherah was "his." Older connotations of the goddess may have continued in the literary record despite the demise of her cult.

The contribution made by the Tel Miqneh (Ekron) inscriptions to this discussion depends on their interpretation. The excavator of the site, S. Gitin, understood the words *ʾšrt* or *qdš* in the inscriptions as the name and title

122. For comparative evidence marshalled in favor of this view, see P. Xella, "Le dieu et 'sa' déesse: l'utilisation des suffixes pronominaux avec des théonymes d'Ebla à Ugarit et à Kuntillet ʿAjrud," *UF* 27 (1995): 599-610; and M. Dietrich, "Die Parhedra in Pantheon von Emar: Miscellenea Emariana (I)," *UF* 29 (1997): 115-22.

123. Zevit, *The Religions of Ancient Israel,* 403 n. 10; Zevit's italics.

("Holy One") of the goddess.[124] Given the Phoenician cognates for these words and the resemblances of the Ekron script with Phoenician writing, others have preferred to view these words respectively as "shrine" and "holy" (place).[125] This is not to deny that the site knew at least one goddess. The goddess called "PTGYH, his lady," is attested in an important inscription from Miqneh.[126] The identity of this goddess is disputed; offered as options are Pidray known from Ugaritic texts, Pothnia (assuming a scribal error) or Pythogaia, both known from the Aegean.[127] However, this figure may have no bearing on the references to *'šrt* and *qdš* in the epigraphic evidence from Miqneh.

In conclusion, I am not opposed in theory to the possibility that Asherah was an Israelite goddess during the monarchy. My chief objection to this view is that it has not been demonstrated, given the plausibility of alternative views. By the same token, the case has not been disproven, and I must concede that I may be wrong. It may be only a matter of time before superior evidence attesting to Asherah's cult in monarchic Israel is discovered.

5. In Retrospect

As the preceding sections illustrate, the landscape of academic research has continued to develop mostly in ways that are intellectually challenging and refreshing. Despite the advances discussed in the first section above and the *desiderata* addressed in the second section, a new edition of *The Early History of God* may serve as an introductory work to Yahweh and other major deities in ancient Israel. In this second edition, I have been able to correct errors, prune some of the more dubious citations, and modify some of the larger discussion. I am also pleased to be able to update the most important bibliography and primary data. Readers interested in a more complete and recent discussion of the issues would benefit from perusing Zevit's important book,

124. Giṭin, "Seventh Century BCE Cultic Elements at Ekron," 248-58; cf. Zevit, *The Religions of Ancient Israel,* 321 n. 126, 374.

125. Hadley, *The Cult of Asherah in Ancient Israel and Judah,* 179-84; Lipiński, *Dieux et déesses,* 421; Smith, "Yahweh and the Other Deities of Ancient Israel," 197-234, and *The Origins of Biblical Monotheism,* 73.

126. S. Gitin, T. Dothan, and J. Naveh, "A Royal Dedicatory Inscription from Eqron," *IEJ* 47/1-2 (1997): 1-16.

127. These options are discussed by R. G. Lehmann, "Studien zur Formgeschichte der 'Eqron-Inschrift des 'KYŠ und den phönizischen Dedikationtexten aus Byblos," *UF* 31 (1999): 255-306, esp. 258-59.

The Religions of Ancient Israel. If readers wish to know more about what I think, my views particularly on polytheism and monotheism are explored in my recent book, *The Origins of Biblical Monotheism* (published in 2001).

In some ways, *The Origins of Biblical Monotheism* reads like a sequel to *The Early History of God.* The former builds on the latter in an effort to develop a more sustained analysis of the development of monotheism in the seventh and sixth centuries. In a sense, *The Origins of Biblical Monotheism* picks up where the discussion of monotheism in chapters 6 and 7 of *The Early History of God* leave off. (Accordingly, some of the processes prior to monotheism, such as convergence and differentiation, hallmarks of *The Early History of God,* are presumed in *The Origins of Biblical Monotheism.*) The new book also revisits the Ugaritic texts and early biblical evidence and makes a number of suggestions about how conceptual unity informing polytheism in the Ugaritic texts may help scholars to understand monotheistic formulations found in the Bible. *The Origins of Biblical Monotheism* also contains more theoretical considerations left aside in *The Eary History of God.* In order to make the connections between the two books easier to follow, I have included numerous citations to *The Origins of Biblical Monotheism* in this second edition of *The Early History of God.* This has also given me the opportunity to fill out some points (such as the original home of Yahweh in Edom/Midian/Teiman and his original profile as a warrior-god as well as the process leading to his assimilation into the highland pantheon, headed by El along with his consort, Asherah, and populated further by Baal and other deities). By the same token, I have advanced a number of further points in this second edition not found in the first edition or in *The Origins of Biblical Monotheism.* Despite their flaws, it is my hope that these two books will contribute toward future studies offering a more sophisticated history of religions analysis and synthesis for ancient Israel.

I would like to close with some acknowledgments and thanks. In retrospect, the aid offered by those recognized in the preface to the first edition is all the more appreciated. Morever, I am grateful to the reviewers of the first edition of the book (G. Ahlström, L. Boadt, D. Edelman, D. N. Freedman, L. K. Handy, R. S. Hendel, R. S. Hess, W. L. Humphreys, T. J. Lewis, O. Loretz, N. Lohfink, S. B. Parker, J. G. Taylor, and Z. Zevit), as well as other scholars who have commented on *The Early History of God* (among others, J. Day, D. V. Edelman, J. Hadley, T. N. D. Mettinger, and K. van der Toorn). All of the responses have been extremely helpful, and I am very grateful for them. I wish also to express my thanks to Eerdmans for its interest in publishing a second edition of this work and for their help in producing it. Patrick Miller generously agreed to provide a foreword to this edition, and I am very grateful to him for his reflections. I am also thankful for the learning I've received from students and colleagues in the Department of Hebrew and Judaic Studies as well as the Religion and Ancient Studies programs at New York University. I wish to "update" my thanks to my family, the joy of my life. My wife, Liz Bloch-Smith, has offered constant professional help and personal support (including suggesting improvements for this preface). Our three children, Benjamin, Rachel, and Shulamit, have contributed in ways more wonderful than they will ever know. The two editions of this book mark their progress thus far in their lives: Benjamin, four years old at the time when the first edition was finished, is now sixteen; Rachel was two, but is now fourteen; and Shula is now ten. Finally, the first edition's dedication to my father, Donald Eugene Smith, feels even more true now than it did in 1990.

New York University
10 February 2002

Mark S. Smith
Department of Hebrew
and Judaic Studies

Acknowledgments (First Edition)

While in residence at the W. F. Albright Institute in Jerusalem in the spring of 1987, I began research on this work in conjunction with a commentary on the Ugaritic Baal cycle. As I delved into the use of parallels to the Baal cycle, the problems attending the often-cited biblical parallels began to require attention in their own right. The character of the biblical parallels, their relationship to one another, and their bearing on Israelite culture generated an investigation separate from my examination of the Baal cycle. This volume is the result of the detour I took. It represents an attempt to synthesize a wide array of information building on the studies of many scholars. It is my great pleasure to acknowledge my debt to those who facilitated my research in various ways.

My family's stay at the Albright Institute during the spring and summer of 1987 was made possible by the American Schools of Oriental Research. Thanks to the congenial and stimulating environment of the Albright, I was able to work well. I wish to acknowledge my great debt of gratitude to its director, Dr. Sy Gitin, his family, and his staff. They were helpful and friendly to my wife, Liz Bloch-Smith, and me, and tolerant of our (then) one-and-a-half-year-old Benjamin, as he became accustomed to running about the hallways and exercising his newly found vocal facility. My visit to the Albright was enhanced further by the help and hospitality of the community of École Biblique et Archéologique Française. Like the warmth of the people living at the Albright, the generosity and friendship offered to me by the École community made East Jerusalem seem like home. Émile Puech, Marcel Sigrist, John Strugnell, Jean-Michel de Tarragon, and Benedict Viviano were especially kind. Other friends in Jerusalem were likewise personally and intellectually generous: Celia and Steve Fassberg, Bella and Jonas Greenfield, Menachem Haran, Ruth Hestrin, Avigdor Hurowitz, Avi Hurwitz, Ami Mazar, Abraham

Malamat, Shalom Paul, Alexander Rofé, Arlene and Steve Rosen, and Aaron Schaffer. The apartment of Charlotte and Mordecai Hopp was always a second home to us. The Association of Theological Schools and the Dorot Foundation provided for my family's living expenses during this term. I am especially grateful to the president of the Dorot Foundation, Joy Underleider-Mayerson, who has long supported my research with financial aid and personal encouragement. Yale University was kind enough to permit my leave of absence for the spring semester of 1987. The spring of 1987 was a wonderful time for me, and I thank all these friends and institutions for making it so.

Upon returning to Yale in the summer of 1987, I benefited from the community of scholars and friends who helped in many ways with my research. I am especially grateful to my colleagues and friends who aided me in this study. Gary Beckman, Bill Hallo, Sarah Morris, Saul Olyan, Marvin Pope, Chris Seitz, and Bob Wilson read an early draft of this manuscript and offered many helpful suggestions. My wife, Liz Bloch-Smith, offered critical questions and observations regarding material culture, especially burials and other realia pertaining to the dead. To Saul Olyan I am especially indebted, as chapter 3 of this study drew heavily from his work on the asherah, which first appeared as a chapter in his dissertation (Harvard University, 1985) and has now been published as a monograph, *Asherah and the Cult of Yahweh in Israel* (1988). Our conversations frequently helped to clarify many points and to stimulate my thinking. I am very grateful to Yale, where my position afforded me the time and resources to conduct research. I wish to thank Douglas Green, Richard Whitekettle, and Stephen Cook, who participated in a semester of the Ugaritic seminar devoted primarily to the texts and topics in this work. Gösta Ahlström, Baruch Halpern, Stephen Happel, Patrick Miller, Dennis Pardee, and Jeffrey Tigay, as well as my father, Donald E. Smith, and my father-in-law, Ted C. Bloch, read a draft of this work and offered many comments and insights. For their generosity with their time and their help, I thank them. I express my gratitude to Stephen Happel, who encouraged me to make this work more accessible to scholars outside the field of biblical studies. Toward this end I added the second section to the Introduction describing the assumptions that biblical scholars customarily make. I am further grateful to Professor Happel for commenting on drafts of this section. I also thank a number of scholars for providing me with access to their work before publication: Marc Brettler, Peter Machinist, Dennis Pardee, and David Petersen. I wish to express a word of great thanks to my editor, John Collins, for offering many valuable suggestions, and to Harper & Row, for including this work in its highly selective academic books program. I also thank Stephen Cook for his assistance with proofreading.

The professional biblical societies greatly aided the completion of this work. Many scholars offered critical questions and suggestions at various seminars and meetings where some of the data and ideas in this study were presented: a faculty seminar at the St. Paul Seminary/School of Divinity of the College of St. Thomas (spring 1985), a lecture at the University of Winnipeg (fall 1985), the Upper Midwest meeting of the Society of Biblical Literature (spring 1986), a graduate seminar of Abraham Malamat at the Hebrew University (spring 1987), and the Old Testament Colloquium at Conception Seminary College (winter 1989). Some of the material in this manuscript was presented at national meetings of the Catholic Biblical Association (summer 1988) and the Society of Biblical Literature (fall 1988). I am gratified that my paper presented at the Society of Biblical Literature's 1988 Annual Meeting was awarded the Mitchell Dahood Memorial Prize, and I wish to thank Doubleday for its sponsorship of the prize. My profound thanks go to all of these groups and the scholars who belong to them. I am also grateful to the American Academy of Religion for providing funding for the preparation of the book's indexes.

I wish to make special mention of my teachers of matters Canaanite and Israelite: Frank Cross, Aloysius Fitzgerald, Jonas Greenfield, Marvin Pope, Franz Rosenthal, and Robert Wilson. Their written works, their teaching, and my discussions with them have often aided my efforts to grasp the nature of Israelite religion. Their command of the ancient world of Israel has guided and inspired me. The specific debt I owe Frank Cross is clearly marked in chapters 1 and 2. My debt to Marvin Pope is especially manifest in chapter 5 and generally reflected in the use of the Ugaritic texts. I hasten to add that I alone am responsible for the views expressed in this volume.

My wife, Liz, and our children, Benjamin (now four) and Rachel (now two), have lived with my pursuit of Israelite religion. I thank them for their patience and love. As I seemed lost sometimes in a faraway time and place, my family always made me feel the goodness of this world. This work is dedicated to my father, Donald E. Smith; I do not have words sufficient to express my love for him.

Abbreviations and Sigla

AB	Anchor Bible.
ABD	D. N. Freedman, ed. *The Anchor Bible Dictionary.* 6 vols. New York: Doubleday, 1992.
AHw	W. von Soden. *Akkadisches Handwörterbuch.* Wiesbaden: O. Harrassowitz, 1959-81.
AION	*Annali dell'istituto orientali di Napoli.*
ALASP	Abhandlungen zur Literatur Alt-Syrien-Palästinas und Mesopotamiens.
AnBib	Analecta biblica.
ANEP	J. B. Pritchard, ed. *The Ancient Near East in Pictures.* 2d ed. Princeton: Princeton Univ. Press, 1969.
ANET	J. B. Pritchard, ed. *Ancient Near Eastern Texts.* 3d ed. Princeton: Princeton Univ. Press, 1969.
AnOr	Analecta Orientalia.
AOAT	Alter Orient und Altes Testament.
AP	A. Cowley. *Aramaic Papyrus of the Fifth Century B.C.* Oxford: Clarendon, 1923; reprinted ed., Osnabrück: Otto Zeller, 1967.
ASOR	American Schools of Oriental Research.
AThANT	Abhandlungen zur Theologie des Alten und Neuen Testaments.
BA	*Biblical Archaeologist.*
BASOR	*Bulletin of the American Schools of Oriental Research.*
BBB	Bonner biblische Beiträge.
BDB	F. Brown, S. R. Driver, and C. A. Briggs. *Hebrew and English Lexicon of the Old Testament.* Oxford: Clarendon, 1972.
BH	Biblical Hebrew.

BiOr — *Bibliotheca Orientalis.*
BKAT — Biblische Kommentar: Altes Testament.
BN — *Biblische Notizen.*
BSOAS — *Bulletin of the School of Oriental and African Studies.*
BZAW — Beihefte zur ZAW.
CAD — I. J Gelb et al. *The Assyrian Dictionary of the Oriental Institute of the University of Chicago.* Chicago: Oriental Institute of the University of Chicago, 1956–.
CBQ — *Catholic Biblical Quarterly.*
CBQMS — Catholic Biblical Quarterly Monograph Series.
CIS — *Corpus Inscriptionum Semiticarum.* Paris: E Reipublicae Typographeo, 1881–.
ConBOT — Coniectanea biblica, Old Testament.
CRAIBL — *Comptes rendus de l'Académie des Inscriptions et Belles-Lettres.*
CRB — Cahiers de la Revue Biblique.
CTA — A. Herdner. *Corpus des tablettes en cunéiformes alphabétiques découvertes à Ras Shamra–Ugarit de 1929 à 1939.* Mission de Ras Shamra 10. Paris: Imprimerie Nationale, 1963.
DDD — *Dictionary of Deities and Demons in the Bible.* Ed. K. van der Toorn, B. Becking, and P. W. van der Horst. 2d extensively revised edition. Leiden/Boston/Köln: Brill; Grand Rapids/ Cambridge, U.K.: Eerdmans, 1999.
DISO — C.-F. Jean and J. Hoftijzer. *Dictionnaire des inscriptions sémitiques de l'ouest.* Leiden: Brill, 1965.
DJD — Discoveries in the Judaean Desert.
E — English in Revised Standard Version (where citation differs from BH text).
EA — El Amarna texts cited according to W. L. Moran. *Les Lettres d'El-Amarna.* Translated by D. Collon and H. Cazelles. Littératures anciennes du proche-orient 13. Paris: Les Éditions du Cerf, 1987.
EAEHL — M. Avi-Yonah and E. Stern, eds. *Encyclopedia of Archaeological Excavations in the Holy Land.* 4 vols. Englewood Cliffs, NJ: Prentice-Hall, 1977.
EI — *Eretz Israel.*
Emar — D. Arnaud, *Recherches au pays d'Aštata. Emar 6.* Volume 3: *Textes sumeriennes et accadiens.* Paris: Éditions Recherche sur les Civilizations, 1986.
EncJud — *Encyclopaedia Judaica.* Jerusalem: Keter, 1973.

FRLANT	Forschungen zur Religion und Literatur des Alten und Neuen Testaments.
GKC	E. Kautsch and A. E. Cowley, eds. *Gesenius' Hebrew Grammar* 2d English ed. Oxford: Clarendon, 1910.
HAT	Handbuch zum Alten Testament.
HdO	Handbuch der Orientalistik.
HKAT	Handkommentar zum Alten Testament.
HSM	Harvard Semitic Monographs.
HSS	Harvard Semitic Studies.
HTR	*Harvard Theological Review.*
ICC	International Critical Commentary.
IDB	G. A. Buttrick et al., eds. *Interpreter's Dictionary of the Bible.* Nashville: Abingdon, 1962.
IDBSup	K. Crim et al., eds. *Interpreter's Dictionary of the Bible, Supplement.* Nashville: Abingdon, 1976.
IEJ	*Israel Exploration Journal.*
IOS	*Israel Oriental Studies.*
JANES	*Journal of the Ancient Near Eastern Society.*
JAOS	*Journal of the American Oriental Society.*
JBL	*Journal of Biblical Literature.*
JCS	*Journal of Cuneiform Studies.*
JJS	*Journal of Jewish Studies.*
JNES	*Journal of Near Eastern Studies.*
JNWSL	*Journal of Northwest Semitic Languages.*
JPOS	*Journal of the Palestine Oriental Society.*
JQR	*Jewish Quarterly Review.*
JSOT	*Journal for the Society of Old Testament.*
JSOTSup	Journal for the Society of Old Testament, Supplement Series.
JSS	*Journal of Semitic Studies.*
KAI	H. Donner and W. Röllig. *Kanaanäische und aramäische Inschriften.* Wiesbaden: O. Harrassowitz, 1964-68.
KTU	M. Dietrich, O. Loretz, and J. Sanmartín, *The Cuneiform Alphabetic Texts from Ugarit, Ras Ibn Hani and Other Places.* ALASP 8. Münster: Ugarit-Verlag, 1995.
LAPO	Littératures anciennes du Proche-Orient.
LXX	Septuagint.
MARI	*Mari Annales Recherches Interdisciplinaires.*
MT	Masoretic Text.
NAB	New American Bible.
OBO	Orbis biblicus et orientalis.

OLP	*Orientalia Lovaniensia Periodica.*
OTL	Old Testament Library.
OTPs	J. H. Charlesworth, ed. *The Old Testament Pseudepigrapha.* 2 vols. Garden City, NY: Doubleday, 1983, 1985.
OTS	*Oudtestamentische Studien.*
PE	K. Mras, ed. *Eusebius Werke,* vol. 8, part 1, *Die Praeparatio evangelica.* Berlin: Akademie Verlag, 1954.
PEQ	*Palestine Exploration Quarterly.*
PRU II	C. F. A. Schaeffer. *Le Palais royale d'Ugarit 2.* Mission de Ras Shamra 7. Paris: Imprimerie Nationale/Librairie C. Klincksieck, 1957.
PRU III	J. Nougayrol. *Le Palais royale d'Ugarit 3: Texts accadiens et hourrites des Archives Est, Ouest et Centrales.* Mission de Ras Shamra 6. Paris: Imprimerie Nationale/Librairie C. Klincksieck, 1955.
PRU IV	J. Nougayrol, *Le Palais royale d'Ugarit 4: Textes accadiens des Archives Sud (Archives internationales).* Mission de Ras Shamra 9. Paris: Imprimerie Nationale, 1956.
PRU VI	J. Nougayrol. *Le Palais royale d'Ugarit 6.* Mission de Ras Shamra 12. Paris: Imprimerie Nationale/Librairie C. Klincksieck, 1970.
RA	*Revue d'Assyriologie et d'Archéologie orientale.*
RB	*Revue biblique.*
RES	*Répertoire d'épigraphie sémitiques.* Paris: La commission du Corpus Inscriptionum Semiticarum, 1900–.
RS	Field number of the Mission de Ras Shamra.
RSF	*Revisti di Studi Fenici.*
RSO	Ras Shamra-Ougarit.
RSV	Revised Standard Version.
SBLDS	Society of Biblical Literature Dissertation Series.
SBLMS	Society of Biblical Literature Monograph Series.
SEL	*Studi epigrafici e linguistici.*
TA	*Tel Aviv.*
UBL	Ugaritisch-biblische Literatur.
UF	*Ugarit-Forschungen.*
Ug V	J. Nougayrol et al. *Ugaritica V: Nouveaux textes accadiens, hourrites et ugaritiques des Archives et Bibliothèques privées d'Ugarit, commentaires des textes historiques.* Mission de Ras Shamra 16. Paris: Imprimerie Nationale/P. Geuthner, 1968.
VT	*Vetus Testamentum.*

VTSup	Vetus Testamentum, Supplements.
WMANT	Wissenschaftliche Monographien zum Alten und Neuen Testament.
WO	*Welt des Orients.*
ZA	*Zeitschrift für Assyriologie.*
ZAH	*Zeitschrift für Althebraistik.*
ZAW	*Zeitschrift für die alttestamentliche Wissenschaft.*
ZDMG	*Zeitschrift für Deutschen Morgenländischen Gesellschaft.*
ZDPV	*Zeitschrift des Deutschen Palästina-Vereins.*
1QIsa[a]	M. Burrows, ed. *The Dead Sea Scrolls of St. Mark's Monastery.* New Haven, CT: American Schools of Oriental Research, 1950. Plates 1-54. F. M. Cross et al., eds. *Scrolls from Qumrân Cave 1: The Great Isaiah Scroll, the Order of the Community, the Pesher to Habakkuk.* From photographs by J. C. Trever. Jerusalem: The Albright Institute of Archaeological Research and the Shrine of the Book, 1972. Pages [13]-[123].

[ ]	Reconstructed letter(s) in lacuna or implied in translation.
< >	Restored letter(s).
*	Unattested form or indication of root.
//	Terms in poetic parallelism.

Introduction

1. The Question of Understanding Israelite Religion

> There has been and is much disagreement among theologians about the god honored among the Hebrews.

The view expressed in the epigraph is as true today as it was when Lydus, a Greek of the sixth century A.D., wrote these words.[1] The role of Yahweh within Israelite religion was an important area of inquiry within biblical studies throughout most of the twentieth century. During this century, the understanding of Yahweh has been shaped strongly by the study of Canaanite deities. The title of a significant work in the field of Israelite religion, W. F. Albright's *Yahweh and the Gods of Canaan*,[2] echoed in the subtitle of this present work, reflects the central place that various "Canaanite" deities have long held in the discussion of Israelite monotheism, which may be defined as the worship and belief in Yahweh and disbelief in the reality of other deities. The study of Canaanite deities in connection with Yahweh was inspired largely by the discovery of numerous ancient texts in the Levant, especially

1. Lydus, *De mensibus* 4.53; for text and translation, see H. W. Attridge and R. A. Oden, Jr., *Philo of Byblos: The Phoenician History,* CBQMS 9 (Washington, DC: Catholic Biblical Association of America, 1979), 70-71.

2. W. F. Albright, *Yahweh and the Gods of Canaan: An Historical Analysis of Two Conflicting Faiths* (Garden City, NY: Doubleday, 1968). Albright (p. vi) dates the preface of the book 1 July 1967. For an interesting retrospective of Albright's thought, see J. A. Miles, Jr., "Understanding Albright: A Revolutionary Etude," *HTR* 69 (1976): 151-75. Albright's title is echoed in the name of J. Day's book, *Yahweh and the Gods and Goddesses of Canaan*, JSOTSup 265 (Sheffield: Sheffield Academic Press, 2001). On the term "Canaanite," see the comments on p. 19 n. 2 below.

the many Ugaritic tablets discovered since 1929 at Ras Shamra on the coast of Syria. The Ugaritic texts, dating to the second half of the second millennium B.C., have provided extensive information about the religion of the Canaanites, the neighbors of Israel whom legal and prophetic texts in the Bible roundly condemn. Thanks to the Ugaritic texts, scholars finally have a native Canaanite source to help reconstruct the relationship between Canaanite and Israelite religion.

The Ugaritic mythological texts largely feature the deities El, the aged and kindly patriarch of the pantheon; his consort and queen mother of the divine family, Asherah; the young storm-god and divine warrior, Baal; his sister, Anat, likewise a martial deity; and finally, the solar deity.[3] Scholars of religion have frequently assumed that because these deities were Canaanite, they were not Israelite. According to this view, Israel had always been essentially monolatrous; Israel worshiped only Yahweh, although it did not deny the existence of other deities. While Israel could tolerate other peoples' worship of their deities, Yahweh was ultimately the most powerful deity in the cosmos.

3. For surveys of these deities, see M. Dahood, "Ancient Semitic Deities in Syria and Palestine," in *Le antiche divinità semitiche,* Studi Semitici 1 (Rome: Centro di Studi Semitici, 1958), 65-94; M. H. Pope and W. Röllig, *Syrien: Die Mythologie der Ugarititer und Phönizier,* Wörterbuch der Mythologie 1/1 (Stuttgart: Ernst Klett, 1965), 217-312; A. Cooper, "Divine Names and Epithets in the Ugaritic Texts," in *Ras Shamra Parallels: The Texts from Ugaritic and the Hebrew Bible,* vol. 3, ed. S. Rummel, AnOr 51 (Rome: Pontificium Institutum Biblicum, 1981), 335-469 and various listings in *DDD.* For the Ugaritic mythological texts with translations, see J. C. L. Gibson, *Canaanite Myths and Legends,* 2d ed. (Edinburgh: T. & T. Clark, 1978); G. del Olmo Lete, *Mitos y leyendas srgún la tradición de Ugarit,* Institución San Jerónimo para la Investigación Biblica, Fuentes de la Ciencia Bíblica 1 (Valencia: Institución San Jeronimo; Madrid: Ediciones Cristianidad, 1981). For translations with notes, see *ANET,* 129-55; A. Caquot, M. Sznycer, and A. Herdner, *Textes ougaritiques, vol. 1, Mythes et lègendes,* LAPO 7 (Paris: Les Éditions du Cerf, 1974); M. D. Coogan, *Stories from Ancient Canaan* (Philadelphia: Westminster, 1978); A. Caquot, J. M. de Tarragon, and J. L. Cunchillos, *Textes ougaritiques: Tome II. textes religieux. rituels. correspondance,* LAPO 14 (Paris: Les Éditions du Cerf, 1989); M. Dietrich and O. Loretz, in *Texte aus der Umwelt des Alten Testaments,* ed. O. Kaiser, Band II (Gütersloh: Gütersloher Verlagshaus Gerd Mohn, 1986-); J. C. de Moor, *An Anthology of Religious Texts from Ugarit,* Nisaba 16 (Leiden: Brill, 1987); D. Pardee et al., in W. W. Hallo, ed., *The Context of Scripture* (Leiden: Brill, 1997), 241-375; S. B. Parker, ed., *Ugaritic Narrative Poetry,* Writings from the Ancient World (Atlanta, GA: Scholars, 1997); and N. Wyatt, *Religious Texts from Ugarit: The Words of Ilimilku and His Colleagues,* The Biblical Seminar 53 (Sheffield: Sheffield Academic Press, 1998). For an introduction to the relations between Ugaritic literature and the Hebrew Bible, see J. C. Greenfield, "The Hebrew Bible and Canaanite Literature," in *The Literary Guide to the Bible,* ed. R. Alter and F. Kermode (Cambridge, MA: Harvard Univ. Press, Belknap Press, 1987), 545-60. For further discussion of Ugaritic and biblical studies, see M. S. Smith, *Untold Stories: The Bible and Ugaritic Studies in the Twentieth Century* (Peabody, MA: Hendrickson Publishers, 2001).

Accordingly, Exodus 15:11 asks, "Who is like you among the gods, O Yahweh?" It was Israel's monolatry that led to the monotheism just before and during the Exile (587-539), when Israel explicitly denied the power of all other deities. Whatever influence other deities manifested in ancient, monolatrous Israel, scholars often considered them syncretistic, peripheral, ephemeral, or part of Israel's "popular religion" and not its "official religion." Israel was essentially monolatrous despite the threat other deities presented.

This view of Israelite religion has been expressed in part or in full by European, American, and Israeli scholars with otherwise widely diverging views, including W. F. Albright, Y. Kaufmann, H. Ringgren, G. Fohrer, G. W. Ahlström, and J. Tigay.[4] This historical perspective on Israelite religion derives largely from biblical historiography manifest in passages such as Exodus 23:23-24 and Judges 3:1-7 (cf. Jer. 2:11). Exodus 34:11-16 provides an extensive example of this view:

> Observe what I command you this day. Behold, I will drive out before you the Amorites, the Canaanites, the Hittites, the Perizzites, the Hivites, and the Jebusites. Take heed to yourself, lest you make a covenant with the inhabitants of the land to which you are going, lest it become a snare in the midst of you. You shall break down their altars, and break their pillars, and cut down their asherim (for you shall worship no other god, for Yahweh, whose name is jealous, is a jealous God), lest you make a covenant with the inhabitants of the land, and when they play the harlot after their gods and sacrifice to their gods and one invites you, you eat of his sacrifice, and you take of their daughters for your sons, and their daughters play the harlot after their gods and make your sons play the harlot after their gods.

The passage asserts four points about Israel. First, Israel's ethnic identity was originally separate from other peoples of the land. Second, Israel was not originally among the peoples in the land. Third, specific cultic objects were

4. Y. Kaufmann, *The Religion of Israel from Its Beginnings to the Babylonian Exile,* trans. and abridged by M. Greenberg (New York: Schocken, 1960), 142-47; H. Ringgren, *Israelite Religion,* trans. D. E. Green (Philadelphia: Fortress, 1966), 42, 58, 99; G. Fohrer, *History of Israelite Religion,* trans. D. E. Green (Nashville and New York: Abingdon, 1972), 127-30; G. W. Ahlström, *Aspects of Syncretism in Israelite Religion,* Horae Soederblomianae V (Lund: Gleerup, 1963), 8; J. Tigay, *You Shall Have No Other Gods: Israelite Religion in the Light of Hebrew Inscriptions,* HSS 31 (Atlanta, GA: Scholars, 1986). Cf. F. M. Cross, *Canaanite Myth and Hebrew Epic: Essays in the History of the Religion of Israel* (Cambridge, MA: Harvard Univ. Press, 1973), 190-91. For discussion, see D. R. Hillers, "Analyzing the Abominable: Our Understanding of Canaanite Religion," *JQR* 75 (1985): 253-69.

alien to Israel. Finally, Yahweh was the only deity of Israel. Some scholarly works have used these biblical claims as elements in their historical reconstructions of Israelite religion. Syncretism of Israelite religion with Canaanite religion remains a historical reconstruction prevalent among biblical scholars. Beyond this scholarly consensus, there has been wide disagreement. Some scholars, such as Y. Kaufmann and J. H. Tigay,[5] argue that neither Baal nor Asherah was hardly a deity in Israel. Other scholars, such as G. W. Ahlström, H. Ringgren, and G. Fohrer,[6] vigorously defend the biblical witness to Israelite worship of Baal and Asherah.

The category of syncretism continues to affect the approach to the issues surrounding deities in ancient Israel. Syncretism, the union of religious phenomenon from two historically separate systems or cultures, remains a standard way of characterizing Israelite interest in deities other than Yahweh, and de-emphasizes the importance of Israelite worship of other deities and practices forbidden in the Bible. For example, K. Spronk relegates practices pertaining to the dead forbidden in the Bible to the realm of "popular religion" and claims that "popular religion" was syncretistic, allowing the influences of Canaanite practices in a way that "official religion" did not permit. This historical reconstruction overlooks the difficulties of historically defining the nature of "official religion."[7] Similarly, J. Tigay, largely depending on the evidence of divine elements in proper names, has followed in the footsteps of Y. Kaufmann in arguing that Israel was essentially monotheistic, or at least monolatrous, during the period of the monarchy (1000-587) and that Israelites hardly worshiped Asherah at all and Baal but briefly. To show that Israel was essentially monotheistic, Tigay cites the overwhelming preponderance of proper names with Yahweh as the divine or theophoric element and the paucity of personal names with theophoric elements other than Yahweh's name.[8]

The distribution of "theophoric" elements — that is, forms of divine names — in proper names lends credence, however, only to the notion that Yahweh was Israel's most popular god, its national deity. There is more to the

5. Y. Kaufmann, *The Religion of Israel,* 134-47; J. H. Tigay, *You Shall Have No Other Gods,* 37-41. See Hillers, "Analyzing the Abominable," 253-69; R. A. Oden, *The Bible Without Theology* (San Francisco: Harper & Row, 1987), 1-39. See also the observations of Morton Smith, "On the Differences between the Culture of Israel and the Major Cultures of the Ancient Near East," *JANES* 5 (1973): 389-95.

6. Ahlström, *Aspects of Syncretism,* 23-24, 50-51; Ringgren, *Israelite Religion,* 24, 42, 95-96, 261; Fohrer, *History of Israelite Religion,* 58, 104.

7. See chapter 5, section 2.

8. Tigay, *You Shall Have No Other Gods,* 12, 65-73, 83-85.

evidence than proper names, which, however suggestive, are notoriously difficult to assess for historical purposes. The giving of names was subject to conventions governed by factors other than religious concerns. Indeed, as D. Pardee has observed,[9] the names of deities contained in proper names are little proof of devotion to those deities. For example, Ugaritic texts rarely, if ever, have proper names with the theophoric element of the goddess Asherah *('aṯrt)*.[10] However, Ugaritic ritual texts indicate this goddess was venerated at ancient Ugarit. Similarly, although Tannit was the most popular goddess in the Punic west, Punic names likewise rarely contain *tnt* as a theophoric element.[11] In general, proper names serve as reliable evidence of religious conditions only when used in conjunction with other information.

While many parameters of the discussion of Israelite religion have remained the same since Albright's *Yahweh and the Gods of Canaan,* there has been a great deal of change. The more than twenty years since the publication of Albright's book have witnessed major epigraphic and archaeological dis-

9. See D. Pardee, "An Evaluation of the Proper Names from Ebla from a West Semitic Perspective: Pantheon Distribution According to Genre," in *Eblaite Personal Names and Semitic Name-Giving,* ed. A. Archi (Rome: Missione Archeologica Italiana in Siria, 1988), 119-51. Pardee collects a number of examples of deities worshiped in cult, but absent from the onomastica. See also K. M. Weiss, D. L. Rossmann, R. Chakraborty, and S. L. Norton, "Wherefore Art Thou, Romeo? Name Frequency Patterns and Their Use in Automated Genealogy Assembly," in *Genealogical Demography,* ed. B. Dyke and W. T. Morrill (New York: Academic Press, 1980), 41-61. For a critique of Tigay's study, see R. Callaway, "The Name Game: Onomastic Evidence and Archaeological Reflections on Religion in Late Judah," *Jian Dao* II (1999): 15-36.

10. See J. A. Emerton, "New Light on Israelite Religion: The Implications from Kuntillet ʿAjrûd," *ZAW* 94 (1982): 16 n. 10; S. Olyan, *Asherah and the Cult of Yahweh in Israel,* SBLMS 34 (Atlanta, GA: Scholars, 1988), 35-36; J. M. Hadley, *The Cult of Asherah in Ancient Israel and Judah: Evidence for a Hebrew Goddess,* University of Cambridge Oriental Publications 57 (Cambridge: Cambridge University Press, 2000), 106-55; and Z. Zevit, *The Religions of Ancient Israel: A Synthesis of Parallactic Approaches* (London/New York: Continuum, 2001), 370-405. F. Gröndahl (*Die Personennamen der Texte aus Ugarit,* Studia Pohl 1 [Rome: Pontifical Biblical Institute, 1967]) lists no proper names with *'aṯrt* as the theophoric element.

11. Olyan, *Asherah and the Cult of Yahweh,* 36-37. For further discussion of Tannit, see D. Harden, *The Phoenicians,* 2d ed. (Middlesex, England/New York: Penguin, 1980), 79; *DISO,* 229; Cross, *Canaanite Myth and Hebrew Epic,* 28; M. Dothan, "A Sign of Tannit from Tel ʿAkko," *IEJ* 24 (1974): 44-49; R. A. Oden, Jr., *Studies in Lucian's De Syria Dea,* HSM 15 (Missoula, MT: Scholars, 1977), 92-93, 141-49; M. Görg, "Zum Namen der punischen Göttin Tinnit," *UF* 12 (1980): 303-6; E. Lipiński, "Notes d'épigraphie phéniciennes et puniques," *OLP* 14 (1983): 129-65; P. Bordreuil, "Tanit du Liban (Nouveaux documents phéniciens III)," in *Phoenicia and the East Mediterranean in the First Millennium B.C.: Proceedings of the Conference Held in Louvain 14-16 November 1985,* Studia Phoenicia V (Louvain: Uitgeverij Peeters, 1987), 79-86; Olyan, *Asherah and the Cult of Yahweh,* 53-54, 59-60; Lipiński, *Dieux et déesses,* 62-64, 199-215, 423-26, 440-46.

coveries. For the Middle and Late Bronze Ages (ca. 1950-1200), the ongoing publication of the Mari letters and Ugaritic texts continue to provide new information bearing on Canaanite religion. For instance, a recently published letter from the city of Mari on the Euphrates River helps to illuminate the political function of storm imagery of Baal at Ugarit and of Yahweh in Israel. New tablets from ancient Emar, modern Meskene in Syria, also provide some data regarding Canaanite religion in the Late Bronze Age (ca. 1550-1200). New Iron Age (ca. 1200-587) data include discoveries both within and outside Israel. Inscriptions from Deir ʿAlla, a Transjordian site located on the Jordan River north of Jericho, lend insights into the religion of Transjordan. The Aramaic version of Psalm 20 in Demotic, a late form of Egyptian, provides information about Baal, among other deities. The Kuntillet ʿAjrûd and Khirbet el-Qôm inscriptions furnish new texts about the asherah forbidden in the Bible. Many scholars have considered the references to the asherah in these inscriptions as evidence of Asherah as an Israelite goddess. The excavations at Carthage have transformed scholarly understanding of child sacrifice in Phoenician and Israelite religion. The recently discovered iconography from Pozo Moro in Spain perhaps provides depictions of the Punic cult of child sacrifice. The growing body of Phoenician and Transjordian inscriptions has helped to focus thinking on the nature of the religions of Israel's immediate neighbors. The Dead Sea Scrolls continue to supply new text-critical readings of important biblical passages. Nonbiblical writings of the Dead Sea Scroll community have been published. These texts reflect religious notions with roots in the Late Bronze or Iron Age, and at some points the texts supply new information about these notions in biblical tradition. A wide variety of archaeological discoveries continues to add important information to the historical record of Israel's culture. In short, the data illuminating the religion of Israel have changed substantially in the last twenty years, and they have helped to produce four major changes in scholarly perspective that inform the present work.

The most significant change involves Israel's cultural identity. Despite the long regnant model that the "Canaanites" and Israelites were people of fundamentally different culture, archaeological data now cast doubt on this view. The material culture of the region exhibits numerous common points between the Israelites and "Canaanites" in the Iron I period (ca. 1200-1000). The record would suggest that the Israelite culture largely overlapped with, and derived from, "Canaanite" culture. (Scholars call the preceding culture "Canaanite" because the Bible refers to it with this term, but this biblical term may be in part a "cover-all" term for the various people in the land.) As noted below in chapter 1, the extrabiblical text from Egypt known as the Merneptah stele also distinguishes Israel and Canaan. In short, Israelite culture was largely "Canaanite" in nature. Given the information available, one cannot maintain a radical cultural separation between "Canaanites" and Israelites for the Iron I period. To be sure, the early history of Israel was extremely complex, and establishing ethnic continuity or discontinuity is impossible for this period. Some distinctions probably existed among the various groups inhabiting the highlands and valleys and coastal regions in Israel's earliest history; information about them is largely unavailable at present. The first section of chapter 1 focuses on the development of Israelite culture from the larger "Canaanite" culture. The remainder of this study focuses on one specific area of this cultural continuum, namely, the literary and religious motifs from Israelite's "Canaanite" heritage that bear on the development of Israelite monolatry.

The change in the scholarly understanding of early Israel's culture has led to the second major change in perspective, which involves the nature of Yahwistic cult. With the change in perspective concerning Israel's "Canaanite" background, long-held notions about Israelite religion are slowly eroding. Baal and Asherah were part of Israel's "Canaanite" heritage, and the process of the emergence of Israelite monolatry was an issue of Israel's breaking with its own "Canaanite" past and not simply one of avoiding "Canaanite" neighbors. Although the biblical witness accurately represented the existence of Israelite worship of Baal and perhaps of Asherah as well, this worship was not so much a case of Israelite syncretism with the religious practices of its "Canaanite" neighbors, as some biblical passages depict it, as it was an instance of old Israelite religion. If syncretism may be said to have been involved at all, it was a syncretism of various religious traditions and practices of Israelites. In short, any syncretism was largely a phenomenon within Israelite culture. In early Israel, the cult of Yahweh generally held sway. However, this statement does not fully characterize pre-exilic Israelite religion as a whole. Rather, Israelite religion apparently included worship of Yahweh, El, Asherah, and Baal.

The shape of this religious spectrum in early Israel changed, due in large measure to two major developments; the first was convergence, and the second was differentiation.[12] Convergence involved the coalescence of vari-

12. For convergence in this early period, see B. Halpern, "'Brisker Pipes Than Poetry': The Development of Israelite Monotheism," in *Judaic Perspectives on Ancient Israel,* ed. J. Neusner, B. A. Levine, and E. S. Frerichs (Philadelphia: Fortress, 1987), 88. That this was a general feature of Israelite society as a whole as argued by Halpern appears unlikely in view of the worship of Baal in ancient Israel (see chapter 2, section 1). Cross uses the term "differentiation" with respect to Canaanite and Israelite religion (*Canaanite Myth and Hebrew Epic,* 71). In

ous deities and/or some of their features into the figure of Yahweh. This development began in the period of the Judges and continued during the first half of the monarchy. At this point, El and Yahweh were identified, and perhaps Asherah no longer continued as an identifiably separate deity. Features belonging to deities such as El, Asherah, and Baal were absorbed into the Yahwistic religion of Israel. This process of absorption is evident in the poetic compositions that a number of scholars consider to be the oldest stratum of Israel's literature.[13] From a linguistic perspective,[14] these poems, including Genesis 49, Judges 5, 2 Samuel 22 (= Psalm 18), 2 Samuel 23:1-7, and Psalms 29 and 68, appear to be older than the poetic compositions in the prophetic books and therefore date at least to the first half of the monarchy; some of them may be older. Judges 5, for example, suggests a premonarchic setting.[15] In these poetic compositions, titles and characteristics originally belonging to various deities secondarily accrued to Yahweh.

Furthermore, if the prophetic critiques of Elijah and Hosea include credible historical information, then Baal was accepted within Israel by Israelites. What the prophets fail to mention is how deities functioned in monarchic Israel. Israelite monolatry developed through conflict and compromise

his discussion of the biblical combination of El and Baal traits in the personage of Yahweh, he uses the term "conflation" (163), which I take to reflect the larger process of convergence. See also Ahlström, "The Travels of the Ark: A Religio-Political Composition," *JNES* 43 (1984): 146-48. For further discussion, see below, especially chapter 1, section 4; chapter 3, section 5; chapter 5; and chapter 6, section 1. In his review of the first edition of this book, S. Parker prefers the term "individuation" to my "differentiation." See Parker, *Hebrew Studies* 33 (1992): 158. For "differentiation," see further G. Emberling, "Ethnicity in Complex Societies: Archaeological Perspectives," *Journal of Archaeological Research* 5/4 (1997): 306, reference courtesy of E. Bloch-Smith; see her relevant piece, "Israelite Ethnicity in Iron I" (tentative title, in preparation).

13. For discussion of the dating of the so-called old poetry, see F. M. Cross and D. N. Freedman, *Studies in Ancient Yahwistic Poetry,* SBLDS 76 (Missoula, MT: Scholars, 1975); Cross, *Canaanite Myth and Hebrew Epic,* 100-103, 121-44, 151-62, 234-37; D. N. Freedman, *Pottery, Poetry, and Prophecy: Studies in Early Hebrew Poetry* (Winona Lake, IN: Eisenbrauns, 1980), 77-178. For a contrary view, see M. H. Floyd, "Oral Tradition as a Problematic Factor in the Historical Interpretation of Poems in the Law and the Prophets" (Ph.D. diss., Claremont Graduate School, 1980), 174-205, 484-93.

14. D. A. Robertson, "Linguistic Evidence in Dating Early Hebrew Poetry" (Ph.D. diss., Yale University, 1966); M. O'Connor, *Hebrew Verse Structure* (Winona Lake, IN: Eisenbrauns, 1980).

15. Cross, *Canaanite Myth and Hebrew Epic,* 100-101. G. Garbini ("Il cantico di Debora," *La parola del passato* 178 [1978]: 5-31) and J. A. Soggin (*Judges: A Commentary,* OTL [Philadelphia: Westminster, 1981], 93) argue for a monarchic date for Judges 5, but some details of background in this chapter suggest an earlier setting (see L. E. Stager, "Archaeology, Ecology, and Social History: Background Themes to the Song of Deborah," in *Congress Volume: Jerusalem 1986,* ed. J. Emerton, VTSup [Leiden: Brill, 1988], 221-34).

between the cults of Yahweh and other deities. Israelite literature incorporated some of the characteristics of other deities into the divine personage of Yahweh. Polemic against deities other than Yahweh even contributed to this process. For although polemic rejected other deities, Yahwistic polemic assumed that Yahweh embodied the positive characteristics of the very deities it was condemning.

The second major process involved differentiation of Israelite cult from its "Canaanite" heritage. Numerous features of early Israelite cult were later rejected as "Canaanite" and non-Yahwistic. This development apparently began first with the rejection of Baal worship in the ninth century, continued in the eighth to sixth centuries with legal and prophetic condemnations of Baal worship, the asherah, solar worship, the high places, practices pertaining to the dead, and other religious features. The two major developments of convergence and differentiation shaped the contours of the distinct monotheism that Israel practiced and defined in the Exile (ca. 587-538) following the final days of the Judean monarchy. Chapter 1 discusses convergence in early ancient Israelite religion in connection with the deities El, Baal, and Asherah. Chapter 2, section 4, illustrates how the martial imagery associated with the goddess Anat was assimilated to Yahweh, although the goddess herself makes no appearance in Israelite texts; in this case, convergence of imagery is indicated, although there is no issue of the cult of this goddess in ancient Israel. Chapters 2, 3, and 4 present examples of both convergence and differentiation in ancient Israel. In these chapters, Baal, the symbol of the asherah, and solar imagery are seen as subject to modification to the cult of Yahweh; varying degrees of convergence or assimilation to the cult of Yahweh can be discerned. All of these three phenomena also reflect the later development of differentiation. As old Canaanite/Israelite features, Baal and the asherah were perceived as non-Yahwistic and therefore non-Israelite. Chapter 5 examines some cultic practices also subject to differentiation: high places, practices pertaining to the dead, and the *mlk* sacrifice. High places and practices pertaining to the dead, originally part of ancient Israel's heritage, were criticized as non-Yahwistic.

The third shift in perspective involves the role of the monarchy (ca. 1000-587) in the processes of convergence and differentiation. The monarchy fostered the inclusion of various deities, or their features, into the cult of Yahweh.[16] The development of a national religion and a national god did not

16. This has been seen by H. Gottlieb ("El und Krt — Jahwe und David. Zum Ursprung des alttestamentlichen Monotheismus," *VT* 24 [1974]: 159-67) and Morton Smith (*Palestinian Parties and Politics That Shaped the Old Testament* [New York: Columbia Univ. Press, 1971], 21-

exclude other deities; indeed, at times they were encouraged. The national or state religions in Mesopotamia and Egypt tolerated other deities; moreover, these religions incorporated the features of various deities into the cult of the state deity, thereby exalting the main deity and the state's own identity. As one example of incorporation, the traits of numerous deities were attributed to Marduk, the god of Babylon, not only in the fifty names that he receives at the end of Enuma Elish, but also in the characterizing of over a dozen deities as aspects of Marduk in a small god list.[17] Assur, the god of the city-state by the same name, was depicted with the iconography of other deities. Similarly, Amun-Re, the divine champion of New Kingdom Egypt, received the attributes of Egypt's more traditional chief deities.[18] A compara-

---

22). Most substantial treatments of the history of religion in Israel comment on the role of the monarchy. For example, see Ringgren, *Israelite Religion,* 57-65, 220-38; Fohrer, *History of Israelite Religion,* 123-50; Cross, *Canaanite Myth and Hebrew Epic,* 219-65; G. Mendenhall, *The Tenth Generation: The Origins of the Biblical Tradition* (Baltimore: Johns Hopkins Univ. Press, 1973), 181, 188-94; G. W. Ahlström, *Royal Administration and National Religion in Ancient Palestine,* Studies in the History of the Ancient Near East 1 (Leiden: Brill, 1982); idem, *Who Were the Israelites?* (Winona Lake, IN: Eisenbrauns, 1986), 85-99; Halpern, "'Brisker Pipes Than Poetry,'" 77-115.

17. See W. G. Lambert, "The Historical Development of the Mesopotamian Pantheon: A Study in Sophisticated Polytheism," in *Unity and Diversity: Essays in the History, Literature, and Religion of the Ancient Near East,* ed. H. Goedicke and J. J. M. Roberts (Baltimore: John Hopkins Univ. Press, 1975), 191-200; idem, "Trees, Snakes and Gods in Ancient Syria and Anatolia," *BSOAS* 48 (1985): 439; A. Livingstone, *Mystical and Mythological Explanatory Works of Assyrian and Babylonian Scholars* (Oxford: Clarendon, 1986), 101, 233; W. Sommerfeld, *Der Aufstieg Marduks,* AOAT 213 (Kevelaer: Butzon & Bercker; Neukirchen-Vluyn: Neukirchener Verlag, 1982), 174-81. On the fifty names of Marduk, see J. Bottéro, "Les noms de Marduk, l'écriture et la 'logique' en Mésopotamie ancienne," in *Essays on the Ancient Near East in Memory of Jacob Joel Finkelstein,* ed. M. de Jong Ellis, Memoirs of the Connecticut Academy of Arts and Sciences (Hamden, CT: Archon Books, 1977), 5-28. For further discussion, see R. S. Hendel, "Aniconism and Anthropomorphism in Ancient Israel," in *The Image and the Book: Iconic Cults, Aniconism, and the Rise of Book Religion in Israel and the Ancient Near East,* ed. K. van der Toorn, Contributions to Biblical Exegesis and Theology 21 (Leuven: Peeters, 1997), 206-12; and M. S. Smith, *The Origins of Biblical Monotheism: Israel's Polytheistic Background and the Ugaritic Texts* (Oxford/New York: Oxford Univ. Press, 2001), 87-88. See further S. Parpola, "Monotheism in Ancient Assyria," in *One God or Many? Conceptions of Divinity in the Ancient World,* ed. B. N. Porter, Transactions of the Casco Bay Assyriological Institute (Bethesda, MD: CDL Press, 2000), 165-209.

18. On Amun-Re, see J. Assman, *Re und Amun: Die Krise des polytheistischen Weltbildes im Ägypten der 18.-20. Dynastie,* OBO 51 (Göttingen: Vandenhoeck & Ruprecht, 1982); G. Posener, "Sur le monothéisme dans l'ancienne Egypte," in *Mélanges biblique et orientaux en l'honneur de M. Henri Cazelles,* ed. A. Caquot and M. Delcor, AOAT 212 (Kevelaer: Butzon & Bercker; Neukirchen-Vluyn: Neukirchener Verlag, 1981), 347-51; cf. D. B. Redford, *Akhenaten: The Heretic King* (Princeton: Princeton Univ. Press, 1984), 158, 176, 205, 225-26, 232; J. C. de

ble process might be seen at work in monarchic Israel. For examples of toleration, one may appeal to either Solomon's concessions to the gods of his foreign wives (1 Kings 11:5, 7-8) or Ahab's sponsorship of Phoenician Baal worship (1 Kings 17–19).[19] In the first half of its existence, the monarchy fostered some features of convergence in exalting Yahweh as the national god. By this exaltation, Yahweh evidently acquired titles and traits originally belonging to other deities.

Moreover, royal religion was both conservative and innovative. It incorporated practices traditional in popular religion, such as the cult of Baal, the symbol of the asherah, high places, and practices pertaining to the dead. During the second half of the monarchy, religious programs patronized by the Judean kings Hezekiah and Josiah contributed to the differentiation of Israelite religion from its "Canaanite" past. Centralization of cult and criticism of various cultic practices reflect substantial changes in royal religious policies following the fall of the northern kingdom. Despite the roles the monarchy played in the development of Israelite monotheism, the monarchy has been perceived as an institution hostile to "pure" Yahwistic cult. If the condemnations in the books of Kings are to be believed, the monarchs of Israel were the most guilty in tolerating and sometimes even importing deities and religious practices allegedly alien to Yahwism. While this viewpoint is partially true, it is partially misleading. The monarchy was responsible for some of the developments leading to the eventual emergence of monotheism. The monarchy generally maintained a special relationship with Yahweh; Yahweh was the national god and patron of the monarchy. Israelite "service" *(*ʿbd)* only to Yahweh in the monarchic period eventually developed into a notion of universal service to Yahweh.[20] Though monotheism was ultimately a product of the Exile, some developments leading to it are evident in a variety of religious expressions dating to the monarchy. Royal influence is abundantly manifest in the political use of storm imagery, which chapter 2, section 3, emphasizes. The royal setting of the asherah is discussed in chapter 3, section 1. Solar imagery in ancient Israel was perhaps in part a royal phenomenon, as explored

---

Moor, "The Crisis of Polytheism in Late Bronze Ugarit," *OTS* 24 (1986): 1-20; J. Baines, "Egyptian Deities in Context: Multiplicity, Unity, and the Problem of Change," in *One God or Many?* ed. B. N. Porter, 9-78, esp. 53-62. See also Halpern, "'Brisker Pipes Than Poetry,'" 79-80.

19. J. Tigay, "Israelite Religion: The Onomastic and Epigraphic Evidence," in *Ancient Israelite Religion: Essays in Honor of Frank Moore Cross,* ed. P. D. Miller, Jr., P. D. Hanson, and S. D. McBride (Philadelphia: Fortress, 1987), 178-79.

20. On this point, see J. P. Floss, *Jahwe dienen — Göttern dienen: Terminologische, literarische und semantische Untersuchung einer theologischen Aussage zum Gottesverhältnis im Alten Testament,* BBB 45 (Cologne and Bern: Peter Hanstein Verlag GmbH, 1975), esp. 140-49.

in chapter 4. Other features in Israelite religion, though not royal in origin, were tolerated by the monarchy and sometimes incorporated into the royal cult; high places and practices pertaining to the dead, discussed in chapter 5, belong to this category.

One caveat regarding the historical reconstruction of the monarchy's role in Israel's religion deserves comment. Because the Hebrew Bible received its fundamental formation in the city of Jerusalem, the biblical information pertaining to royal religious policy derives largely from the southern kingdom. As a result, it is not possible to provide a balanced view of the religious practices of the northern monarchy except in those cases that held importance for southern tradents. The institution of bull iconography by Jeroboam I in the cities of Dan and Bethel (1 Kings 12:28-30) and the royal patronization of the cult of Phoenician Baal by Ahab and his Tyrian wife, Jezebel (1 Kings 17–19), evidently appeared in biblical books produced in the southern capital because these practices contained evidence of the northern kingdom's apostasy. Many of the religious practices studied in the following chapters appear to be features general to both kingdoms (including the asherah, the high places, and religious customs pertaining to the dead) or specific to Judah (such as solar imagery for Yahweh). Religious contributions made by the monarchy examined in this study are thus often decidedly Judean in character.

The fourth change in outlook reflects the tremendous interest expressed in goddesses in Israelite religion. As the title of Albright's *Yahweh and the Gods of Canaan* illustrates, goddesses have not featured nearly as prominently as gods in the secondary literature pertaining to ancient Israel. This is due to the relative paucity of primary material bearing on goddesses in ancient Israel. The features of the gods, El and Baal, are more frequently attested in biblical descriptions of Yahweh than the imprint of the goddesses, Asherah and Anat. Fortunately, recent interest in ancient goddesses and their place in Israelite religion has sparked greater scrutiny of the ancient sources for pertinent information. Furthermore, inscriptions from Kuntillet ʿAjrûd and Khirbet el-Qôm (and Ekron, according to some scholars) furnish further data concerning one goddess, Asherah, or at least her symbol, the asherah, and have compelled scholars to reexamine the roles of goddesses in Israel. The goddesses Asherah, Astarte, and Anat are discussed in various parts of the present study. Chapter 1, section 4, and chapter 3 are devoted to Asherah and her symbol, the asherah. Chapter 3, section 4, addresses the evidence concerning Astarte in ancient Israel. Chapter 2, section 4, presents the data bearing on the literary influence that traditions pertaining to the goddess Anat may have exercised on some descriptions of Yahweh, although it appears that Anat was not a goddess at any time in ancient Israel. Other goddesses receive brief notice: the Phoenician figures Tannit and *tntʿštrt,* the biblical "Queen of Heaven" (Jer. 7:18; 44:17-25), and Mesopotamian Ishtar. Chapter 3, section 5, discusses personified Wisdom (Proverbs 1–9; Ben Sira 1:20; 4:13; 24:12-17; Baruch 4:1), another female figure often included by scholars in this divine company.

The present work utilizes the recent additions of data and major changes in perspective in order to illuminate broad trends underlying the development of various features of Israelite religion. Scholars have long recognized how the Ugaritic corpus provides evidence of the literature, the mythology, and the religion of the Canaanites, which constituted the background from which Israelite religion largely emerged. Indeed, many scholarly studies have treated individual aspects of the Canaanite contributions to Israelite religion. The present work examines the Canaanite and Israelite data in some detail and inquires into the fundamental relationship between Canaanite and Israelite religion. The task involves more than drawing parallels between Canaanite and Israelite texts and iconography. Rather, it requires situating Canaanite deities and their cultic symbols and imagery within the context of the complex historical development of the cult of Yahweh. Early Israel initially witnessed a spectrum of religious worship that included the cults of various Canaanite deities. Inscriptional and biblical evidence reflects the overwhelming religious hegemony of Yahweh for nearly all periods of Israelite history. Texts, iconography, archaeology, and other data further document the complex character of this hegemony over the course of the Iron Age. By the end of the monarchy much of the spectrum of religious practice had largely disappeared; monolatrous Yahwism was the norm in Israel, setting the stage for the emergence of Israelite monotheism.[21] As chapters 2 through 5 illustrate, the period of the monarchy produced the conditions for the gradual development of monotheism. With a view to the information provided in the first five chapters, chapter 6 offers a historical overview of the development of convergence, monolatry, and monotheism in ancient Israel. Chapter 7 pre-

21. See Ahlström, *Royal Administration,* 69; M. S. Smith, "God Male and Female in the Old Testament: Yahweh and His Asherah," *Theological Studies* 48 (1987): 338. Halpern ("'Brisker Pipes Than Poetry,'" 85, 87, 88, 91, 96, 101) equates Israel's monolatrous henotheism (i.e., worship of one deity without denying the existence of other deities) with monotheism and calls the monolatrous henotheistic religion of monarchic Israel "unselfconsciously monotheistic." For a study of this terminology, see D. L. Petersen, "Israel and Monotheism: The Unfinished Agenda," in *Canon, Theology, and Old Testament Interpretation: Essays in Honor of Brevard S. Childs,* ed. G. M. Tucker, D. L. Petersen, and R. R. Wilson (Philadelphia: Fortress, 1988), 92-107. See also the discussion in chapter 6.

sents some major historical and theological issues presented by the historical picture drawn in chapter 6. The information contained in this study illustrates the complex factors involved in the emergence of Israelite monotheism, one of the greatest contributions of ancient Israel to Western civilization.

2. Presuppositions in This Study

Before presenting the historical data bearing on the development of the cult of Yahweh, it may be valuable to state at the outset some of the methodological presuppositions inherent in this investigation.[22] The most important assumptions regard the nature of the Bible. The Bible, the main source for the history of ancient Israel, is not a history book in the modern sense. Nonetheless, the Bible contains much information about history, and indeed the books running from Joshua through 2 Chronicles may rightly be called the works of ancient Israelite historians. As B. Halpern comments, the authors of these biblical books were no less historians than Herodotus or Thucydides.[23] The biblical historians presented a picture of ancient Israel based on information that they viewed as historically true. There are other similarities between the historiography of the ancient biblical authors and that of modern scholars of Israelite religion. Both ancient and modern scholars have tried to identify the periods to which the various parts belong; both sift through all the pieces of biblical books to assess the historical nature and accuracy of the information contained in them. Both ancient and modern scholars have attempted to arrange information before them in chronological order and to narrate accordingly a history of Israel. Modern scholars attempt to arrange biblical books and the blocks of material within them in order so as to understand various periods of Israel's history. Like the ancient scribes of Israel, modern scholars also bring other data to bear on interpreting the history of Israel. They incorporate sources or material from other genres of literature or other sources to enable their history writing. Like modern historians, biblical writers provided background information from time to time (e.g., 1 Sam. 28:3; 1 Kings 18:3b; 2 Kings 9:14b-15a; 15:12) or "historical" explanations of the events that they describe (e.g., 2 Kings 13:5-6; 17:7-23). Biblical and mod-

22. See G. A. Herion, "The Impact of Modern and Social Science Assumptions on the Reconstruction of Israelite Religion," *JSOT* 34 (1986): 3-33; and J. Berlinerblau, "The 'Popular Religion' Paradigm in Old Testament Research: A Sociological Critique," *JSOT* 60 (1993): 3-26.

23. B. Halpern, *The First Historians: The Hebrew Bible and History* (San Francisco: Harper & Row, 1988), 3-35; cf. M. Brettler, *The Creation of History in Ancient Israel* (London/New York: Routledge, 1995). See also the discussion above on pp. xxvi-xxviii.

ern authors alike have supplied footnotes for their studies. The difference is that biblical authors incorporated their footnotes into their text (e.g., 1 Kings 14:19, 29; 15:7, 23, 31; 16:14, 20; 22:45; 2 Kings 1:18; 10:34; 12:19; 13:8, 12; 14:15, 28; 15:6, 11, 15, 21, 26, 31, 36; 16:19; 20:20; 21:17; 23:28).

There are, however, major differences between the historiography of the Bible and modern historiography. In rendering a picture of ancient Israel, modern historians customarily avoid the heavily theological interpretations of events that lace biblical historiography. At the same time, one must recognize that like the ancient historians of Israel, modern historians investigating biblical history often have a personal, theological interest in their subject, even if they attempt to maintain a critical distance from the subject. Indeed, the research of modern scholars is dictated in large measure by both the concern with historical accuracy and scholars' religious interest in the biblical record. Modern scholars are sensitive to the different types of texts included in the Bible and their separate histories. They have recognized how unevenly biblical material is distributed over the history of ancient Israel. The sources for the years from the fall of the northern kingdom (ca. 722) down to the fall of the southern kingdom (ca. 587) heavily outweigh the sources for either the period of the Judges (ca. 1200-1000) or the initial stages of the monarchy (ca. 1000-722). As a result, much more is known about the late monarchy than either the period of the Judges or the first half of the monarchy. Moreover, the bulk of the data derives from the southern kingdom, and therefore there are great gaps in information regarding the northern kingdom. Besides large gaps in primary data, there are other problems. The historical reconstruction drawn in the following chapters is complicated further by the long time frame and the culturally and topographically diverse areas from which the data derive. For example, the northern and southern kingdoms exhibited many cultural divergencies in pottery, tomb types, language, and social institutions. Further regional differences within the northern and southern kingdoms are even more difficult to grasp, since there is little information available for such specific regional features. Finally, transitions between periods based on the archaeological record remain obscure; they were far more complex than the textual record indicates.[24] Indeed, A. Faust has noted that despite long-term continuities, the eleventh to early tenth century witnessed some break in material culture as well as significant rural highland abandonment.[25]

24. For the Late Bronze–Iron I transition, see below p. 21 n. 9. For the Iron I–Iron II transition, see A. Faust, "Abandonment, Urbanization, Resettlement and the Formation of the Israelite State," *Near Eastern Archaeology* (in press).

25. For discussion and evidence, see A. Faust, "Abandonment, Urbanization, Resettle-

After testing the historical setting of biblical passages, biblical scholars study the information provided by various passages for potential interrelationships. Often such relationships are unclear, tenuous, or nonexistent. This stage of investigation resembles working with a puzzle that is missing many or most of its pieces.[26] Worse yet, scholars do not know how many pieces there are. It is clear that many or probably most of the pieces are missing, but there is no way to verify the extent of the gaps in data. Commentators try to overcome these limitations by consulting other sources: archaeology, iconography, and inscriptions. These sources suffer from many of the same limitations found in the biblical record, however. From a synthesis of all these sources, a partial picture of ancient Israel emerges.

Studying Israelite religion involves recognizing the character of ancient religion manifest in the biblical record. This study often focuses on large-scale developments and examines religion in its institutional expressions, as the biblical record provides information mostly about Israel's institutions — religious, social, and royal. For many people today, religion is a private matter kept separate from politics. In striking contrast, religion depicted in the Hebrew Bible is primarily not a private matter but a communal one, a national one, with major social and political implications. The Torah or Pentateuch, consisting of the first five books of the Bible, relates Israel's national origins as well as the legal, social, and cultic norms by which Israelites were called to live. The narrative books of Joshua through 2 Chronicles provide a national history down to the fall of the southern kingdom. The prophetic books detail religious problems with the northern or southern kingdom as a whole, though sometimes focusing on the religious problems among specific groups of people. The wisdom books and other works of the Writings (Ketubim) offer instruction in everyday norms and the difficulties of Israelite existence. The Bible often presents a general picture of ancient Israel and its religion. The present work often depends on this sort of picture insofar as it relies on correlating religious features with developments within political and social institutions.

There are not only problems with the historical record, but also difficulties with modern methods and perspectives. In the analysis of the available data, conscious and unconscious assumptions are made. Furthermore, presenting data inevitably involves making choices. The examination of Israelite

---

ment and the Formation of the Israelite State," and E. M. Bloch-Smith, "Israelite Ethnicity in Iron I" (in preparation). I do not accept the cause put forth by Faust for these developments.

26. For illustrations of problems inherent in historical reconstructions, see D. H. Fischer, *Historians' Fallacies: Toward a Logic of Historical Thought* (New York: Harper & Row, 1970).

religion in the present work has concentrated more on the literary data than on archaeological information. Because contemporary interests dictate the subjects of some parts of this study, the data are inevitably shaped by contemporary considerations. Monotheism is not only a question for the scholarly investigation of ancient Israel; ancient Israelite monotheism continues to elicit interest among adherents to Judaism and Christianity, two of the great monotheistic traditions of today. Similarly, renewed interest in the Northwest Semitic goddesses and in gender language applied to Yahweh in the Hebrew Bible affects the treatment of these historical issues in chapters 1 and 3.

The study of Israelite religion often involves studying practices more than credal beliefs because the Bible more frequently stresses correct practices than correct beliefs or internal attitudes. Christian scholars, however, tend to focus more on beliefs or internal attitudes because Christian theology has often emphasized this aspect of religion. The study of Israelite monotheism is complicated by this factor, as monotheism has usually been defined as a matter of belief in one deity whereas monolatry has been understood as a matter of practice, specifically, the worship of only one deity, sometimes coupled with a tolerance for other peoples' worship of their deities. However, if ancient Israelite religion is to be viewed primarily as a matter of practice, then the modern distinction between monotheism and monolatry is problematic.[27] Nonetheless, the distinction is retained in this study for two reasons. First, the appearance of both monolatry and monotheism remains a matter of current interest. Second, the distinction between the two phenomena emerged within Israelite religion.

Finally, the modern study of Israelite religion considers both what some biblical sources consider "normative" and what appears to be outside the norms set by biblical laws or prophetic criticisms. Although the Bible and the religious claims made in it are entirely relevant to the task of reconstructing the history of Israelite religion, they do not represent the sum of Israelite faith in Yahweh. All religious data, including the Bible, inscriptions, iconography, and other archaeological data, are pertinent to the attempt to understand the religion of ancient Israel. The notion of an essence of a religion apart from the sum total of a people's religious beliefs, words, and actions constitutes a secondary abstraction. When expressions about a religious essence of ancient Israel are based on biblical statements about religious norms, the expressions represent statements of personal faith and not historical description. Biblical

27. For a critical treatment of issues pertaining to the definition, terminology, and understanding of monotheism in Israel, see Halpern, "'Brisker Pipes Than Poetry,'" 75-115; Petersen, "Israel and Monotheism," 92-107.

statements and sometimes contemporary claims about religious syncretism constitute one type of attempt to make distinctions between a normative, religious essence of Israel, on the one hand, and illegitimate or non-Israelite practices infecting Israelite religion, on the other. Although it is historically true that some practices were secondarily incorporated into the religion of Israel from Israel's neighbors, other practices classified as being the result of syncretism belonged to Israel's ancient religious heritage. Both original and borrowed features constitute legitimate subjects of historical inquiry. Ancient Israelite religion included both officially sanctioned practices and practices not sanctioned by various authorities; both official and popular religion belong to any historical description of Israelite religion. The historical enterprise examines the historical limitations and presuppositions of biblical claims. The task of reconstructing the cult of Yahweh includes biblical claims and sets them within a wider framework that accounts for the available information. The data in the attested sources indicate a pluralism of religious practice in ancient Israel that led sometimes to conflict about the nature of correct Yahwistic practice. It is precisely this conflict that produced the differentiation of Israelite religion from its Canaanite heritage during the second half of the monarchy. As a result of this conflict, some elements of faith appear transformed or muted in the Bible in a variety of ways. Anthropomorphic descriptions of Yahweh and language of the goddess may constitute examples of this change. Both were part of Israel's ancient traditions; both were considerably modified during the process of differentiation.[28]

Because of these considerations about ancient historical evidence and about modern methods used to reconstruct Israelite religion, the picture presented in the following chapters is necessarily a partial and subjective one.

28. Cf. Day, *Yahweh and the Gods and Goddesses of Canaan,* 226-33.

CHAPTER 1

Deities in Israel in the Period of the Judges

1. Israel's "Canaanite" Heritage

Early Israelite culture cannot be separated easily from the culture of "Canaan."[1] The highlands of Israel in the Iron Age (ca. 1200-587) reflect continuity with the "Canaanite" (or better, West Semitic[2]) culture during the preceding period both in the highlands and in the contemporary cities on the coast and in the valleys.[3] This continuity is reflected in scripts, for one example.

1. On the environment and social organization of early Israel, see L. E. Stager, "The Archaeology of the Family in Ancient Israel," *BASOR* 260 (1985): 1-35; C. Meyers, "Of Seasons and Soldiers: A Topographical Appraisal of the Premonarchic Tribes of Galilee," *BASOR* 252 (1983): 47-59; Ahlström, *Who Were the Israelites?* 2-83; J. W. Rogerson, "Was Israel a Fragmentary Society?" *JSOT* 36 (1986): 17-26; and E. Bloch-Smith and B. Alpert Nakhai, "A Landscape Comes to Life: The Iron Age I," *Near Eastern Archaeology* 62/2 (1999): 62-92, 101-27. On judicial administration in early Israel, see R. R. Wilson, "Enforcing the Covenant: The Mechanisms of Judicial Authority in Early Israel," *The Quest for the Kingdom of God: Studies in Honor of George E. Mendenhall,* ed. H. B. Huffmon, F. A. Spina, and A. R. W. Green (Winona Lake, IN: Eisenbrauns, 1983), 59-75. The traditional designation, "period of the Judges," is employed without adherence to the notion that this label accurately characterizes the period of Israelite history (ca. 1200-1000). For the historiographical issues involved with this label, see A. D. H. Mayes, "The Period of the Judges and the Rise of the Monarchy," in *Israelite and Judaean History,* ed. J. H. Hayes and J. M. Miller, OTL (Philadelphia: Westminster, 1977), 285-331.

2. In this edition, I have generally used the more tradition label, "Canaanite." However, "Canaanite" as a term of contrast with "Israelite" is more a product of biblical historiography than historical record. I prefer instead the term, "West Semitic," since it does not reinscribe the ideology of biblical historiography. For discussion, see M. S. Smith, *Untold Stories: The Bible and Ugaritic Studies in the Twentieth Century* (Peabody, MA: Hendrickson Publishers, 2001), 196-97. See further O. Loretz, "Ugariter, 'Kanaanäer' und 'Israeliten,'" *UF* 24 (1992): 249-58.

3. See Stager, "Archaeology of the Family in Ancient Israel," 1-35; J. Callaway, "A New Perspective on the Hill Country Settlement of Canaan in Iron Age I," in *Palestine in the Bronze and Iron Ages: Papers in Honour of Olga Tufnell,* ed. J. N. Tubb (London: Institute of Archaeology, 1985), 31-49.

Both linear and cuneiform alphabetic scripts are attested in inscriptions in the highlands as well as in the valleys and on the coast during both the Late Bronze (ca. 1550-1200) and Iron I (ca. 1200-1000) periods.[4] This continuity is visible also in language. Though Hebrew and Canaanite are the linguistic labels applied to the languages of the two periods in this region,[5] they cannot be easily distinguished in the Iron I period. For example, most scholars argue that the Gezer Calendar was written in Hebrew, but E. Y. Kutscher labels its language Canaanite.[6] Canaanite and Hebrew so closely overlap that the ability to distinguish them is premised more on historical information than linguistic criteria.[7] The ancient awareness of the close linguistic relationship, if

4. On the continuity of noncuneiform alphabetic scripts between the highlands and the valleys and coast, see the references below in n. 30. On alphabetic cuneiform texts with a comparable distribution, see A. R. Millard, "The Ugaritic and Canaanite Alphabets — Some Notes," *UF* 11 (1979): 613-16.

5. For the scholarly views regarding the relationships among Northwest Semitic languages, see J. C. Greenfield, "Amurrite, Ugaritic and Canaanite," in *Proceedings of the International Conference on Semitic Studies Held in Jerusalem, 19-23 July 1965* (Jerusalem: The Israel Academy of Sciences and Humanities, 1969), 92-101; W. R. Garr, *Dialect Geography of Syria-Palestine, 1000-586 B.C.E.* (Philadelphia: Univ. of Pennsylvania Press, 1985), 2-6. For a listing of pertinent works, see 241-60.

6. E. Y. Kutscher, *A History of the Hebrew Language* (Jerusalem: Magnes; Leiden: Brill, 1982), 67. D. Pardee proposes that the Gezer Calendar is possibly Phoenician (review of *Textbook of Syrian Semitic Inscriptions,* vol. 3, *Phoenician Inscriptions, Including Inscriptions in the Mixed Dialect of Arslan Tash,* by J. C. L. Gibson, *JNES* 46 [1987]: 139 n. 20). This classification is based on comparing the proleptic suffixes in lines 1 and 2 of the Gezer Calendar, in Phoenician inscriptions, and in late biblical Hebrew (Ezek. 10:3; 42:14; Prov. 13:4; Ezra 3:12; Job 29:3). The suffixes in the Gezer Calendar are notoriously difficult, however, and other, albeit less convincing, proposals for them have been made. Moreover, the anticipatory or proleptic suffix may represent a survival in both Phoenician and Hebrew (see Garr, *Dialect Geography,* 63, 108, 167-68).

7. For "Canaan" and "Canaanite" as terms applied to both material culture and language, see the following discussions: B. Maisler (Mazar), "Canaan and the Canaanites," *BASOR* 102 (1946): 7-12; W. F. Albright, "The Role of the Canaanites in the History of Civilization," in *The Bible and the Ancient Near East: Essays in Honor of William Foxwell Albright,* ed. G. E. Wright (Garden City, NY: Doubleday, 1961), 328-420; J. C. L. Gibson, "Observations on Some Important Ethnic Terms in the Pentateuch," *JNES* 20 (1961): 217-38; M. C. Astour, "The Origin of the Terms 'Canaan,' 'Phoenician' and 'Purple,'" *JNES* 24 (1965): 346-50; A. F. Rainey, "A Canaanite at Ugarit," *IEJ* 13 (1963): 43-45; idem, "The Kingdom of Ugarit," *BA* 28/4 (1965): 105-7 (reprinted in *The Biblical Archaeologist Reader 3,* ed. E. F. Campbell, Jr., and D. N. Freedman [Garden City, NY: Doubleday, Anchor Books, 1970], 79-80); idem, "Observations on Ugaritic Grammar," *UF* 3 (1971): 171; idem, "Toponymic Problems (cont.)," *TA* 6 (1979): 161; idem, "Toponymic Problems (cont.)," *TA* 9 (1982): 131-32; R. de Vaux, "Le Pays de Canaan," *JAOS* 88 (1968): 23-30; idem, *Histoire ancienne d'Israël: Des origines à l'installation en Canaan* (Paris: Gabalda, 1971), 124-26 (translation: *The Early History of Israel,* trans. D. Smith [Philadelphia: Westminster, 1978], 126-28); A. R. Millard, "The Canaanites," in *Peoples of Old Testament Times,*

not identity, between Canaanite and Hebrew is reflected in the postexilic oracle of Isaiah 19:18, which includes Hebrew in the designation "the language of Canaan" (*śĕpat kĕnaʿan;* cf. *yĕhûdît,* "Judean," in 2 Kings 18:26, 28; Isa. 36:11, 13; 2 Chron. 32:18; Neh. 13:24).[8]

Similarly, Canaanite and Israelite material culture cannot be distinguished by specific features in the Judges period.[9] For example, some Iron I

---

ed. D. J. Wiseman (Oxford: Clarendon, 1973), 29-52; M. Görg, "Der Name 'Kanaan' in aegyptischer Wiedergabe," *BN* 18 (1982): 26-27; M. Weippert, "Kinaḫḫi," *BN* 27 (1985): 18-21; idem, "Kanaan," *Reallexikon der Assyriologie* 5:352-55. See N. P. Lemche, *The Canaanites and Their Land: The Tradition of the Canaanites,* JSOTSup 110 (Sheffield: JSOT, 1991). See the critiques of A. Rainey, "Who Is a Canaanite? A Review of the Textual Evidence," *BASOR* 304 (1996): 1-15; N. Na'aman, "The Canaanites and Their Land: A Rejoinder," *UF* 26 (1994): 397-418. See Lemche's responses in "Greater Canaan: The Implications of a Correct Reading of EA 151:49-67," *BASOR* 310 (1998): 19-24, and "Where Should We Look for Canaan? A Reply to Nadav Na'aman," *UF* 28 (1996): 767-72. See also O. Fleming, "'The Storm God of Canaan' at Emar," *UF* 26 (1994): 127-30; R. Hess, "Occurrences of 'Canaan' in Late Bronze Age Archites of the West Semitic World," *IOS* 18 (1998): 365-72; idem, "Canaan and Canaanites at Alalakh," *UF* 31 (1999): 225-36; and N. Na'aman, "Four Notes on the Size of Late Bronze Age Canaan," *BASOR* 313 (1999): 31-38. See also the comments in Smith, *Untold Stories,* 196-97. Late Bronze Age "Canaan" as a geographical unit refers to the Egyptian province generally and to the coast in particular (Maisler, "Canaan and the Canaanites," 11). The northern limit of Canaan ran somewhere south of the kingdom of Ugarit and north of Byblos (see Rainey, "Kingdom of Ugarit," 106; idem, "Toponymic Problems (cont.)," *TA* 9 [1982]: 131). Canaanite merchants are distinguished at Ugarit as foreigners (Rainey, "A Canaanite at Ugarit," 43-45; S. E. Loewenstamm, "Ugarit and the Bible II," *Biblica* 59 [1978]: 117). The relationship between Ugaritic and Canaanite language is more complex (see the works cited in n. 5 and the remarks of Albright, *Yahweh and the Gods of Canaan,* 116 n. 15). Second-century coins minted in Laodicea (Latakia) bear the inscription "Of Laodicea, mother in Canaan" (G. F. Hill, *A Catalogue of the Greek Coins of Phoenicia* [London: Longmans, 1910], pl. 50). In the homeland, the term "Canaanite" is attested as late as the New Testament (Matt 15:22; cf. Mark 7:26).

8. O. Kaiser, *Isaiah 13–39; A Commentary,* trans. R. A. Wilson, OTL (Philadelphia: Westminster, 1974), 106-7; R. E. Clements, *Isaiah 1–39,* New Century Bible Commentary (Grand Rapids, MI: Eerdmans; London: Marshall, Morgan & Scott, 1980), 171; H. M. Orlinsky, "The Biblical Concept of the Land of Israel," *EI* 18 (1986 = N. Avigad Volume): 55* n. 17. On this verse, see further D. Barthélemy, *Critique Textuelle de l'Ancien Testament: Isaïe, Jérémie, Lamentations,* OBO 50/2 (Fribourg: Éditions Universitaires; Göttingen: Vandenhoeck & Ruprecht, 1986), 1.143-50.

9. See the survey in Bloch-Smith and Alpert-Nakhai, "A Landscape Comes to Life," 62-92, 101-27. See also A. Mazar, "The Iron Age I," in *The Archaeology of Ancient Israel,* ed. A. Ben-Tor, trans. R. Greenberg (New Haven/London: Yale Univ. Press/The Open University of Israel, 1992), 258-301; S. Bunimovitz, "Socio-Political Transformations in the Central Hill Country in the Late Bronze–Iron I Transition," in *From Nomadism to Monarchy: Archaeological and Historical Aspects of Early Israel,* ed. I. Finkelstein and N. Na'aman (Jerusalem: Yad Izhak Ben-Zri/Israel Exploration Society; Washington, DC: Biblical Archaeological Society, 1994), 179-202; and Dever, *What Did the Biblical Writers Know and When Did They Know It?* 108-24. See some help-

(ca. 1200-1000) cooking pots and storage jars as attested at Giloh represent a pottery tradition continuous with the Late Bronze Age.[10] Items such as the four-room house, collared-rim store jar, and hewn cisterns, once thought to distinguish the Israelite culture of the highlands from the Canaanite culture of the coast and valleys, are now attested on the coast, in the valleys, or in Transjordan.[11] Both indigenous tradition and influence from the coast and valleys are represented also in burial patterns. Multiple primary burials in caves continued in the hill country from the Late Bronze Age throughout the Iron Age. Arcosolia and bench tombs, two types of rock-cut tombs, are initially attested on the coast, and appeared also in the highlands in the Iron I period.[12]

The Canaanite (or, West Semitic) background of Israel's culture extended to the realm of religion. This is evident from the terminology for cultic sacrifices and personnel. BH sacrificial language with corresponding

---

ful cautions expressed by S. Bunimovitz and A. Faust, "Chronological Separation, Geographical Segregation, or Ethnic Demarcation? Ethnography and the Iron Age Low Chronology," *BASOR* 332 (2001): 1-10. For economic considerations, see R. F. Muth, "Economic Influences on Early Israel," *JSOT* 75 (1997): 59-75.

10. See A. Mazar, "Giloh: An Early Israelite Settlement Site Near Jerusalem," *IEJ* 31 (1981): 20-27, 32-33; Ahlström, *Who Were the Israelites?* 26, 28; I. Finkelstein, *The Archaeology of the Israelite Settlement* (Jerusalem: Israel Exploration Society, 1988), 270-91, 337.

11. For a lack of diagnostic features distinguishing Canaanite and Israelite material culture in the Judges period, see Ahlström, *Who Were the Israelites?* 28-35; Callaway, "A New Perspective," 37-41; W. G. Dever, "The Contribution of Archaeology to the Study of Canaanite and Early Israelite Religion," in *Ancient Israelite Religion: Essays in Honor of Frank Moore Cross,* ed. P. D. Miller, Jr., P. D. Hanson, and S. D. McBride (Philadelphia: Fortress, 1987), 235; M. M. Ibrahim, "The Collared Rim Jar of the Early Iron Age," in *Archaeology and the Levant: Essays in Honor of Kathleen Kenyon,* ed. R. Moorey and P. Parr (Warminster, England: Aris & Philips, 1978), 116-26; A. Schoors, "The Israelite Conquest: Textual Evidence in the Archaeological Argument," in *The Land of Israel: Cross-Roads of Civilizations,* ed. E. Lipiński, Orientalia Lovansiensia Analecta 19 (Louvain: Uitgeverij Peeters, 1985), 78-92. See also G. and O. van Beek, "Canaanite-Phoenician Architecture: The Development and Distribution of Two Styles," *EI* 15 (1981): 70*-74*. See also the continuity of the practice of terrace agriculture; see S. Gibson, "Agricultural Terraces and Settlement Expansion in the Highlands of Early Iron Age Palestine: Is There Any Correlation between the Two?" in *Studies in the Archaeology of the Iron Age in Israel and Jordan,* ed. A. Mazar, with the assistance of G. Mathias, JSOTSup 331 (Sheffield: Sheffield Academic Press, 2001), 113-46.

12. R. Gonen, "Regional Patterns and Burial Customs in Late Bronze Age Canaan," *Bulletin of the Anglo-Israel Archaeological Society* (1984-85): 70-74; E. M. Bloch-Smith, "Burials, Israelite," *ABD* 1.785-89; idem, *Judahite Burial Practices and Beliefs about the Dead,* JSOTSup 123, JSOT/ASOR Monograph Series 7 (Sheffield: Sheffield Academic Press, 1992). See also her essay, "The Cult of the Dead in Judah: Interpreting the Material Remains," *JBL* 111 (1992): 213-24. See further R. Tappy, "Did the Dead Ever Die in Biblical Judah?" *BASOR* 298 (1995): 59-68.

terms in Ugaritic and/or Phoenician includes *zebaḥ*, "slaughtered offering," a biblical term applied to sacrifices in the cults of both Yahweh (Gen. 46:1; Exod. 10:25; 18:12; Hos. 3:4; 6:6; 9:4; Amos 5:25) and Baal (2 Kings 10:19, 24; cf. KTU 1.116.1; 1.127; 1.148; KAI 69:12, 14; 74:10); *zebaḥ hayyāmîm*, "the annual slaughtered offering" (1 Sam. 1:21; 2:19; 20:6; cf. KAI 26 A II:19–III:2; C IV:2-5); *šĕlāmîm*, "offering of well-being/greeting"[13] (Leviticus 3; cf. KTU 1.105.9; 109; KAI 69:3; 51 obv.:5-6; 120:2); *neder*, offering of a vow (Numbers 30; Deuteronomy 12; cf. Ugaritic *ndr*, KTU 1.127.2; cf. *md̠r*, 1.119.30; KAI 155:1; 156; cf. 18:1; 45:1); *minḥāh*, "tribute offering" (Lev. 2:1-16; cf. CIS 14:5; KAI 69:14; 145:12-13); *kālîl*, "holocaust" (Deut. 33:10; Lev. 6:15-16; 1 Sam. 7:9; Ps. 51:21; cf. Deut. 13:17; cf. KTU 1.115.10; KAI 69:3, 5, 7; 74:5).[14] Other terms have been viewed as semantic equivalents in Hebrew and Ugaritic. It is assumed, for example, that BH *ʿôlāh* (Leviticus 1; cf. Judg. 11:30, 39) is semantically equivalent with Ugaritic *šrp* (KTU 1.105.9, 15; 1.106.2; 1.109); both denote an offering entirely consumed by fire. The *ʿôlāh* sacrifice belonged not only to the cult of Yahweh in Jerusalem and elsewhere but also to the cult of Baal in Samaria (2 Kings 10:24; cf. *ʿlt* in KAI 159:8). A ritual of general expiation was not only an Israelite feature (e.g., Leviticus 16; 17:11; cf. Gen. 32:21 for a noncultic example); it was also a Ugaritic phenomenon (KTU 1.40).[15] Both Ugaritic texts (1.46.1; 1.168.9) and biblical rituals (Leviticus 4–5) provide for divine forgiveness *(*slḥ/*slḥ)*. This incidence of highly specialized sacrificial terms suggests a common West Semitic heritage.

Although other terminological parallels between Israelite and Ugaritic and Phoenician texts are found also in Mesopotamian culture, these links further mark the closely related Israelite and Canaanite cultures. Biblical names with a Canaanite background for cult personnel include "priest," *kōhēn* (2 Kings 10:19; cf. KTU 4.29.1; 4.38.1; 4.68.72), "dedicated servants," *nĕtûnîm/nĕtunîm* (Num. 3:9; 8:19) and *nĕtînîm* (Ezra 2:43, 58, 70; 7:7; 8:17, 20; Neh. 3:26, 31; 7:46, 60, 72; 10:29; 11:3, 21; cf. 1 Chron. 9:2; cf. Ugaritic *ytnm* in KTU 4.93.1), and *qādēš*, a cultic functionary of some sort in both Is-

13. See B. A. Levine, *The JPS Torah Commentary: Leviticus ויקרא* (Philadelphia/New York/Jerusalem: The Jewish Publication Society, 1989), 15.

14. See Fohrer, *History of Israelite Religion*, 58-59; B. Levine, *In the Presence of the Lord: A Study of Cult and Some Cultic Terms in Ancient Israel* (Leiden: Brill, 1974); J. M. de Tarragon, *Le Culte à Ugarit*, CRB 19 (Paris: Gabalda, 1980); M. Weinfeld, "Social and Cultic Institutions in the Priestly Source Against Their Ancient Near Eastern Background," in *Proceedings of the Eighth World Congress of Jewish Studies* (Jerusalem: World Union of Jewish Studies, 1983), 95-129.

15. See J. C. de Moor and P. Sanders, "An Ugaritic Expiation Rite and Its Old Testament Parallels," *UF* 23 (1991): 283-300.

raelite religion (Deut. 23:18 [E 17]; 2 Kings 14:24; 15:12; 22:47; 23:7; Job 36:14) and Ugaritic cult (KTU 1.112.21; 4.29.3; 4.36; 4.38.2; 4.68.73).[16] Similarly, BH *hakkōhēn haggādôl,* "chief priest" (Lev. 21:10; Num. 35:25-28; Josh. 20:6; 2 Kings 12:11; 22:4, 8; Neh. 3:1, 20; 13:28; 2 Chron. 34:9; Hag. 1:1, 12, 14; 2:2, 4; Zech. 3:1, 8; 6:11) compares closely with Ugaritic *rb khnm,* "chief of the priests" (KTU 1.6 VI 55-56). Furthermore, the "tent of meeting" *('ōhel mô'ēd)* derived from Canaanite prototypes (2 Sam. 7:6; KTU 1.4 IV 20-26).[17] To be sure, parallels in terminology do not establish parallels in cultural setting in each of these cases.[18] Yet cultural continuity appears likely in these instances. It is evident from many areas of culture that Israelite society drew very heavily from Canaanite culture.[19]

16. Regarding cultic personnel at Ugarit, see J. M. de Tarragon, *Le Culte à Ugarit d'après les textes de la pratique en cunéiformes Alphabétiques,* CRB 19 (Paris: Gabalda, 1980), 131-48; M. Heltzer, *The Internal Organization of the Kingdom of Ugarit (Royal Service System, Taxes, Royal Economy, Arms and Administration)* (Wiesbaden: Dr. Ludwig Reichert Verlag, 1982), 131-39. For a synopsis of cultic personnel at Ugarit, see D. M. Clements, *Sources for Ugaritic Ritual and Sacrifice, Vol. I, Ugaritic and Ugaritic Akkadian Texts,* AOAT 284/1 (Münster: Ugarit-Verlag, 2001), 1086-89. For a general presentation of Ugaritic ritual, see G. del Olmo Lete, *Canaanite Religion according to the Liturgical Texts of Ugaritic,* trans. W. G. E. Watson (Bethesda, MD: CDL Press, 1999). For in-depth study of the Ugaritic ritual texts, see the magisterial work of D. Pardee, *Les textes rituels,* 2 vols., RSO XII (Paris: Édition Recherche sur les Civilisations, 2000). An English translation of the rituals is to appear from Pardee in the Writing in the Ancient World series. Concerning Ugaritic *ytnm,* BH *nĕtûnîm* and *nĕtînîm,* see B. A. Levine, "The *Nĕthînîm,*" *JBL* 82 (1963): 207-12; E. Puech, "The Tel el-Fûl Jar and the *Nĕtînîm,*" *BASOR* 261 (1986): 69-72. On *qdš,* see M. I. Gruber, "Hebrew *qĕdēšāh* and Her Canaanite and Akkadian Cognates," *UF* 18 (1986): 133; see also the references in n. 18.

17. On the Ugaritic parallels to BH *'ōhel mô'ēd,* see chapter 1, section 2.

18. The interpretation of BH *qĕdēšāh* is a good example of how cultural equivalences have been wrongly drawn on the basis of etymological cognates. According to Gruber ("Hebrew *qĕdēšāh,*" 133-48), scholars have incorrectly imputed a cultic background to BH *qĕdēšāh,* "prostitute" (Gen. 38:21-22; Deut. 23:18[E 17]; Hos. 4:14), and a sexual meaning to its cognates, Ugaritic *qdšt* and Akkadian *qadištu.* In this way, BH *qĕdēšāh* and its cognates have been viewed as terms for cultic prostitutes. Based on his examination of the extant evidence, Gruber concludes, on the contrary, that BH *qĕdēšāh* refers to a (secular) prostitute, while its Ugaritic and Akkadian cognates refer to cultic functionaries whose roles do not include sexual activities. See further the discussions of J. G. Westenholz, "Tamar, *Qĕdēšā, Qadištu,* and Sacred Prostitutions in Mesopotamia," *HTR* 82/3 (1989): 245-65; and P. A. Bird, *Missing Persons and Mistaken Identities: Women and Gender in Ancient Israel,* Overtures to Biblical Theology (Minneapolis: Fortress, 1997), 206-8, 233-36. See further S. Ackerman, *Warrior Dancer, Seductress, Queen: Women in Judges and Biblical Israel,* The Anchor Bible Reference Library (New York: Doubleday, 1998), 156, 176 n. 92.

19. This is not to suggest that the transition from the Late Bronze to the Iron I in the highlands was simple. The archaeology of this transition is immensely complicated, and beyond the scope of this discussion. For treatments of this subject, see the works cited in n. 9.

The evidence of the similarities between Canaanite and Israelite societies has led to a major change in the general understanding of the relationship between these two societies. Rather than viewing them as two separate cultures, some scholars define Israelite culture as a subset of Canaanite culture.[20] There are, however, some Israelite features that are unattested in Canaanite sources. These include the old tradition of Yahweh's southern sanctuary, variously called Sinai (Deut. 33:2; cf. Judg. 5:5; Ps. 68:9), Paran (Deut. 33:2; Hab. 3:3), Edom (Judg. 5:4), and Teiman (Hab. 3:3 and in the Kuntillet ʿAjrûd inscriptions; cf. Amos 1:12; Ezek. 25:13),[21] and Israel's early tradition of the Exodus from Egypt (Exod. 15:4).[22] Neither of these features appears to be Canaanite.[23]

That Israel in some form was distinguished from Canaan ca. 1200 is clear from an inscribed monument of the pharaoh Merneptah. This stele dates to the fifth year of the pharaoh's reign (ca. 1208) and mentions both Israel and Canaan:

> The princes are prostrate, saying: "Mercy!"
> Not one raises his head among the Nine Bows.

20. See M. D. Coogan, "Canaanite Origins and Lineage: Reflections on the Religion of Ancient Israel," in *Ancient Israelite Religion: Essays in Honor of Frank Moore Cross,* ed. P. D. Miller, Jr., P. D. Hanson, and S. D. McBride, 115.

21. For the traditions of the southern sanctuary, see chapter 2, section 2.

22. On the development of the traditions of the Exodus and the wandering in the wilderness, see B. S. Childs, *The Book of Exodus,* OTL (Philadelphia: Westminster, 1974), 218-30, 254-64.

23. Ringgren, *Israelite Religion,* 43-44. The Canaaanite background of the name of Yahweh is contraverted. According to Cross and Freedman Yahweh was a shortened form of a title of El, which became a divine name (Cross, *Canaanite Myth and Hebrew Epic,* 60-72; idem, "Reuben, First-Born of Jacob," *ZAW* 100 [1988]: 57-63; Freedman, *Pottery, Poetry, and Prophecy,* 132-46, 119-20). For criticisms of this theory, see Ringgren, *Israelite Religion,* 68; Childs, *The Book of Exodus,* 62-64; A. Gibson, *Biblical Semantic Logic: A Preliminary Analysis* (Oxford: Basil Blackwell, 1981), 71-73, 159-64. For the argument that the name of Yahweh may be related to a place name in the region to the south of Canaan mentioned in Late Bronze Age Egyptian records, see R. Giveon, "Toponymes Ouest-Asiatiques à Soleb," *VT* 14 (1964): 244; S. Herrman, *Israel in Egypt,* Studies in Biblical Theology 11/27 (London: SCM, 1973), 56-86; cf. M. C. Astour, "Yahweh in Egyptian Topographic Lists," in *Festschrift Elmar Edel: 12 Marz 1979,* ed. M. Görg and E. Pusch, Aegypten und Altes Testament 1 (Bamberg: M. Görg, 1979), 17-34; Ahlström, *Who Were the Israelites?* 58-60; R. J. Hess, "The Divine Name Yahweh in Late Bronze Age Sources?" *UF* 23 (1991): 180-82. For further discussion of the issues, see D. B. Redford, "The Ashkelon Relief at Karnak and the Israel Stela," *IEJ* 36 (1986): 199-200; M. Weinfeld, "The Tribal League at Sinai," in *Ancient Israelite Religion: Essays in Honor of Frank Moore Cross,* ed. P. D. Miller, Jr., P. D. Hanson, and S. D. McBride, 303-14; Finkelstein, *Archaeology of the Israelite Settlement,* 345.

Desolation is for Tehenu; Hatti is pacified;
Plundered is the Canaan with every evil;
Carried off is Ashkelon; seized upon is Gezer;
Yanoam is made as that which does not exist;
Israel is laid waste, his seed is not;
Hurru is become a widow for Egypt!
All lands together, they are pacified;
Everyone who is restless, he has been bound.[24]

The purpose of this passage was to celebrate Egyptian power over various lands in Syro-Palestine. Hatti and Hurru stand for the whole region of Syro-Palestine; Canaan and Israel represent smaller units within the area, and Gezer, Ashkelon, and Yanoam are three cities within the region. In this hymn to the power of the pharaoh, all these places stand under Egyptian rule. The text distinguishes between Israel and Canaan, as they constitute two different terms in the text. Some scholars note that the two terms are further distinguished. The word "Canaan" is written with a special linguistic feature called a determinative, denoting land. "Israel" is written with the determinative for people. Drawing historical conclusions from this difference in the scribal use of the two determinatives has proven problematic. On the one hand, if the determinatives were used accurately by the Egyptian scribe who wrote this text, then Israel as a people was established by 1200 B.C. On the other hand, some scholars believe that scribes did not use the two different determinatives consistently in other texts and therefore challenge the accuracy of their use in the Merneptah stele.[25] If the determinatives were used correctly, Israel stands for a people living in the region of the highlands rather than designating the geographical area of the highlands. In any case, Israel and Canaan are differentiated in the text, and in some way they represented different entities

24. *ANET,* 378. For the text, see K. A. Kitchen, *Ramesside Inscriptions: Historical and Biographical,* vol. 4 (Oxford: Basil Blackwell, 1982), 12-19. For further information, see M. Lichtheim, *Ancient Egyptian Literature,* vol. 2, *The New Kingdom* (Berkeley and Los Angeles: Univ. of California Press, 1976), 73-78. For further discussion, see D. Redford, "The Ashkelon Relief at Karnak and the Israel Stela," 188-200; A. R. Schulman, "The Great Historical Inscription of Mernepta at Karnak: A Partial Reappraisal," *Journal of the American Research Center in Egypt* 24 (1987): 21-34; M. Hasel, "Israel in the Merneptah Stela," *BASOR* 296 (1994): 45-61. For an analysis of the text, see A. Niccacci, "La Stèle d'Israël. Grammaire et stratégie de communication," in *Études Égyptologiques et Bibliques à la mémoire du Père B. Couroyer,* ed. M. Sigrist, CRB 36 (Paris: Gabalda, 1997), 43-107. For further commentary (especially a critique of Hasel's article), see A. Rainey, "Israel in Merneptah's Inscription and Reliefs," *IEJ* 51 (2001): 57-75.

25. For discussion, see *ANET,* 378 n. 18; G. W. Ahlström and D. Edelman, "Merneptah's Israel," *JNES* 44 (1985): 59-61; Ahlström, *Who Were the Israelites?* 37-42.

to the Egyptian scribe who inscribed the Merneptah stele. Israel was differentiated as early as 1200 from its Canaanite forebears.

Iron I evidence currently at the disposal of scholars presents a dilemma. On the one hand, the historical understanding of the period has been tremendously enhanced by archaeological research.[26] On the other hand, the data do not answer many of the important questions regarding early Israel. It is at present impossible to establish, on the basis of archaeological information, distinctions between Israelites and Canaanites in the Iron I period. The archaeological evidence does not provide a clear set of criteria for distinguishing an Israelite site from a Canaanite one, although a collocation of features (e.g., four-room houses, collared-rim store jars, hewn cisterns) in an Iron I site in the central highlands continues to be taken as a sign of an Israelite settlement. Inscriptional evidence is likewise of limited help in this regard, since down to the tenth century the languages and scripts of the epigraphic sources do not provide distinctions between the two cultures.

Biblical evidence is similarly problematic. Though it contains much historical information, the accuracy of this information is complicated by centuries of textual transmission and interpretation. Indeed, the narrative material of the Hebrew Bible pertaining to the Iron I period dates largely from the latter half of the monarchy, removed at least two or three centuries from the events of the Iron I period that the texts relate.[27] Moreover, in some cases the biblical record complicates interpretational matters. The difficulty of distinguishing between Israelites and Canaanites is exacerbated by biblical references to several groups besides Israelites and Canaanites. Gibeonites (Josh. 9:15; cf. 2 Sam. 21), Jerahmeelites (1 Sam. 27:10; 30:29), Kenites (Judg. 1:16; 4:11; 1 Sam. 27:10; 30:29), the descendants of Rahab (Josh. 6:25), Caleb the Kenizzite (Josh. 14:13-14; 21:12), and the Canaanite cities of Hepher and Tirzah became part of Israel (cf. Exod. 6:15).[28] Presumably other groups and places were absorbed into Israel as well. Furthermore, other groups are mentioned as being dispossessed of the land by the Israelites: "Hittites, Hivites,

26. See the valuable survey by E. Bloch-Smith and B. A. Nakhai, "A Landscape Comes to Life: The Iron Age I," *Near Eastern Archaeology* 62 (1999): 62-92, 101-27.

27. For a recent discussion of various positions on the development of Israelite historical material, see Halpern, *The First Historians;* see also chapter 1, section 3.

28. Smith, *Palestinian Parties and Politics*, 16, 211 n. 15; D. Sperling, "Israel's Religion in the Ancient Near East," in *Jewish Spirituality: From the Bible Through the Middle Ages*, ed. A. Green, World Spirituality: An Encyclopedic History of the Religious Quest 13 (New York: Crossroad, 1987), 9. Smith would include Midianites on the basis of Num. 10:29f. and Moabites on the basis of Num. 25:1-5. While it is possible that Midianites and Moabites were components in the population of early Israel, the sources cited do not support this reconstruction.

Perizzites, Girgashites, Amorites, and Jebusites" (Josh. 3:10; 9:1; 11:3; 12:8). While some of these group names may be suspect and reflect a later attempt to reconstruct the history of Israel's early development in the land, the point that some of them indicate the complex social composition of highlands Israel remains valid. Finally, current attempts to distinguish Israel from Canaan in the Iron I period are marked by their own modern limitations. To pose only one difficulty, although Israelite and Canaanite societies cannot be distinguished on the basis of archaeological evidence,[29] archaeological features do not constitute all the criteria for making historical distinctions; even if there were not a single criterion for establishing clear distinctions based on material culture (and at present there is no such criterion), some early Israelites may have perceived themselves as radically different from Canaanites. Information bearing on such perceptions is at present unavailable for the Iron I period, although it might be inferred from older biblical texts such as Judges 5. From the evidence that is available, one may conclude that although largely Canaanite according to currently available cultural data, Israel expressed a distinct sense of origins and deity and possessed largely distinct geographical holdings in the hill country by the end of the Iron I period. The Canaanite character of Israelite culture largely shaped the many ways ancient Israelites communicated their religious understanding of Yahweh. This point may be extended: the people of the highlands who came to be known as Israel comprised numerous groups, including Canaanites, whose heritage marked every aspect of Israelite society. In sum, Iron I Israel was largely Canaanite in character.

Israel inherited local cultural traditions from the Late Bronze Age, and its culture was largely continuous with the Canaanite culture of the coast and valleys during the Iron I period. The realm of religion was no different. Although one may not identify the local deities prior to and during the emergence of Israel by equating Ugaritic religion with Canaanite religion, the Ugaritic evidence is pertinent to the study of Canaanite religion since inscriptions from the Late Bronze Age and the Iron I period in Canaan indicate that the deities of the land included El, Baal, Asherah, and Anat, all major divinities known from the Ugaritic texts. The proper name *'y'l*, "where is El?" is contained in a twelfth-century inscription from Qubur el-Walaydah, which lies about ten kilometers southeast of Gaza.[30] The Lachish ewer, dated to the

29. See D. Esse, review of *The Archaeology of the Israelite Settlement*, by I. Finkelstein, *Biblical Archaeologist Review* 14/5 (1988): 6-9.

30. See F. M. Cross, "Newly Found Inscriptions in Old Canaanite and Early Phoenician Scripts," *BASOR* 238 (1980): 2-3; E. Puech, "Origine de l'alphabet," *RB* 93 (1986): 174. On this

thirteenth century, contains an inscription probably referring to this goddess: *mtn. šy [l] [rb]ty 'lt,* "mattan. An offering [to] my [la]dy, 'Elat."[31] The words, *rbt,* "lady" (literally, "great one," marked with a feminine ending) and *'lt,* "goddess," are regular, though not exclusive, titles of Asherah in the Ugaritic texts,[32] and these epithets in the Lachish ewer probably refer to her as well. An arrowhead from El-Khadr near Bethlehem dating to ca. 1100 reads *bn ʿnt,* "son of Anat."[33] Baal is mentioned in a fifteenth-century Taanach letter and in a fourteenth-century El-Amarna letter from Tyre (EA 147:13-15).[34] The element **bʿl* occurs also in an inscription from Lachish,[35] either as divine name or as an element contained in personal names. Other deities enjoyed cultic devotion in late second millennium Canaan. For example, *'lʾb,* the divine ancestral god, and *bʿlt,* "the Lady," are known from late second millennium inscriptions from Lachish.[36] Given that Ugaritic and biblical texts attest so

---

type of name, see W. F. Albright, "Northwest Semitic Names in a List of Egyptian Slaves from the Eighteenth Century B.C.," *JAOS* 74 (1954): 225-26; idem, "An Ostracon from Calah and the North-Israelite Diaspora," *BASOR* 149 (1958): 34 n. 12; and H. B. Huffmon, *Amorite Personal Names* (Baltimore: Johns Hopkins Univ. Press, 1965), 161. For issues concerning the dating of these inscriptions, see R. Wallenfels, "Redating the Byblian Inscriptions," *JANES* 15 (1983): 97-100.

31. On the Taanach letter, see *ANET,* 490. Concerning the inscription on the Lachish ewer, see F. M. Cross, "The Evolution of the Proto-Canaanite Alphabet," *BASOR* 134 (1954): 21; idem, "The Origin and Early Evolution of the Alphabet," *EI* 8 (1967 = E. L. Sukenik Volume), 16*; Puech, "Origine de l'alphabet," 178-80; idem, "The Canaanite Inscriptions of Lachish and Their Religious Background," *TA* 13-14 (1986-87): 17-18. In the first article, Cross offers a second possible translation: "A gift: a lamb for my Lady 'Elat."

32. Cross, "Evolution of the Proto-Canaanite Alphabet," 20 n. 17. In CTA 3.2(KTU 1.3 II).18, *'ilt* refers to the goddess Anat; otherwise it refers to Athirat (1.4[1.1 IV].14; 3.5.45 = 1.3 V 37; 4.1.8 = 1.4 I 7; 4.4[1.4 IV].49; 6.1[1.61].40; 15.3 [1.15 III].26; 14.4.198, 202 = 1.14 IV 35, 39). A neo-Punic inscription bears a dedication *lhrbt l'lt,* "to the Lady, the Goddess" (G. A. Cook, *A Textbook of North Semitic Inscriptions* [Oxford: Clarendon, 1903], 158, cf. 135). See also the name Abdi-Ashirta (meaning "servant of Asherah") of Amurru in the EA letters (see B. Halpern, *The Emergence of Israel in Canaan,* SBLMS 29 [Chico, CA: Scholars, 1983], 58-62, 69-78).

33. Cross, "Old Canaanite and Early Phoenician Scripts," 7. On the arrowheads of this period, see T. C. Mitchell, "Another Palestinian Inscribed Arrowhead," in *Palestine in the Bronze and Iron Ages: Papers in Honour of Olga Tufnell,* ed. J. N. Tubb, 136-53.

34. See A. E. Glock, "Texts and Archaeology at Tell Taʿanak," *Berytus* 31 (1983): 59-61. The theophoric element of *bʿl* may lie behind dIM attested as the theophoric element in the Canaanite names of some senders of El Amarna letters, e.g., EA 249-250, 256, and 258. See R. Hess, "Divine Names in the Amarna Texts," *UF* 18 (1986): 154. The name *bʿly* is attested in a ca. twelfth-century inscription from Shiqmana (see A. Lemaire, "Notes d'épigraphie nord-ouest sémitique," *Semitica* 30 [1980]: 17-32).

35. Puech, "The Canaanite Inscriptions," 17.

36. Puech, "The Canaanite Inscriptions," 17-22.

many of the same deities, religious practices, and notions, the Ugaritic texts may be used with caution for religious material in the West Semitic sphere which Israelite tradition inherited.

According to biblical tradition, these deities continued in various ways during the period of the Judges within Israel. (While few, if any, of the following texts actually date to the premonarchic period, they may reflect earlier religious conditions, or at least help to suggest some of the range in the deities worshiped in premonarchic Israel.) The god of Shechem in Judges 9:46 (see 8:33) is called *'ēl bĕrît,* which scholars have identified as a title of El.[37] Religious devotion to Asherah perhaps lies behind Genesis 49:25. The asherah, the symbol named after the goddess Asherah, is explicitly described in Judges 6:25-26. The word *baʿal* forms the theophoric element in the biblical name Jerubbaal (Judg. 6:32; 8:35). Two members of the family of Saul, Eshbaal (1 Chron. 8:33; 9:39) and Meribbaal (1 Chron. 8:34; 9:40), likewise have names containing the element *baʿal.* Only one proper name, Shamgar ben Anat (Judg. 5:6), attests to the name of Anat in the period of the Judges. The lack of either inscriptional or biblical evidence for Anat would suggest the absence of a cult devoted to her. During the Judges period, the major deities in the territory of Israel included Yahweh, El, Baal, and perhaps Asherah.

Some scholars have used this evidence to demonstrate that Israel in the period of the Judges was heavily "syncretistic," insofar as it incorporated Canaanite elements into an Israelite religion that was originally non-Canaanite.[38] Indeed, some biblical texts view Israel's protohistory at Sinai as a time when Canaanite elements would have been alien to Yahwism. For example, Deuteronomy 32 expresses life in the wilderness in the following terms: "the Lord alone did lead him [Israel], and there was no foreign god with him" (v. 12; see also vv. 8, 17).[39] The claim is potentially misleading on two counts.

37. On *'ēl bĕrît,* see Cross, *Canaanite Myth and Hebrew Epic,* 39, 44; T. J. Lewis, "The Identity and Function of El/Baal Berith," *JBL* 115 (1996): 401-23; and L. E. Stager, "The Fortress-Temple at Shechem and the 'House of El, Lord of the Covenant,'" in *Realia Dei: Essays in Archaeology and Biblical Interpretation in Honor of Edward F. Campbell, Jr. at His Retirement,* ed. P. H. Williams, Jr., and T. Hiebert, Scholars Press Homage Series 23 (Atlanta, GA: Scholars, 1999), 228-49.

38. See Kaufmann, *The Religion of Israel,* 229-31; cf. the biblical evidence that Kaufmann (229 n. 7) dismisses.

39. The secondary literature exhibits little consensus concerning the date of Deuteronomy 32. Some commentators, citing archaic poetic features, favor a date in the first half of the monarchy or earlier (see P. K. Skehan, "The Structure of the Song of Moses in Deuteronomy (Dt 32:1-43)," *CBQ* 13 [1951]: 153-63 ; idem, *Studies in Israelite Poetry and Wisdom,* CBQMS 1 [Washington, DC: Catholic Biblical Association of America, 1971], 67-77; Cross, *Canaanite Myth and Hebrew Epic,* 264 n. 193; Freedman, *Pottery, Poetry, and Prophecy,* 99-101). Other writ-

First, religious elements identified as "Canaanite" were not "syncretistic," at least not in the sense that such elements were not original to Israel. The biblical historiography in Deuteronomy 32 omits any reflection of the fact that Israel's cultural heritage was largely Canaanite; indeed, it implicitly denies this idea. Second, the evidence that the Canaanite deities, El, Baal, or Asherah, were the object of Israelite religious devotion separate from the cult of Yahweh in the period of the Judges is scant. Both of these claims are largely extensions of biblical historiography: because the historical works of the Bible view the religion of the Judges period in this way, then some scholars have concluded that the biblical view represents historical reality.[40] However, in various ways, El, Baal, and Asherah (or at least the symbol named after her, the asherah) were integrally related to Yahweh and the cult of this deity during the period of the Judges.

In sum, the Israelites may have perceived themselves as a people different from the Canaanites. Separate religious traditions of Yahweh, separate traditions of origins in Egypt for at least some component of Israel, and separate geographical holdings in the hill country contributed to the Israelites' sense of difference from their Canaanite neighbors inhabiting the coast and the valleys. Nonetheless, Israelite and Canaanite cultures shared a great deal in common, and religion was no exception. Deities and their cults in Iron Age Israel represented aspects of the cultural continuity with the indigenous Late Bronze Age culture and the contemporary urban culture on the coast and in the valleys. The examples of El, Baal, and the symbol of the asherah illustrate this continuity for the period of the Judges.

---

ers prefer an exilic or postexilic date (see G. von Rad, *Deuteronomy: A Commentary,* trans. D. Barton, OTL [London: SCM, 1966], 200; A. D. H. Mayes, *Deuteronomy,* New Century Bible [London: Oliphants, 1979], 382). Yahweh's choice of Israel in MT Deut. 32:8-9 need not be viewed as a late feature. A comparable concept is attested in the Wen-Amun tale dated to ca. 1100. In this story, the ruler of Byblos, Zakar-Baʿl, tells Wen-Amun: "Now when Amon founded all lands, in founding them he founded first the land of Egypt" (*ANET,* 27; M. Lichtheim, *Ancient Egyptian Literature,* vol. 2, 227). According to von Rad, the mixture of literary material (wisdom, prophetic, etc.) does not favor an early date. Moreover, commentators have noted the presence of originally northern elements (e.g., the mention of Jacob in v. 9) and southern components (the divine appellative of "rock"), presupposing a setting when these features had come together. This combination of features, too, would support a date in the eighth century or later, according to A. Reichert ("The Song of Moses (Dt. 32) and the Quest for the Deuteronomic Psalmody," in *Proceedings of the Ninth World Congress of Jewish Studies: Division A, The Period of the Bible* [Jerusalem: World Union of Jewish Studies, 1986], 57-58). For the evidence for a later date, see Olyan, *Asherah and the Cult of Yahweh,* 72 n. 7. For a recent survey, see P. Sanders, *The Provenance of Deuteronomy 32,* OTS 37 (Leiden: Brill, 1996).

40. See n. 5 above.

2. Yahweh and El

The original god of Israel was El. This reconstruction may be inferred from two pieces of information. First, the name of Israel is not a Yahwistic name with the divine element of Yahweh, but an El name, with the element, **'ēl.* This fact would suggest that El was the original chief god of the group named Israel.[41] Second, Genesis 49:24-25 presents a series of El epithets separate from the mention of Yahweh in verse 18 (discussed in section 3 below). Yet early on, Yahweh is understood as Israel's god in distinction to El. Deuteronomy 32:8-9 casts Yahweh in the role of one of the sons of El, here called *'elyôn:*[42]

> When the Most High *('elyôn)* gave to the nations their inheritance,
> when he separated humanity,
> he fixed the boundaries of the peoples
> according to the number of divine beings.[43]
> For Yahweh's portion is his people,
> Jacob his allotted heritage.

This passage presents an order in which each deity received its own nation. Israel was the nation that Yahweh received. It also suggests that Yahweh, originally a warrior-god from Sinai/Paran/Edom/Teiman,[44] was known separately from El at an early point in early Israel.[45] Perhaps due to trade with

41. G. W. Ahlström, "Where Did the Israelites Live?" *JNES* 41 (1982): 134.

42. On *'elyôn* as a title of El, see section 4 below.

43. MT reads *bĕnê yiśrā'ēl,* whereas LXX *aggelōn theou* and Qumran *bny 'lhym* (cf. Symmachus and Old Latin). For the DSS evidence, see the discussion by J. A. Duncan, in *Qumran Cave 4. IX: Deuteronomy, Joshua, Judges, Kings,* ed. E. Ulrich and F. M. Cross, DJD XIV (Oxford: Clarendon, 1995), 90. See also P. K. Skehan, "A Fragment of the 'Song of Moses' (Deut. 32) from Qumran," *BASOR* 136 (1954): 12-15; R. Meyer, "Die Bedeutung von Deuteronomium 32, 8f. 43 (4Q) für die Auslegung Mosesliedes," in *Verbannung und Theologie Israels im 6. und 5. jahrhundert v. Chr. Wilhelm Rudolph zum 70. Geburtstage,* ed. A. Kuschke (Tübingen: J. C. B. Mohr, 1961), 197-209. E. Tov, *Textual Criticism of the Hebrew Bible* (Minneapolis: Fortress; Assen/Maastricht: Van Gorcum, 1992), 269; A. Schenker, "Le monothéisme israélite: un dieu qui transcende le monde et les dieux," *Biblica* 78 (1997): 438. Skehan (*Studies,* 69) notes that Ben Sira 17:17, reflecting later exegesis of Deut. 32:8, implies a divine ruler for every nation.

44. See above for the biblical references to these locations, and n. 82 below.

45. For discussion of Yahweh's original people, his importation from Edom and his secondary adoption into the highlands religion, see K. van der Toorn, *Family Religion in Babylonia, Syria and Israel* (Leiden: Brill, 1996), 266-315, esp. 281-86; and "Yahweh," *DDD,* 910-19, and Smith, *The Origins of Biblical Monotheism,* 135-48. See below n. 82. The background of the name of Yahweh is disputed. For a present discussion of the form, see J. Tropper, "Der

Edom/Midian, Yahweh entered secondarily into the Israelite highland religion. Passages such as Deuteronomy 32:8-9 suggest a literary vestige of the initial assimilation of Yahweh, the southern warrior-god, into the larger highland pantheism, headed by El; other texts point to Asherah (El's consort) and to Baal and other deities as members of this pantheon. In time, El and Yahweh were identified, while Yahweh and Baal co-existed and later competed as warrior-gods. As the following chapter (section 2) suggests, one element in this competition involved Yahweh's assimilation of language and motifs originally associated with Baal.

One indication that Yahweh and El were identified at an early stage is that there are no biblical polemics against El. At an early point, Israelite tradition identified El with Yahweh or presupposed this equation.[46] It is for this reason that the Hebrew Bible so rarely distinguishes between El and Yahweh.[47] The development of the name El *(ʾēl)* into a generic noun meaning

---

Gottesname **Yahwa,*" *VT* 51 (2001): 81-106. For earlier proposals, see K. van der Toorn, "Yahweh," *DDD,* 913-16. For a recent defense of Yahweh as a title of El, see M. Dijkstra, "El, de God van Israël — Israël, het volk van YHWH. Over de van het Jahwisme in Oud-Israël," in *Eén God alleen . . . ? Over monothëisme in Oud-Israël en de verering van de godin Asjera,* ed. B. Becking and M. Dijkstra (Kampen: Kok, 1998), 59-92; and his article, "El, YHWH and Their Asherah: On Continuity and Discontinuity in Canaanite and Ancient Israelite Religion," in *Ugarit: Eine ostmediterranes Kulturzentrum in Alten Orient. Ergebnisse und Perspektiven der Forschung; Band I: Ugarit und seine altorientalische Umwelt,* ed. M. Dietrich and O. Loretz, ALASP 7 (Münster: Ugarit-Verlag, 1995), 43-73. Like earlier advocates of this view, Dijkstra has not marshalled evidence for the identification of Yahweh as a title of El. A plausible case for the Midianite-Edomite background of Yahweh has been made by K. van der Toorn, but the argument for the importation of Yahweh-cult under Saul due to his Edomite background is speculative. See van der Toorn, *Family Religion,* 266-86.

46. O. Eissfeldt, "El and Yahweh," *JSS* 1 (1956): 25-37; Cross, *Canaanite Myth and Hebrew Epic,* 44-75. For the possible attestation of El at Ebla as *DINGER* in an offering list, see W. G. Lambert, "Old Testament Mythology in Its Ancient Near Eastern Context," in *Congress Volume: Jerusalem 1986,* ed. J. Emerton, VTSup 40 (Leiden: Brill, 1988), 131. Cf. *DINGER-lì* in Emar 282:16.

47. Cross, *Canaanite Myth and Hebrew Epic,* 44. For various views as to how the identification between Yahweh and El occurred, see Cooper, "Divine Names and Epithets in the Ugaritic Texts," 337-42; and C. E. L'Heureux, "Searching for the Origins of God," in *Traditions in Transformation: Turning Points in Biblical Faith,* Festschrift Honoring Frank Moore Cross, ed. B. Halpern and J. D. Levenson (Winona Lake, IN: Eisenbrauns, 1981), 33-44. Ezekiel 28 represents an exception to the fact that the biblical tradition does not distinguish between El and Yahweh, but the god in this satire on the city of Tyre is the Tyrian El and not the El indigenous to Israel's Canaanite tradition. On this chapter, see Pope, *El in the Ugaritic Texts,* VTSup 2 (Leiden: Brill, 1955), 97-103; R. R. Wilson, "The Death of the King of Tyre: The Editorial History of Ezekiel 28," in *Love and Death in the Ancient Near East: Essays in Honor of Marvin H. Pope,* ed. J. H. Marks and R. M. Good (Guilford, CT: Four Quarters, 1987), 211-18, esp. 213-14; Greenfield, "The Hebrew

"god" also was compatible with the loss of El's distinct character in Israelite religious texts. One biblical text exhibits the assimilation of the meaning of the word *'ēl* quite strongly, namely Joshua 22:22 (cf. Pss. 10:12; 50:1):[48]

'ēl 'ĕlōhîm yhwh	God of gods is Yahweh,
'ēl 'ĕlōhîm yhwh	God of gods is Yahweh.

The first word in each clause in this verse reflects the development of the name of the god El into a generic noun meaning "god." In this verse the noun forms part of a superlative expression proclaiming the incomparable divine status of Yahweh. The phrase "god of gods" may be compared to other superlative expressions of this type in the Bible such as "king of kings" (Dan. 2:37; Ezra 7:12), the name of the biblical book "Song of Songs" (Song of Songs 1:1), and the opening words of the first speech in Ecclesiastes, "vanity of vanities" (Eccles. 1:2).[49]

The priestly theological treatment of Israel's early religious history in Exodus 6:2-3 identifies the old god El Shadday with Yahweh. In this passage Yahweh appears to Moses: "And God said to Moses, 'I am Yahweh. I appeared to Abraham, to Isaac, and to Jacob, as El Shadday, but by my name Yahweh I did not make myself known to them.'" This passage reflects the fact that Yahweh was unknown to the patriarchs. Rather, they worshiped the Canaanite god, El. Inscriptional texts from Deir ʿAlla, a site north of Jericho across the Jordan River, attest to the epithet *shadday.* In these inscriptions the *shadday* epithet is not applied to the great god, El. The author of Exodus 6:2-3 perhaps did not know of or make this distinction; rather, he identified Yahweh with the traditions of the great Canaanite god, El.[50]

Bible and Canaanite Literature," 554; H. R. Page, Jr., *The Myth of Cosmic Rebellion: A Study of Its Reflexes in Ugaritic and Biblical Literature,* VTSup 65 (Leiden/New York/Köln: Brill, 1996), 140-58; and D. E. Callendar, Jr., *Adam in Myth and History: Ancient Israelite Perspectives on the Primal Human,* HSS 48 (Winona Lake, IN: Eisenbrauns, 2000), 179-89. Recognizing that Ezekiel 28 refers to Tyrian El would provide further confirmation that El was a Tyrian god although under a different name (e.g. Bethel, see below).

48. See J. J. M. Roberts, "El," *IDBSup,* 255-58. For a recent treatment of BH *'ĕlōhîm,* see J. S. Burnett, *A Reassessment of Biblical Elohim,* SBLDS 183 (Atlanta, GA: Scholars, 2001).

49. M. H. Pope, *Song of Songs,* AB 7C (Garden City, NY: Doubleday, 1977), 294-95.

50. See Cross, *Canaanite Myth and Hebrew Epic,* 47 n. 15, 52-60, 86 n. 17, 298; Childs, *The Book of Exodus,* 111-14; Freedman, *Pottery, Poetry, and Prophecy,* 86; J. A. Hackett, "Some Observations on the Balaam Traditions at Deir ʿAlla," *BA* 49 (1986): 216-22; idem, "Religious Traditions in Israelite Transjordan," in *Ancient Israelite Religion: Essays in Honor of Frank Moore Cross,* ed. P. D. Miller, Jr., P. D. Hanson, and S. D. McBride, 125-36. Cf. O. Loretz, "Der kanaanäische Ursprung des biblischen Gottesnames *El Šaddaj,*" *UF* 11 (1979): 420-21; E. A. Knauf, "El Šaddai — der Gott Abrahams?" *BN* 29 (1985): 97-103. For the *editio princeps* of the

J. Tigay's recent study of inscriptional onamastica is compatible with the historical reconstruction of the identification of El with Yahweh in early Israelite tradition.[51] Tigay lists all proper names with theophoric elements. Found in Israelite inscriptions, all dating after the beginning of the monarchy, are 557 names with Yahweh as the divine element, 77 names with **'l*, a handful of names with the divine component **b'l*, and no names referring to the goddesses Anat or Asherah. The few proper names with the divine names of Anat and Asherah do not reflect a cult to these deities; Baal may be an exception. The names with the element of the name of El historically reflect the identification of Yahweh and El by the time these names may appear in the attested inscriptions. Just as no cult is attested for Anat (and perhaps Asherah) in Israelite religion, so also there is no distinct cult attested for El except in his identity as Yahweh.

In Israel the characteristics and epithets of El became part of the repertoire of descriptions of Yahweh. In both texts and iconography, El is an elderly bearded figure enthroned,[52] sometimes before individual deities (KTU

Deir 'Alla texts, see J. Hoftijzer and G. van der Kooij, *Aramaic Texts from Deir 'Alla* (Leiden: Brill, 1976). For bibliography pertaining to the Deir 'Alla texts up to 1984, see W. E. Aufrecht, "A Bibliography of the Deir 'Alla Plaster Texts," *Newsletter for Targumic and Cognate Studies*, Supplement 2 (1985): 1-7. The *šdym* in Deut. 32:16-17 and Ps. 106:37 may not be demons (cf. Akkadian *šēdu*), but a group of deities corresponding to *šdyn* in the Deir 'Alla texts (for discussion, see J. A. Hackett, *The Balaam Texts from Deir 'Alla*, HSM 31 [Chico, CA: Scholars, 1984], 85-89; idem, "Religious Traditions," 133). Might they be the military retinue of El Shadday? For further discussion, see below section 5.

51. Tigay, *You Shall Have No Other Gods*, 12, 65-73, 83-85. These totals for Yahweh and El names compare with only twenty-six plausible non-Yahweh-El names. Some of the twenty-six cases may be Yahwistic (such as *ṭbšlm*, "[divine] ally is good"[?], so Tigay, 69) or belong to foreigners. The relative popularity of El names in fact stems from their being considered Yahwistic names. Z. Zevit ("A Chapter in the History of Israelite Proper Names," *BASOR* 250 [1983]: 1-16) notes that no names with *-yh/-yhw* occur before the tenth century, perhaps reflecting the relatively late development of Yahweh's cult in Canaan/Israel (cf. Smith, *Palestinian Parties and Politics*, 21). See also S. I. L. Norin, *Sein Name allein ist hoch: Das Jhw-haltige Suffix althebraischer Personnennamen untersucht mit besonderer Berücksichtigung der alttestamentlichen Redaktionsgeschichte*, ConBOT 24 (Lund: Gleerup, 1986). For the limitations on using proper names as evidence of religious practice, see introduction. On onornastic lag, see Tigay, *You Shall Have No Other Gods*, 17.

52. For descriptions of El, see Pope, *El in the Ugaritic Texts*, 34-35; and W. Herrmann, "El," *DDD*, 274-80. See further W. Herrmann, "Wann werde Jahwe zum Schöpfer der Welt," *UF* 23 (1991): 166-80. Ugaritic examples of iconography of the bearded El include *ANEP*, no. 493, and the drinking mug from Ugarit. For discussion, see C. F. A. Schaeffer, "Neue Entdeckungen in Ugarit," *Archiv für Orientsforschung* 20 (1963): 206-16, esp. fig. 30; idem, "Le culte d'El à Ras Shamra et le veau d'or," *CRAIBL* 1966, 327-28; idem, "Nouveaux témoinages du culte d'El et de Baal à Ras Shamra et ailleurs en Syrie-Palestine," *Syria* 43 (1966): 1-19, esp. fig. 1; M. H. Pope,

1.3 V; 1.4 IV-V), sometimes before the divine council (KTU 1.2 I), known by a variety of expressions; this feature is attested also in Phoenician inscriptions (KAI 4:4-5; 14:9, 22; 26 A III 19; 27:12; cf. KTU 1.4 III 14). In KTU 1.10 III 6 El is called *drd<r>*, "ageless one," and in KTU 1.3 V and 1.4 V, Anat and Asherah both affirm the eternity of his wisdom.[53] His eternity is also expressed in his epithet, *ʾab šnm*, "father of years."[54] In KTU 1.4 V 3-4 Asherah

---

"The Scene on the Drinking Mug from Ugarit," in *Near Eastern Studies in Honor of William Foxwell Albright*, ed. H. Goedicke (Baltimore: Johns Hopkins Univ. Press, 1971), 393-405; Cross, *Canaanite Myth and Hebrew Epic*, 35-36. These pieces of iconography of El are the closest analogues to the metal enthroned male figures with hand upraised from Ugarit, Jezzin (Lebanon), Byblos, Tell Abu Hawam, Beth-Shemesh, and elsewhere (see O. Negbi, *Canaanite Gods in Metal: An Archaeological Study of Ancient Syro-Palestinian Figurines* [Tel Aviv: Tel Aviv Univ. Institute of Archaeology, 1976], 42-56, nos. 1441, 1443, 1446, 1447, 1450). See further the discussions of W. Herrmann, "El," *DDD*, 274-80; and Smith, *The Origins of Biblical Monotheism*, 41-66. Note the debate over El as primarily an Aramean god between I. Kottsieper, "El — ein aramäischer Gott? — Eine Antwort," *BN* 94 (1998): 87-98, and C. Maier and J. Tropper, "El — ein aramäischer Gott," *BN* 93 (1998): 77-88, who reject this thesis of Kottsieper. For further discussion of the divine assembly in Canaanite and Israelite tradition, see chapter 3, section 5.

53. Cross (*Canaanite Myth and Hebrew Epic*, 21) argues that *ʿlm* is an epithet especially appropriate to El. The evidence is quite restricted, however. El's wisdom is called *ʿm ʿlm*, "for eternity" (KTU 1.3 V 31; 1.4 IV 42). The related word, *ʿllmn*, in KTU 1.1 V 5 may refer to El, but the context is too broken to provide confirmation. Cross interprets the occurrence of *ʿlm* in KTU 1.108.1 also as a title of El. The first line of the text presents *rpʾu mlk ʿlm* and the second line calls this figure *ʾil*. Cross regards *ʾil* in line 2 as El and not generically as "god," and identifies *rpʾu mlk ʿlm* with El. For the problems underlying this interpretation, see chapter 5, sections 2 and 3. The term *ʿlm* is an epithet suitable also to Ugaritic deities other than El. Baal's kingship is called *ʿlm* in KTU 1.2 IV 10. The phrase *zbl mlk ʿllmy* in KTU 1.22 I 10 is problematic. The word *ʿllmy* appears to be a form of **ʿlm*, "eternal one" (R. M. Good, "Geminated Sonants, Word Stress, and Energic in *-nn/-.nn* in Ugaritic," *UF* 13 [1981]: 118-19). Where BH *ʿôlām* appears with other elements of imagery attested for El in the Ugaritic texts, the BH use of *ʿôlām* may be traced back to El.

54. For further discussions of *ʾab šnm* as "father of years," see Pope, *El in the Ugaritic Texts*, 32-33; Cross, *Canaanite Myth and Hebrew Epic*, 16 n. 24; Greenfield, "The Hebrew Bible and Canaanite Literature," 555; E. Ullendorff, "Ugaritic Marginalia IV," *EI* 14 (1978 = H. L. Ginsberg Volume): 23*. The title, *ʾab šnm*, has been interpreted in other ways for two reasons. First, the plural of years is otherwise expressed by the feminine form *šnt*. In this case the use of the masculine plural is a frozen form. Second, *šnm* appears in KTU 1.114.18-19 as the second element in the double-name of the divine personage, *ṯkmn w-šnm*, who accompanies El, stricken with severe drunkenness, to his home. This role is treated as a filial duty in 1.17 I 31-32. Therefore, it has been inferred that *ṯkmn w-šnm* is a son of El and that El's title, *ʾab šnm*, refers to El's paternity of this figure. For these alternative views, see *ANET*, 129 n. 1; C. H. Gordon, "El, Father of *šnm*," *JNES* 35 (1976): 261-62; J. Gray, *The Biblical Doctrine of the Reign of God* (Edinburgh: T. & T. Clark, 1979), 235, esp. n. 201; A. Jirku, "Šnm (Schunama) der Sohn des Gottes 'Il," *ZAW* 82 (1970): 278-79; J. C. de Moor, "Studies in the New Alphabetic Texts from Ras Shamra I," *UF* 1 (1969): 79; Pope, *El in the Ugaritic Texts*, 33, 61, 81.

addresses El: "You are great, O El, and indeed, wise; your hoary beard instructs you" *(rbt 'ilm lḥkmt šbt dqnk ltsrk)*. Anat's threats in 1.3 V 24-25 and 1.18 I 11-12 likewise mention El's gray beard. Similarly, Yahweh is described as the aged patriarchal god (Ps. 102:28; Job 36:26; Isa. 40:28; cf. Ps. 90:10; Isa. 57:15; Hab. 3:6; Dan. 6:26; 2 Esdras 8:20; Tobit 13:6, 10; Ben Sira 18:30), enthroned amidst the assembly of divine beings (1 Kings 22:19; Isa. 6:1-8; cf. Pss. 29:1-2; 82:1; 89:5-8; Isa. 14:13; Jer. 23:18, 22; Zechariah 3; Dan. 3:25).[55] Later biblical texts continued the long tradition of aged Yahweh enthroned before the heavenly hosts. Daniel 7:9-14, 22, describes a bearded Yahweh as the "ancient of days," and "the Most High." He is enthroned amid the assembly of heavenly hosts, called in verse 18 "the holy ones of the Most High," *qaddîšê 'elyônîn* (cf. 2 Esdras 2:42-48; Revelation 7). This description for the angelic hosts derives from the older usage of Hebrew *qĕdōšîm*, "holy ones," for the divine council (Ps. 89:6; Hos. 12:1; Zech. 14:5; cf. KAI 4:5, 7; 14:9, 22; 27:12). The tradition of the enthroned bearded god appears also in a Persian period coin marked *yhd*, "Yehud."[56] The iconography belongs to a god, apparently Yahweh.

The Canaanite/Israelite tradition of the divine council derived from the setting of the royal court[57] and evolved in accordance with the court termi-

55. For surveys of the terminology of the divine council in Akkadian, Ugaritic, Phoenician, and Hebrew, see E. T. Mullen, *The Divine Council in Canaanite and Early Hebrew Literature*, HSM 24 (Chico, CA: Scholars, 1980); A. Cooper, "Divine Names and Epithets in the Ugaritic Texts," 431-41.

56. See D. V. Edelman, "Tracking Observance of the Aniconic Tradition Through Numismatics," in *The Triumph of Elohim: From Yahwisms to Judaisms*, ed. D. V. Edelman (Grand Rapids, MI: Eerdmans, 1996), 185-225, esp. 190-204, with drawings of the coin's two sides on p. 225.

57. The language describing the Ugaritic divine court includes many further elements derived from royal realia of the second millennium. Royal treaty terminology for tribute *('argmn)* and royal gifts from an inferior king to a superior king *(mnḥ)* appear in KTU 1.2 I 37-38 (cf. KTU 3.1.24-25; 4.91.1). The language of *'bd*, literally "slave," but in the context of an inferior to a superior, a "servant," appears also in KTU 1.2 I 36 and 1.5 II 12 (cf. *PRU IV*, p. 49, line 12; 2 Sam. 16:7; see J. C. Greenfield, "Some Aspects of Treaty Terminology in the Bible," *Fourth World Congress of Jewish Studies: Papers*, vol. 1 [Jerusalem: World Union of Jewish Studies, 1967], 117-19; F. C. Fensham, "Notes on Treaty Terminology in Ugaritic Epics," *UF* 11 [1979]: 265-74; A. Rainey, *The Scribe of Ugarit* [Jerusalem: Israel Academy of Sciences and Humanities, 1969], 141-42). The use of *b'l* as a title of Yamm in KTU 1.2 I 17-19//33-35 and Mot in 1.5 II 12 reflects the diplomatic title for a superior king (3.1.26). The messengers' insistence on having Baal's gold *(pḏ)* in 1.2 I 19//35 reflects a routine demand from one monarch to the king whom he is besieging (cf. KTU 1.3 III 46-47; 1 Kings 20:2-4; for the interpretation of *pḏ*, see del Olmo Lete, *Mitos y leyendas*, 609). The protocols of messengers and their presentations of their messages reflect the language of royal international correspondence. The formulas introducing

nology of the dominant royal power. During the Israelite monarchy, the imagery of the divine council continued from its Late Bronze Age antecedents. M. Brettler has observed that the Israelite monarchy also had a distinct impact on some features of the divine council.[58] Roles in the divine council in Canaanite and early Israelite literature were generally not individuated, but one exception was "the commander of the army of Yahweh" *(śar ṣĕbāʾ yhwh)* in Joshua 5:13-15, which, according to Brettler, was based on the comparable role in the Israelite army (1 Sam. 17:55; 1 Kings 1:19; cf. Judg. 4:7). Similarly, the divine "destroyer," *mašḥît,* of Exodus 12:13 and 1 Chronicles 21:15 (cf. Isa. 54:16; Jer. 22:7), may be traced ultimately to the military *mašḥît* of 1 Samuel 13:17 and 14:15, perhaps as a class of fighters personified or individualized and secondarily incorporated into the divine realm.[59] The *mašḥîtîm* appear either singly or as a plurality acting on behalf of their divine Lord. Two of the mysterious divine figures in Genesis are evidently *mašḥîtîm,* since they apply this very term to themselves in Gen. 19:13. Other features of the divine council in Israelite literature reflect later political developments. According to Brettler, *mĕšārēt,* "servant," applied first to royal officials in the postexilic period (e.g., 1 Chron. 27:1; 28:1; 2 Chron. 17:19; 22:8; Esther 1:10; 2:2), and sec-

---

Yamm's message in 1.2 I 16//33 are common in royal letters. For further discussion of these parallels, see J. F. Ross, "The Prophet as Yahweh's Messenger," *Israel's Prophetic Heritage: Essays in Honor of James Muilenburg,* ed. B. W. Anderson and W. Harrelson (New York: Harper, 1962), 98-107 (reprinted in *Prophecy in Israel: Search for an Identity,* ed. D. L. Petersen, Issues in Religion and Theology 10 (Philadelphia: Fortress; London: SPCK, 1987, 112-21). Similarly, *lḥt,* etymologically derived from "tablet," means "message," in both human and divine passages (1.2 I 26; see D. Pardee, "A New Ugaritic Letter," *BiOr* 34 [1977], 7-8) and not "insult" or the like (for this view, see del Olmo Lete, *Mitos y leyendas,* 571-72). Other terminology within descriptions of the heavenly court appear to have derived directly from a royal setting. Baal's approach to El *bḥnt,* "with his graciousness" in KTU 1.17 I 16 has been modeled on the act of intercession before the king in the Ugaritic court. In a secular setting, one person asks another to "intercede for me before the king" (KTU 2.15.3; cf. KAI 10:9-10). On this comparison, see J. W. Watts, "*Ḥnt:* An Ugaritic Formula of Intercession," *UF* 21 (1989): 443-49.

58. M. Brettler, *God Is King: Understanding an Israelite Metaphor,* JSOTSup 76 (Sheffield: JSOT, 1989), 102-9. Professor Brettler suggested the formulation regarding the *mašḥît.* On aspects of the divine council in the prophetic literature, see J. S. Holladay, "Assyrian Statecraft and the Prophets of Israel," *HTR* 63 (1970): 29-51 (reprinted in *Prophecy in Israel: Search for an Identity,* ed. D. L. Petersen, 122-43).

59. See the view of R. de Vaux and B. Mazar that the Philistine *mašḥîtîm* in 1 Sam. 13:5, 31:2 may be characterized as mobile strike-forces; cited in P. Machinist, "Biblical Traditions: The Philistines and Israelite History," in *The Sea Peoples and Their World: A Reassessment,* ed. E. D. Oren, University Museum Monograph 108, University Museum Symposium Series 11 (Philadelphia: The University Museum, University of Pennsylvania, 2000), 58, 71 n. 29. See further p. 123 n. 64 below.

ondarily referred to angels in a postexilic text, Psalm 103:21 (cf. Ps. 104:4).[60] Some biblical innovations in terminology of the heavenly court in the postexilic period may have been modeled on the court of the reigning Mesopotamian power. The depiction of the *satan* in Job 1–2 and Zechariah 3 has been traced to neo-Babylonian or Persian bureaucracies.[61] Similarly, J. Teixidor has suggested that the angelic term, *ʿîr,* "watcher" (e.g., Dan. 4:10, 14, 20), was based on spies who watched over the empire on behalf of the Persian ruler.[62]

El and Yahweh exhibit a similar compassionate disposition toward humanity. Like "Kind El, the Compassionate" *(lṭpn ʾil dpʾid),* the "father of humanity" *(ʾab ʾadm),* Yahweh is a "merciful and gracious god," *ʾēl-rāḥûm wĕḥannūn* (Exod. 34:6; Ps. 86:15), and father (Deut. 32:6; Isa. 63:16, 64:7; Jer. 3:4, 19; 31:9; Mal. 1:6, 2:10; cf. Exod. 4:22; Hos. 11:1). Both El and Yahweh appear to humans in dream-visions and function as their divine patron.[63] Like El (KTU 1.16 V-VI), Yahweh is a healing god (Gen. 20:17; Num. 12:13; 2 Kings 20:5, 8; Ps. 107:20; cf. personal name, *rĕpāʾēl,* in 1 Chron. 26:7). Moreover, the description of Yahweh's dwelling-place as a "tent" (*ʾōhel;* e.g., Pss. 15:1; 27:6; 91:10; 132:3), called in the Pentateuchal traditions the "tent of meeting" (*ʾōhel môʿēd;* Exod. 33:7-11; Num. 12:5, 10; Deut. 31:14, 15) recalls the tent of El, explicitly described in the Canaanite narrative of Elkunirsa.[64] The tabernacle of Yahweh has *qĕrāšîm,* usually understood as "boards" (Exodus 26–40; Num. 3:36; 4:31), while the dwelling of El is called *qrš,* perhaps "tabernacle" or "pavilion" (KTU 1.2 III 5; 1.3 V 8; 1.4 IV 24; 1.17 V 49). Furthermore, the dwelling of El is set amid the cosmic waters (KTU 1.2 III 4; 1.3 V 6; 1.4 IV 20-22; 1.17 V 47-48), a theme evoked in de-

60. Brettler, *God Is King,* 106-7, 109.

61. See A. L. Oppenheim, "'The Eyes of the Lord,'" *JAOS* 88 (1968): 173-80; C. L. Meyers and E. M. Meyers, *Haggai, Zechariah 1–8,* AB 25B (Garden City, NY: Doubleday, 1987), 184; P. L. Day, *An Adversary in Heaven: śāṭān in the Hebrew Bible,* HSM 43 (Atlanta, GA: Scholars, 1988), 39-43; Brettler, *God Is King,* 105, 109. On the *satan,* see further N. Forsyth, *The Old Enemy: Satan and the Combat Myth* (Princeton: Princeton Univ. Press, 1987), 107-23.

62. J. Teixidor, review of *The Genesis Apocryphon of Qumran Cave I: A Commentary,* by J. A. Fitzmyer, *JAOS* 87 (1967): 634; cf. Day, *An Adversary in Heaven,* 42.

63. See Pope, *El in the Ugaritic Texts,* 25-54; idem, "Ups and Downs in El's Amours," *UF* 11 (1979 = C. F. A. Schaeffer Festschrift): 701-8; Cross, *Canaanite Myth and Hebrew Epic,* 13-43; P. D. Miller, "Aspects of the Religion of Israel," in *Ancient Israelite Religion; Essays in Honor of Frank Moore Cross,* ed. P. D. Miller, Jr., P. D. Hanson, and S. D. McBride, 55; Greenfield, "The Hebrew Bible and Canaanite Literature," 547-48. For El and Baal as coregents, see *PE* 1.10.31 (Attridge and Oden, *Philo of Byblos,* 54-55). Compatibility between El and Baal is likewise evident in KTU 1.15 II and 1.17 I-II.

64. *ANET,* 519.

scriptions of Yahweh's abode in Jerusalem (Pss. 47:5; 87; Isa. 33:20-22; Ezek. 47:1-12; Joel 4:18; Zech. 14:8).[65]

65. Studies of El's abode include: Pope, *El in the Ugaritic Texts,* 62-72; idem, "The Scene on the Drinking Mug from Ugarit," in *Near Eastern Studies in Honor of William Foxwell Albright,* 393-405; O. Kaiser, *Die mythische Bedeutung des Meeres in Ugarit, Aegypten und Israel,* BZAW 80 (Berlin: Töpelmann, 1961), 42-56; E. Lipiński, "El's Abode: Mythological Traditions related to Mt. Hermon and to the Mountains of Armenia," *OLP* 2 (1971): 13-69; R. J. Clifford, "The Tent of El and the Israelite Tent of Meeting," *CBQ* 33 (1971): 221-27; idem, *The Cosmic Mountain in Canaan and the Old Testament,* HSM 4 (Cambridge, MA: Harvard Univ. Press, 1972), 35-37; Cross, *Canaanite Myth and Hebrew Epic,* 36-39; idem, "The Priestly Tabernacle in Light of Recent Research," in *Temple and High Places in Biblical Times: Proceedings of the Colloquium in Honor of the Centennial of Hebrew Union College, Jewish Institute of Religion, Jerusalem, 14-16 March 1977* (Jerusalem: Hebrew Union College, Jewish Institute of Religion, 1981), 177-78; P. K. McCarter, "The River Ordeal in Israelite Literature," *HTR* 66 (1973): 403-12; Mullen, *The Divine Council,* 128-68; M. Weinfeld, "Social and Cultic Institutions in the Priestly Source Against Their Ancient Near Eastern Background," in *Proceedings of the Eighth World Congress of Jewish Studies, Jerusalem, 16-21 August 1981* (Jerusalem: World Union of Jewish Studies, Perry Foundation for Biblical Research, 1983), 103-4; M. S. Smith, "Mt. *Ll* in KTU 1.2 I 19-20," *UF* 18 (1986): 458; Greenfield, "The Hebrew Bible and Canaanite Literature," 548, 554. See also the important contribution by D. E. Fleming, "Mari's Large Public Tent and the Priestly Tent Sanctuary," *VT* 50 (2000): 485-98. The new Mari evidence discussed by Fleming adds to the cultural background of El's tent and the tent-shrine (tabernacle) of Yahweh. A number of commentators (e.g., Cross, Clifford, Greenfield, Mullen) identify El's abode with the seat of the divine council in Ugaritic tradition. Iconography on a seal from Mari perhaps bolsters this identification (A. Vanel, *L'Iconographie du Dieu de l'Orage dans le Proche-Orient Ancien jusqu'à VIIe Siècle avant J.-C.,* CRB 7 [Paris: Gabalda, 1965], 73-74; O. Keel, *The Symbolism of the Biblical World: Ancient Near Eastern Iconography and the Book of Psalms* [New York: Seabury, 1978], fig. 42). O. Keel describes the scene: The seal depicts "a god of the type of El enthroned, between the spring of two streams, on a mountain. He is flanked by two vegetation goddesses who grow out from the waters. A fourth figure, a warlike god, appears thrusting into the stream with a spear" ("Ancient Seals and the Bible," *JAOS* 106 [1986]: 309). This seal apparently combines at least two scenes that are distinguished in the Baal cycle. El in his abode and Baal piercing the waters constitute two separate mythologems or mythological scenes. Discrepancies in the Ugaritic descriptions of the two caution against an identification of the settings of El's abode and the divine council, at least for Ugaritic tradition (Pope, *El in the Ugaritic Texts,* 69), if not for Canaanite tradition generally — although Ugaritic literature may assume the identification without expressing it explicitly. If the two were not identified in Ugaritic literature or Canaanite literature generally, the conflation of the scene of the divine council with the heavenly abode as found in biblical tradition would belong to a point in Canaanite literary tradition later than the Ugaritic literary texts. On the traditions of El and his waters at Hierapolis, see H. W. Attridge and R. A. Oden, *The Syrian Goddess (De Dea Syria) Attributed to Lucian,* Society of Biblical Literature Texts and Translations 9, Graeco-Roman Religion Series 1 (Missoula, MT: Scholars, 1976), 4, 8 n. 14; Oden, *Studies,* 32-33, 124-26, 142. For Mesopotamian iconography of the waters flowing from the vase held by Ea/Enki, see E. D. van Buren, *The Flowing Vase and the God with Streams* (Berlin: Hans Schoetz und Co., GMBH,

The characteristics of Yahweh in Deuteronomy 32:6-7 include some motifs that can be traced to traditional descriptions of El:

> Do you thus requite Yahweh,
> you foolish and senseless *(lōʾ ḥākām)* people?
> Is he not your father *(ʾābîkā),* who created you *(qānekā)*
> who made you and established you *(wayĕkōnĕnekā)?*
> Remember the days of old *(ʿôlām),*
> consider the years of many generations *(šĕnôt dôr-wādôr);*
> ask your father, and he will show you;
> your elders and they will tell you.

As J. C. Greenfield notes,[66] almost every line of this passage contains an element familiar from descriptions of El, known as "Bull El his Father, El the king who establishes him," *ṯr ʾil ʾabh ʾil mlk dyknnh* (KTU 1.3 V 35-36; 1.4 I 4-15, etc.). Like El, Yahweh is the father *(*ʾab)* who establishes *(*kwn)* and creates *(*qny).* The verb *qny* recalls the epithet "El, creator of the earth," *ʾl qny ʾrṣ.* Second-millennium Canaanite tradition, preserved in a Hittite text, attributes this title to El.[67] Genesis 14:19 likewise applies this title to *ʾēl ʿelyôn,* itself an old El epithet. The phrase is also found in a neo-Punic inscription from Leptis Magna in Libya (KAI 129:1). While Deuteronomy 32:6-7 applies some traditional traits of El to Yahweh, it also employs other features of El as a foil to the people's character, according to Greenfield. The people, for example, are "senseless" *(lōʾ ḥākām),* unlike El. Finally, "eternity" *(ʿôlām)* evokes El's same epithet, and "the years of many generations" *(šĕnôt dôr-wādôr)* echoes El's title, *ʾab šnm,* "father of years."

Like some descriptions of Yahweh, some of Yahweh's epithets can be traced to those of El. Traditions concerning the cultic site of Shechem illustrate the cultural process lying behind the Yahwistic inclusion of old titles of El, or stated differently, the Yahwistic assimilation to old cultic sites of El. In the city of Shechem the local god was *ʾēl bĕrît,* "El of the covenant" (Judg. 9:46; cf. 8:33; 9:4). This word *ʾilbrt* appears as a Late Bronze Age title for El in

---

Verlagsbuchhandlung, 1933), 9-10; idem, *Symbols of the Gods in Mesopotamian Art,* AnOr 23 (Rome: Pontificium Institutum Biblicum, 1945), 131-33.

66. Greenfield, "The Hebrew Bible and Canaanite Literature," 554.

67. See *ANET,* 519. On this title, see P. D. Miller, Jr., "El, the Creator of the Earth," *BASOR* 239 (1980): 43-46. For the Luvian correspondences for this title, see E. Laroche, "Études sur les Hieroglyphes Hittites," *Syria* 31 (1954): 102-3. Cf. Asherah's Ugaritic title, *qnyt ʾilm,* "creatress of the gods," and Dagan's title at Emar, *EN qu-ù-ni,* "lord of creation" (Emar 373:88′, 379:5′, 381:15 and 382:16; my thanks go to Mr. Douglas Green for bringing these references to my attention).

KTU 1.128.14-15.[68] In the patriarchal narratives, the god of Shechem, *'ēl*, is called *'ĕlōhê yiśrā'ēl*, "the god of Israel," and is presumed to be Yahweh.[69] In this case, a process of reinterpretation appears to be at work. In the early history of Israel, when the cult of Shechem became Yahwistic, it inherited and continued the El traditions of that site.[70] Hence Yahweh received the title *'ēl bĕrît*, the old title of El. This record illustrates up to a point how Canaanite/Israelite traditions were transmitted. Israelite knowledge of the religious traditions of other deities was not due only to contact between Israel and its Phoenician neighbors in the Iron Age. Rather, as a function of the identification of Yahweh-El at cultic sites of El such as Shechem and Jerusalem, the old religious lore of a deity such as El was inherited by the Yahwistic priesthood in Israel. Ezekiel 16:3a proclaims accordingly: "Thus says the Lord God to Jerusa-

68. P. C. Craigie, "*El brt. El dn* (RS 24. 278, 14-15)," *UF* 5 (1973): 278-79; Cross, *Canaanite Myth and Hebrew Epic*, 39, 44; K. A. Kitchen, "Egypt, Ugarit, Qatna and Covenant," *UF* 11 (1979): 458; Lewis, "The Identity and Function of El/Baal Berith," 408, 416; Stager, "The Fortress-Temple," 239.

69. Fohrer, *History of Israelite Religion*, 38.

70. See R. Boling, *Judges*, AB 6A (Garden City, NY: Doubleday, 1975), 180. The complex tradition history surrounding the cult of Shechem perhaps points also to its antiquity (see G. E. Wright, *Shechem: The Biography of a Biblical City* [New York: McGraw-Hill, 1965], 123-58; L. Toombs and G. E. Wright, "The Fourth Campaign at Balatah (Shechem)," *BASOR* 169 [1963]: 28, 30; L. Toombs, "Shechem: Problems of the Early Israelite Era," in *Symposia Celebrating the Seventy-Fifth Anniversary of the Founding of the American Schools of Oriental Research (1900-1975)*, ed. F. M. Cross [Cambridge, MA: American Schools of Oriental Research, 1979], 69-83). The peaceful relationship between the Israelites and Shechemites in Josh. 24:25-26 has spawned theories positing an early emergence of Israel in the vicinity of Shechem. Genesis 34 depicts a violent period in the early relationships between the clan of Jacob and the natives of Shechem. The history of relations between the various members of the population was undoubtedly complex. See A. de Pury, "Genèse XXXIV et l'histoire," *RB* 71 (1969): 5-49; A. Lemaire, "Asriel, *śr'l*, Israël et l'origine de la conféderation Israelite," *VT* 23 (1973): 239-43; idem, "Les Benê Jacob: Essai d'interprétation historique d'une tradition patriarcale," *RB* 85 (1978): 321-37; cf. de Vaux, *The Early History of Israel*, 800-804; Freedman, *Pottery, Poetry, and Prophecy*, 84, 88, 164, 172, 176; G. W. Ahlström, "Another Moses Tradition," *JNES* 39 (1980): 65-69, esp. 66; idem, *Who Were the Israelites?* 40, 66-70; and Halpern, *The Emergence*, 81-94, 228. Because at Shechem no destruction levels can be dated to the time shortly before 1200 and continuous repair of Late Bronze Age fortifications into the Iron I period are attested, Ahlström argues that the Shechemite kingdom of Labayu known from the Amarna letters continued down through Gideon's time. The archaeological evidence, especially from surveys, could be wedded to such a theory; see I. Finkelstein, *The Archaeology of the Period of the Settlement and Judges* (Tel Aviv: Hakkibutz Hameuchad, 1986) (Heb.); idem, *'Izbet Sarṭah: An Early Iron Age Site Near Rosh Ha'ayin, Israel*, BAR International Series 299 (Oxford: BAR, 1986), esp. 205-13; idem, *The Archaeology of the Israelite Settlement*; B. Mazar, "The Early Israelite Settlement in the Hill Country," *BASOR* 241 (1981): 75-85; Stager, "The Archaeology of the Family in Ancient Israel," 24, and "The Fortress-Temple," 228-49.

lem: Your origin and your birth are of the land of the Canaanites." Israelite inclusion of Yahweh into the older figure of El was not syncretistic insofar as El belonged to Israel's original religious heritage. If syncretism was involved, it was a syncretism of various Israelite notions, and one that the prophets ultimately applauded. B. Vawter remarks: "The very fact that the prophets fought Canaanization would make them advocates of the 'syncretism' by which pagan titles were appropriated to Yahweh."[71] Yet even this "Canaanization," to use Vawter's term, was part of Israel's heritage.

3. Yahweh and Baal

It is assumed sometimes that in the period of the Judges religious devotion to Baal competed with the cult of Yahweh.[72] The basis for this claim is grounded in the criticism that the books of Judges (2:11-13; 3:7) and 1 Samuel (7:3-4; 12:10) direct against Baal. The story of Gideon in Judges 6 functions as a paradigmatic story designed to illustrate how true Yahwists in the early phase of Israel's history eradicated devotion to Baal and Asherah (see vv. 25-32). Indeed, in the story Gideon's name is changed from Jerubbaal, a name with *baʿal* as its theophoric element.

The historical picture of Israelite treatment of Baal is difficult to reconstruct. It may be clarified by distinguishing between the older material and the use that the tradents of the book of Judges made of this material. Their later viewpoint is embedded in the polemics of Judges 2–3, a secondary stage of the book, dating probably to the second half of the monarchy.[73] Textual hints in the book of Judges point to the monarchy as the period of redaction (which involved editing and supplementing received tradition). The final verse of Judges (21:25) relates the period of the Judges from a monarchist perspective: "in those days there was no king in Israel; each man did what was right in his own eyes." It is possible to pinpoint more precisely the time frame for the redaction of the book of Judges. Judges 18:30 relates the historical development of the priesthood in the tribe of Dan: "and Jonathan the son of Gershom, son of Moses, and his sons were priests to the tribe of the Danites until the day of the captivity of the land."[74] The temporal phrase, *ʿad-yôm*

71. B. Vawter, "The Canaanite Background of Genesis 49," *CBQ* 17 (1955): 12 n. 40.

72. A. S. Kapelrud, *Baal in the Ras Shamra Texts* (Copenhagen: Gad, 1952), 64-93; Pope, *El in the Ugaritic Texts,* 32, 35-42.

73. On these passages, see Boling, *Judges,* 30, 74; Soggin, *Judges,* 39, 41-44, 45.

74. For Judg. 18:30, read "Moses" instead of MT "Manasseh" (for the evidence of the versions and rabbinic sources, see D. Barthélemy, *Critique Textuelle de l'Ancien Testament,* 2 vols.,

gělôt hā'āreṣ, "until the day of exile of the land," would refer either to the captivity of the northern kingdom in 722, which included the territory of the tribe of Dan, or less likely the exile of the southern kingdom in 587. Given the royal perspective of Judges 21:25, the exile of the northern kingdom is evidently intended. In this case, the redaction of the book of Judges belongs to the eighth century or later. The later polemics in Judges 2 and 3 function as the initial elements in the cyclic pattern underlying the structure of many of the Judges stories: the Israelites sin against God, who in turn leaves them prey to their enemies; the Israelites cry out to God to save them, at which time God sends a judge to deliver them from their enemies.[75]

The information about Baal and the asherah in Judges 6 appears to be older, as it is integrated into the fabric of the story. The older information contained in this chapter was available to tradents and probably served as the historical source for the later polemics. If this material is older, does it then attest to Israelite acceptance of Baal and Asherah in the Judges period? The redaction of the later tradents manifest in Judges 2–3 indicates that they answered this question in the affirmative. Despite problems with this conclusion, it is in fact a reasonable conclusion, yet it may mask the larger picture. The tradents assumed that in the Judges period Baal and Asherah were distinctive deities worshiped by Israelites at expense to the cult of Yahweh. To be sure, worship of the Phoenician storm-god Baal at the expense of Yahweh's cult occurred during of the reign of Ahab, yet that does not appear to have been the case in the time of the Judges. Despite the picture that later tradents constructed, some older elements, especially the proper names with the element **ba'al* in Judges 6 and elsewhere may suggest a different situation. The

---

OBO 50/1 [Fribourg: Éditions Universitaires; Göttingen: Vandenhoeck & Ruprecht, 1982], 1.115-16). See the discussion of S. Weitzman, "Reopening the Case of the Suspiciously Suspended Nun in Judges 18:30," *CBQ* 61 (1999): 429-47. On Judges 18, see Soggin, *Judges*, 276-78; D. G. Schley, *Shiloh: A Biblical City in Tradition and History*, JSOTSup 63 (Sheffield: JSOT, 1988). On the function of related phrases in Judges, see B. S. Childs, "A Study of the Formula, 'Until This Day,'" *JBL* 82 (1963): 272-92; B. O. Long, "Framing Repetitions in Biblical Historiography," *JBL* 106 (1987): 397-98.

75. On this cycle, see W. Richter, *Die Bearbeitungen des 'Retterbuches' in der deuteronomischen Epoche*, BBB 21 (Bonn: P. Hanstein, 1964), 65-68; A. Malamat, "Charismatic Leadership in Early Israel," in *Magnalia Dei, The Mighty Acts of God: Essays on the Bible and Archaeology in Memory of G. Ernest Wright*, ed. F. M. Cross, W. E. Lemke, and P. D. Miller, Jr. (Garden City, NY: Doubleday, 1976), 155; A. D. H. Mayes, "The Period of the Judges and the Rise of the Monarchy," in *Israelite and Judaean History*, ed. J. H. Hayes and J. M. Miller, OTL (Philadelphia: Westminster, 1977), 290; Soggin, *Judges*, 43-44; Ahlström, *Who Were the Israelites?* 75; Halpern, *The First Historians*, 121-43; and M. Brettler, "The Book of Judges: Literature as Politics," *JBL* 108 (1989): 395-418.

evidence may point to a more complex picture, in which the cult of the old Canaanite god Baal was deemed tolerable by some Israelites.

The tradents' treatment of the name of Jerubbaal in Judges 6–7 exposes the religious problem. The tradents altered the original Baalistic import of the name, which means "may Baal contend." The name of the Byblian king Rib-Addi illustrates the original significance of Jerubbaal's name, since the name Rib-Addi has essentially the same elements as the name of Jerubbaal. Both names have the same verbal base or root, **ryb*, "to contend," and both have a name of the Canaanite storm-god. The name Addu appears as Haddu in Ugaritic texts where Haddu stands in parallelism with Baal. In the second millennium, Baal was an epithet of Haddu. Like the name Jerubbaal, the name Rib-Addi means "may Addu contend." Judges 7:32 reinterprets the name of Jerubbaal negatively as an anti-Baal name: "let Baal plead against him, because he has thrown down his altar." The negative interpretation of the name as anti-Baal shows the tradents' assumption that the theophoric element refers to the god Baal.[76] Likewise, 2 Samuel 11:21 reflects a negative view of the name of Jerubbaal. The verse refers to Jerubbaal as Jerubbeshet, substituting for *baʿal* the element **bešet*, a play on *bôšet*, "shame." Jeremiah 3:24 refers to Baal precisely as *habbôšet*, "the Shame" (cf. 11:13; Hos. 9:10).[77] Albright argued that the name of Gideon, based on the root **gdʿ*, "to hew," functioned in the text to indicate Jerubbaal's role as a destroyer of Baal's altar and the asherah. Albright therefore suggested that Jerubbaal was the original and perhaps the only name of this figure (although two historical figures may stand behind the two names). Some confirmation for Albright's conclusion is provided in 1 Samuel 12:11. The verse offers a partial list of judges who saved

76. Albright, *Archaeology and the Religion of Israel* (Baltimore: Johns Hopkins Univ. Press, 1956), 160; idem, *The Biblical Period from Abraham to Ezra* (New York: Harper & Row, 1963), 42; idem, *Yahweh and the Gods of Canaan*, 199-200, esp. n. 101; Ringgren, *Israelite Religion*, 44; J. A. Emerton, "Gideon and Jerubbaal," *Journal of Theological Studies* 27 (1976): 289-312; U. Oldenburg, *The Conflict Between El and Baʿal in Canaanite Religion* (Leiden: Brill, 1969), 179. For an attempt to compare the element **bôšet* in these names with Akkadian *baštu*, "dignity, pride, honor," see M. Tsevat, "Ishbosheth and Congeners: The Names and Their Study," *Hebrew Union College Annual* 34 (1975): 71-87; for criticisms of this position, see P. K. McCarter, *II Samuel*, AB 9 (Garden City, NY: Doubleday, 1984), 84-85. The view of Tsevat has received new support from G. J. Hamilton, "New Evidence for the Authenticity of *bšt* in Hebrew Personal Names and for Its Use as a Divine Epithet in Biblical Texts," *CBQ* 60 (1998): 228-50. See further S. Schorch, *Euphemismen in der Hebräischen Bibel*, Orientalia Biblica et Christiana 12 (Wiesbaden: Harrassowitz, 2000), 78 n. 201. Assuming Hamilton's view of the origins of the **bšt* element is correctly "protective spirit," it remains possible that it was secondarily understood in these contexts as "shame."

77. See Cooper, "Divine Names and Epithets in the Ugaritic Texts," 359-60.

Israel; the recitation gives Gideon's name only as Jerubbaal.[78] The editorial gloss in Judges 7:1 also reflects the independent tradition regarding Jerubbaal. The chapter begins its story, "Then Jerubbaal (that is, Gideon) . . ." Some proper names with *baʿal* as the theophoric element probably did refer to the god Baal, which would explain the redactor's alterations. Such ambiguity underlies some proper names with *baʿal* as the theophoric element, which may be either a Baal or a Yahweh name. For example, like Jerubbaal, the name *baʿal ḥānān,* the royal overseer of olive and sycamore trees under David in 1 Chronicles 27:28 (cf. Gen. 36:38-39), is ambiguous. The name means either "Baal is gracious," referring to the divinity Baal, or "the lord is gracious," referring to Yahweh.

The presupposition that *baʿal* refers to a god, Baal, not only underlies the change of Jerubbaal to Jerubbeshet in 2 Samuel 11:21 but also informs the fact that the names of Eshbaal ("man [?] of Baal/lord") and Meribbaal ("Baal/lord is advocate/my master") in 1 Chronicles 8–9 were altered to Ishboshet ("man [?] of shame") and Mephiboshet (from **mippîbôšet,* "from the mouth [?] of shame") in 2 Samuel 2–4. The changes in these names reflect the supposition that these names witnessed to an acceptance of Baal.[79] However, Eshbaal and Meribbaal belonged to the clan of Saul, in which Yahwistic names are also attested, such as Jonathan, the son of Saul. Why would a Yahwistic family give Baal names, if Baal were a god inimical to Yahweh? The answer is perhaps implicit in the name of another family member provided in the genealogy of Saul's clan in 1 Chronicles 8:30 and 9:36. In this verse, Baal is the name of Saul's uncle. The name is hypocoristic (i.e. lacking a divine name), and is usually interpreted as "(Yahweh is) lord." This name belongs also to a Reubenite (1 Chron. 5:5). Direct analogies are provided by the name *bĕʿalyāh,* "Yah is lord" (1 Chron. 12:6) and *ywbʿl,* "Yaw is lord," attested in a seal inscription.[80] These names point to three possibilities. In Saul's family, either *baʿal* was a title for Yahweh, or Baal was acceptable in royal, Yahwistic circles, or both.[81] The same range of possible interpretations underlies the names of Eshbaal and Meribbaal; both were possibly Yahwistic names, later understood as anti-Yahwistic in import. The later defensiveness over these

78. Ahlström, "Another Moses Tradition," 65-69.

79. See Albright, *Archaeology and the Religion of Israel,* 113, 207 n. 62; idem, *The Biblical Period,* 38; Tigay, *You Shall Have No Other Gods,* 8 n. 10; cf. Oldenburg, *The Conflict,* 181 n. 4. For textual and philological discussions of the names, see McCarter, *II Samuel,* 82, 85-87, 124-25, 128. See n. 77 above.

80. N. Avigad, "Hebrew Seals and Sealings and Their Significance for Biblical Research," in *Congress Volume: Jerusalem 1986,* ed. J. Emerton, VTSup 40 (Leiden: Brill, 1988), 8.

81. Ringgren, *Israelite Religion,* 44.

names points to the fact that the language of Baal, though criticized during the monarchy, was used during the Judges period. Furthermore, the characteristics of Baal and Yahweh probably overlapped. There is indirect evidence for this conclusion in what is considered Israel's oldest poetry. Some passages, for example, Judges 5:4-5 and Psalm 29, use imagery characteristic of Baal to describe Yahweh as the divine warrior fighting to deliver Israel.[82] In short, the conflict between Yahweh and Baal was a problem of the monarchic period and not the period of the Judges.[83]

The religious issue of the Judges period requires further explanation. If in early Israel El and Yahweh were identified, and the cults of Baal and Yahweh coexisted, the question why the cults of Baal and Yahweh were considered irreconcilable beginning in the ninth century needs to be addressed. To anticipate the discussion of the next chapter, El was not a threat to the cult of Yahweh in ancient Israel. Phoenician Baal, on the contrary, represented a threat in the ninth century and onward, especially thanks to the efforts of Ahab and Jezebel to elevate him in the northern kingdom.[84] This situation was the perspective through which the later tradents of Judges viewed the religious material in Judges 6–7. In Israel during the Judges period, however, Baal was probably no more a threat than El. Later tradition did not view the figure of Baal in these terms; indeed, later sources treat Baal as a threat to Yahwism from the era of the Judges down to the period of the monarchy. While this historical witness to Baal in Israelite circles is probably correct, the polemical cast of the witness is not. Baal was probably not the threat in the Judges period or the tenth century that later tradents considered him. It was the traumatic events of the ninth century and afterwards that shaped the perspective of the tradents.

4. Yahweh and Asherah

Just as there is little evidence for El as a separate Israelite god in the era of the Judges, so Asherah is poorly attested as a separate Israelite goddess in this

82. See chapter 2, section 2. It is possible that the application of storm-imagery (in the rain storm) was secondary to Yahweh, who after all is said to derive from Midian/Teiman/Paran, a region not particularly known for its rain-storms. See Smith, *The Origins of Biblical Monotheism,* 145-46. If correct, the application of storm-imagery, made under the appropriation of Baal imagery, would still be quite early, probably premonarchic. J. Day (*Yahweh and the Gods and Goddesses of Canaan,* 91-116) has stressed the secondary appropriation of Baal imagery by Yahweh.

83. Ringgren, *Israelite Religion,* 44.

84. See chapter 2, section 1.

period. Arguments for Asherah as a goddess in this period rest on Judges 6 and elsewhere where she is mentioned with Baal. Yet the story in Judges 6 focuses much more attention on Baal worship and none on Asherah. Only the asherah, the symbol that bears the name of the goddess, is criticized. Furthermore, unlike *ʾēl* and *baʿal, ʾăšērāh* does not appear as the theophoric element in Hebrew proper names.[85] In recent years it has been claimed that Asherah was an Israelite goddess and the consort of Yahweh, because her name or at least the cultic item symbolizing her, the asherah, appears in the eighth-century inscriptions from Kuntillet ʿAjrûd and Khirbet el-Qôm. To anticipate that discussion,[86] **ʾšrth* in these inscriptions refers to the symbol originally named after the goddess, although during the eighth century it may not have symbolized the goddess. This conclusion does not address, however, the issue of whether Asherah was distinguished as a separate goddess and consort of Yahweh in the period of the Judges. Indeed, it may be argued that her symbol was part of the cult of Yahweh in this period, but it did not symbolize a goddess. Just as El and Baal and their imagery were adapted to the cult of Yahweh, the asherah was a symbol in Yahwistic cult in this period.

There is one passage that may point to Asherah as an Israelite goddess at some point in early Israel. Genesis 49 reports Jacob's blessings to his twelve sons. B. Vawter, D. N. Freedman, and M. O'Connor argue that verses 24-26, part of the blessings to Joseph, represent a series of divine epithets, including two titles of Asherah.[87] MT reads:

wattēšeb bĕʾêtān qaštô
wayyāpōzzû zĕrōʿê yādāyw
mîdê ʾăbîr yaʿăqōb
miššām rōʿeh ʾeben yiśrāʾēl
mēʾēl ʾābîkā wĕyaʿzĕrekkā
wĕʾēt šadday wîbārĕkekkā
birkōt šāmayim mēʿāl
birkōt tĕhôm rōbeṣet tāḥat

85. For this point, see Olyan, *Asherah and the Cult of Yahweh,* 35-36.

86. See chapter 3, section 3.

87. Vawter, "The Canaanite Background," 12-17; Freedman, "'Who Is Like Thee Among the Gods?' The Religion of Early Israel," in *Ancient Israelite Religion: Essays in Honor of Frank Moore Cross,* ed. P. D. Miller, Jr., P. D. Hanson, and S. D. McBride, 324-25; O'Connor, *Hebrew Verse Structure,* 177-78. For the question of the etymology of *šadday,* see Albright, "The Names Shaddai and Abram," *JBL* 54 (1935): 173-204; Ringgren, *Israelite Religion,* 22; Cross, *Canaanite Myth and Hebrew Epic,* 52-56; and references in n. 50 above.

birkōt šādayim wārāḥam
birkōt 'ābîkā gābĕrû 'al
birkōt hôray 'ad-
ta'ăwat gib'ōt 'ôlām
tihyênâ lĕrō'š yôsēp
ûlqodqōd nĕzîr 'eḥāyw

The following translation departs from the MT and instead reflects the proposal of B. Vawter that four pairs of divine entities are invoked from verse 24d through verse 26c:

His bow stayed taut,
His hands were agile,
By the Bull of Jacob,
By the strength of the Shepherd, the Stone of Israel,
By El, your Father, who helps you,
By Shadday who blesses you
With the blessings of Heavens, from above,
The blessings of the Deep, crouching below,
The blessings of Breasts-and-Womb,
The blessings of your Father, Hero and Almighty,
The blessings of the Eternal Mountains,
The delight of the Everlasting Hills,
May they be on the head of Joseph,
On the crown of the chosen of his brothers.[88]

Within verses 24-26 Vawter sees four sets of divine epithets: (a) *'ăbîr ya'ăqōb,* "Bull[89] of Jacob," and *rō'eh 'eben yiśrā'ēl,* "Shepherd, Stone of Israel";

88. Many emendations have been proposed for these verses. For the text-critical issues, see Vawter, "The Canaanite Background," 16; Cross and Freedman, *Studies in Ancient Yahwistic Poetry,* 75-76, 91-92 nn. 78-83. In v. 24a, MT understands Joseph as the referent (so RSV, New Jewish Publication Society version; cf. NAB), but many commentators take Joseph's enemies as the referent (so O'Connor, *Hebrew Verse Structure,* 177). This translation emends MT *gābĕrû* to *gibbôr* and MT *hôray* to *harĕrê* in v. 26. In the attempt to make *birkōt 'ābîkā gābĕrû* more consistent with the customary interpretation of *birkōt šādayim wārāḥam* as an expression of natural fertility, some commentators emend the former expression to *birkōt 'ābîb wĕgib'ōl* (e.g., E. A. Speiser, *Genesis,* AB I [Garden City, NY: Doubleday, 1964], 369-70); there is no text-critical basis for this change. The blessings of vv. 25b-26a are translated as syntactically dependent on *wîbārĕkekkā.* It is possible to read them as the subject of the verb in v. 26b (so O'Connor, *Hebrew Verse Structure,* 177).

89. I am not inclined to separate the semantics of *'ăbîr/'abbîr,* as N. Sarna maintains (Sarna, *The JPS Torah Commentary: Genesis* בראשית [Philadelphia/New York/Jerusalem: The

(b) *ʾēl ʾābîkā wĕyaʿzĕrekkā,* "El, your father, who saves you," and *šadday wîbārĕkekkā,* "Shadday who blesses you"; (c) *šāmayim mēʿāl,* "Heaven above," and *tĕhôm rōbeṣet tāḥat,* "Deep crouching below"; and (d) *šādayim wārāḥam,* "Breasts-and-Womb," and *ʾābîkā gibbôr wāʿāl,* "your Father, Hero and Almighty." Most of these epithets, including "Father" and "Shadday," are attributed elsewhere to Yahweh-El. "Bull of Jacob" is a title of Yahweh in Psalm 132:2, 5; Isaiah 49:26; 60:16 (cf. Isa. 1:4). The pair of Heaven and Deep is described in similar fashion in Deuteronomy 33:13. There *ṭal,* "dew," occurs in the same syntactic position as *ʿāl,* "above," in Genesis 49:25c (cf. Gen. 27:28a). Genesis 27:39 combines differently the various terms associated with Heaven in these verses: *ûmiṭṭal haššāyim mēʿāl,* "from the dew of Heaven from above." O'Connor understands verse 26a as a series of epithets and translates "the blessings of your father, Hero and Almighty." Instead of MT *gābĕrû ʿal* (so RSV), **gbr* is understood as a noun, *w-* is taken as the conjunction, and ʿl is read as a short form of the divine epithet, *ʿly.*[90] Verse 25e also contains epithets: "the blessings of Breasts-and-Womb." This reading of verse 25e is compelling, given the pairs of epithets in the preceding cola. Indeed, the titles of verse 25e are paired with the title "your father" of verse 26a, which recalls a standard El epithet.

The phrase *šādayim wārāḥam* in verse 25e echoes Ugaritic titles of the goddesses Asherah and Anat.[91] The word *rḥm* is associated with the goddess Anat in KTU 1.6 II 27, 1.15 II 6, and 1.23.16. In KTU 1.23.13 and 28, this title refers to Anat in her pairing with Asherah.[92] In an invocation in KTU 1.23.23-24, the "beautiful gods" *(ʾilm nʿmm)* are characterized as receiving nourishment from Asherah and Anat:[93]

Jewish Publication Society, 1989], 343, 372 n. 49), based on Sarna's early study, "The Divine Title 'ʾabhîr yaʿăqôbh,'" in *Essays on the Occasion of the 70th Anniversary of Dropsie University* [Philadelphia: Dropsie Univ. Press, 1979], 389-98). For *ʾăbîr* as "bull," see P. D. Miller, "Animal Names as Designations in Ugaritic and Hebrew," *UF* 11 (1979): 177-86; see also Cross, *Canaanite Myth and Hebrew Epic,* 4-5, n. 6.

90. On *ʿly* as an epithet, see chapter 2, section 2.

91. Vawter, "The Canaanite Background," 16-17.

92. See *rḥmt* for "young women" also in the Mesha stele (KAI 181:17). For discussion, see P. Bordreuil, "A propos de l'Inscription de Meshaʿ deux notes," in *The World of the Arameans III: Studies in Language and Literature in Honour of Paul-Eugène Dion,* ed. P. M. Michèle Daviau, J. W. Wevers, and M. Weigl, JSOTSup 326 (Sheffield: Sheffield Academic Press, 2001), 158-61.

93. On KTU 1.23, see Pope, "Mid Rock and Scrub: A Ugaritic Parallel to Exodus 7:19," in *Biblical and Near Eastern Studies: Essays in Honor of W. S. Lasor,* ed. G. Tuttle (Grand Rapids, MI: Eerdmans, 1978), 146-50; del Olmo Lete, *Mitos y leyendas,* 427-48; R. Ratner and B. Zuckerman, "'A Kid in Milk'?: New Photographs of KTU 1.23, Line 14," *Hebrew Union College Annual* 57 (1986): 15-60. The reconstruction of [*ʾagzr ym bn*] is suggested by the parallel phrases in lines 58-59 and 61. The pairing of *ʾaṯrt wrḥm* in line 13 and *ʾaṯrt wrḥmy* in line 28 is the basis for the reconstruction of line 24b.

'iqr'an 'ilm nʿmm	I would invoke the beautiful gods,
['agzr ym bn] ym	[voracious ones of the sea, sons of] the sea,
ynqm b'ap ḏd	who suck from the teat of the breast
'aṯrt [wrḥmy]	of Asherah [and Rahmay]

The description of the "beautiful gods" is paralled in KTU 1.23-61, which refers to a goddess with the word *št,* "lady," perhaps a title of Anat elsewhere in Ugaritic (KTU 1.18 IV 27; 1.19 IV 53).[94] In Genesis 49:25e-26a, "Breasts-and-Womb" might be a title attributed to a goddess, paired with the standard male imagery of El as father. This pair would belong to a larger sequence of paired epithets including titles of El. The question of which goddess might be involved is not too difficult to establish. The epithets do not belong to Anat, as her cult is unattested for Iron Age Israel or Phoenicia. Astarte could be the goddess of Genesis 49:25, since her name is associated with natural fertility, which is the setting for the epithets in this passage. More specifically, the expression *ʿaštĕrôt ṣō'n* refers to the young of animals (Deut. 7:13; 28:4, 18, 51)[95] and derives from the goddess's name in construct with *ṣō'n,* a collective term for small animals such as sheep and goats.[96] Moreover, there are later references to Astarte in biblical literature (Judg. 2:13; 10:6). The strongest evidence, however, supports Asherah as the goddess evoked by the female epithets in Genesis 49:25. The Ugaritic background of the epithets favors Asherah. Furthermore, the pairing of *šādayim wārāḥam* with El would further point to Asherah, since Asherah is the goddess paired with him in the Ugaritic texts. Other interpretations are posssible for *šādayim wārāḥam.* These terms meaning "breasts and womb" could be interpreted in purely natural terms, as signs of natural fertility. This interpretation represents the traditional view of the terms and is reflected in most modern translations (e.g., RSV, NAB, New Jewish Publication Society). The word *šdym* could be translated differently and understood to refer to "mountains" cognate with Akkadian *šadû,* and *rāḥam* could be understood in another way, perhaps as "winds," the plural of Hebrew *rûaḥ.* The first alternative would fit well with

94. For interpretations of *št,* see del Olmo Lete, *Mitos y leyendas,* 633-34. See further P. Merlo, "Über die Ergänzung ‚<št> in KTU 1.23:59," *UF* 28 (1996): 491-94.

95. *BDB,* 800; Albright, *Yahweh and the Gods of Canaan,* 185; H. L. Ginsberg, "The North-Canaanite Myth of Anath and Aqhat," *BASOR* 97 (1945): 9; Oden, *Studies,* 80; J. M. Hadley, "The Fertility of the Flock? The De-Personalization of Astarte in the Old Testament," in *On Reading Prophetic Texts: Gender-Specific and Related Studies in Memory of Fokkelien van Dijk-Hemmes,* ed. B. Becking and M. Dijkstra (Leiden: Brill, 1996), 115-33.

96. See B. A. Levine, "Ugaritic Descriptive Rituals," *Journal of Cuneiform Studies* 17 (1963): 105-11.

the setting of natural fertility in these verses. The second alternative would comport with the cosmic terms, "Heaven" and "Deeps" in the preceding bicolon and "Eternal Mountains" and "Everlasting Hills" in the following line. The pairing with El, however, favors the interpretation of *šādayim wārāḥam* as the epithets of Asherah. If this interpretation of Genesis 49:24-26 is correct, then El and Asherah were Israelite deities distinguished from Yahweh, who is invoked separately in verse 18.[97] This chapter might then represent a tradition or early stage in Israel's religious history in which El and Yahweh were not identified and Asherah stood as an identifiable goddess.

In subsequent tradition, the titles of El in this passage were treated differently from *šādayim wārāḥam.* In the period of the monarchy, the male titles of El as well as Baal were regarded as epithets of Yahweh, as their attestations in Deuteronomy 33:26-27 and Psalm 18 (2 Sam. 22):14-16 show. The female imagery of Genesis 49:25e suffered a different fate in the history of the tradition. It was not directly assimilated to Yahweh in the way that male epithets were. Rather, these epithets were not applied to Yahweh and, as chapter 3 shows, female language for the divine appears infrequently and indirectly in biblical texts. The history of interpretation of Genesis 49:25e also illustrates the way that this female language was treated. Modern translations and commentaries generally treat the language of "Breasts-and-Womb" in purely natural terms, despite the cluster of divine epithets surrounding this phrase. S. Olyan has demonstrated that Asherah was a goddess paired with El, and this pairing was bequeathed to Israelite religion by virtue of the Yahweh-El identification.[98] This reconstruction is consistent with the evidence of Genesis 49:25. However, the subsequent history of the female language seems to differ. In some quarters devotion to the goddess may have persisted, but neither biblical information nor inscriptional material unambiguously confirms this historical reconstruction. Rather, the explicit cult of the goddess may not have endured. The maternal language, originally deriving from the goddess and made cultically present through the symbol of the asherah, did not refer to the goddess later in the cult of Yahweh. The titles and imagery belonging to El and Baal in Genesis 49:24-26 raise a further question about the nature of conflation of deities in early Israel. While later tradition presumed that these verses describe Yahweh, the god treated in these verses appears to be a different god, since Yahweh is invoked in a separate section in verse 18.

One further piece of evidence, a cultic stand from the site of Taanach,

97. The authenticity of this invocation has been doubted (so Freedman, *Pottery, Poetry, and Prophecy,* 85; cf. O'Connor, *Hebrew Verse Structure,* 175).

98. Olyan, *Asherah and the Cult of Yahweh,* 38-61.

may point to Israelite devotion to Asherah in the early monarchy. Dated to the tenth century by its excavators, this square hollow stand has four levels or registers depicting a number of divine symbols.[99] The bottom level depicts a naked female figure with each of her hands resting on the heads of lions (or lionesses) flanking her. This figure could be Anat, Asherah, or Astarte, but the attestation of Astarte's cult in this period and her iconography with the lion in Egypt might favor the identification of the female figure here with her. The second lowest register has an opening in the middle flanked by two sphinxes with a lion's body, bird's wings, and a female head. The next register has a sacred tree, composed of a heavy central trunk sprouting symmetrically three pairs of curling branches. Two ibexes stand on their hind legs, and both face the tree in the center. On the outside of the two ibexes are two lions. The symbol of the tree is an asherah, the tree named after the goddess Asherah. The top register depicts a young four-legged animal, either a bovine, such as an ox or a young bull without horns (BH *ʿēgel*). This animal may have represented either Baal or Yahweh in tenth-century Taanach. Finally, above the animal appears a solar disk, the symbol of the sun deity that appears with major gods in the iconography of this period. In short, assuming the correct dating of the stand to the tenth century, the stand attests to polytheism in this area. The Taanach stand suggests that at the beginning of Iron II (ca. 1000-587), the city maintained the worship of a god, either Yahweh or Baal, a goddess, probably Astarte, and the devotion to the asherah, possibly at this juncture symbolizing the goddess Asherah. The significance of the stand for understanding Israelite

99. For a picture of the stand, see A. E. Glock, "Taanach," *EAEHL* 4:1142. For a detailed discussion of the stand, see R. Hestrin, "The Cult Stand from Taʿanach and Its Religious Background," in *Studia Phoenicia V: Phoenicia and the East Mediterranean in the First Millennium B.C., Proceedings of the Conference Held in Leuven 14-16 November 1985*, ed. E. Lipiński, Orientalia Lovaniensia Analecta 22 (Louvain: Uitgeverij Peeters, 1987), 62-77. Tigay (*You Shall Have No Other Gods*, 92-93) argues for the Caananite provenience of the stand. J. G. Taylor argues that the stand is Israelite and that Asherah is depicted in registers 2 and 4 and Yahweh in registers 1 and 3. ("Yahweh and Asherah at Tenth Century Taanach," *Newsletter for Ugaritic Studies* 37/38 [1987]: 16-18; "The Two Earliest Representations of Yahweh," in *Ascribe to the Lord: Biblical and Other Studies in Memory of Peter C. Craigie*, ed. L. Eslinger and G. Taylor, JSOTSup 67 [Sheffield: JSOT, 1988], 557-66). For assessments, see Hadley, *The Cult of Asherah in Ancient Israel and Judah*, 169-76; and Miller, *The Religion of Ancient Israel*, 43-45. See also the important study of P. Beck, "The Cult-Stands from Taanach: Aspects of the Iconographic Tradition of Early Iron Age Cult Objects in Palestine," in *From Nomadism to Monarchy: Archaeological and Historical Aspects of Early Israel*, ed. I. Finkelstein and N. Na'aman (Jerusalem: Yad Izhak Ben-Zvi/Israel Exploration Society; Washington, DC: Biblical Archaeology Society, 1994), 352-81. For further discussion of the iconography of this stand, see also below chapter 2, section 2; chapter 3, section 4; chapter 4, section 3. For archaeological discussion of Taanach in the Iron Age, see Finkelstein, *Archaeology of the Israelite Settlement*, 88-89.

religion in the early years of the monarchy hinges in part on the accuracy of the dating of the stand by its excavators. If the stand is dated correctly, then it might constitute evidence for Israelite religion. Judges 1:27 would suggest that the city remained at least partially Canaanite down to the monarchy. Afterwards following the rise of the Davidic dynasty, the city became Israelite. Solomon's organization of the nation lists Taanach and Megiddo in the fifth district (1 Kings 4:12). Though politically identified as Israelite, the city may have continued its Canaanite cultic traditions, which flourished in the valleys and the coast in the Late Bronze Age. Dated to the early monarchy, the stand would appear to provide evidence for Israelite polytheism (including Asherah), continuous with earlier Canaanite traditions.

That Anat was not a goddess in Iron Age Israel seems clear. Apart from proper names, evidence for her cult is virtually nonexistent. As section 4 of chapter 2 discusses, her imagery also became part of the repertoire of martial descriptions for Yahweh. Solar worship in this early period is likewise difficult to establish. Solar imagery for Yahweh developed during the period of the monarchy, perhaps through the influence of monarchic religious ideology.[100] The geographical distribution of these deities can be pinpointed minimally. The cult of Yahweh and the symbol, the asherah, appear from later data to be general features of both northern and southern religion. The northern evidence for El seems clear from his cult in Shechem. Jerusalem probably represents another cultic site where the royal cult of Yahweh assumed the indigenous traditions of El. The monarchic solar imagery for Yahweh seems to be strictly a southern development, a special feature of the royal Judean cult. The information about Baal stems from largely northern sources, but he was apparently popular in both kingdoms. Evidence for Astarte is extremely rare in the period of the Judges. Moreover, the biblical evidence may stem from a later, southern polemic against this goddess.

5. Convergence of Divine Imagery

Some of the older Israelite poems juxtapose imagery associated with El and Baal in the Ugaritic texts and apply this juxtaposition of attributes to Yahweh. It was noted that Genesis 49:25-26, for example, exhibits language deriving from El and Asherah. According to F. M. Cross,[101] Deuteronomy 33:26-27[102]

100. Ringgren, *Israelite Religion,* 62, 97-98. On solar language, see chapter 4.

101. Cross, *Canaanite Myth and Hebrew Epic,* 157 n. 52; cf. 163.

102. The dating of Deuteronomy 33 varies significantly. Scholars arguing for a pre-

mixes El and Baal epithets.[103] Verse 26 describes Yahweh in storm language traditional to Baal[104] while verse 27 applies to Yahweh the phrase, *'ĕlōhê qedem,* "the ancient god," a description reflecting El's great age:

> There is none like God, O Jeshurun,
> who rides *(rōkēb)* through the heavens *(šāmayim)* to your help,
> and in his majesty through the skies.
> The eternal God *('ĕlōhê qedem)* is your dwelling place . . .

Psalm 18 (2 Sam. 22):14-16 (E 13-15) likewise juxtaposes El and Baal imagery or titles for Yahweh:[105]

> Yahweh also thundered in the heavens,
> and the Most High *('elyôn)* uttered his voice,
> hailstones and coals of fire.
> And he sent out his arrows,
> and scattered them;
> he flashed forth lightnings,

---

monarchic date include I. L. Seeligman, "A Psalm from Pre-Regal Times," *VT* 14 (1964): 90; Cross, *Canaanite Myth and Hebrew Epic,* 123; Freedman, *Pottery, Poetry, and Prophecy,* 90-92. H. Seebass argues for a Davidic setting for the poem ("Die Stämmeliste von Dtn XXXIII," *VT* 27 [1977]: 158-69). Von Rad (*Deuteronomy,* 208) dates Deuteronomy 33 to the ninth or early eighth century. Other scholars who propose an eighth-century dating include Mayes, *Deuteronomy,* 397; G. A. Smith, *The Book of Deuteronomy,* The Cambridge Bible (Cambridge: Cambridge Univ. Press, 1918), 361; C. Steuenagel, *Das Deuteronomium,* Göttingen Handbuch zum Alten Testament (Göttingen: Vandenhoeck & Ruprecht, 1923), 173; and R. Tournay, "Le Psaume et les Bénédictions de Möise (Deutéronome, XXXIII)," *RB* 65 (1958): 208. The later dates proposed for the formation of the chapter do not preclude an earlier date for vv. 26-27.

103. In view of the evidence pertaining to the conflation of El and Baal between the Ugaritic sources and the earliest biblical traditions, it may be queried whether the Israelite traditions created the conflation of divine imagery or inherited it (see the discussions of Genesis 49 in sections 4 and 5). Such a question is impossible to answer unless the character of Yahweh prior to contact with El or Baal (if there was any such period) can be determined. In the oldest Israelite traditions describing the march of the divine warrior, Yahweh appears primarily as a storm deity with El epithets. Despite some scholarly claims to the contrary (see P. D. Miller, *The Divine Warrior in Early Israel,* HSM 5 [Cambridge, MA: Harvard Univ. Press, 1973], 48-58; J. J. M. Roberts, *The Earliest Semitic Pantheon: A Study of the Semitic Deities Attested in Mesopotamia before Ur III* [Baltimore: Johns Hopkins Univ. Press, 1972], 95-96 n. 233), El is not attested clearly as a warrior figure in the extant textual material. If the approach taken in this section is correct, it would serve to explain the fundamental compatibility of Yahweh with Baal during the Judges period and the early monarchy (see chapter 2).

104. See chapter 2, section 2.

105. Regarding the date and function of Psalm 18, see Cross, *Canaanite Myth and Hebrew Epic,* 158-59.

and routed them.
Then the channels of the sea *(ʾăpîqê mayim)* were seen . . .

This passage bears two explicit hallmarks of El language within a passage primarily describing a storm theophany of the type predicated of Baal in Ugaritic literature. The title *ʿelyôn* is an old epithet of El.[106] In Genesis 14:19 it occurs as a title of the god of the patriarchs, and it appears in the older poetic compositions for the god of Israel (see also Num. 24:4; cf. Deut. 32:8). It is a common divine title in the Psalter (Pss. 93; 21:8; 46:5; 50:14; 57:3; 73:11; 77:11; 78:17, 35, 56; 83:19; 91:1, 9; 92:2; 107:11). In Psalm 82:6 it appears in the phrase *bĕnê ʿelyôn.* There it refers to other deities and reflects El's role as father of the gods. The "channels of the sea" *(ăpîqê mayim)* perhaps echo the description of the waters of El's abode, called *mbk nhrm//ʾapq thmtm,* "springs of the two rivers//the channels of the double-deeps" (KTU 1.2 III 4; 1.3 V 14; 1.4 IV 21-22; 1.5 VI 1*; 1.6 I 34; 1.17 VI 48; cf. 1.100.2-3).[107] Besides the features associated with El in Canaanite tradition, Psalm 18:14-16 describes Yahweh as a divine warrior, manifesting his divine weaponry in the storm like Baal in the Ugaritic texts.

In these passages, Deuteronomy 33:26-27, Psalm 18 (2 Sam. 22):14-16, as well as Genesis 49:25-26, imagery regularly applied to El and Baal in Northwest Semitic literature was attributed to Yahweh at a relatively early point in Israel's religious history. Moreover, in applying this imagery to Yahweh, these passages combine or conflate the imagery of more than one Canaanite deity. Other poetic passages treated in subsequent chapters, such as Psalm 68 and Deuteronomy 32, offer further examples of conflation or convergence of divine language associated with a variety of deities in Canaanite literature. Such convergence in Israel's earliest history occurs in other forms. The modes and content of revelation appropriate to El and Baal appear in conflated form in the earliest levels of biblical tradition.[108] Likewise, Psalm 27 describes the divine dwelling in terms used of El's and Baal's homes in Canaanite tradition. Psalm 27:6 calls Yahweh's home a tent *(*ʾōhel)* like El's

106. Scholars differ whether *ʿelyôn* was originally an epithet of El or a secondary accretion to El (see Gen. 14:18). On this issue, see Cross, *Canaanite Myth and Hebrew Epic,* 50-52; cf. R. Rendtorff, "The Background of the Title עֶלְיוֹן in Gen xiv," in *Fourth World Congress of Jewish Studies: Papers,* vol. 1 (Jerusalem: World Union of Jewish Studies, 1967), 167-70. *PE* 1.10.15 differentiates beween El and Elioun *(ʿelyôn),* but this may represent a Hellenistic attempt to imitate classical accounts (for text and translation, see Attridge and Oden, *Philo of Byblos,* 46-47). For further discussion, see Pope, *El in the Ugaritic Texts,* 55-57.

107. See above, section 2.

108. Cross, *Canaanite Myth and Hebrew Epic,* 186.

dwelling in the Elkunirsa myth. Psalm 27:4 calls Yahweh's home a "house" *(bêt),* language more characteristic of Baal's abode (KTU 1.4 VII 42) than El's dwelling (cf. KTU 1.114). As J. C. Greenfield has noted,[109] other terms in Psalm 27 evoking language of Baal's home include *nōʿam* in verse 4 and *yiṣpĕnēnî (*ṣpn)* in verse 5.

6. Convergence in Israelite Religion

Israel's major deities in the period of the Judges were not numerous. Genesis 49:25-26 possibly point to an early stage when Israel knew three deities, El, Asherah, and Yahweh. In addition, Baal constituted a fourth deity in Israel's early religious history. This situation changed by the period of the early monarchy. Yahweh and El were identified, and at some point, devotion to the goddess Asherah did not continue as an identifiably separate cult. After this point, polytheism in the Judges period other than devotion to Baal is difficult to document. In general, the oldest stages of Israel's religious literature exhibit some limited signs of Yahweh having assimilated the imagery of the primary deities. These conclusions cannot be stated without qualification, inasmuch as the data is incomplete and possibly not representative. Indeed, because of the incomplete picture of this period, perhaps it should be concluded that Israel was more polytheistic in the period of the Judges.

Other religious developments within the cult of Yahweh may have played a role in accenting Yahwistic monolatry during various periods. According to P. D. Miller,[110] these features include Israel's imageless or aniconic tradition, the influence of the Ten Commandments in Israel's religious tradition, and polemics against *ʾĕlōhîm ʾăḥērîm,* "other gods" (Exod. 20:3; Deut. 5:7), and *ʾĕlōhîm ḥădāšîm,* "new gods" (Judg. 5:8; cf. Ps. 44:21), as well as de-

109. Greenfield, "The Hebrew Bible and Canaanite Literature," 551-54.

110. P. D. Miller, "Israelite Religion," in *The Hebrew Bible and Its Modern Interpreters,* ed. D. A. Knight and G. M. Tucker (Philadelphia: Fortress; Decatur, GA: Scholars, 1985), 212. On Israel's aniconic requirement, see W. W. Hallo, "Texts, Statues and the Cult of the Divine King," in *Congress Volume: Jerusalem 1986,* ed. J. Emerton, VTSup 40 (Leiden: Brill, 1988), 54-66; Halpern, "'Brisker Pipes Than Poetry,'" 82, 83, 100, 101, 109-10 nn. 25-26; R. S. Hendel, "The Social Origins of the Aniconic Tradition in Early Israel," *CBQ* 50 (1988): 365-82; T. Mettinger, "The Veto on Images and the Aniconic God in Ancient Israel," in *Religious Symbols and Their Functions,* ed. H. Biezais (Stockholm: Almqvist & Wiksell International, 1979), 15-29. Concerning "other gods," especially within the context of the Ten Commandments, see Childs, *The Book of Exodus,* 403-4. See discussion on pp. xvi-xvii; chapter 3, section 3; chapter 6, section 1.

nials of other gods (Deut. 32:39; 1 Sam. 2:2). Although numerous polemics against images (e.g., Isa. 2:8; 10:10; 30:22; 31:7; 40:19; 42:19; Jer. 1:16; 8:19; Micah 1:7; Nahum 1:14) would bring into question the claim that the aniconic requirement exercised influence on other apects of Israelite religion, presumably these features helped to mold ideas of monolatry early in Israel's history.[111] Moreover, the prophetic criticisms against images belong largely to the eighth century, leaving open the question of the later influence of the aniconic requirement. As chapter 6 illustrates, centralization of cult and the rise of writing as an authoritative medium also contributed to the development of Israelite monolatry in the period of the monarchy. These features of Israelite religion generally distinguish it from Israel's neighbors, as far as the evidence indicates.

The convergence of titles and imagery of deities to the personage of Yahweh appears to have been part of a wider religious development of conflation of religious motifs in Israelite tradition. Two examples of this general religious development illustrate it. The biblical and extrabiblical traditions of Shadday perhaps witness to a regional influence on the cult of Yahweh. The epithet appears twice in the stories in Numbers 22–24 pertaining to the prophet seer Balaam (Num. 24:4, 16).[112] A non-Israelite initially hired to curse the Israelites moving through Moab, Balaam in the end proclaims a blessing upon them. The Deir ʿAlla texts likewise suggest that **šd(y)* was a divine epithet at home in Transjordan. These texts describe an oracle of Balaam witnessing to divinities called *šdyn, shaddays.* The *šdyn* deities in these texts diverge from material known about El or Yahweh from either Ugaritic or generally from the Bible. It would appear from both the biblical attestation to the title El Shadday in Numbers 24 and the reference to the *šdyn* in the Deir ʿAlla texts that this divine epithet was traditional to the region of Transjordan. The epithet was a title for El during the period of the

111. See the important study of T. N. D. Mettinger, *No Graven Image? Israelite Aniconism in Its Ancient Near Eastern Context,* ConBOT 42 (Stockholm: Almqvist & Wiksell, 1995). See the responses in *The Image and the Book: Iconic Cults, Aniconism, and the Rise of Book Religion in Israel and the Ancient Near East,* ed. K. van der Toorn, Contributions to Biblical Exegesis and Theology 21 (Leuven: Peeters, 1997); and T. J. Lewis, "Divine Images: Aniconism in Ancient Israel," *JAOS* 118 (1998): 36-53. Based on the lack of divine images in what are plausibly identified as Israelite sites, R. S. Hendel would argue for aniconism as a feature that distinguishes early Israel from Canaanite culture; see Hendel, "The Social Origins of the Aniconic Tradition in Early Israel," 367-68, and his review of *The Early History of God,* in *CBQ* 54 (1992): 132-33. Other scholars locate aniconism considerably later. See B. B. Schmidt, "The Aniconic Tradition: On Reading Images and Viewing Texts," pp. 75-105, and Edelman, "Tracking Observance of the Aniconic Tradition Through Numismatics."

112. See n. 50 above.

monarchy, appearing, for example, in Genesis 49:25. The priestly tradition reflects the further assimilation of this title into the repertoire of epithets for Yahweh (Gen. 17:1; 28:3; 35:11; 43:14; cf. Ezek. 10:5), and attaches the name to Bethel (Gen. 48:3).

In Israelite religious tradition, the waters of El's abode apparently underwent two major alterations. First of all, they appear in two different ways in biblical tradition.[113] As in the examples of Genesis 49:25d and Deuteronomy 33:13b noted above, these waters are life-giving. In Isaiah 33:20-22; Ezekiel 47:1-12; Joel 4:18; Zechariah 14:8 (cf. Gen. 2:10; 2 Esdras 5:25-26; 1 Enoch 26), they issue from beneath the Temple. As noted above in the case of Psalm 18 (2 Sam. 22):16, the waters also appear in biblical tradition as underworld waters (see also Job 28:11;[114] 38:16-17; 2 Esdras 4:7-8). Second, the underworld setting of the waters was perhaps originally alien to the mythologem.[115] The examples of El Shadday and the waters of El's home illustrate that despite the explicit identification between Yahweh and El made in some biblical passages, the relationship between the traditions of El and Yahweh was highly complex. Indeed, Canaanite religious traditions exhibit substantial modifications in their Israelite forms. By and large, it is difficult, if not impossible, to identify the specific socio-political forces behind the process of convergence. One of the major instances cited above is Psalm 18 (= 2 Samuel 22), which is clearly a royal thanksgiving. From this example, it is evident that the monarchy either generated or inherited (and then used) the convergence of divine imagery in order to elevate the national god. Indeed, the vast bulk of biblical texts date to the monarchic period or later, and the ascendant position of Yahweh as the national god under the monarchy would make convergence of divine imagery a powerful ideology political tool. Yet, given the lack of information, the premonarchic period cannot be ruled out entirely as the older context for convergence, at least to some degree.

113. See above, section 2.

114. Besides the underworld streams in Job 28, Greenfield ("The Hebrew Bible and Canaanite Literature," 556) notes two other Ugaritic motifs clustered in Job 28, the references in vv. 14 and 22 to Yamm and Mot, both called the "beloved of El" in Ugaritic literature, and the larger issue of the location of wisdom, a feature of El in Ugaritic mythology. On El's abode, see above.

115. A. J. Wensinck, *The Ocean in the Literatures of the Western Semites* (Amsterdam: Johannes Muller, 1918), 4-49; T. H. Gaster, "Dead, Abode of the," *IDB* 1:787.

7. Israel and Its Neighbors

The immediate neighbors of Israel that emerged by the early first millennium exhibit ten or fewer deities, according to the meager data.[116] At first glance, Ammon does not appear to reflect a relatively small group of deities. Based on the theophoric elements in proper names, K. Jackson lists ten Ammonite deities: *'b, 'dn, 'l, 'nrt, bl, hm, mlk, nny, 'm* and *šmš*.[117] Some of these elements, such as *'b* and *'dn*, are presumably titles, however. Biblical sources presuppose that *mlk* or Milkom was the national Ammonite god (1 Kings 11:5, 33; Jer. 49:1, 3; cf. 2 Sam. 12:30; 1 Chron. 20:2; Zeph. 1:5). Ammonite proper names show a preponderance of the theophoric element **'l*,[118] which might suggest a close relationship between El and Milkom in Ammonite religion. Perhaps the two were identified, like El and Yahweh in Israelite religion.[119] The patron god of the Moabite dynasty was Chemosh (KAI 181:3, 5, 9, 12, 13, 14, 18, 19, 32, 33; 1 Kings 11:7; Jer. 48:13).[120] The

116. J. Wellhausen, *Prolegomena to the History of Ancient Israel* (Edinburgh: A. & C. Black, 1885; reprinted, New York: Meridian Books, 1957; reprinted, Gloucester, MA: Peter Smith, 1973), 440; Cross, cited in Halpern, *The Emergence*, 102; Halpern, "'Brisker Pipes Than Poetry,'" 79, 84.

117. Jackson, "Ammonite Personal Names in the Context of the West Semitic Onomasticon," in *The Word of the Lord Shall Go Forth: Essays in Honor of David Noel Freedman in Celebration of His Sixtieth Birthday*, ed. C. L. Meyers and M. O'Connor, American Schools of Oriental Research Special Volume Series No. 1 (Winona Lake, IN: Eisenbrauns, 1983), 518. See further L. M. Muntingh, "What Did the Ammonites' Deities Mean to Them? The Concept of Deity as Revealed in Ammonite Personal Names," in *"Feet on Level Ground": A South African Tribute of Old Testament Essays in Honor of Gerhard Hasel*, ed. K. van Wyk (Berrien Center, MI: Hester, 1996), 193-300. W. E. Aufrecht interprets the name *'nmwt* as the root **'ny* plus the divine name Mot, "Death" ("The Ammonite Language of the Iron Age," *BASOR* 266 [1987]: 92). Concerning the limitations on using names to reconstruct religion, see introduction.

118. Jackson, *The Ammonite Language of the Iron Age*, HSM 27 (Chico, CA: Scholars, 1973), 95-98; idem, "Ammonite Personal Names," 518. On *mlkm* in inscriptions, see also N. Avigad, "Some Decorated West Semitic Seals," *IEJ* 35 (1985): 5. See further E. Puech, "Milcom," *DDD*, 575-76.

119. See Tigay, *You Shall Have No Other Gods*, 19 n. 60.

120. On Chemosh, see H. P. Müller, "Chemosh," *DDD*, 186-89. See also W. Aufrecht and W. D. Shury, "Three Iron Age Seals: Moabite, Aramaic and Hebrew," *IEJ* 47 (1997): 58. See also U. Worschech, "Der Gott Kemosch. Versuch einer Characterisierung," *UF* 24 (1992): 393-401. On the historical circumstances of Chemosh in Moabite history, see N. Na'aman, "King Mesha and the Foundation of the Moabite Monarchy," *IEJ* 47 (1997): 83-92. For the broader context of culture in Moab, see S. Timm, *Moab zwischen den Mächten: Studien zu historischen Denkmälern und Texten*, Ägypten und Altes Testament 17 (Wiesbaden: Harrassowitz, 1989). Cf. K. van Wyk, *Squatters in Moab: A Study in Iconography, History, Epigraphy, Orthography, Ethnography, Religion and Linguistics of the ANE* (Berrien Center, MI: Louis Hester, 1996); see

name Ashtar-Chemosh appears once (KAI 181:17). Otherwise, the deities of Moab are little known.[121]

The case for Edom perhaps parallels the religious situation of early Israel more closely. The national god of Edom was Qaws, attested in inscriptional material from Qitmit and the writings of Josephus (*Antiquities* 15.253).[122] This divine name appears as the theophoric element in several Edomite, Nabatean, and Arabic names, including those of Edomite kings.[123] El (Gen. 36:39), Baal (Gen. 36:38), and Hadad (1 Kings 11:14-21; Gen. 36:35-36) also appear as theophoric elements in Edomite proper names. Some of these names were possibly old Canaanite deities that continued into first millennium Edomite religion, although like the name of Anat in Israelite names, these theophoric elements may not point to cultic devotion to these deities. A head of a goddess, presumed to be Edomite, was excavated at Qitmit.[124] As an aside, it should be noted that biblical information about the Edomites in these passages may suggest a high level of cultural interaction in early Israel. This interaction would further explain the origins and incorporation of the cult of Yahweh into the highlands of Israel in the Iron I period from Edom/Midian/Teiman/Paran, a tradition that perdured despite later hostilities between Israelites and Edomites.[125]

The Phoenician city-states of Byblos, Sidon, and Tyre manifest fewer than ten deities. Byblos' deities were Baal Shamem (KAI 4:3), *bʿl ʾdr* (KAI 9 B 5), *bʿl* (KAI 12:4), and *bʿlt gbl,* "the lady of Byblos" (KAI 5:1; 6:2; 7:3).[126] The

the critical review of W. Aufrecht, *CBQ* 60 (1998): 132-34. For Moabite figurines, see U. Worschech, "Pferd, Göttin und Stier: Funde zur moabitischen Religion aus el-Bālūʿ (Jordanien)," *UF* 24 (1992): 385-91.

121. See the El and Baal PNs listed for Moabite seals in M. Heltzer, "The Recently Published West Semitic Inscribed Stamp Seals," *UF* 31 (1999): 216-17.

122. See E. A. Knauf, "Qôs," *DDD*, 674-77. For a useful survey of what is known about Moab, see *BA* 60/4 (1997).

123. See I. Beit-Arieh and B. Cresson, "An Edomite Ostracon from Horvat ʿUza," *TA* 12 (1985): 96-100; C. M. Bennett, "Fouilles d'Umm el-Biyara," *RB* 73 (1966): 400; B. Oded, "Egyptian References to the Edomite Deity Qaus," *Andrew University Seminary Studies* 9 (1971): 47-50; T. C. Vriezen, "The Edomitic Deity Qaus," *Oudtestamentische Studien* 14 (1965): 330-53. For Josephus, *Antiquities* 15.253, see R. Marcus, *Josephus, vol. 8, Jewish Antiquities, Books 15-17,* Loeb Classical Library (London: W. Heinemann; Cambridge, MA: Harvard Univ. Press, 1963), 118-19.

124. P. Beck, "A Head of a Goddess from Qitmit," *Qadmoniot* 19 (1986): 79-81.

125. See van der Toorn, *Family Religion,* 281-86; and Smith, *The Origins of Biblical Monotheism,* 145-46. See above, pp. 25, 32-33.

126. On Baal Shamem, see chapter 2, section 1. The goddess, *hrbt bʿlt gbl,* "the Dame, the Lady of Byblos" (KAI 10:2, 3, 7, 15), is known in the second millennium as ^{d}*NIN ša URU gu-ub-la* (EA 68:4), ^{d}*NIN ša URU gub-la* (EA 73:3-4, 74:2-30), etc. (see Hess, "Divine Names,"

dynastic god of Byblos was Baal Shamem, and the other deities perhaps were older Canaanite divinities.[127] Sidonian deities included Eshmun (KAI 14–16) and Astarte (KAI 13:1; 1 Kings 11:5).[128] Sidonian inscriptions also mention

151). For the divine title *b'lt* in the proto-Sinaitic inscription 347, see Albright, *The Proto-Sinaitic Inscriptions and Their Decipherment* (Cambridge: Harvard Univ. Press, 1966), 17; Cross, "The Early Alphabetic Inscriptions from Sinai and Their Development," *BASOR* 110 (1948): 6-22; idem, "Origin and Early Evolution," 8*-24*. She has been identified with either Astarte or Asherah. The identification of "the Lady of Byblos" with Astarte is founded on inferences drawn from classical sources. According to Plutarch (*De Iside et Osiride,* para. 15, 3), the queen of Byblos is called Astarte according to some (J. G. Griffiths, *Plutarch's De Iside et Osiride* [n.p.: University of Wales; printed at Cambridge: Cambridge Univ. Press, 1970], 140-41). An identification of Astarte as the goddess of Byblos might be inferred also from the description of Aphrodite at Byblos in *De Dea Syria,* para. 6 (Attridge and Oden, *De Dea Syria,* 13). Aphrodite is equated with Astarte in other sources, such as *PE* 1.10.32 (Attridge and Oden, *Philo of Byblos,* 54-55). Cross ("Origin and Early Evolution of the Alphabet," 8*; *Canaanite Myth and Hebrew Epic,* 28-29 n. 90) and R. A. Oden ("Ba'al Šamem and 'Ēl," *CBQ* 39 [1977]: 460) argue for an identification of the *b'lt gbl* with Asherah, largely based on common functions, but it is possible that Astarte exercised these functions in first-millennium Phoenicia. J. W. Betlyon (*The Coinage and Mints of Phoenicia: The Pre-Alexandrine Period,* HSM 26 [Chico, CA: Scholars, 1980], 115, 139-40) argues for a syncretism of features of the three great goddesses in the "lady of Byblos." For Astarte at Ashkelon, see 1 Sam. 31:10. Herodotus, *History* 1.105 (A. D. Godley, *Herodotus,* vol. 1, books 1 and 2, Loeb Classical Library [Cambridge: Harvard Univ. Press; William Heinemann, 1920], 136-37) refers to the "temple of Aphrodite Ourania" in Ashkelon, a reference to Astarte. Olyan ("Some Observations Concerning the Identity of the Queen of Heaven," *UF* 19 [1987]: 168-69) has noted an inscription from Delos where Aphrodite Ourania is identified with Astarte of Palestine: "To the heavenly Zeus and to Astarte of Palestine/Aphrodite of the Heavens, gods with hearing," *Dii Ourioi kai Astartei Palaistinei Aproditei Ouraniai theois epekoois* (P. Rouseel and M. Launey, *Inscriptions de Delos,* 2 vols. [Paris: Honore Champion, 1937], no. 2305). Inscription no. 1719 reads similarly with some restoration. There is no evidence for the names of Asherah and Anat on the Phoenician mainland. For further discussion, see E. Lipiński, *Dieux et déesses de l'univers phénicien et puniques,* Orientalia Lovaniensa Analecta 64 (Leuven: Uitgeverij Peeters/& Departement Oosterse Studies, 1995), 70-76; C. Bonnet, *Astarté: Dossier documentaire et perspectives historiques,* Contributi all Storia della Religione Fenicio-Punica II, Collezione di Studi Fenici 37 (Rome: Consiglio Nazionale delle Ricerche, 1996), 19-30.

127. Concerning *b'l 'dr,* see Olyan, *Asherah and the Cult of Yahweh,* 64-68. See also F. M. Cross, "A Recently Published Phoenician Inscription of the Persian Period from Byblos," *IEJ* 29 (1979): 41, 43; and Lipiński, *Dieux et déesses,* 88-89, 261-62, 418.

128. For Astarte at Sidon, see also *De Dea Syria,* para. 4 (see Attridge and Oden, *De Dea Syria,* 13); cf. 1 Kings 11:5, 33; 2 Kings 23:13. For discussion and further primary sources, see Lipiński, *Dieux et déesses,* 128-54; Bonnet, *Astarté,* 30-36. Claims for Asherah as a Sidonian goddess during the Persian period are circumstantial. J. W. Betlyon ("The Cult of 'Ašerah/'Ēlat at Sidon," *JNES* 44 [1985]: 53-56) argues that the title of *'lt ṣr,* "goddess of Tyre," appearing on Sidonian coins points to a cult of Asherah since *'lt* is best attested as an epithet of Asherah in the Ugaritic texts, though not exclusively (see above, n. 32). An epithet as general as *'lt* perhaps ap-

Resheph (KAI 15) and the Rephaim (13:7; 14:8). The treaty of Esarhaddon with Baal II of Tyre lists in order the deities of Tyre as Bethel, Anat-Bethel, Baal Shamem, Baal-Malaga, Baal-Saphon, Melqart, Eshmun, and Astarte.[129] The initial position of Bethel would point to his status as the primary god of the Tyrian pantheon. That Bethel is a secondary hypostasis of El has been argued by M. Barré.[130] The depiction of Tyrian El in Ezekiel 28 would comport with this conclusion. Baal Shamem is also mentioned in a Tyrian inscription (KAI 18). Astarte is attested in KAI 17:1 from nearby Umm el-ʿAmed. Inscriptions from nearby Sarepta include the deities *šdrpʾ* and *tntʿštrt*, perhaps a combination of the names of two goddesses, Tannit and Astarte.[131] The collectivity of

plied to the main goddess of a locality. Astarte is clearly the most important goddess of Persian-period Sidon. Similarly, *rbt*, an epithet applied in the Ugaritic texts for Asherah, is attributed to Astarte in the Persian-period Phoenician inscriptions from Sidon and elsewhere (see chapter 3, section 4). There is no attestation to Asherah either separately or as the theophoric element in proper names from Sidon. In contrast, Astarte is attested in proper names (see Betlyon, *The Coinage and Mints*, 3-20). On Eshmun, see S. Ribichini, "Eshmun," *DDD*, 306-9; and P. Xella, "Les plus anciens témoignages sur le dieu Eshmoun: Un mise au point," in *The World of the Aramaeans II: Studies in History and Archaeology in Honour of Paul-Eugène Dion*, ed. P. M. Michèle Daviau, J. W. Wevers, and M. Weigl, JSOTSup 325 (Sheffield: Sheffield Academic Press, 2001), 230-42; and "Eshmun von Sidon: Der phönizische Aklepios," in *Mesopotamica-Ugaritica-Biblica: Festschrift für Kurt Bergerhof zur Vollendung seines 70. Lebensjahres am 7. Mai 1992*, ed. M. Dietrich and O. Loretz, AOAT (Kevalaer: Butzon & Bercker; Neukirchen-Vluyn: Neukirchener Verlag, 1993), 481-98.

129. For Astarte at Tyre, see the treaty of Esarhaddon with Baal II of Tyre (*ANET*, 534), the late classical witnesses of *PE* 1.10.32 (Attridge and Oden, *Philo of Byblos*, 54-55) and Josephus, *Antiquities* 8.146 (H. St.J. Thackeray and R. Marcus, *Josephus*, vol. 5, *Jewish Antiquities, Books 5-8*, Loeb Classical Library [Cambridge, MA: Harvard Univ. Press; London: William Heinemann, 1934], 650-51) and *Contra Apionem* 1.118, 123 (Thackeray, *Josephus: The Life, Against Apion*, Loeb Classical Library [Cambridge, MA: Harvard Univ. Press; London: William Heinemann, 1926], 210-13). According to Josephus (*Contra Apionem* 1.123; Thackeray, *Josephus: The Life*, 224-25), King Ethbaal was a priest of Astarte. Astarte appears as the theophoric element in proper names from Tyre (J. B. Pritchard, *Palestinian Figurines in Relation to Certain Goddesses Known Through Literature* [New Haven: American Oriental Society, 1943], 71). Her name appears also as an element in Tyrian royal names recorded in Josephus (*Contra Apionem* 1.157; H. St.J. Thackeray, *Josephus: The Life*, 224-25). For Hellenistic and Roman evidence for Astarte at Tyre, see H. Seyrig, "Antiquités syriennes," *Syria* 40 (1963): 19-28. For an overview, see Bonnet, *Astarté*, 37-44.

130. M. L. Barré, *The God-List in the Treaty between Hannibal and Philip V of Macedonia* (Baltimore: Johns Hopkins Univ. Press, 1983), 48-49. However, see the critique by K. van der Toorn, "Anat-Yahu, Some Other Deities, and the Jews of Elephantine," *Numen* 39 (1992): 80-101.

131. For discussion of these deities, see B. Peckham, "Phoenicia and the Religion of Israel: The Epigraphic Evidence," in *Ancient Israelite Religion: Essays in Honor of Frank Moore Cross*, ed. P. D. Miller, Jr., P. D. Hanson, and S. D. McBride, 80-81. See also the references in nn. 128 and 129 above.

deities, the divine council, is attested in Phoenician inscriptions from Byblos (KAI 4:4-5, 7), Sidon (KAI 14:9, 22), and Karatepe (KAI 26 A III 19).

On the basis of the little available evidence, it would appear that the first-millennium neighbors of Israel did not maintain cultic devotion on the same scale as the second-millennium religion in the Levant. While more than two hundred deities are attested at Ugarit, the texts for the first-millennium states in the region attest to ten or fewer deities. It might be presumed that in Israel and among its neighbors there were other deities to which the extant texts do not witness. Indeed, it might be argued that if the same number and variety of texts were available for early Israel or its neighbors as from Ugarit, the number of deities in them would approximate the number of deities in the Ugaritic texts. This argument by extrapolation to the Ugaritic texts may represent no better or no worse an argument from silence than one that would conclude a relative paucity of deities from the little evidence of Israelite and other first-millennium Northwest Semitic texts. In the final analysis, deriving historical claims on the basis of the actually attested texts (especially for the early period) is highly problematic. While it can be claimed only that the deities attested for Israel are relatively few in number, it remains possible that first-millennium Levantine religion differed in this respect from its second-millennium antecedents, and Israel was part of this development.

In conclusion, according to the available evidence, Israelite religion in its earliest form did not contrast markedly with the religions of its Levantine neighbors in either number or configuration of deities. Rather, the number of deities in Israel was relatively typical for the region. Furthermore, as they did in the religions of surrounding states, some old Canaanite deities continued within an Israelite pantheon dominated by a national god. Like some of the Phoenician city-states and perhaps Edom, earliest Israel knew El, Baal, a new dynastic or national god, the divine council, a partial divinization of deceased ancestors (Rephaim), and perhaps the cult of a goddess. Similarly, during the period of the Judges, Yahweh held hegemony over a complex religion that preserved some old Canaanite components through an identification with El, a continuation of the concepts of the divine council and partially divinized ancestors, a coexistence with Baal, and perhaps an early toleration for Asherah and subsequent assimilation of her cult and symbol, the asherah. This state of affairs was not to hold for the period of the monarchy.

CHAPTER 2

Yahweh and Baal

1. Baal Worship in Israel

According to the biblical record, the worship of Baal threatened Israel from the period of the Judges down to the monarchy.[1] It is assumed in 1 Kings 11:4 that this was the case for Solomon's reign. Names with *baʿal* as the theophoric element, such as Jerubbaal, Eshbaal, and Meribbaal, have been taken to indicate that Israelite society, including some royal circles, viewed the worship of Baal as a legitimate practice. Indeed, some scholars interpret these names as evidence both that *baʿal* was a title for Yahweh and that the cult of Baal coexisted with the cult of Yahweh.[2] Inscriptions from Samaria, the capital city of the northern kingdom, provide an important witness for the ninth or eighth century. These inscriptions, called the Samaria ostraca, contain at least five names with the theophoric element of *baʿal* as opposed to nine names with the Yahweh component.[3] By way of contrast, no personal names with

1. For secondary literature up to 1975, see Cooper, "Divine Names and Epithets in the Ugaritic Texts," 350-52; see also M. H. Pope, "Baal Worship," *EncJud* 4:7-12; R. Rendtorff, "El, Baʿal und Jahwe: Erwägungen zum Verhältnis von kanaanäischer und israelitischer Religion," *ZAW* 78 (1966): 277-92; E. Gaál, "Tuthmösis III as Storm-God?" *Studia Aegyptica* 3 (1977): 29-37; D. Kinet, *Baʿal und Jahwe: Ein Beitrag zur Theologie des Hoseabuches*, Europaische Hochschulschriften 23/87 (Frankfurt/Bern: Lang, 1977); A. Saviv, "Baal and Baalism in Scripture," *Beth Mikra* 29 (1983/84): 128-32 (Heb.). On Baal in sources prior to Ugaritic material, see K. Koch, "Zur Entstehung der Baʿal-Verehrung," *UF* 11 (1979 = C. F. A. Schaeffer Festschrift): 465-79; G. Pettinato, "Pre-Ugaritic Documentation of Baʿal," in *The Bible World: Essays in Honor of Cyrus H. Gordon*, ed. G. Rendsburg, A. Adler, M. Arfa, and N. H. Winter (New York: KTAV, 1980), 203-9; W. Herrmann, "Baal," *DDD*, 132-39; cf. E. Sollberger, *Administrative Texts Chiefly Concerning Textiles: L. 2752*, Archiv Reali di Ebla Testi 8 (Rome: Missione Archeologica Italiana in Siria, 1986), 9-10.

2. See chapter 1, section 3.

3. On the Baal names in the Samaria ostraca, see Pope, "Baal Worship," 11; R. Lawton, "Israelite Personal Names on Pre-Exilic Hebrew Inscriptions," *Biblica* 65 (1984): 332, 335, 341;

ba'al as the theophoric element are extant from Judah. These data have prompted some scholarly speculation about the widespread acceptance of Baal from the period of the Judges down through the fall of the northern kingdom in 722, especially in the north.[4]

According to 1 Kings 17–19, the ninth century marked a critical time for the cult of Baal in Israel. The biblical and extrabiblical sources provide a wide array of information pertaining to the cult of Baal in Israel and Phoenicia during this period. The biblical record dramatically presents the spread of the cult of Phoenician Baal in Samaria. Jezebel, daughter of Ittobaal, king of Tyre, and wife of Ahab, king of the northern kingdom, strongly sponsored the worship of Baal (1 Kings 16:31). First, Ahab built a temple to Baal, which is said to have been in Samaria (1 Kings 16:32). From 2 Kings 13:6, it is clear that Baal had his own temple in the environs of Samaria, apart from the cult of the national god, Yahweh (cf. 1 Kings 16:32; 2 Kings 10:21-27).[5] Ahab also erected an asherah, whose location and relationship to Baal are not specified. Elijah, the enemy of Ahab, and the measures that Ahab and Jezebel took to support the worship of Baal in the capital are presented in 1 Kings 17–19. Jezebel persecuted the prophets of Yahweh (1 Kings 18:3), but provided in-

I. T. Kaufman, "The Samaria Ostraca: A Study in Ancient Hebrew Paleography" (Ph.D. diss., Harvard University, 1966); idem, "The Samaria Ostraca: An Early Witness to Hebrew Writing," *BA* 45 (1982): 229-39; Tigay, *You Shall Have No Other Gods,* 65-66. The names are *'bb'l,* "Baal/lord is father" (2:4); *b'l',* "Baal/lord" (1:7); *b'lzmr,* "Baal/lord is strong" (or "Baal/lord sings," 12:2-3); *b'l'zkr,* "Baal/lord remembers" (37:3); and *mrb'l,* "Baal/lord is strong(?)" (2:7); cf. *[t]ṣb'l*(?) in Mesad Hashavyahu (see Tigay, *You Shall Have No Other Gods,* 66). On the background of the ostraca, see also A. F. Rainey, "The *Sitz im Leben* of the Samaria Ostraca," *TA* 6 (1979): 91-94; cf. W. H. Shea, "Israelite Chronology and the Samaria Ostraca," *ZDPV* 101 (1985): 9-20. See also the Phoenician name *b'lplṭ* from Tel Dan (J. Naveh, "Inscriptions of the Biblical Period," in *Recent Archaeology in the Land of Israel,* ed. H. Shanks and B. Mazar [Jerusalem: Biblical Archaeology Society and Israel Exploration Society, 1985], 64); the Hebrew name *blntn* (**bêl-nātan* from **ba'al-nātan*) in an eighth-century Aramaic inscription from Calah (so Albright, "An Ostracon," 34 n. 15, 35). Albright interprets the theophoric element in this name as a title of Yahweh, but the name seems to be non-Yahwistic.

4. Pope, "Baal Worship," 11-12. See also A. Rainey, "The Toponyms of Eretz Israel," *BASOR* 231 (1978): 1-17; B. Rosen, "Early Israelite Cultic Centres in the Hill Country," *VT* 38 (1988): 114-17.

5. Olyan, *Asherah and the Cult of Yahweh,* 6. For further discussion, see Y. Yadin, "The 'House of Baal' of Ahab and Jezebel in Samaria, and that of Athalia in Judah," in *Archaeology in the Levant: Essays for Kathleen Kenyon,* ed. R. Moorey and P. Parr (Warminster, England: Aris & Phillips, 1978), 127-35; cf. B. Halpern, "'The Excremental Vision': The Doomed Priests of Doom in Isaiah 28," *Hebrew Annual Review* 10 (1986): 117 n. 14. See also H. D. Hoffmann, *Reform und Reformen: Untersuchungen zu einem Grundthema der deuteronomistischen Geschichtsschreibung,* AThANT 66 (Zurich: Theologischer Verlag, 1980), 42-43.

come to the prophets of Baal and Asherah (1 Kings 18:19).[6] Later, in a speech to Yahweh, Elijah says that he is the only prophet of Yahweh to have escaped Ahab and Jezebel (1 Kings 19:10).

To judge from the biblical sources, the baal of Jezebel was a god with power over the rain, like Ugaritic Baal. In 1 Kings 17–19 is stressed Yahweh's power over nature, which corresponds to various phenomena associated with Baal in the Ugaritic texts.[7] These powers include dominion over the storm (1 Kings 17:1-17; 18:41-46).[8] The prophets of "the *baal*" compete with Elijah on Mount Carmel to see whose god truly has power over nature (1 Kings 18). One of the functions of 1 Kings 17–19 is to prove that Yahweh has power over all of these phenomena, but unlike the baal of Jezebel, Yahweh transcends these manifestations of divine power (1 Kings 19, esp. v. 11).[9] Jezebel's own name, *'îzebel,* "where is the Prince?" (e.g., 1 Kings 16:31; 18:4f.; 19:1; 21:5f.; 2 Kings 9:7), recalls the specific wording of human concern expressed over Baal's death, attested in the Ugaritic Baal cycle (KTU 1.6 IV 4-5).[10]

6. Numerous scholars treat the reference to the prophets of Asherah in 1 Kings 18:19 as a secondary gloss. See chapter 3, section 1, for discussion.

7. For older discussions, see A. Alt, "Das Gottesurteil auf dem Karmel," *Kleine Schriften zur Geschichte des Volkes Israel: Zweiter Band* (Munich: C. H. Beck'sche Verlagsbuchhandlung, 1953), 135-49; K. Galling, "Der Gott Karmel und die Achtung der fremden Gotter," *Geschichte und Altes Testament,* ed. W. F. Albright (Tübingen: J. C. B. Mohr [Paul Siebeck], 1953), 105-26; H. H. Rowley, "Elijah on Mount Carmel," *Bulletin of the John Rylands Library* 43 (1960-61): 190-219; D. R. Ap-Thomas, "Elijah on Mount Carmel," *PEQ* 92 (1960): 146-55; Kaufmann, *The Religion of Israel,* 273-75; O. Eissfeldt, "Jahve und Baal," *Kleine Schriften: Erster Band,* ed. R. Sellheim and F. Maass (Tübingen: J. C. B. Mohr [Paul Siebeck], 1962), 1-12; and Albright, *The Biblical Period,* 38, 42, 70-71. See also Cross, *Canaanite Myth and Hebrew Epic,* 190-94; F. C. Fensham, "A Few Observations on the Polarization Between Yahweh and Baal in I Kings 17–19," *ZAW* 92 (1980): 227-36; Peckham, "Phoenicia and the Religion of Israel," 80, 87; C. Bonnet, *Melqart: Cultes et Mythes de l'Héraclès & Tyrien en Méditerranée,* Studia Phoenicia 8 (Louvain: Uitgeverij Peeters/Presses Universitaires de Namur, 1988), 139-43; Olyan, *Asherah and the Cult of Yahweh,* 8, 38, 62; M. Beck, *Elia und die Monolatrie, Ein Beitrag zur religionsgeschichtlichen Ruckfrage nach dem vorschriftprophetischen Jahwe-Glauben,* BZAW 281 (Berlin/New York: de Gruyter, 1999). On 1 Kings 18, see also chapter 3, section 1.

8. Cf. Fensham, "A Few Observations," 233-34; cf. Bonnet, *Melqart,* 143.

9. Cross, *Canaanite Myth and Hebrew Epic,* 190-94.

10. Jezebel's name, *'îzebel,* consists of two elements, *'y,* "where?" and *zebel,* "prince" (with distortion from **zĕbul;* see *BDB,* 33). For **zbl* in names, see *zbl* (P. Mosca and J. Russel, "A Phoenician Inscription from Cebel Ireis Dagi in Rough Cilicia," *Epigraphica Anatolia* 9 [1987]: 1-27), *šmzbl,* "name is prince" (KAI 34:4), *b'l'zbl* (KAI 67:1-2), and *beelzeboul* (Mark 3:22; Matt. 12:27; Luke 11:18). For the element **'î* in names, cf. *'î-kābôd,* "where is Glory?" (1 Sam. 4:21), *'î'ezer,* "where is Help?" (Num. 26:30), *'îtāmār,* "where is Tamar?" (Exod. 6:23, etc.), and *'b'l,* "where is Baal?" (A. Berthier and R. Charlier, *Le Sanctuaire punique d'El-Hofra à Constantine: Texte* [Paris: Arts et Metiers Graphiques, 1955], 106, text 141, line 2).

That the biblical baal was a Phoenician god with power over the storm may be deduced from extrabiblical texts. The baal is identified either with Melqart[11] or Baal Shamem.[12] Nothing in the meager Phoenician sources bearing on this god directly contradicts an identification with Melqart. Perhaps he was the main city god of Tyre, since in KAI 47:1 he is called the "lord of Tyre" *(bʿl ṣr)*.[13] Furthermore, it might be argued that the baal of Jezebel should be Melqart, since his name means "king of the city," presumably referring to Tyre (although this point perhaps presupposes that his name and cult originated at Tyre, a conclusion beyond the scope of the currently available information). A primary feature of his cult seems to be his "awakening" from death.[14] Melqart is the Herakles whom Josephus calls the "dead hero" *(hērōi enagizousi)* who receives offerings. Josephus (*Antiquities* 8.146) also mentions that Hiram "brought about the resurrection of Herakles" *(tou hērakleous egersin epoiēsato)*. The title "raiser of Herakles" *(egerse[itēn tou] hērakleou[s])* occurs in a Roman period inscription from Philadelphia. This cult likely underlies the title *mqm ʾlm*, "the raiser of the god(s)," in a second-century Phoenician inscription from Rhodes (KAI 44:2). Arguments identifying the Baal of 1 Kings 17–19 with Melqart rely largely on viewing the taunt of 1 Kings

11. Albright, *Yahweh and the Gods of Canaan*, 243-44; R. de Vaux, *The Bible and the Ancient Near East*, trans. D. McHugh (Garden City, NY: Doubleday, 1971), 238-51; Bonnet, *Melqart*, 139-43. Oden ("Baʿal Šamem and ʾĒl," 457-73) identifies Baal Shamem with El, which does not comport with the attestation of Baal Shamem and *ʾl qn ʾrṣ* as separate gods in KAI 26 A III 18. For further criticisms, see Barré, *The God-List*, 56-57.

12. Eissfeldt, "Jahve und Baal," 1-12; Ringgren, *Israelite Religion*, 42, 261; B. Mazar, *The Early Biblical Period: Historical Essays*, ed. S. Ahituv and B. A. Levine (Jerusalem: Israel Exploration Society, 1986), 79-80; Barré, *The God-List*, 56; Olyan, *Asherah and the Cult of Yahweh*, 62-64; H. Niehr, "JHWH in der Rolle des Baalšamem," in *Ein Gott allein?* ed. W. Dietrich and M. A. Klopfenstein, 307-26; and W. Röllig, "Baal-Shamem," *DDD*, 149-51.

13. See also "Melqart in Tyre" *(mlqrt bṣr)*, which appears in a Phoenician inscription (P. Bordreuil, "Attestations inédité de Melqart, Baal Hamon et Baal Saphon à Tyr (Nouveaux documents religieux phéniciens II)," in *Religio Phoenicia: Acta Colloquii Namurcensis habiti diebus 14 et 15 mensis Decembris anni 1984*, ed. C. Bonnet, E. Lipiński, and P. Marchetti, Studia Phoenicia 4 [Namur: Société des études classiques, 1986], 77-82). My thanks go to Professor Olyan for bringing this article to my attention.

14. For the text of Josephus, *Antiquities* 8.146, see Thackeray and Marcus, *Josephus*, vol. 5, *Jewish Antiquities, Books 5–8*, 650. For details regarding *mqm ʾlm*, "the awakener of god(s)," in KAI 44:2, see de Vaux, *The Bible and the Ancient Near East*, 247-49; J. C. L. Gibson, *Textbook of Syrian Semitic Inscriptions*, vol. 3, *Phoenician Inscriptions* (Oxford: Clarendon, 1982), 144-47; Bonnet, *Melqart*, 143, 377. Concerning Baal Shamem and Melqart at Tyre in the Hellenistic and Roman periods, see also Seyrig, "Antiquités syriennes," 19-28. For Greek descriptions of Herakles, see de Vaux, *The Bible and the Ancient Near East*, 247, 250; and Gibson, *Textbook of Syrian Semitic Inscriptions*, vol. 3, 145-46. See further the works discussed in n. 15 below.

18:27 as an allusion to this rite of "awakening." Yet the ancient Near Eastern notion of the "sleeping god" in this verse is wider than the specific cult of Melqart. Sleep is attributed to deities in Mesopotamia, Egypt, and Canaan, including Yahweh (Pss. 44:24[E 23]; 78:65).[15] There is no evidence indicating that Melqart was a storm-god, although appeal might be made to his lineage presented in Philo of Byblos (*PE* 1.10.27): "Demarous had a son Melkarthos, who is also known as Herakles."[16] From this connection between Melqart and Demarous, a title of Baal Haddu in the Ugaritic texts,[17] it might be inferred that the nature of Melqart was meteorological.

The evidence for Baal Shamem is manifestly meteorological. Attested in Phoenician inscriptions at Byblos (KAI 4:3), Umm el-ʿAmed (KAI 18:1, 7), Karatepe (KAI 26 A III 18), Kition (RES 1519b), Carthage (KAI 78:2), and Sardinia (KAI 64:1), Baal Shamem had power over the storm, which is mentioned in a curse in the treaty between Esarhaddon and Baal II of Tyre. The treaty invokes three "b̆aals" — Baal Shamem, Baal-Malaga, and Baal-Saphon — to bring an "evil wind" upon Baal II if he violates the treaty: "May Baal Shamem, Baal Malaga and Baal Saphon raise an evil wind against your ships, to undo their moorings, tear out their mooring pole, may a strong wave sink them in the sea, a violent tide [. . .] against you."[18] This curse invokes all three gods to wield their power of the storm (cf. Jonah 1:4). According to Philo of Byblos (*PE* 1.10.7), *beelsamēn* was a storm-god, associated with the sun in the heavens and equated with Zeus,[19] although Baal Shamem's solar characteris-

15. For the motif of the "sleeping god" in ancient Near Eastern literature, see B. Batto, "The Sleeping God: An Ancient Near Eastern Motif of Divine Sovereignty," *Biblica* 68 (1987): 153-77; T. McAlpine, *Sleep Divine and Human in the Old Testament,* JSOTSup 38 (Sheffield: JSOT, 1987), 181-90; and A. Mrozek and S. Votto, "The Motif of the Sleeping Divinity," *Biblica* 80 (1999): 415-19. If the motifs in 1 Kings 18:27, including the sleeping god, were intended to refer specifically to Melqart, it is possible that a conflation of the figures Baal Shamem and Melqart lies behind the portrait of Jezebel's god in 1 Kings 18. For the so-called "dying and rising gods," see Smith, *The Origins of Biblical Monotheism,* 104-31; and T. N. D. Mettinger, *The Riddle of Resurrection: "Dying and Rising Gods" in the Ancient Near East,* ConBOT 50 (Stockholm: Almqvist & Wiksell International, 2001). Mettinger beautifully surveys the ancient evidence as well as the modern debate. Mettinger believes that this category has more merit than recent treatments (such as mine) have considered.

16. Attridge and Oden, *Philo of Byblos,* 52-53.

17. Pope, *El in the Ugaritic Texts,* 47 n. 95, 56.

18. *ANET,* 534. On the three baals in the treaty of Esarhaddon, see Barré, *The God-List,* 50-56. Baal Saphon appears with Baal Hamon in a Phoenician text dated to the sixth century and originating in the region of Tyre (Bordreuil, "Attestations inédités," 82-86).

19. See Attridge and Oden, *Philo of Byblos,* 40-41; Olyan, *Asherah and the Cult of Yahweh,* 62. Bull iconography surviving on Tyrian coins dating to the Persian period (Betlyon, *The Coinage and Mints,* 43-44) perhaps constitutes a further element supporting the identification of Baal Shamem as a storm-god.

tic apparently was a later product.[20] That Baal Shamem and not Melqart was the patron god of Ahab and Jezebel may be inferred from the proper names attested for the Tyrian royal family. The onomasticon of the Tyrian royal house bears no names with Melqart. There is only one exception to **bʿl* as the theophoric element in royal proper names from Tyre.[21]

That Baal Shamem and not Melqart was a threat in Israel in the pre-exilic period might be inferred from the fact that the god in question is called "the baal" (1 Kings 18:19, 22, 25, 26, 40). The invocation of Baal Shamem in the Aramaic version of Psalm 20 written in Demotic may also provide evidence of this god in Israelite religion.[22] This version of Psalm 20 belongs to a papyrus dating to the second century known as Papyrus Amherst Egyptian no. 63 (column XI, lines 11-19). The text, which may have come from Edfu, shows some Egyptian influence, specifically the mention of the god Horus. The text may secondarily reflect genuine Israelite features. M. Weinfeld argues that the psalm was originally Canaanite or northern Israelite.[23] For Weinfeld, the references to Baal Shamem, El-Bethel, and Mount Saphon reflect an original Canaanite or northern Israelite setting, perhaps Bethel. The biblical version of Psalm 20 would reflect a southern version, which secondarily imported the psalm into the cult of Yahweh. In this case, the Aramaic

20. M. Avi-Yonah, "Mount Carmel and the God of Baalbek," *IEJ* 2 (1952): 121; Oden, "Baʿal Šamem and ʾĒl," 464; Attridge and Oden, *Philo of Byblos*, 81 n. 49. For further examples, see Zeus Heliopolis (see n. 27) and Adonis in Macrobius, *Saturnalia* 1.21.1 (P. V. Davies, *Macrobius: The Saturnalia* [New York: Columbia Univ. Press, 1969], 141). See also Macrobius, *Saturnalia* 1.17 (Davies, *Macrobius*, 114-27).

21. Citing Menander of Ephesus, Josephus (*Contra Apionem* 2.112-14, 157 [Thackeray, *Josephus: The Life*, 210-19, 224-51; cf. *Antiquities* 8.144-49 [Thackeray and Marcus, *Josephus*, vol. 5, *Antiquities, Books 5–8*, 648-53]).

22. C. F. Nims and R. C. Steiner, "A Paganized Version of Psalm 20:2-6 from the Aramaic Text in Demotic Script," *JAOS* 103 (1983 = S. N. Kramer Festschrift): 261-74. For a different view of the relationship between the Demotic version and MT, see Z. Zevit, "The Common Origin of the Demotic Prayer to Horus and Psalm 20," *JAOS* (1990): 213-28.

23. M. Weinfeld, "The Pagan Version of Psalm 20:2-6 — Vicissitudes of a Psalmodic Creation in Israel and Its Neighbours," *EI* 18 (1985 = N. Avigad volume): 130-40, 70*; Nims and Steiner, "A Paganized Version," 269-72. See further R. Steiner, "Papyrus Amherst 63: A New Source for the Language, Literature, Religion, and History of the Aramaeans," in *Studea Aramaica: New Sources and New Approaches; Papers Delivered at the London Conference of the Institute of Jewish Studies University College London 26th-28th June 1991*, ed. M. J. Geller, J. C. Greenfield, and M. P. Weitzman with the assistance of V. T. Mathias, JSS Supplement 4 (Oxford: Oxford Univ. Press, 1995), 205-7. For a convenient translation, see R. C. Steiner, "The Aramaic Text in Demotic Script," in *The Context of Scripture*, vol. 1, *Canonical Compositions from the Biblical World*, ed. W. W. Hallo and K. L. Younger, Jr. (Leiden/New York/Köln: Brill, 1997), 309-27.

version may have derived from a northern Israelite predecessor. If so, the reference to Baal Shamem might reflect the impact of this god in Israelite religion.

Some scholars identify the baal of Jezebel with the baal of Carmel, perhaps as his local manifestation at Carmel.[24] Like Baal Shamem, the baal of Carmel appears to be a storm-god. A second-century inscription from Carmel on a statue identifies the god of Carmel as Zeus Heliopolis.[25] At Baalbek, Zeus Heliopolis had both solar and storm characteristics. According to Macrobius (*Saturnalia* 1.23.19), this Zeus Heliopolis was a solarized form of the Assyrian storm-god, Adad.[26] As with Baal Shamem, the solar characteristic of Adad is a secondary development. Macrobius (*Saturnalia* 1.23.10) identifies the cult of Zeus Heliopolis with a solarized worship of Jupiter. The text provides further description:

> The Assyrians, too, in a city called Heliopolis, worship the sun with an elaborate ritual under the name of Heliopolis, calling him "Zeus of Heliopolis." The statue of the god was brought from the Egyptian town also called Heliopolis, when Senemur (who was perhaps the same as Senepos) was king of Egypt . . . the identification of this god with Jupiter and the sun is clear from the form of the ceremonial and from the appearance of the statue.[27]

In sum, the biblical evidence suggests that the Phoenician baal of Ahab and Jezebel was a storm-god. The extrabiblical evidence indicates that the baal of Carmel and Baal Shamem were also storm-gods, whereas Melqart does not appear to have been a storm-god. From the available data, following O. Eissfeldt, Baal Shamem was the baal of Jezebel.

Some reason for the adoption of the Phoenician baal by the northern monarchy may be tentatively suggested. The coexistence of cult to Yahweh and Baal prior to and up to the ninth century may have suggested to Ahab and his successors that elevating Baal in Israel would not represent a radical innovation. Ahab's religious policies presumably would have appealed to

24. Eissfeldt, "Jahve und Baal," 1-12.

25. Avi-Yonah, "Mount Carmel," 118-24; Albright, *Yahweh and the Gods of Canaan*, 229-30; Cross, *Canaanite Myth and Hebrew Epic*, 7 n. 13, 8 n. 16; Olyan, *Asherah and the Cult of Yahweh*, 62.

26. Avi-Yonah, "Mount Carmel," 121.

27. Davies, *Macrobius*, 151. For text, translation, and notes, see also H. Bornecque, *Macrobe: Les Saturnales*, vol. 1, books 1–3 (Paris: Librairie Garnier Frères, 1937), 236-37; J. Willis, *Ambrosii Theodosii Macrobii: Saturnalia* (Leipzig: BSB B. G. Teubner Verlagsgesellschaft, 1970), 126. For 1.23.19, see Davies, *Macrobius*, 152. Cf. 1.17.66-67 (Davies, *Macrobius*, 126).

those "Canaanites" living in Israelite cities during the monarchy, if these "Canaanites" represent a historical witness to those descendents of the old Canaanite cities that the Israelites are said not to have held originally (Josh. 16:10; 17:12-13; Judg. 1:27-35);[28] however, this witness is difficult to assess for historical value. The religious program of Ahab and Jezebel represented a theopolitical vision in continuity with the traditional compatibility of Yahweh and Baal. Up to this time both Yahweh and Baal had cults in the northern kingdom. Whereas Yahweh was the main god of the northern kingdom and divine patron of the royal dynasty in the north, Baal also enjoyed cultic devotion. Ahab and Jezebel perhaps created a different theopolitical vision. While the cult of Yahweh continued in the northern kingdom, Baal perhaps was elevated as the patron god of the northern monarchy, thus creating some sort of theopolitical unity between the kingdom of the north and the city of Tyre.

It would appear from various statements in the biblical text that although Ahab and Jezebel attempted to promote Baal, there may have been initially no corresponding royal attempt to rid the north of the cult of Yahweh, although the complaints of Elijah (1 Kings 18:22) give that impression. Ahab was not quite the apostate from Yahwism that the biblical polemics of 1 Kings 16:30-33 and 21:25-26 present. Ahab's sons, Ahaziah (1 Kings 22:40) and Joram (2 Kings 1:17; 8:25), bear Yahwistic names. After his conflict with Elijah, Ahab consults Yahwistic prophets (1 Kings 20:13-15, 22, 28). In the presence of Elijah, whom he calls "my enemy" (1 Kings 21:20), Ahab repents (1 Kings 21:27-29), which requires a postponement of divine punishment. The historical narratives depicting Ahab and Jezebel as opponents to the cult of Yahweh contain a considerable degree of negative typecasting. The theopolitical vision of Ahab and Jezebel perhaps did not initially include the eradication of the cult of Yahweh, but it would appear that some cost was involved, at least within the royal cult. This situation likely provoked the severe reaction against the Phoenician baal represented in the Elijah cycle (1 Kings 17–19). The perspective of Elijah represents a third theopolitical vision reacting against the royal program. This reaction perhaps issued subsequently in the persecution of Yahwistic prophets on the part of Ahab and Jezebel. Both the evidence for royal support for Yahweh and Baal and the reports of royal persecution of Yahwistic prophets are historically plausible.[29]

28. On the monarchic date of these references, see chapter 1, section 3.

29. Smith, *Palestinian Parties and Politics,* 34. See further W. M. Schniedewind, "History and Interpretation: The Religion of Ahab and Manasseh in the Book of Kings," *CBQ* 55 (1993): 649-61.

According to historical sources, support for Baal was severely ruptured at this juncture in Israelite history. Jehu managed the slaughter of Baal's royal and prophetic supporters and the destruction of the Baal temple in Samaria (2 Kings 10), and Jehoiada the priest oversaw the death of Athaliah and the destruction of another temple of Baal (2 Kings 11). Jehu's reform was not as systematic as the texts might suggest, however. Jehu did not fully eradicate Baal worship.[30] Confirmation for this viewpoint comes from inscriptional and biblical sources. The Kuntillet ʿAjrûd inscriptions contain the names of Baal and Yahweh in the same group of texts. Dismissing such attestations to the god Baal because the script may be "Phoenician" appears injudicious.[31] Indeed, the texts bear "vowel letters" (or *matres lectionis*),[32] which constitute a writing convention found in Hebrew, but not in Phoenician. Unlike Hebrew, Phoenician does not use letters to mark vowels.[33]

References in Hosea to "the baal" (2:10 [E 8]; 2:18 [E 16]; 13:1; cf. 7:16) and "the baals" (2:15 [E 13]; 2:19 [E 17]; 11:2) add further evidence of Baal worship in the northern kingdom. Hosea 2:16 (E 18) begins a section that recalls imagery especially reminiscent of Baal. According to some scholars,[34] Hosea 2:18 (E 16) plays on *baʿal* as a title of Yahweh and indicates that some northern Israelites did not distinguish between Yahweh and Baal. The verse declares, "And in that day, says Yahweh, you will call me, 'My husband,' and no longer will you call me, 'My *baʿal*.'"[35] The substitution of Yahweh for Baal

30. On the political circumstances surrounding Jehu's accession and reform, see H. Donner, "The Separate States of Israel and Judah," *Israelite and Judaean History,* ed. J. H. Hayes and J. M. Miller, OTL (Philadelphia: Westminster, 1977), 407-13; G. W. Ahlström, "The Battle of Ramoth-Gilead in 841 B.C.," *"Wünschet Jerusalem Frieden": Collected Communications to the 12th Congress of the International Organization for the Study of the Old Testament, Jerusalem 1986,* ed. M. Augustin and K. D. Schunk, Beiträge zur Erforschung des Alten Testaments und des antiken Judentums 13 (New York: Peter Lang, 1988), 157-66.

31. So Z. Meshel, *Kuntillet ʿAjrûd: A Religious Centre from the Time of the Judaean Monarchy,* Museum Catalog 175 (Jerusalem: The Israel Museum, 1978), 19, English section 12-13.

32. J. Tigay, "Israelite Religion: The Onomastic and Epigraphic Evidence," in *Ancient Israelite Religion: Essays in Honor of Frank Moore Cross,* ed. P. D. Miller, Jr., P. D. Hanson, and S. D. McBride, 177, 192 n. 115.

33. F. M. Cross and D. N. Freedman, *Early Hebrew Orthography* (New Haven: American Oriental Society, 1952), 11-20. On the script of the Kuntillet ʿAjrûd inscriptions, see chapter 3, section 3.

34. See F. I. Andersen and D. N. Freedman, *Hosea,* AB 24 (Garden City, NY: Doubleday, 1980), 278-79. The material in Hosea is quite complex literarily; in connection to the question of the references to Baal in Hosea, see T. Hentrich, "Die Kritik Hoseas an der kanaanäischen Religion. Eine redaktionsgeschichtliche Analyse" (Ph.D. diss., Université de Montréal, 1999).

35. See chapter 1, section 3. On the redactional stage of Hos. 2:21-23, see H. W. Wolff, *Hosea: A Commentary on the Book of the Prophet Hosea,* trans. G. Stansell, Hermeneia (Philadel-

continues dramatically in Hosea 2:23-24 (E 21-23). These verses echo Baal's message to Anat in KTU 1.3 III 13-31 (cf. 1.3 IV 7-20). In this speech, Baal announces to Anat that the word that he understands will be revealed to humanity who does not yet know it. In the context of the narrative, this word is the message of the cosmic fertility that will occur when Baal's palace is built on his home on Mount Sapan. Upon the completion of his palace, Baal creates his meteorological manifestation of the storm from the palace, which issues in cosmic blessing (KTU 1.4 V-VII). Part of the message to Anat describes the cosmic communication between the Heavens and the Deeps, an image for cosmic fertility[36] (cf. Gen. 49:25; Deut. 33:13):

dm rgm ʾiṯ ly w ʾargmk	For I have a word I will tell you,
hwt w ʾaṯnyk	A message I will recount to you,
rgm ʿṣ w lḫšt ʾabn	A word of tree and whisper of stone,
tʾant šmm ʿm ʾarṣ	Converse of Heaven with Earth,
thmt ʿmn kbkbm	Of Deeps to the Stars.
ʾabn brq dl tdʿ šmm	I understand the lightning Heaven does not know,
rgm ltdʿ nšm	The word humans do not know,
wltbn hmlt ʾarṣ	And Earth's masses do not understand.
ʾatm wʾank ʾibǵyh	Come and I will reveal it,
btk ǵry ʾil ṣpn	In the midst of my mountain, Divine Sapan,
bqdš bǵr nḥlty	In the holy place, on the mount of my possession,
bnʿm bgbʿ tlʾiyt	In the pleasant place, on the hill of my victory.

With victory in hand, Baal's message presages a glorious natural paradise on earth through the agency of his fructifying rains.

---

phia: Fortress, 1974), 47; G. A. Yee, *Composition and Tradition in the Book of Hosea: A Redaction Critical Investigation,* SBLDS 102 (Atlanta, GA: Scholars, 1987), 87-88. On Hosea 2, see also M. A. Freedman, "Israel's Response in Hosea 2:17b: 'You are my Husband,'" *JBL* 99 (1980): 199-204.

36. Andersen and Freedman, *Hosea,* 286-87; B. Batto, "The Covenant of Peace: A Neglected Ancient Near Eastern Motif," *CBQ* 49 (1987): 187-211, esp. 189, 200. For the context of CTA 3.3.15-28 (= KTU 1.3 III 18-31) and the meaning of **ʿnh* in Hos. 2:21-23, see M. S. Smith, "Baal's Cosmic Secret," *UF* 16 (1985): 295-98; cf. Freedman, "Israel's Response," 199-204; Batto, "The Covenant of Peace," 199. For the pair "Heaven" and "Deep" in another context of earthly fertility, see Gen. 27:39; 49:25; Deut. 33:13. According to Hab. 3:10, "Deep gave forth its voice," *nātan tĕhôm qôlô.* The phrase is highly reminiscent of Baal's giving forth of his holy voice in KTU 1.4 VII 29 and Yahweh in various biblical passages, including Joel 4:16 (E 3:16) and Amos 1:2. The application of this image to Deep in Hab. 3:10 perhaps represents an extension of this motif generally attributed to the storm-god in Ugaritic and Israelite literature (see chapter 2, section 2).

Hosea 2:23-24 (E 21-22) bears a similar message, which also utilizes the language of cosmic speech or "answering":[37]

wĕhāyāh bayyôm hahû'	And it will be on that day,
'eʿĕneh nĕ'um yhwh	I will answer — oracle of Yahweh —
'eʿĕneh 'et-haššāmāyim	I will answer the heavens,
wĕhēm yaʿănû 'et-hā'āreṣ	And they shall answer the earth;
wĕhā'āreṣ taʿăneh	And the earth shall answer
'et-haddāgān wĕ'et-hattîrôš	With the grain, the wine
wĕ'et-hayyiṣhār	and the oil,
wĕhēm yaʿănû 'et-yizrĕʿe(')l	And they shall answer Jezreel.

Like Baal's victory over the forces of destruction, one day Yahweh's "answering" will produce cosmic bounty for Israel (cf. Hos. 14:9). Like Baal's word to Anat, the message of Yahweh will traverse the heavens and the earth, which will explode with universal fertility. For Hosea 2, this cosmic speech communicates the natural fertility, a blessing that issues from the covenant between Yahweh and Israel (v. 20). The words of Hosea 2:23-24 bear the freight of Canaanite literary tradition, evoking, like Hosea 2:18, the imagery of the storm-god Baal and his divine blessings on the cosmos.

Despite royal attempts at reform, Baal worship continued. Although Jehoram, the son of Ahab, undertook a program of reform (2 Kings 3:2) and Athaliah and Mattan, the priest of Baal, were murdered (2 Kings 11:18), royal devotion to Baal persisted. Ahaz fostered Baal worship (2 Chron. 28:2). According to Jeremiah 23:13, Baal worship led to the fall of Samaria and the northern kingdom. The verse declares, "And among the prophets of Samaria I saw an unsavory thing; they prophesied by Baal and led astray my people, Israel." Jeremiah 23:27 further condemns Israelite prophecy by Baal. Hezekiah sought to eliminate worship of Baal, but his son, Manasseh, rendered royal support to his cult (2 Kings 21:3; 2 Chron. 33:3). Finally, Josiah purged the Jerusalem temple of cultic paraphernalia designed for Baal (2 Kings 23:4; cf. Zeph. 1:4). Prophetic polemic from the end of the southern kingdom also claims that the monarchy permitted religious devotion to Baal down to its final days (Jer. 2:8; 7:9; 9:13; 12:16). From the cumulative evidence it appears that on the whole Baal was an accepted Israelite god, that criticism of his cult began in the ninth or eighth century, and that despite prophetic and Deuteronomistic criticism, this god remained popular through the end of the southern kingdom. There is no evidence that prior to the ninth century Baal was considered a major threat to the cult of Yahweh.

37. See Yee, *Composition and Tradition,* 88-90.

The word *baʿal* exhibits a complex development in biblical and extrabiblical sources. The Hebrew terms "the baal" *(habbaʿal)* and "the baals" *(habbĕʿālîm)* represent the god Baal, his manifestation at a variety of cult sites, and various divine "lords" or gods. Baal Hermon, Baal Lebanon, and Baal Saphon, the Ugaritic storm-god (cf. KAI 50, 69; Exod. 14:2, 9; Num. 33:7), appear to be Canaanite storm-gods.[38] The baal of Carmel in 1 Kings 18, the Phoenician baal of Ahab and Jezebel, and the baal criticized by Hosea were also storm-gods, perhaps the same one. The grouping of various storm-gods known by the name Baal is attested in the treaty of Esarhaddon with Baal of Tyre and also at Ugarit and in an Egyptian-Hittite treaty. CTA 29 (KTU 1.47).6-11 and KTU 1.118.5-10 list six baals *(bʿlm)* after Baal Saphon (*bʿl ṣpn;* cf. KTU 1.148.3-4, 11-12). An Akkadian version of the same text from Ugarit, RS 20.24,[39] lists the storm-god six times (^{d}IM *II-VII*) after the weather-god called "lord of Mount Hazzi" (^{d}IM *be-el ḫuršân ḫazi*).[40] Similarly, in the treaty (ca. 1280) between Ramses II and the Hittite king, Hattusilis, the divine witnesses include both "Seth [i.e., Baal], lord of the sky" and Seth of various towns.[41] The mention of "this Hadad" *(hdd zn)* in one of the Panammu inscriptions (KAI 213:14, 16) reflects an awareness of multiple Hadads.

Hosea plays on the relationship between the great god Baal, his manifestations in numerous cult sites, and finally the generic use of his name to refer to other "lords."[42] Hosea 2:18-19 (E 16-17) makes explicit the connection between "the baal" and the generic phrase for gods, "the baals." Seventh- and sixth-century attestations to the term "the baals" reflect the widespread, but not exclusively generic, use of the expression. Jeremiah 23:13 indicates that

38. See *ANET,* 534. For discussion, see Cross, *Canaanite Myth and Hebrew Epic,* 28 n. 86; Peckham, "Phoenicia and the Religion of Israel," 89-90 nn. 11-13. For later evidence from Philo of Byblos, see Attridge and Oden, *Philo of Byblos,* 82 n. 55.

39. See Nougayrol, *Ug V,* 45-46; de Tarragon, *Le Culte à Ugarit,* 157; J. F. Healey, "The Akkadian 'Pantheon' List from Ugarit," *SEL* 2 (1985): 115-25.

40. According to Nougayrol (*Ug V,* 48) these *bʿlm* constitute Baal's military escort. Nougayrol further allows for the possibility that these baals are baals of various local sanctuaries. R. J. Clifford (*The Cosmic Mountain,* 65) also surmises these are the baals at local sanctuaries. J. C. de Moor ("The Semitic Pantheon of Ugarit," *UF* 2 [1970]: 219) likewise identifies these *bʿlm* with *bʿl ṣpn,* but discounts them as various baals at local sanctuaries. The reference to *bʿlm* in this manner differs from allusions to *bʿl, bʿl ṣpn,* or *bʿl ʾugrt* in other texts and would appear to differ in some way from all three of these baals.

41. *ANET,* 201. This sort of delineation of the storm-god is found also in Hittite treaties discovered at Ras Shamra (see *Ug V,* 48). It is by no means certain, however, that groups of multiple ^{d}IM in Hittite lists of gods refer to local variants or manifestations of the storm-god.

42. Cf. B. Halpern, "'Brisker Poetry Than Pipes,'" 84, 92-94.

the west Semitic storm-god, Baal, continued to be known as a deity in Israel. At the same time, two sections of Jeremiah criticize Baal worship, "for as many as your cities are your gods, O Judah" (2:28; cf. 11:13). Jeremiah mixes the singular, "the baal" (2:8; 7:9; 11:13, 17; 32:29), with the plural, "the baals" (2:23; 9:14). The plurals, "the baals," in Jeremiah 2:23 and 9:14, like "the baals and the asherahs" in Judges 3:7 and "the baals and the astartes" in Judges 2:13, 10:6, 1 Samuel 7:4 and 12:10, reflect a further development in the use of the term "the baals."[43] These expressions indicate that the designation of "baal"

43. Andersen and Freedman, *Hosea*, 256-58. Besides the manifestation of the deity at various locales, there are other types of plural forms of deities in Northwest Semitic literature, mostly attested in Ugaritic and Phoenician. Plural forms of deity may reflect a divine vanguard of a deity. This constitutes a less likely interpretation of "the baals," since after six references to *bʿlm*, CTA 29.12 (= KTU 1.118.11) lists *ʾil tʿḏr bʿl*, "Baal's divine helpers," perhaps equivalent with his vanguard described in KTU 1.5 V 7-9. This idea may apply to enigmatic plural references to *ršpm*, cognate with the West Semitic god Resheph. Ugaritic attests to both *ršpm* and to several *ršp* combined with a place name (P. Xella, "KTU 1.91 [RS 19.15] e i sacrifici del re," *UF* 11 [1979]: 833-38). The plural *ršpm* in KTU 1.91.11 are described entering *bt mlk*, the royal palace or royal sanctuary/chapel. According to de Tarragon (*Le Culte à Ugarit*, 167), this description refers to the procession of cult statues into a sanctuary. Sidonian inscriptions (KAI 15:2; RES 289:2, 290:3, 302 B:5) mention *ʾrṣ ršpm*, "the land of reshephs" (cf. *ʾrqršp* in KAI 214:11). Following Albright, H. Donner and W. Röllig (*Kanaanäische und Aramäische Inschriften*, vol. 2, *Kommentar* [Wiesbaden: Otto Harrassowitz, 1973], 24) interpret *ršpm* as a general collectivity of deities like the Rephaim (see below). Might *ʾrṣ* refer, like *šmm rmm* in the preceding line of KAI 15:2, to a sacred "district," in this case perhaps figuratively to the "underworld," hence a cemetery? (See G. C. Picard, "From the Foundation of Carthage to the Barcid Revolution," *Archaeologia Viva* 1/2 [1968-69]: 152.) Fulco (*The Canaanite God Rešep* [New Haven, CT: American Oriental Society, 1976], 47) renders *ʾrṣ ršpm* "Land of the Warriors." Ugaritic and Phoenician *ršpm* may designate a martial vanguard. An Egyptian description of the army of Ramses III is compatible with this view: "the chariot-warriors are as mighty as Rashaps" (*ANET*, 250 n. 27). BH *rešep* appears as part of a theophanic vanguard (Deut. 32:24; Hab. 3:5) and as a term for sparks and fiery arrows (Ps. 76:3; Job 5:7; Song of Songs 8:6; cf. Aramaic *rišpāʾ*, "flame"). On Resheph, see also P. Xella, "Le dieu Rashaph à Ugarit," *Les annales archaeologiques arabes syriennes* 29-30 (1979-80): 145-62; Cooper, "Divine Names and Epithets in the Ugaritic Texts," 413-15; Y. Yadin, "New Gleanings on Resheph from Ugarit," in *Biblical and Related Studies Presented to Samuel Iwry*, ed. A. Kort and S. Morschauer (Winona Lake, IN: Eisenbrauns, 1985), 259-74; Greenfield, "The Hebrew Bible and Canaanite Literature," 549). Other collective groups of deities in Ugaritic include *rpʾum*, the *mlkm* and the *kṯrt*. The term *gṯrm* in KTU 1.112.18-20 may belong to this category (as a title for the Rephaim like *mlkm?* cf. *gṯr* as title of *rpʾu mlk ʿlm* in KTU 1.108.1-2; see de Tarragon, *Le Culte à Ugarit*, 159, 176; chapter 5, sections 2 and 3). De Moor ("The Semitic Pantheon," 226) interprets some Ugaritic divine names (e.g., *ʾilhm, bʿlm, mtm, nhrm,* and sometimes *ʾilm*) with mimation as instances of plural of majesty (might the place name *ʿănātôt* in Jer. 1:1 be explained along these lines?) See also the "Baali-Zaphon," attested in New Kingdom Egypt (*ANET*, 250). J. A. Wilson interprets this phrase as either a plural of majesty or a collective noun (*ANET*, 250 n. 12). Bethel (*Ba-a-a-ti-ilī*^{meš}) and

in the period of the late monarchy came to signify all "the baals" or various gods of the land, with different cults and identities. This usage perhaps compares with *ilāni u ištarāti*, an Akkadian phrase for "gods and goddesses" based on the word for "god" plus the generic use of the plural form of the proper name of the goddess Ishtar.[44]

Anat-Bethel (^{d}*A-na(?)-ti-Ba-[a]-[a-ti-il]*^{meš}) found in the treaty of Baal of Tyre with Esarhaddon are marked as plural forms (R. Borger, *Die Inschriften Asarhaddons Königs von Assyrien*, Archiv für Orientsforschung Beiheft 9 [Graz: Weidner, 1956; reprinted, Osnabrück: Biblio-Verlag, 1967], 109, col. 4, line 6; *ANET*, 491; Barré, *The God-List*, 46-47). BH *'ĕlōhîm* may be understood as a plural of majesty or the like (see *GKC*, para. 124 g-h; Ginsberg, *The Israelian Heritage of Judaism* [New York: The Jewish Theological Seminary of America, 1982], 35; A. E. Draffkorn Kilmer, "*Ilāni/Elohîm*," *JBL* 76 [1957]: 216-17; Ahlström, *Who Were the Israelites?* 94; cf. Roberts, *The Earliest Semitic Pantheon*, 134-35). The remarks in Philo of Byblos (*PE* 1.10.20) may be noted in this connection: "Now the allies of Elos, i.e., Kronos, were called 'eloim,' as the ones named after Kronos would be 'Kronians,'" *hoi de summachoi Ēlou tou Kronou Elōeim epeklēlēsan hos an Kronioi houtoi ēsan hoi legomenoi epi Kronou* (Attridge and Oden, *Philo of Byblos*, 50-51). However, Burnett (*A Reassessment of Biblical Elohim*, 19-24, 57-58) rejects the plural of majesty in favor of the plural of abstraction. The resulting understanding (and translation of *'ĕlōhîm* ("divinity") is not preferable to understanding (and translation) resulting from interpreting *'ĕlōhîm* as a plural of majesty ("godhead"). Still Burnett's arguments specifically about *'ĕlōhîm* as a plural of abstraction have much to commend them. For further discussion of such divine groups, see Smith, *The Origins of Biblical Monotheism*, 67-68; and note further I. Kottsieper, "'ŠTRM — eine südarabische Gottheit in der Scharonebene," *ZAW* 113 (2001): 245-50.

44. On *ilāni u ištarāti*, see *CAD* I:272; *AHw*, 399-400; Cooper, "Divine Names and Epithets in the Ugaritic Texts," 342, 404. The genericization of West Semitic deities for common nouns occurred in a variety of ways. The name of Dagon (Roberts, *The Earliest Semitic Pantheon*, 18-19) became a BH word for "grain," *dāgôn* (*BDB*, 186). BH *'aštĕrôt (haṣ)ṣō'n*, referring to young sheep and goats in Deut. 7:13 and 28:4, 18, 51, represents the generic usage of Astarte's fertility (*BDB*, 800; Albright, *Yahweh and the Gods of Canaan*, 185; H. L. Ginsberg, "The North-Canaanite Myth of Anath and Aqhat," 9; Oden, *Studies*, 80). BH *rešep* as a demon (Deut. 32:24; Hab. 3:5), disease (Ps. 78:48), and sparks and fiery arrows (Ps. 76:3; Job 5:7; Song of Songs 8:6) can be traced to the Canaanite god by the same name (see the preceding note). For evidence of *rĕšāpîm* in rabbinic sources as a breed of birds, see E. Lipiński, "*R^{e}šāfîm:* From God to Birds of Prey," in *Mythos im Alten Testament und seiner Umwelt: Festschrift für Hans-Peter Müller zum 65. Geburstag*, ed. A. Lange, H. Lichtenberger, and D. Römheld, BZAW 278 (Berlin/New York, 1999), 255-59. In Arabic, the names of Baal and Mot denote types of soil relating to the qualities of the gods who gave their names to these types (W. R. Smith, *The Religion of the Semites: The Fundamental Institutions*, Burnett Lectures 1888-1889, rev. ed. [London: Adam & Charles Black, 1894; reprint, New York: Schocken, 1972], 97; T. H. Gaster, *Thespis: Ritual, Myth, and Drama in the Ancient Near East*, rev. ed. [Garden City, NY: Doubleday, 1961], 124-25). Gaster would add Athtar to this list, but Robertson Smith questions this attribution (*Religion of the Semites*, 99 n. 2). The expressions "house of Baal" and "field of the house of Baal" refer to a well-watered field in the Mishnah (*Sebi'it* 2:9; *Terumot* 10:11, *Baba Batra* 3:1; see Smith, *Religion of the Semites*, 96-97, 99 n. 2, 102). According to G. Dossin, at Mari the name of Shamash was used as a

Biblical tradition grouped and conflated a number of different gods as "baals," just as it apparently conflated various El traditions and grouped and conflated the asherahs with the astartes. The plural form of "the baals" *(habbĕʿālîm)* refers to the divine "lords" or gods of various places, some surviving in the Iron Age only in the form of place names.[45] These would include Baal (1 Chron. 4:33), Baal Gad (Josh. 11:17; 12:7; 13:5), Baal Hamon (Song of Songs 8:11), Baal Hazor (2 Sam. 13:23), Baal Hermon (Deut. 3:9; Judg. 3:3; 1 Chron. 5:23), Baal Lebanon (2 Kings 19:23; Ps. 29:5-6), Baal Maʿon (Num. 32:38; 1 Chron. 5:8; Ezek. 25:9; cf. KAI 181:3, 30), Baal Peor (Num. 25:3, 5; Deut. 4:3; Ps. 106:28; cf. Hos. 9:10), Baal Perazim (2 Sam. 5:20; 1 Chron. 14:11), Baal Shalisha (2 Kings 4:42), and Baal Tamar (Judg. 20:33).[46] These baals included different manifestations of the storm-god in various locales, with cult traditions presumably as varied as for El or for Yahweh in their various sanctuaries.[47]

The descriptions of Baal and baals in 1 Kings 17–19, Hosea 2, and other biblical texts raise a final issue concerning Baal's character in ancient Israel. In the Ugaritic sources Baal's meteorological manifestations are expressions of his martial power. In contrast, 1 Kings 17–19 and Hosea 2 deplore belief in Baal's ability to produce rains, but these and other biblical passages are silent on the martial import of his manifestation. Indeed, no biblical text expresses ideas about Baal's status as a warrior. Yahweh had perhaps exhibited and possibly usurped this role at such an early point for the tradents of Israel's religious literature. This conclusion might be inferred from the numerous similarities between Baal and Yahweh that many scholars have long observed.

---

word for "god" ("Le Pantheon de Mari," in *Studia Mariana,* vol. 4 [Leiden: Brill, 1950], 46). For the possibility that *ʿannôt* in Exod. 32:18 derived from the name of the goddess Anat, see H. L. Ginsberg, "The North-Canaanite Myth," 9. Albright (*Yahweh and the Gods of Canaan,* 187) interprets **ʾašmannîm* (written with waw in 1QIsa[a]) in Isa 59:10 as an abstract plural meaning "health," deriving from the name of the god Eshmun. The development of *ʾl* for "god" from El/Ilu has been discussed in connection with the process of genericization (see A. R. Millard, review of *The Earliest Semitic Pantheon,* by J. J. M. Roberts, *JSS* 19 [1974]: 89). The generic usage does not appear to apply to the divine name *mlk* (see chapter 5, section 3).

45. The form *habbĕʿālîm* is not singular with an added or enclitic mem (so Boling, *Judges,* 74).

46. On the difficulties attending the interpretation of Baal Hamon, see Pope, *Song of Songs,* 686-88. Concerning Baal Peor, see chapter 5, section 2. According to Ps. 106:34-38, the cult of Baal-Peor involved child sacrifice, on which see below chapter 5.

47. See McCarter, "Aspects of the Religion of the Israelite Monarchy: Biblical and Epigraphic Data," in *Ancient Israelite Religion: Essays in Honor of Frank Moore Cross,* ed. P. D. Miller, Jr., P. D. Hanson, and S. D. McBride, 139-43.

2. Imagery of Baal and Yahweh

Various West Semitic descriptions emphasize either Baal's theophany in the storm (KTU 1.4 V 6-9, 1.6 III 6f., 12f., 1.19 I 42-46) or his role as warrior (KTU 1.2 IV, 1.5 I 1-5, 1.119.26-29, 34-36; RS 16.144.9[48]). These two dimensions of Baal are explicitly linked in KTU 1.4 VII 29-35, 1.101.1-4, and EA 147.13-15 as well as some iconography.[49] F. M. Cross treats different descriptions of Baal as a single *Gattung* with four elements, which appear in these passages in varying degrees. The four components are: *(a)* the march of the divine warrior, *(b)* the convulsing of nature as the divine warrior manifests his power, *(c)* the return of the divine warrior to his holy mountain to assume divine kingship, and *(d)* the utterance of the divine warrior's "voice" (i.e., thunder) from his palace, providing rains that fertilize the earth.[50] Biblical material deriding other deities reserves power over the storm for Yahweh (Jer. 10:11-16; 14:22; Amos 4:7; 5:8; 9:6). Biblical descriptions of Yahweh as storm-god (1 Sam. 12:18; Psalm 29; Job 38:25-27, 34-38) and divine warrior (Pss. 50:1-3; 97:1-6; 98:1-2; 104:1-4; Deut. 33:2; Judges 4–5; Job 26:11-13; Isa. 42:10-15, etc.) exhibit this underlying unity and pattern explicitly in Psalm 18 (= 2 Sam. 22):6-19, 68:7-10, and 86:9-19.[51] Psalm 29, 1 Kings 19, and 2 Esdras 13:1-4 dramatize the meteorological progression underlying the imagery of Yahweh as warrior. All three passages presuppose the image of the storm

48. *PRU III*, 76.

49. *ANEP*, 168 and 307, no. 490. For EA 147:13-15, see W. L. Moran, *Les Lettres d'El-Amarna*, trans. D. Collon and H. Cazelles, LAPO 13 (Paris: Les Éditions du Cerf, 1987), 378-80. For general discussions, see Cross, *Canaanite Myth and Hebrew Epic*, 147-51; Miller, *The Divine Warrior*, 24-48; M. Weinfeld, "Divine Intervention in War in Ancient Israel and in the Ancient Near East," in *History, Historiography and Interpretation: Studies in Biblical and Cuneiform Literatures*, ed. H. Tadmor and M. Weinfeld (Jerusalem: Magnes, 1983), 121-47; S. Moon-Kang, *Divine War in the Old Testament and the Ancient Near East*, BZAW 177 (Berlin/New York: de Gruyter, 1989), 77-79; and C. Kloos, *Yhwh's Combat with the Sea: A Canaanite Tradition in the Religion of Ancient Israel* (Amsterdam: G. A. van Oorschot; Leiden: Brill, 1986), 42-52. For further pertinent iconography, see the depictions of the Late Bronze Age Syrian "smiting god"; see A. Vanel, *L'Iconographie du dieu de l'orage, dans le proche-orient ancien jusqu'au VIIe siècle avant J.-C.*, CRB 3 (Paris: Gabalda, 1965), 69-110; O. Negbi, *Canaanite Gods in Metal: An Archaeological Study of Ancient Syro-Palestinian Figurines* (Tel Aviv: Tel Aviv University, Institute of Archaeology, 1976), 29-36; I. Cornelius, *The Iconography of the Canaanite Gods Reshef and Ba'al: Late Bronze Age I Periods (c. 1500-1000 BCE)*, OBO 140 (Fribourg: Universitätsverlag; Göttingen: Vandenhoeck & Ruprecht, 1994); Keel and Uehlinger, *Gods, Goddesses and Images of God*, 60, 76-78, 135-36, 138 & 140 n. 8.

50. Cross, *Canaanite Myth and Hebrew Epic*, 162-63. See also Pope, "Baal Worship," 12.

51. Cross, *Canaanite Myth and Hebrew Epic*, 151-63; Moon-Kang, *Divine War*, 204-22; Kloos, *Yhwh's Combat with the Sea.*

moving eastward from the Mediterranean Sea to the coast. In 1 Kings 19 and 2 Esdras 13:1-4 this force is portrayed with human imagery. The procession of the divine warrior is accompanied by a contingent of lesser divine beings (Deut. 32:34; 33:2; Hab. 3:5; KTU 1.5 V 6-9; cf. Judg. 5:20). The Ugaritic antecedent to Resheph in Yahweh's entourage in Habakkuk 3:5 may be KTU 1.82.1-3, which perhaps includes Resheph as a warrior with Baal against *tnn,* related to biblical *tannînîm.*[52] Though the power of other Near Eastern warrior-gods was manifest in the storm (e.g., Amun, Ningirsu/Ninurta, Marduk, and Addu/Adad),[53] the proximity of terminology and imagery between the Ugaritic and biblical evidence points to an indigenous cultural influence on meteorological descriptions of Yahweh.

Israelite tradition modified its Canaanite heritage by molding the march of the divine warrior specifically to the element of Yahweh's southern sanctuary, variously called Sinai (Deut. 33:2; cf. Judg. 5:5; Ps. 68:9), Paran (Deut. 33:2; Hab. 3:3), Edom (Judg. 5:4), and Teiman (Hab. 3:3[54] and in the Kuntillet ʿAjrûd inscriptions; cf. Amos 1:12; Ezek. 25:13). This modification may underlie the difference between Baal's epithet *rkb ʿrpt,* "cloud-rider" (e.g., CTA 2.4[KTU 1.2 IV].8), and Yahweh's title, *rōkēb bāʿărābôt,* "rider over the steppes," in Psalm 68:5 (cf. Deut. 33:26; Ps. 104:3),[55] although a shared background for this feature is evident from other descriptions of Baal and Yahweh. The notion of Baal riding on a winged war chariot is implicit in *mdl,* one element in Baal's meteorological entourage in KTU 1.5 V 6-11.[56] Psalm

52. J. Day, *God's Conflict with the Dragon and the Sea,* University of Cambridge Oriental Publications 35 (Cambridge: Cambridge Univ. Press, 1985), 105-6.

53. See M. Weinfeld, "'Rider of the Clouds' and 'Gatherer of the Clouds,'" *JANES* 5 (1975 = T. H. Gaster Festschrift): 421-26; idem, "Divine Intervention," 121-24; Moon-Kang, *Divine War,* 23-48; T. Hiebert, *God of My Victory: The Ancient Hymn of Habakkuk* 3, HSM 38 (Atlanta, GA: Scholars, 1986), 93.

54. Cross, *Canaanite Myth and Hebrew Epic,* 101-2; idem, "Reuben, First-Born of Jacob," 57-63; Miller, *Divine Warrior,* 160-61; Hiebert, *God of My Victory,* 83-92. These poems are thought to belong to the older strata of Israelite literature (see introduction, section 1).

55. A. R. Johnson, *Sacral Kingship in Ancient Israel,* 2d ed. (Cardiff: Univ. of Wales, 1967), 78 n. 6; J. Gray, "A Cantata of the Autumn Festival: Psalm LXVIII," *JSS* 22 (1977): 7, 9, 21 n. 4; Day, *God's Conflict,* 31. Although BH *bāʿărābôt* is interpreted as "steppes" instead of "clouds," Yahweh nonetheless is regarded as riding on a cloud in this passage (see Day, *God's Conflict,* 32). For other suggestions, see Cooper, "Divine Names and Epithets in the Ugaritic Texts," 458-60.

56. See J. C. Greenfield, "Ugaritic *mdl* and Its Cognates," *Biblica* 45 (1964): 527-34; Weinfeld, "'Rider of the Clouds,'" 421-26; J. Day, "Echoes of Baal's Seven Thunders and Lightnings in Psalm xxix and Habakkuk iii 9 and the Identity of the Seraphim in Isaiah vi," *VT* 29 (1979): 147 n. 18; R. M. Good, "Some Draught Terms Relating to Draught and Riding Animals," *UF* 16 (1984): 80-81. Day (*God's Conflict,* 33 n. 93) also compares Enlil's commission to Ishkur: "Let the seven winds be harnessed before you like a team, harness the winds before you"

77:19 refers to the wheels in Yahweh's storm theophany, which presumes a divine war chariot. Psalm 18 (2 Sam. 22):11 presents Yahweh riding on the wind surrounded by storm clouds. This image forms the basis for the description of the divine chariot in Ezekiel 1 and 10. Psalm 65:12 (E 11) likewise presupposes the storm-chariot image: "You crown your bounteous year, and your tracks drip with fatness." Similarly, Yahweh's storm chariot is the image presumed by Habakkuk 3:8 and 15:

> Was your wrath against the rivers, O Yahweh?
> Was your anger against the rivers,
> or your indignation against the sea,
> when you rode upon your horses,
> upon your chariot of victory?
> You trampled the sea with your horses,
> the surging of the mighty waters.

The description of Yahweh's horses fits into the larger context of the storm theophany directed against the cosmic enemies, Sea and River. (The horses in this verse are unrelated to the horses dedicated to the sun in 2 Kings 23:11, unless there was a coalescence of the chariot imagery of the storm and the sun.[57]) The motif of chariot-riding storm-god with his divine entourage extends in Israelite tradition to the divine armies of Yahweh riding on chariots with horses (2 Kings 2:11; 6:17).

Other features originally attributed to Baal also accrued to Yahweh. Albright and other scholars[58] have argued the epithet *ʿly,* "the Most High," belonging to Baal in the Ugaritic texts (KTU 1.16 III 6, 8; cf. RS 18.22.4′), ap-

---

(*ANET,* 578). See also the seven winds in Marduk's weaponry in Enuma Elish 4:46-47 (*ANET,* 66). Cf. A. A. Weider, "Ugaritic-Hebrew Lexicographical Notes," *JBL* 84 (1965): 164.

57. Cf. Ahlström, *Royal Administration,* 70 n. 130.

58. Albright, *The Biblical Period,* 18; Dahood, *Psalms I: 1–50,* AB 16 (Garden City, NY: Doubleday, 1965), xxiii, xxv, xxxvi, 45, 79, 89, 117, 194, 251; idem, *Psalms II: 51–100,* AB 17 (Garden City, NY: Doubleday, 1968), xxxix, 38, 149, 303; idem, *Psalms III: 101–150,* AB 17A (Garden City, NY: Doubleday, 1970), xxxix-xl, 188, 201, 229, 293, 295, 310, 320, 341; Freedman, *Pottery, Poetry, and Prophecy,* 78-79, 261; Cross, *Canaanite Myth and Hebrew Epic,* 234 n. 66; Cooper, "Divine Names and Epithets in the Ugaritic Texts," 451-58. On *ʿly* in RS 18.22.4′, see *PRU VI,* 55; and J. Huehnergard, *Ugaritic Vocabulary in Syllabic Transcription,* HSS 32 (Atlanta, GA: Scholars, 1987), 160. Freedman (*Pottery, Poetry, and Prophecy,* 95) and G. Rendsburg ("The Northern Origin of 'the Last Words of David' (2 Sam. 23, 1-7)," *Biblica* 69 [1988]: 119) interpret *ʿāl* in 2 Sam. 23:1 as an epithet. Citing the reading *ʾl* in 4QSam[a], Cross (*Canaanite Myth and Hebrew Epic,* 52 n. 31, 234 n. 66) and McCarter (*II Samuel,* 477) reject this interpretation of 2 Sam. 23:1 (see E. C. Ulrich, *The Qumran Text of Samuel and Josephus,* HSM 19 [Missoula, MT: Scholars, 1978], 113-14; Barthélemy, *Critique Textuelle de l'Ancien Testament,* 1.310).

pears as a title of Yahweh in 1 Samuel 2:10, 2 Samuel 23:1, Psalms 18 (2 Sam. 22):14 and 68:6, 30, 35 (cf. Dan. 3:26, 32; 4:14, 21, 22, 29, 31; 5:18, 21; 7:25), in the biblical hypocoristicon *ʿēlî*, the name of the priest of Shiloh,[59] and in Hebrew inscriptional personal names *yhwʿly*, "Yahu is Most High," *ywʿly*, "Yaw is Most High," *ʿlyhw*, "Most High is Yahu," and *ʿlyw*, "Most High is Yaw."[60]

The bull iconography that Jeroboam I sponsored in Dan and Bethel (1 Kings 12:28-31) has been attributed to the influence of Baal in the northern kingdom. This imagery represented an old northern tradition of divine iconography for Yahweh used probably as a rival symbol to the traditional royal iconography of the cherubim of the Jerusalem temple.[61] The old northern tradition of bull iconography for Yahweh is reflected in the name *ʿglyw*, which may be translated, "Young bull is Yaw," in Samaria ostracon 41:1.[62] The ca. twelfth-century bull figurine discovered at a site in the hill country of Ephraim and the young bull depicted on the tenth-century Taanach stand likewise involve the iconography of a god, either Yahweh or Baal.[63] Newer discoveries have yielded iconography of a deity on a bull on a ninth-century plaque from Dan and an

59. The name *ʿēlî* does not indicate that he was a priest of a deity *ʿly* other than Yahweh (so Ahlström, "The Travels of the Ark," 142; idem, *Who Were the Israelites?* 78), but rather that *ʿly*, a title of Baal in the Ugaritic texts, had become a title of Yahweh in ancient Israel.

60. N. Avigad, *Hebrew Bullae from the Time of Jeremiah: Remnants of a Burnt Archive* (Jerusalem: Israel Exploration Society, 1986), 45, 93-94.

61. Cross, *Canaanite Myth and Hebrew Epic*, 73-75. See also Ahlström, *Royal Administration*, 69 n. 91; and K. Koenen, "Eherne Schlage und goldenes Kalb: Eine Vergleich der Überlieferungen," *ZAW* 111 (1999): 353-72. For the Exodus as a northern "charter myth," see van der Toorn, *Family Religion*, 287-315; see also A. Cooper and B. Goldstein, "Exodus and *Maṣṣôt* in History and Tradition," Maarav 8/2 (1992): 15-37.

62. On the reading of the name, see J. C. L. Gibson, *Textbook of Syrian Semitic Inscriptions*, vol. 1, *Hebrew and Moabite Inscriptions* (Oxford: Clarendon, 1971), 10, 12; Ahlström, "An Archaeological Picture of Iron Age Religion in Ancient Palestine," *Studia Orientalia* 55 (1984): 11; Tigay, *You Shall Have No Other Gods*, 59. In a private communication, Tigay mentions that the PN may be moot, if **ʿgl* means "to speed, hasten." Yet this verbal meaning is rare, if not unattested, for Hebrew, at least in the biblical period.

63. For a discussion of the bull site, see A. Mazar, "The 'Bull Site' — An Iron Age I Open Cult Place," *BASOR* 247 (1982): 27-42; R. Wenning and E. Zenger, "Ein bäuerliches Baal-Heiligtum im samarischen Gebirge aus der Zeit der Anfänge Israels," *ZDPV* 102 (1986): 75-86. For a defense of the site as Israelite, see A. Mazar, "On Cult Places and Early Israelites: A Response to Michael Coogan," *Biblical Archaeologist Review* 15/4 (1988): 45. In contrast, I. Finkelstein ("Two Notes on Northern Samaria: The ʿEinun Pottery and the Date of the 'Bull Site,'" *PEQ* 130 [1998]: 94-98) regards the bull site as Middle Bronze. Besides calf iconography, the solar disk and a goddess are depicted on the Taanach stand, and if one were to assume its Israelite provenience, it would constitute an example of the polytheistic religious belief in Israel; cf. R. Hestrin, "Cult Stand from Taʿanach," *EAEHL* 4:61-77; and chapter 1, section 4; chapter 4, section 3.

eighth-century stele from Bethsaida.[64] Indeed, evidence for Yahweh as bull appears in Amherst Papyrus 63 (column XI): "Horus-Yaho, our bull is with us. May the lord of Bethel answer us on the morrow."[65] Despite later syncretism with Horus, the text apparently preserves a prayer to Yahweh in his emblem-animal as a bull invoked as the patron-god of Bethel. The further question is whether these depictions were specific to either El or Baal (or both) in the Iron Age. The language has been thought also to derive from El, frequently called "bull" *(ṯr)* in the Ugaritic texts. There is some evidence pointing to the application of this iconography to El in the Iron Age. The title, *'ăbîr yaʿăqōb,* "bull of Jacob" (Gen. 49:24; Ps. 132:2, 4), derived from the bovine imagery of El. The image of Yahweh having horns "like the horns of the wild ox" *(kĕtôʿăpōt rĕ'ēm)* in Numbers 24:8 also belongs to this background. Other Late Bronze and Iron I iconographic evidence might favor a connection with Baal.[66] The reference to kissing Baal in 1 Kings 19:18 and the allusion to kissing calves in Hosea 13:2[67] would seem to bolster the Baalistic background to the bull iconography in the northern kingdom. However, the mention of kissing bulls in the apparent context of the Bethel cult in Papyrus Amherst 63 (column V) would point to the Yahwistic background of this practice.[68] It is also possible that a number of major gods could be regarded as "the divine bull,"[69] as this title applies also to Ashim-Bethel in Papyrus Amherst 63 (column XV).[70] The polemics against the

64. For the Tel Dan plaque B, see A. Biran, "Two Bronze Plaques and the *Ḥuṣṣot* of Dan," *IEJ* 49 (1999): 43-54. For the Bethsaida stele, see M. Bernett and O. Keel, *Mond, Stier und Kult am Stadttor, Die Stele von Betsaida (et-Tell),* OBO 161 (Fribourg: Universitätsverlag; Göttingen: Vandenhoeck & Ruprecht, 1998); Keel, *Goddesses and Trees, New Moon and Yahweh: Ancient Near Eastern Art and the Hebrew Bible,* JSOTSup 261 (Sheffield: Sheffield Academic Press, 1998), 115-20; and T. Ornan, "The Bull and Its Two Masters: Moon and Storm Deities in Relation to the Bull in Ancient Near Eastern Art," *IEJ* 51 (2001): 1-26.

65. See Steiner, "The Aramaic Text in Demotic Script," 310, 318. Steiner also compares the speech of Abijah in 2 Chronicles 13 (esp. vv. 8, 10, 12).

66. See Cooper, "Divine Names and Epithets in the Ugaritic Texts," 361; Mazar, "The 'Bull Site,'" 27-32; Hestrin, "Cult Stand from Taʿanach," 75. See further the discussion of D. Fleming, "If El is a Bull, Who is a Calf? Reflections on Religion in Second-Millennium Syria-Palestine," *EI* 26 (1999): 52*-63*.

67. Perhaps the motif of "kissing" in Hos. 13:2 should be compared with *naššĕqû-bar,* "kiss purely (?)" in Ps. 2:12, although C. A. and E. G. Briggs (*A Critical and Exegetical Commentary on the Book of Psalms,* vol. 1, ICC [Edinburgh: T. & T. Clark, 1906], 17) compare Job 31:26-28 (see chapter 4 n. 13 below).

68. See Steiner, "The Aramaic Text in Demotic Script," 313.

69. So T. J. Lewis (personal communication).

70. See Steiner, "The Aramaic Text in Demotic Script," 321. This text may provide background to the *'ašmat* of Samaria in Amos 8:14 and Eshem-Bethel, a compound divine name attested at Elephantine. See M. Cogan, "Ashima," *DDD,* 105-6.

calf in Samaria in Hosea 8:5 and 10:5 may reflect indignation at the Yahwistic symbol that was associated also with Baal. Similarly, Tobit 1:5 (LXX Vaticanus and Alexandrinus) mentions the worship of "the Baal the calf" *(tē Baal tē damalei)* in the northern kingdom. Despite the evidence for the attribution of "bull" to Baal in the first millennium, a genetic solution tracing the imagery specifically to either El or Baal may not be applicable. B. Vawter argues that "bull" means no more than chief "male,"[71] a point perhaps supported by the secular use of this term in KTU 1.15 IV 6, 8, 17, 19 and 4.360.3.[72] The anti-Baalistic polemic of Hosea 13:2 and Tobit 1:5 may also constitute a secondary rejection of this Yahwistic symbol, because bull iconography may have represented both gods in the larger environment of Phoenicia and the northern kingdom. In any case, the Canaanite tradition of the bull iconography ultimately provides the background for this rendering of Yahweh.

Common to both Yahweh and Baal was also a constellation of motifs surrounding their martial and meteorological natures. The best-known and oldest of these motifs is perhaps the defeat of cosmic foes who are variously termed Leviathan, *ʿqltn, tnn,* the seven-headed beast, Yamm, and Mot. A second-millennium seal from Mari depicts a god thrusting a spear into waters, apparently representing the conflict of the West Semitic war-god with the cosmic waters (cf. the piercing, **ḥll,* of the serpent in Job 26:13 and of *tannîn* in Isa. 51:9).[73] This conflict corresponds at Ugarit with Baal's struggle with Yamm in KTU 1.2 IV, although Yamm appears as Anat's adversary in KTU 1.3 III 43. Yamm appears as a destructive force in the Ugaritic texts (KTU 1.14 I 19-20; cf. 1.2 IV 3-4) and a proud antagonist to the divine warrior in the biblical record (Job 38:11; Ps. 89:10 [E 9]). Baal's victory over Yamm in KTU 1.2 IV 27-34 presents the possibility of Yamm's annihilation (**kly;* cf. KTU 1.3 III 38-39, 46) and then proclaims his death, an image that appears rarely in biblical material (Rev. 21:1; cf. Testament of Moses 10:6).[74] Various biblical texts depict the divine defeat of Yamm with other images: the stilling *(*šbḥ/*rgʿ)* of Yamm (Pss. 65:8 [E 7]; 89:10 [E 9]; Job 26:11); the crushing[75] *(*prr)* of

71. Vawter, "The Canaanite Background," 4.

72. For this usage, see P. D. Miller, "Animal Names as Designations in Ugaritic and Hebrew," *UF* 2 (1970): 180.

73. On this seal, see chapter 1 n. 66.

74. For a discussion of the verbs in KTU 1.2 IV 27, see J. C. de Moor, *The Seasonal Pattern in the Ugaritic Myth of Baʿlu: According to the Version of Ilimilku,* AOAT 16 (Kevelaer: Butzon & Bercker; Neukirchen: Neukirchener Verlag des Erziehungsvereins, 1971), 138-39; E. L. Greenstein, "The Snaring of Sea in the Baal Epic," *Maarav* 3/2 (1982): 195-216.

75. Citing **prr,* "crush, batter," in Mishnaic Hebrew and Akkadian, J. C. Greenfield (review of *The Ras Shamra Discoveries and the Old Testament,* by A. S. Kapelrud, *JAOS* 87 [1967]:

Yamm (Ps. 74:13; cf. the crushing, **dk'*, of Rahab in Ps. 89:11 [E 10]); the drying up *(*ḥrb)* of Yamm (Isa. 51:10); the establishment of a boundary *(gĕbûl)* for Yamm (Ps. 104:9; Jer. 5:22; cf. Prov. 8:29); the placement of a guard *(mišmār)* over Yamm (Job 7:12); and the closing of Yamm behind doors (Job 38:8, 10); compare the hacking of Rahab into pieces (**ḥṣb;* Isa. 51:9); and the scattering *(*pzr)* of cosmic enemies (Ps. 89:11 [E 10]).

A seal from Tel Asmar (ca. 2200) depicts a god battling a seven-headed dragon, a foe identified as Baal's enemy in CTA 5.1(KTU 1.5 I).3 (and reconstructed in 30) and Yahweh's adversary in Psalm 74:13 and Revelation 13:1.[76] A shell plaque of unknown provenance depicts a god kneeling before a fiery seven-headed dragon.[77] Leviathan, Baal's enemy mentioned in CTA 5.1(KTU 1.5 I).1 (and reconstructed in 28), appears as Yahweh's opponent and creature in Isaiah 27:1, Job 3:8, 26:13, 40:25 (E 41:1), Psalm 104:26, and 2 Esdras 6:49, 52.[78] In Psalm 74:13-14 (cf. Ezek. 32:2), both Leviathan and the *tannînîm* have multiple heads, the latter known as Anat's enemy in 1.83.9-10 and in a list of cosmic foes in CTA 3.3(D).35-39 (= KTU 1.3 III 38-42). This Ugaritic list includes "Sea," Yamm//"River," Nahar, Baal's great enemy in CTA 2.4 (KTU 1.2 IV). In Isaiah 11:15 the traditions of Sea//River and the seven-headed dragon appear in conflated form:

> And the Yahweh will utterly destroy the tongue of the sea of Egypt, and will wave his hand over the River with his scorching wind, and smite it into seven channels that men may cross dry-shod.

Here the destruction of Egypt combines both mythic motifs with the ancient tradition of crossing the Red Sea in Egypt. The seven-headed figure is attested

---

632) rejects the common rendering of *pôrartā* in Ps. 74:13 as "split, divide" (RSV; cf. New American Bible: "stirred up"; New Jewish Publication Society: "drove back").

76. See C. H. Gordon, "Leviathan: Symbol of Evil," in *Biblical Motifs: Origins and Transformations,* ed. A. Altmann (Cambridge, MA: Harvard Univ. Press, 1966), 4, pl. 1; J. C. Greenfield, "Notes on Some Aramaic and Mandaic Magic Bowls," *JANES* 5 (1973 = T. H. Gaster volume): 151; E. Williams-Forte, "The Snake and the Tree in the Iconography and Texts of Syria during the Bronze Age," in *Ancient Seals and the Bible,* ed. L. Gorelick and E. Williams-Forte (Malibu, CA: Undena, 1983), 18-43; G. Rendsburg, "*UT* 68 and the Tell Asmar Seal," *Orientalia* 53 (1984): 448-52. For iconographic evidence for the Syrian warrior-god piercing a serpent, see also Vanel, *L'Iconographie du Dieu,* 126; Keel, "Ancient Seals and the Bible," 309.

77. *ANEP,* 218, no. 671.

78. H. Ringgren, "Ugarit und das Alte Testament: Einige methodologische Erwägungen," *UF* 11 (1979): 719-20; Cooper, "Divine Names and Epithets in the Ugaritic Texts," 388-91; O. Loretz, "Der Tod Baals als Rache Mot für die Vernichtung Leviathans in KTU 1.5 I 1-8," *UF* 12 (1980): 404-5; D. A. Diewart, "Job 7:12: Yam, Tannin and the Surveillance of Job," *JBL* 106 (1987): 203-15.

in other biblical passages. In Psalm 89:10 the seven-headed figure is Rahab, mentioned in Isaiah 51:9-11 in the company of *tannîn* and Yamm. The seven-headed enemy also appears in Revelation 12:3, 13:1, 17:3 and in extrabiblical material, including *Qiddushin* 29b, Odes of Solomon 22:5, and *Pistis Sophia* 66.[79] Yamm appears in late apocalyptic writing as the source of the destructive beasts symbolizing successive empires (Dan. 7:3). J. Day has suggested that this imagery developed from the symbolization of political states hostile to Israel as beasts.[80] For example, Rahab stands for Egypt (Isa. 30:7; Ps. 87:4), the River for Assyria (Isa. 8:5-8; cf. 17:12-14), *tannîn* for Babylon (Jer. 51:34).[81] This type of equation is at work in a less explicit way in Psalm 18 (2 Sam. 22):4-18. In this composition, monarchic victory over political enemies (vv. 4, 18) is described in terms of a storm theophany over cosmic waters (vv. 8-17). Because of the political use of the cosmic enemies, Day suspects that a political allusion lies behind the figure of Leviathan in Isaiah 27:1.[82]

Finally, the figure of Mot, "Death," is attested in KTU 1.4 VIII–1.6 and 2.10 and in several biblical passages, including Isaiah 25:8, 28:15 and 18, Jeremiah 9:20, Hosea 13:14, Habakkuk 2:5, Psalm 18(2 Sam. 22):5-6, Revelation 21:4 (cf. Odes of Solomon 15:9; 29:4).[83] Biblical Mot is personified as a

79. Cross, *Canaanite Myth and Hebrew Epic,* 113-16, 119-20; Cooper, "Divine Names and Epithets in the Ugaritic Texts," 369-83; S. Rummel, "Narrative Structures in the Ugaritic Texts," in *Ras Shamra Parallels,* vol. 3, ed. S. Rummel, AnOr 51 (Rome: Pontifical Biblical Institute, 1981), 233-75; S. E. Loewenstamm, "The Ugaritic Myth of the Sea and Its Biblical Counterparts," *EI* 14 (1978): 96-101 = *Comparative Studies in Biblical and Oriental Literatures,* AOAT 204 (Kevelaer: Butzon & Bercker; Neukirchen-Vluyn: Neukirchener Verlag, 1980), 346-61; Day, *God's Conflict,* 18-61, esp. 24. The tradition of Yamm has been presumed to be older than the extant Ugaritic tablets of the Baal cycle dating to the fourteenth century. Cross (*Canaanite Myth and Hebrew Epic,* 113), for example, dates the earliest oral forms of the cycle to no later than the Middle Bronze Age (1800-1500). This point has been recently confirmed by a Mari letter discussed below. For further discussion, see M. S. Smith, *The Ugaritic Baal Cycle: Volume I, Introduction with Text, Translation and Commentary of KTU 1.1-1.2,* VTSup 55 (Leiden/New York/Köln: Brill, 1994), 105-14.

80. Day, *God's Conflict,* 151-78.

81. Day, *God's Conflict,* 88.

82. Day, *God's Conflict,* 112, 142-45.

83. Cooper, "Divine Names and Epithets in the Ugaritic Texts," 392-400. For the name of the god Mot as the theophoric element in Eblaitic proper names, see Lambert, "Old Testament Mythology," 132; F. Pomponio, "I nomi divini nei testi di Ebla," *UF* 15 (1983): 152. Personal names from Emar likewise have this god as the theophoric element: *iliya-mut* (Emar 109:46; 279:25; 319:8), *mutu* (Emar 32:25; 99:15), and *mu[tu?]-re'ú* (J. Huehnergard, "The Vicinity of Emar," *Revue Assyriologique* 77 [1983]: 23, text 4, line 27; cf. Eblaite name *re-u*$_9$*-mu-tù* in Pomponio, "I nomi divini," 152). Mesopotamian tradition occasionally personifies death in the figure of *mūtu,* "death," but it does not appear as a literary character (see *CAD* M/2: 317-18). The absence of an epic figure of death in Mesopotamian tradition is conspicuous, since there is

demon, in the manner of Ugaritic Mot in KTU 1.127 and Mesopotamian *mūtu*. As J. Tigay has observed, this background would explain the description of Mot in Jeremiah 9:20 better than either U. Cassuto's recourse to the episode of the window in Baal's palace (KTU 1.4 V-VII) or S. Paul's comparison with the Mesopotamian demon Lamashtu.[84] Biblical descriptions of the east wind as an instrument of divine destruction may have derived from the imagery of Mot in Canaanite tradition, although mythological dependency is not necessarily indicated in this instance. The juxtaposition of the east wind and personified Death in Hosea 13:14-15 may presuppose the mythological background of Mot as manifest in the sirocco.[85]

Like the motif of the divine foes, the biblical motif of the divine mountainous abode derives primarily from the Northwest Semitic tradition of di-

---

a plethora of motifs in the Baal-Mot section of the Baal cycle (KTU 1.4 VIII–1.6, not simply 1.5-6, as it is customarily characterized) also in Mesopotamian literary texts, such as the descent of the hero to the netherworld, the return of the hero from the netherworld, descriptions of the netherworld, and the searching and lamenting of the consort for the hero. It may be suggested tentatively that the older narrative of the hero's death appears transformed in West Semitic tradition as a story of conflict between the hero and personified death. The new form of the story may have been modeled on the conflict narrative between Baal and Yamm. Some of the points of contact between the Baal-Yamm and Baal-Mot stories have already been observed (see Rummel, "Narrative Structures in the Ugaritic Texts," 241-42). The date of this transformation is impossible to fix, although the personal names with Mot as the theophoric element from Ebla might suggest a date prior to the extant Ugaritic literary corpus. For further details, see M. S. Smith, "Death in Jeremiah IX, 20," *UF* 19 (1987): 291-93. The biblical names *ʿazmawet,* meaning "Death is strong" (2 Sam. 23:31; 1 Chron. 27:25), and *ʾăḥîmôt,* "my [divine] brother is Death" (1 Chron. 6:10), might suggest the continuation of the god Mot into Israelite religion (see McCarter, *II Samuel,* 498). One might appeal as well to personifications of Death in biblical texts as evidence of devotion to the god of death. On Mot in Ugaritic and biblical literature, see N. Tromp, *Primitive Conceptions of Death and the Netherworld in the Old Testament,* Biblica et Orientalia 21 (Rome: Pontifical Biblical Institute, 1969), 99-107; Cooper, "Divine Names and Epithets in the Ugaritic Texts," 392-400; see also J. C. de Moor, "'O death, where is thy sting?'" in *Ascribe to the Lord: Biblical and Other Studies in Memory of Peter C. Craigie,* ed. L. Eslinger and G. Taylor, JSOTSup 67 (Sheffield: JSOT, 1988), 99-107.

84. For discussion and references, see Tigay, *You Shall Have No Other Gods,* 70; F. Saracino, "Ger. 9, 20, un polmone ugaritico e la forza di Mot," *AION* 44 (1984): 539-43; Smith, "Death in Jeremiah IX, 20," 289-91; cf. J. L. Cunchillos, "Le dieu Mut, guerrier de El," *Syria* 62 (1985): 205-18. See also H. Tawil, "ʿAzazel the Prince of the Steppe: A Comparative Study," *ZAW* 92 (1980): 43-59.

85. For the possible Canaanite background for Mot manifest in the east wind, see de Moor, *Seasonal Pattern,* 115, 173-76, 180, 187-89, 207, 228, 238-39; M. S. Smith, "Interpreting the Baal Cycle," *UF* 17 (1985): 331. See now the important study of A. Fitzgerald, *The Lord of the East Wind,* CBQMS 34 (Washington, DC: The Catholic Biblical Association of America, 2002, in press), 182. Cf. S. A. Wiggins, "The Weather Under Baal: Meteorology in KTU 1.1-6," *UF* 32 (2000): 577-98.

vinely inhabited mountains, especially the Baal's mountainous home of Sapan (*ṣpn*), modern Jebel el-Aqraʿ. This dependency on language connected with Sapan in Ugaritic tradition is especially manifest in the identification of Mount Zion as *yarkĕtê ṣāpôn,* "the recesses of the north," in Psalm 48:3 (cf. Isa. 14:13) and the MT's apparent substitution of Zion for *ṣpn* in the Aramaic version of Psalm 20:3 written in Demotic.[86] According to Josephus (*Antiquities* 7.174), Belsephon was a city in the territory of Ephraim.[87] Saphon is the site of conflict between Baal and his cosmic enemies, Yamm (KTU 1.1 V 5, 18) and Mot (KTU 1.6 VI 12). The same mountain, modern Jebel el-Aqraʿ, Mount Hazzi in Hittite tradition, occurs in the narrative of conflict between the storm-god and Ullikumi.[88] In classical tradition, the same peak, Mons Cassius, was one site of conflict between Zeus and Typhon (Apollodorus, *The Library* 1.6.3; Strabo, *Geography* 16.2.7).[89] Herodotus (*History* 3.5) records that Typhon was buried by the Sirbonian Sea, which was adjacent to the Egyptian Mount Saphon.[90] Similarly, Zion is the place where Yahweh will take up battle (Joel 3:9-17, 19-21; Zech. 14:4; 2 Esdras 13:35; cf. Isa. 66:18-21; Ezekiel 38-39). The descriptions of Yahweh's taking his stand as warrior on top of Mount Zion (Isa. 31:4; Zech. 14:4; 2 Esdras 13:35) also echo depictions of the Hittite and Syrian storm-gods standing with each foot on a moun-

86. Gaster, *Thespis,* 181-83; Clifford, *The Cosmic Mountain,* 142-44; A. Robinson, "Zion and *Sāphôn* in Psalm XLVIII 3," *VT* 24 (1974): 118-23; M. Astour, "Place Names," in *Ras Shamra Parallels II,* ed. L. Fisher, AnOr 50 (Rome: Pontifical Biblical Institute, 1975), 318-24; J. J. M. Roberts, "*Ṣapôn* in Job 28:7," *Biblica* 56 (1975): 554-57; Mullen, *The Divine Council,* 154-55. Cf. divinized Mount Hazzi (= Saphon) in Emar 472:58′, 473:9′, and 474:21′; **ṣpn* as a theophoric element in the Phoenician name *bdṣpn* (CIS 108). For Baal Saphon in Egyptian and Phoenician sources, see R. Stadelmann, *Syrisch-Palästinensische Gottheiten in Ägypten,* Probleme der Ågyptologie 5 (Leiden: Brill, 1967), 32-47; Pope, "Baal-Hadad," in Pope and Röllig, *Syrien,* 257-58; W. Fauth, "Das Kasion-Gebirge und Zeus Kasios. Die antike Tradition und ihre vorderorientalischen Grundlagen," *UF* 22 (1990): 105-18. According to Achilles Tatius, *Adventures* 3.6, "at Pelusium [in Egypt] is the holy statue of Zeus of Mount Casius; in it the god is represented so young that he seems more like Apollo" (W. Gaselee, *Achilles Tatius,* Loeb Classical Library [London: William Heinemann; New York: G. P. Putnam's Sons, 1917], 146-47). On the Demotic text of Psalm 20, see nn. 22 and 23 above.

87. Thackeray and Marcus, *Josephus, Antiquities V,* 454-55.

88. *ANET,* 123; H. G. Güterbock, "The Song of Ullikumi," *Journal of Cuneiform Studies* 5 (1951): 145; Clifford, *The Cosmic Mountain,* 59-60.

89. J. G. Frazer, *Apollodorus: The Library,* Loeb Classical Library (London: William Heinemann; New York: G. P. Putnam's Sons, 1921), 1.48-49; H. L. Jones, *The Geography of Strabo 8,* Loeb Classical Library (Cambridge, MA: Harvard Univ. Press; London: William Heinemann, 1930), 244-45. See Day, *God's Conflict,* 32.

90. A. D. Godley, *Herodotus,* vol. 2, *Books 3 and 4,* Loeb Classical Library (Cambridge, MA: Harvard Univ. Press; London: William Heinemann, 1921), 8-9; Day, *God's Conflict,* 33 n. 92.

tain.[91] Saphon and Zion share a number of epithets. For example, KTU 1.3 III 13-31 (cf. IV 7-20), cited in full in the previous section, applies *qdš*, "holy place," *nʿm*, "pleasant place," and *nḥlt*, "inheritance," to Baal's mountain. Similarly, Psalms 46:5 and 48:2 describe Zion as **qōdeš* (cf. Exod. 15:13; Pss. 87:1; 93:5; KAI 17:1, 78:5 [?]), while Psalm 27:4 calls Yahweh's mountain *nōʿam* (cf. Ps. 16:6).[92] As Greenfield has observed, *nōʿam* in Psalm 27:4 is followed in the next verse by wordplay or paronomasia on the root **ṣpn*.[93] Yahweh's mountain is called a *naḥălāh*, "portion" (Ps. 79:1; Jer. 12:7; cf. Exod. 15:17; Ps. 16:6). The epithets for Zion and the way they are listed together in Psalm 48:2-3 likewise recall the titles for Sapan in KTU 1.3 III 29-31.[94]

The mountainous temple home from which Baal utters his voice and rains lavishly upon the earth (KTU 1.4 V-VII) appears not only in descriptions of Yahweh roaring from Zion (Joel 3:16; Amos 1:2) or giving forth rains (Isa. 30:19; Jer. 3:3; 5:24; 10:13; 14:4; 51:16; Amos 4:7) but also in postexilic discussions of the rebuilding of the temple in Jerusalem. The tradition of the temple home that guarantees the life-giving rains underlies the relationship between tithe and temple in Malachi 3:10. This passage reflects the notion that payment of the tithe to the temple would induce Yahweh to open the windows of heaven and pour down crop-producing rains. Similarly, Haggai 1:7-11 attributes drought and scarcity to the failure to rebuild the temple.[95]

91. For examples of the Anatolian storm-god standing on mountains in Hittite iconography, see R. L. Alexander, "The Mountain-God at Eflatun Pinar," *Anatolian Studies* 2 (1968): 77-85; idem, "A Hittite Cylinder Seal in the Fitzwilliam Museum," *Anatolian Studies* 25 (1975): 111-17; H. G. Güterbock, in K. Bittel et al., *Das hethitische Felsheiligtum Yazilikaya* (Berlin: Gebr. Mann Verlag, 1975), 169-70, Tafel 42d; Lambert, "Trees, Snakes and Gods," 443. For this iconography on Hittite seals from Ras Shamra, see C. F. A. Schaeffer, *Ugaritica 3: Sceaux et cylindres hittites, epée gravée du cartouche de Mineptah, tablettes chypro-minoennes et autres découvertes nouvelles de Ras Shamra*, Mission de Ras Shamra 8 (Paris: Geuthner, 1956), 24-25 figs. 32-33, 48-49 figs. 66-67, and 50 figs. 68-69. For iconography of the Syrian warrior-god standing on a mountain, see Vanel, *L'Iconographie du Dieu*, 39, 61, 79, 83, 114, 118, 162. See also M. Dijkstra, "The Weather-God on Two Mountains," *UF* 23 (1991): 127-40.

92. Greenfield, "The Hebrew Bible and Canaanite Literature," 553-54.

93. For literary play on the name of Baal's mountain in Hos. 13:12, Ps. 27:5, and Job 26:7-8, see Greenfield, "The Hebrew Bible and Canaanite Literature," 551, 553-54.

94. Clifford, *The Cosmic Mountain*, 143 n. 63; J. Levenson, *Theology of the Program of the Restoration of Ezekiel 40–48*, HSM 10 (Missoula, MT: Scholars, 1976), 15-16. For further Ugaritic connections with Psalm 48, see also M. L. Barré, "The Seven Epithets of Zion in Ps 48, 2-3," *Biblica* 69 (1988): 557-63; M. S. Smith, "God and Zion: Form and Meaning in Psalm 48," *SEL* 6 (1989): 67-77.

95. See Pope, "Baal Worship," 12. See G. Anderson, *Sacrifices and Offerings in Ancient Israel: Studies in Their Social and Political Importance*, HSM 41 (Atlanta, GA: Scholars, 1987), 91-122.

Yahweh's role as the divine source of rain appears elsewhere in postexilic prophecy (Zech. 10:1). Joel 4 (E 3) presents various aspects of the mountain tradition. It is the divine home (4:17 [E 3:17]), the location of Yahweh's roar (4:16 [E 3:16]), the site of divine battle (4:9-15 [E 3:9-15]) with heavenly hosts (4:11-13 [E 3:11-13]; cf. 2:1-11), and the origin of the divine rains issuing in terrestrial fertility (4:18 [E 3:18]).

In sum, the motifs associated with Baal in Canaanite literature are widely manifest in Israelite religion. The Baal cycle (KTU 1.1-6) presents the sequence of defeating the enemy, Sea, followed by the building of the divine palace for the divine warrior, and concluding with the vanquishing of the enemy, Death. This pattern of features appears in a wide variety of biblical texts describing divine presence and action. Rabbinic aggadah and Christian literature continue these motifs. Indeed, the defeat of Sea, the building of the heavenly palace, and the destruction of death belong to the future divine transformation of the world in Revelation 21:1-4. These motifs are of further importance for the long life that some of them enjoyed; for example, the motif of Leviathan is attested in religious documents into the modern period.[96]

3. The Role of the Monarchy

The presentation of Yahweh in imagery associated with Baal in Canaanite tradition played a role in Israel's politics. Yahweh, a tribal god of the highlands, emerged as the national god of Israel (1 Kings 20:23).[97] As in Mesopotamia and Egypt, this god became the divine "king" (Ps. 10:16; cf. Exod. 15:18;

96. In rabbinic tradition Leviathan was identified as a big fish (*Leviticus Rabbah* 22:10; David Kimchi on Isa. 27A). As in 2 Baruch 29:4-8, later rabbinic sources mention Leviathan as food for the righteous at the messianic banquet (*Baba Batra* 75b; *Leviticus Rabbah* 22:10; *Midrash Tehillim* 18). Leviathan was invoked in two Aramaic bowls (see Gordon, "Leviathan: Symbol of Evil," 8; J. C. Greenfield, "Notes on Some Aramaic and Mandaic Magic Bowls," 151). On Leviathan in Arabic tradition, see Wensinck, *The Ocean*, 3, 25. Leviathan was portrayed in thirteenth- and fourteenth-century Hebrew manuscripts and on Seder plates in fifteenth-century Jewish communities in northern Italy (see J. Guttmann, "Leviathan, Behemoth and Ziz: Jewish Messianic Symbols in Art," in *No Graven Images: Studies in Art and the Hebrew Bible*, ed. J. Gutmann [New York: KTAV, 1971], 225-30). Leviathan has come into modern parlance as the largest or most massive thing of its kind, including various large sea animals or seagoing vessels, inspiring the title of Thomas Hobbes's treatise on the state, *Leviathan* (1651 English edition; 1668 Latin edition).

97. See Fohrer, *History of Israelite Religion*, 125; Ahlström, "The Travels of the Ark," 141-48; Stager, "Archaeology of the Family in Ancient Israel," 1.

1 Sam. 8:7; Pss. 47:9; 93:1; 96:10; 97:1; 99:1; 146:10, etc.) and national god.[98] In order to describe the powerful god that brought them to prominence, the Davidic dynasts drew on older, traditional language used for the divine warrior, known from Judges 5:3-5 and elsewhere (cf. 1 Sam. 7:10; 12:18).[99] A dramatic example of the patron god fighting on behalf of the Davidic king is Psalm 18 (= 2 Sam. 22). Verses 8-19 describe Yahweh in terms associated with Baal's battle (KTU 1.2 IV; cf. 1.4 VII 8-9, 38-39), fighting for the king and saving him from destruction. Verses 29-45 depict Yahweh's enabling the monarch to conquer his enemies in battle.[100] Psalm 2, a royal psalm, alludes to the enemies who stand against Yahweh and "his anointed," the king.[101] Psalm 89 likewise parallels the victorious power of Yahweh in verses 5-18 with the divine favor that Yahweh bestows upon the Davidic monarch in verses 19-37. In verse 26 Yahweh extends his power to the monarch in language associated with the god Baal: "I will set his hand on Sea and his right hand on River(s)." As many commentators have observed,[102] Sea and River(s) are titles of Baal's enemy in the first major section of the Ugaritic Baal cycle (KTU 1.1-2). The

98. See J. A. Soggin, "The Davidic-Solomonic Kingdom," in *Israelite and Judaean History,* ed. J. H. Hayes and J. M. Miller, OTL (London: SCM, 1977), 361-63, 370-73.

99. Moon-Kang (*Divine War,* 224) describes the political dimensions of the divine warrior: "the traditions and the historical and annalistic records of the Davidic battles show that the idea of YHWH's help and intervention in the battles began to appear in the rising period of the Davidic kingdom." Cross, Freedman, and others date Exodus 15, Hab. 3:3-15, and other biblical compositions to the premonarchic period, while some commentators prefer a monarchic date, conforming more closely to the point that the monarchy played a significant role in the patterning of Yahweh after Baal (for the range of opinions on Exodus 15, see Moon-Kang, *Divine War,* 115-16 n. 9; for the dates proposed for Hab. 3:3-15, see Hiebert, *God of My Victory,* 119-20; cf. Floyd, "Oral Tradition," 272-300). The premonarchic date of the Song of Deborah in Judges 5 is more secure (see Moon-Kang, *Divine War,* 179-80; and Floyd, "Oral Tradition," 233-66).

100. Concerning Psalm 18 = 2 Samuel 22, see chapter 1, section 5.

101. On the political aspects of Psalm 2, see H. J. Kraus, *Psalms 1–59: A Commentary,* trans. H. C. Oswald (Minneapolis, MN: Augsburg, 1988), 125-32.

102. G. W. Ahlström, *Psalm 89: Eine Liturgie aus dem Ritual des leidenden Königs* (Lund: Håkan Ohlssons Boktryckeri, 1959), 108-9; Cross, *Canaanite Myth and Hebrew Epic,* 258; Clifford, "Psalm 89: A Lament over the Davidic Ruler's Continued Failure," *HTR* 73 (1980): 35-47; P. G. Mosca, "Ugarit and Daniel 7: A Missing Link," *Biblica* 67 (1986): 496-517. For the political significance of Psalm 89, see further Cross, *Canaanite Myth and Hebrew Epic,* 160-62, 257-61. Despite the suggestive parallel of Yamm's title *ṯpṭ nhr,* "Judge River," there are no text-critical grounds for interpreting BH *nhrwt* in the singular, although the word might be interpreted as a plural of majesty (for discussion, see U. Cassuto, *Biblical and Oriental Studies,* vol. 2, *Bible and Ancient Oriental Texts,* trans. I. Abrahams (Jerusalem: Magnes, 1975], 84; Dahood, *Psalms II,* 120-21). In texts dating to New Kingdom Egypt, the military prowess of the pharaoh is compared with Baal's martial abilities (see EA 147:13-15; *ANET,* 249-50; M. Lichtheim, *Ancient Egyptian Literature,* vol. 3, 65, 67, 69, 71; Gaál, "Tuthmōsis as a Storm-God?" 29-37).

psalm thus draws on the imagery of Yahweh's victory over Sea and other cosmic enemies in verses 9-10 and extends this imagery to the king in verse 26 at a time of royal decline, indicated by verses 38-51. Psalm 72:8 likewise alludes to Sea and River in describing the expanse of the Davidic territory: "May he have dominion from sea to sea, and from the River to the ends of the earth!" *(wĕyērd miyyām ʿad-yām ûminnāhār ʿad-ʾapsê-ʾāreṣ).*[103] While "the River" historically refers to the Euphrates, it may also evoke the mythic pair of "Sea" and "River." It appears that 2 Samuel 5:20 plays on the storm imagery of Baal. After his defeat of the Philistines at Baal-perazim, David is quoted as saying, "The Lord has broken through my enemies before me, like a bursting flood." The same verse then gives these words as the basis for the place-name: "Therefore the name of that place is called Baal-perazim."[104]

Other motifs known from the Ugaritic traditions of Baal appear in Israelite royal theology. J. J. M. Roberts has argued that the Baal motifs of divine warrior and his mountain developed within the Zion tradition during the reigns of David and Solomon.[105] According to T. N. D. Mettinger,[106] the divine title *ṣbʾt* accrued to Yahweh during the reign of David and expressed Yahweh's functions as divine patron and national god of the Davidic dynasty. S. Moon-Kang attributes the same function and setting to the divine titles *gbr* and *ʿzr.*[107] That the theological self-understanding of the dynasty and not simply worship of Baal inspired this divine warrior language in Israel may be deduced from the fact that the language of the divine warrior emerged independently in various ancient Near Eastern locales, and not infrequently under the impetus of newly emerging political units.[108] The inclusion of traditional language of the

103. The use of the singular **nāhār* in Ps. 72:8 differs strikingly from the general use of the plural in BH texts containing the cosmic terms "Sea" and "River" (see the previous note). On this verse, see H. J. Kraus, *Psalmen 60–150,* BKAT 15/2 (Neukirchen-Vluyn: Neukirchener Verlag des Erziehungsvereins, 1972), 498.

104. On 2 Sam. 5:20, see McCarter, *II Samuel,* 154. See also A. Mazar, "Three Israelite Sites in the Hills of Judah and Ephraim," *BA* 45 (1982): 170.

105. J. J. M. Roberts, "Zion in the Theology of the Davidic-Solomonic Empire," in *Studies in the Period of David and Solomon and Other Essays: Papers Read at the International Symposium for Biblical Studies, Tokyo, 5-7 December 1979,* ed. T. Ishida (Winona Lake, IN: Eisenbrauns, 1982), 93-108. See also Moon-Kang, *Divine War,* 202. Freedman (*Pottery, Poetry, and Prophecy,* 79, 93-107) characterizes the tenth century and following as a period of "monarchic syncretism" with respect to divine titles (e.g., *ʿly;* see above section 2).

106. T. N. D. Mettinger, "YHWH SABAOTH — The Heavenly King on the Cherubim Throne," in *Studies in the Period of David and Solomon and Other Essays: Papers Read at the International Symposium for Biblical Studies, Tokyo, 5-7 December 1979,* ed. T. Ishida, 117.

107. Moon-Kang, *Divine War,* 197-98.

108. Moon-Kang, *Divine War.*

warrior-god suited Yahweh, the patron deity of a newly emerging nation-state. The concept of Yahweh as the divine warrior therefore did not derive simply from the worship of Baal; it was also the product of the Davidic polity. Indeed, it may be surmised that Baal continued to be popular in Israel precisely because the monarchy embraced his titles and imagery to describe its patron god. The Iron Age development of the Mesopotamian city gods, Marduk of Babylon and Assur of Assur, illustrates further the dependency of martial language for Yahweh on the Israelite/Canaanite literary tradition. Like Yahweh, these two warrior deities had cults that gave expression to the newly emerging military powers in Babylon and Assur.[109] These two gods were attributed imagery found in the literary traditions of the local regions. Similarly, biblical descriptions of Yahweh, the national deity of the newly emerging state, drew on the traditions of the Israelite/Canaanite matrix.

Scholars have long focused on the parallels between Baal in the Ugaritic texts and Yahweh in biblical material. Not only can the imagery and titles of Yahweh as storm-god be found in the Ugaritic texts; the political background of these descriptions of Yahweh can also be traced to the second-millennium west Semitic material from the city of Mari on the Euphrates River. A second-millennium letter from Mari confirms the political function of the storm-god's conflict with the cosmic sea. The letter, which dates toward the end of the reign of the king Zimri-Lim of Mari, is addressed to him by the prophet Nur-Sin of Aleppo. Quoting the storm-god Adad, the text states: "When you [Zimri-Lim] sat on the throne of your father, I gave you the weapon(s) with which I fought against Sea *(tâmtum).*"[110] This text provides the first external textual witness to the West Semitic conflict myth in the Middle Bronze Age. In the version from Mari, the storm-god is identified as Addu, the Akkadian equivalent to Haddu *(hd),* equivalent to Baal in Ugaritic mythic texts. A list of divinities at Ugarit also supplies the equivalence of Addu with Baal.[111] The god ^{d}IM *be-el ḫuršân ḫazi,*

109. See Introduction, section 1; and the following discussion.

110. J. M. Durand, "Le mythologème du combat entre le dieu de l'orage et la mer en Mésopotamie," *MARI* 7 (1993): 41-61; P. Bordreuil and D. Pardee, "Le combat de Baʿlu avec Yammu d'après les textes ougaritiques," *MARI* 7 (1993): 63-70; Smith, *The Origins of Biblical Monotheism,* 158-59. Concerning the prophet Nur-Sin of Aleppo, see B. Lafont, "Le roi de Mari et les prophètes du dieu Adad," *Revue assyriologique* 78 (1984): 7-18.

111. RS 20.24 and RS 1929.17 (KTU 1.47), treated by Nougayrol, *Ug V,* 44-45, 47-48; cf. the readings in KTU 1.47 and 1.118. See F. B. Knutson, "Divine Names and Epithets in the Akkadian Texts," in *Ras Shamra Parallels: The Texts from Ugarit and the Hebrew Bible,* vol. 3, ed. S. Rummel, AnOr 51 (Rome: Pontificium Institutum Biblicum, 1981), 474-76. On Ugaritic *hd,* see M. H. Pope, "Baal-Hadad," in Pope and Röllig, *Syrien,* 253-54; P. J. van Zijl, *Baal: A Study of the Texts in Connexion with Baal in the Ugaritic Epics,* AOAT 10 (Kevelaer: Butzon und Bercker; Neukirchen-Vluyn: Neukirchener Verlag des Erziehungsvereins, 1972), 346-51; Cross, *Canaan-*

"Adad, lord of mount Hazzi," corresponds to *bʿl ṣpn*, "Baal Saphon." The same lists provides the correlation of *ym*, "Yamm" (Sea), and ᵈ*tâmtum*, "Tiamat" (Sea). A comparable witness to the deified sea occurs in an Akkadian text from Ras Shamra. In RS 17.33 obv. 4′, the list of deities serving as witnesses to a treaty between the Hittite king Mursilis and his Ugaritic royal vassal Niqmepa includes [ᵈA].*AB.BA.GAL*, that is, *[tâ]mtu rabitu*, "the great Sea."[112] The West Semitic deity of the cosmic ocean is also attested at Mari. Some proper names at Mari include *ym* as the theophoric element.[113] According to A. Malamat, the offering that Yahdun-Lim of Mari makes to the "Ocean" *(a-ab-ba)* at the Mediterranean Sea reflects the West Semitic cult of the sea-god.[114] A text from Emar attests to offerings to Yamm (ᵈ*Ia-a-mi*).[115]

By contrast with the conflict between Baal and Yamm portrayed in the Baal cycle (KTU 1.2 IV), the Mari text focuses on the human, political function of the cosmic weapons as gifts from the storm-god to the king. The power of the storm-god, the king's patron, reinforces the power of the king. Divine weapons elsewhere play an important role in expressing royal power. In both Old Babylonian and neo-Assyrian texts, kings are described as wielding the weapons of particular martial gods.[116] One letter preserved at Mari was sent to Yashub-Yahad, king of Dir, from Yarim-lim, king of Aleppo. In this letter Yarim-lim declares, "I will show you the terrible weapons of Addu (*GIŠ.TUKUL.ḪI.A.* ᵈIM) and of Yarim-lim."[117] In these texts, the king dem-

ite Myth and Hebrew Epic, 10-11, 58. On *hd* especially in first-millennium sources, see J. C. Greenfield, "Aspects of Aramaean Religion," in *Ancient Israelite Religion: Essays in Honor of Frank Moore Cross*, ed. P. D. Miller, Jr., P. D. Hanson, and S. D. McBride, 67-70.

112. *PRU IV*, 85.

113. See Huffmon, *Amorite Personal Names*, 120, 124, 210; I. J. Gelb, *A Computer-Aided Analysis of Amorite*, Assyriological Studies 21 (Chicago: Oriental Institute of the University of Chicago, 1980), 272-73; J. M. Durand, "Différentes questions à propos de la Religion," *MARI* 5 (1987): 613-14. Cf. the name *aḫiyami* at Taanach (see A. E. Glock, "Texts and Archaeology at Tell Taʿannak," *Berytus* 31 [1983]: 60).

114. See A. Malamat, "ʾlhwtw šl hym htykwn btqst prh-ʾwgryty" [The Divinity of the Mediterranean Sea in a pre-Ugaritic text]," in *Mhqrym bmqrʾ: ywsʾym lʾwr bmlʾt mʾh šnh lhwldtw šl mʺd qʿswṭw* [Research in the Bible; Published on the occasion of the hundredth anniversary of the birth of M. D. Cassuto] (Jerusalem: Magnes, 1987), 184-88; cf. Malamat, "Campaigns to the Mediterranean by Iahdunlim and Early Mesopotamian Rulers," in *Studies in Honor of Benno Landsberger on His Seventy-fifth Birthday, April 21, 1965*, Assyriological Studies 16 (Chicago: Univ. of Chicago Press, 1965), 367.

115. Emar 373:92′: *a-na* ᵈ*INANNA ša a-bi u* ᵈ*Ia-a-mi 2 ta-pal x[*, "à Astarté de la Mer et à Iammu, les deux pai[res . . . ditto" (an offering).

116. *CAD* K:52-55.

117. G. Dossin, "Une lettre de Iarîm-Lim, roi d'Alep, à Iasub-Iahad, roi de Dîr," *Syria* 33 (1956): 67, line 32; *CAD* K:54; D. Charpin, "De la Joie à l'Orage," *MARI* 5 (1987): 661.

onstrates his great power by invoking the power of the divine weapon. The Mari letter citing the words of Nur-Sin of Aleppo mentions the power of the divine weapons of Addu, but it also refers to the West Semitic conflict myth. The divine gift of weapons enhances the relationship between the patron god and his king by invoking the patron god's victory over the cosmic enemy. The power of the king over his enemies mirrors on the cosmic level the victory of the storm-god over his adversary.

The Baal cycle indicates that the martial language for Yahweh derived from the Canaanite sphere. That this mythic material was employed in such a political manner in the Canaanite sphere is less evident from the Baal cycle. Kingship, however, is a central concern of the Ugaritic Baal cycle, which may point to a political use for the Baal-Yamm conflict (and perhaps for the whole of the cycle), similar to the political function of the Mari letter.[118] The production of the Baal cycle may have served the function of reinforcing the kingship not only of the god Baal but also the Ugaritic dynasty. Indeed, the names of the Ugaritic kings reflect the special relationship between Baal and the Ugaritic dynasty. The kings Niqmaddu I and II took an Addu name. The name *nqmd* consists of two parts, the verb **nqm* and the theophoric element *(h)d;* it may be translated "Addu avenged."[119] Another dynast bears the name *yʿḏrd,* which means "May Addu help."[120] It may be noted that only these three dynasts have names with theophoric elements, and in all three instances the theophoric element is *(h)d.* The dynasty perhaps considered Baal/Haddu to be its special divine patron, and the transmission and final production of the Baal cycle may have resulted in part from the political values that it expressed on behalf of the dynasty.

Comparable political contexts have been proposed for the Enuma Elish, a Mesopotamian work exhibiting many similarities with the Baal cycle.[121] T. Jacobsen proposes that the similarities are due to dependence. He argues that the conflict between Marduk and Tiamat was modeled on a West Semitic

118. See Smith, "Interpreting the Baal Cycle," 330-31 n. 95. King Arḫalbu's invocations of Baal in RS 16.144.9, 12-13 (*PRU III*, 76) are perhaps pertinent: ^{d}*Baʿlu (IŠKUR) li-ra-ḫi-iṣ-šu,* "may Baal inundate him"; ^{d}*Baʿlu (IŠKUR) bel (EN) ḫuršân (ḪUR.SAG) Ḫazi li-ra-ḫi-iṣ-šu,* "may Baal, the lord of Mount Hazzi, inundate him." See further discussion of the Baal cycle in this context in Smith, *The Ugaritic Baal Cycle,* 105-14.

119. The dissimilation of /dd/ to /nd/ in the theophoric element **andu* in *ni-iq/niq-ma-an-du* is not exceptional (see Roberts, *The Earliest Semitic Pantheon,* 13). On **nqm,* see W. T. Pitard, "Amarna *ekēmu* and Hebrew *nāqam,*" *Maarav* 3/1 (1982): 5-25.

120. Gröndahl, *Die Personennamen,* 17, 68.

121. For proposals for the historical setting of Enuma Elish, see T. W. Mann, *Divine Presence and Guidance in Israelite Traditions: The Typology of Exaltation* (Baltimore: Johns Hopkins Univ. Press, 1977), 48-51.

version of the conflict tradition, as attested in the Baal cycle.[122] Like the Mari letter, Enuma Elish features Tiamat as the cosmic sea, but unlike the Mari letter, Enuma Elish presents Marduk, the Babylonian divine patron, as Tiamat's enemy. The equivalence between Marduk and Addu is expressly made in Enuma Elish 7:119, where Marduk's forty-seventh name is Addu.[123] Likewise, this equivalence is attested in another text delineating various deities as aspects of Marduk: "Adad (is) Marduk of rain."[124] The common Amorite traditions underlying the dynasties of Ugarit, Mari, and Babylon would appear to bolster Jacobsen's view.[125] Behind the Ugaritic myth of Baal and Yamm, and

122. T. Jacobsen, "The Battle Between Marduk and Tiamat," *JAOS* 88 (1968): 104-8; idem, "Religious Drama in Ancient Mesopotamia," in *Unity and Diversity,* ed. H. Goedicke and J. J. M. Roberts (Baltimore: Johns Hopkins Univ. Press, 1975), 75-76. It has been argued also that the West Semitic conflict myth was transmitted through Mesopotamia to India, reflected in material in the Rig Veda concerning the storm-god, Indra, who defeats the cosmic enemy, Vrtra (so A. K. Lahiri, *Vedic Vrtra* [Delhi: Motital Banarsidass, 1984]; for texts 1.32, 1.85, 1.165, 1.170, and 1.171, see W. O'Flaherty, *The Rig Veda: An Anthology* [Middlesex, England: Penguin, 1981], 148-51, 167-72; H. D. Velankar, "Hymns to Indra in Mandala I," *Journal of Bombay University* 20/2 [1950]: 17-34). Gaster long ago compared the West Semitic, East Semitic, and Vedic material (*Thespis,* 150, 164-65, 170). The evidence rests largely on the comparison between the storm-gods, Baal and Indra. Both gods defeat a cosmic enemy with the aid of divine weapons fashioned by a craftsman-god. Furthermore, like Marduk (cf. Enuma Elish 4:39-40; see *ANET,* 66), both storm-gods are described as having meteorological helpers (see O'Flaherty, *The Rig Veda,* 167-72). Baal's meteorological entourage includes "your clouds, your winds, your chariots (?), your rains, . . . your seven youths, your eight lads" (KTU 1.5 V 6-9). Indra's entourage includes his assistants, the Maruts; they are youthful warriors, riding chariots that produce rains (O'Flaherty, *The Rig Veda,* 166-72). On this point, see further N. Wyatt, "Baal's Seven Boars," *UF* 19 (1987): 391-98. It is interesting to note the observation of M. Müller (*Vedic Hymns: Part 1, Hymns to Maruts, Rudra, Vâya, and Vâtra,* The Sacred Books of the East 32 [Oxford: At the Clarendon, 1891], 58) that the description of the Maruts tossing clouds across the sea is unexpected for an inland people. This is precisely the type of argument that Jacobsen employs for his theory of transmission of the West Semitic conflict myth to Mesopotamia. The theory espoused by Lahiri, however, is marred by poor data and problematic historical reconstructions (J. A. Santucci, review of *Vedic Vrtra,* by A. K. Lahiri, *Religious Studies Review* 14/1 [1988]: 89; see also J. Z. Smith, review of *God's Battle with the Monster: A Study in Biblical Imagery,* by M. K. Wakeman, *JBL* 94 [1975]: 442-44; Wyatt, "Baal's Seven Boars," 396-98). The craftsman-god is absent from Enuma Elish, casting some doubt on this text as the middle step in the transmission of the conflict myth.

123. *ANET,* 72; F. M. Th. Böhl, "Die fünfzig Namen des Marduk," *Archiv für Orientforschung* 11 (1936): 210. On the fifty names of Marduk, see also Bottéro, "Les noms de Marduk," 5-28. That the divine hero varied according to locale is evident from the Assyrian version that substitutes Assur for Marduk (see *ANET,* 62 n. 28). I thank Professor Olyan for bringing this point to my attention.

124. On this text, see Böhl, "Die fünfzig Namen des Marduk," 210; Lambert, "Historical Development of the Mesopotamian Pantheon," 198.

125. Further evidence of the common Amorite traditions behind the Ugaritic and Babylo-

explicit in the Mari letter, is a political function of divine support for a human monarch. To judge from its biblical attestations, the political use of the conflict myth belonged to the Canaanite patrimony of monarchic Israel. It was noted that the cosmic enemies appear as political symbols for states hostile to Israel, for example, Rahab for Egypt (Isa. 30:7; Ps. 87:4). The background for the equation of political enemies with cosmic ones may perhaps be located in the parallelism between the enemies of the god and king, illustrated in Israelite tradition by Psalm 18 (2 Sam 22):17-18 and in earlier West Semitic tradition in the Mari letter.

In view of the political background for motifs associated with the storm-god at Ugarit, Mari, Babylon, and Israel, scholarly reconstructions for the setting of the language describing Yahweh's storm theophany deserve some further consideration. Some scholars have argued that the Feast of Tabernacles every fall (Exod. 23:16; 34:22) included the enthronement of Yahweh.[126] According to S. Mowinckel,[127] the theory's most vigorous proponent,

---

nian dynasties includes their common tribal ancestor, Ugaritic *ddn/dtn* (see KTU 1.15 III 2-4, 13-15; 1.124.4; 1.161.10), and *di-ta-nu* in the genealogy of the Hammurapi dynasty of Babylon and *di-ta-na* and *di-da-a-nu* of Assyrian King List A. For the evidence, see E. Lipiński, "Ditanu," in *Studies in the Bible and the Ancient Near East Presented to Samuel E. Loewenstamm,* ed. Y. Avishur and J. Blau (Jerusalem: E. Rubinstein's Publishing House, 1978), 91-99; J. C. de Moor, "Rapi'uma — Rephaim," *ZAW* 88 (1968): 332-33; K. A. Kitchen, "The King List of Ugarit," *UF* 9 (1977): 142; M. H. Pope, "Notes on the Rephaim Texts from Ugarit," in *Essays on the Ancient Near East in Memory of Jacob Joel Finkelstein,* ed. M. de Jong Ellis, Memoirs of the Connecticut Academy of Arts and Sciences (Hamden, CT: Archon Books, 1977), 179; D. Pardee, "Visiting Ditanu — The Text of RS 24.272," *UF* 15 (1981): 127-40; B. Levine and J. M. de Tarragon, "Dead Kings and Rephaim: The Patrons of the Ugaritic Dynasty," *JAOS* 104 (1984): 655. On the genealogy of the Hammurapi dynasty, see J. J. Finkelstein, "The Genealogy of the Hammurapi Dynasty," *JCS* 20 (1966): 95-118; W. G. Lambert, "Another Look at Hammurabi's Ancestors," *JCS* 22 (1968-69): 1-2. Concerning the Assyrian King List, see I. J. Gelb, "Two Assyrian King Lists," *JNES* 13 (1954): 209-30, esp. 210 line 5, 211 line 4; A. R. Millard, "Fragments of Historical Texts from Nineveh: Middle Assyrian and Later Kings," *Iraq* 32 (1970): 167-76, especially 175 line 5. See also A. Malamat, "King Lists of the Old Babylonian Period and Biblical Genealogies," *JAOS* 88 (1968): 163-73; and R. R. Wilson, *Genealogy and History in the Biblical World,* Yale Near Eastern Researches 7 (New Haven: Yale Univ. Press, 1977), 87-100, 107-14. See also the names of two monarchs of the first dynasty of Babylon, *sa-am-su/si-di-ta-nu,* and the name of one ruler in the ancestral line, *a-bi-di-ta-an* (Lipiński, "Ditanu," 92-93). The name of Ammi-ditana occurs in the genealogy of the Hammurapi dynasty and in the Ras Shamra recension of *ḪAR-ra = ḫubullu* (B. Landsberger, E. Reiner, and M. Civil, *Materials for the Sumerian Lexicon XI: The Series Ḫar-ra = ḫubullu, Tablets 20-24* [Rome: Pontificium Institutum Biblicum, 1974], 48, col. 4, lines 20-21, and 52, line 26). The latter attests to *di-da-na* as well (Landsberger, Reiner, and Civil, *Materials,* 48, col. 4, line 22, and 52, line 28).

126. Day, *God's Conflict,* 18-37.

127. S. Mowinckel, *The Psalms in Israel's Worship,* 2 vols. (Oxford: Basil Blackwell, 1962), 1.16-92, 2.222-50; see also Gaster, *Thespis,* 442-59.

the enthronement aspect of the festival is reflected in numerous psalms containing the motif of Yahweh's battle, often in the storm, against the cosmic enemies. These texts include Psalms 65, 93, and 96–99. The burden of proof for this theory has fallen largely on two pieces of data. The superscription of Psalm 29 in the Septuagint associates this psalm with the Feast of Tabernacles. Zechariah 14:16-17 specifically refers to the celebration of Yahweh's kingship in connection with the Feast of Tabernacles:

> Then every one that survives of all the nations that have come against Jerusalem shall go up year after year to worship the King, Yahweh of hosts, and to keep the feast of booths. And if any of the families of the earth do not go up to Jerusalem to worship the King, the Yahweh of hosts, there will be no rain upon them.

As J. Day notes,[128] the reference to rain in verse 17 accords with the motif of Yahweh's control over the cosmic enemies of the water. Although this passage is postexilic, some of its motifs may have enjoyed a long history in Israelite tradition. A pre-exilic setting for the celebration of divine kingship in the context of Tabernacles is plausible. The setting of Psalm 65, which celebrates in the temple the bounty of the autumn harvest, is possibly a Tabernacles psalm. Day observes that Psalm 65:6-9 (E 5-8) recalls Yahweh's victory over the cosmic waters.[129] It may be further noted that the motif of verse 9 (E 8) is precisely a meteorological one. The "signs" witnessed at the ends of the earth are the thundering of the heavens and earth that announce the imminent arrival of the life-supporting rains (cf. KTU 1.15 III 2-11; cf. 1.3 III 13-31, IV 7-20). Psalm 65 and Zechariah 14:16-17 indicate the meteorological importance of rain in the early autumn. That divine power over the waters was celebrated in the autumnal feast in Jerusalem would seem evident from Psalm 65 and might be inferred from other psalms.[130] While some psalms celebrating Yahweh's kingship may not belong to this setting, and although too much has been made of the theory of the New Year festival, the Feast of Tabernacles perhaps included some celebration of divine kingship manifest in the divine climatic weaponry that subdues the cosmic waters.

This political background for the imagery pitting Yahweh against the

128. E. S. Gerstenberger, "The Lyrical Literature," in *The Hebrew Bible and Its Modern Interpreters*, ed. D. A. Knight and G. M. Tucker (Philadelphia: Fortress; Decatur, GA: Scholars, 1985), 430; Day, *God's Conflict*, 20.

129. Day, *God's Conflict*, 22.

130. See now the magisterial work on meteorology and biblical poems (especially the Psalms) by A. Fitzgerald, *The Lord of the East Wind.*

cosmic waters may have antecedents within Canaanite culture. Meteorological theories of the sort proposed for some biblical psalms have been offered for the Baal cycle as well. T. H. Gaster and J. C. de Moor associate various points of the cycle with various times of year, including the fall.[131] Though de Moor's attempt to correlate the Baal cycle with one annual cycle has not met with acceptance, Gaster's association of two parts in the Baal cycle with the fall seems more probable. Building on Gaster's work, M. S. Smith has argued further that each of the three major sections of the Baal cycle, namely, the Baal-Yamm conflict (KTU 1.1-2), the building of Baal's palace (1.3-4), and the Baal-Mot (1.5-6), draws on the weather of the fall, specifically the arrival of the rains. Internal evidence points to all three sections building toward the appearance of rain that had been previously lacking. The meteorological imagery lying behind the weapons called *ṣmdm* in KTU 1.2 IV has been noted by many scholars. Y. Yadin argued on the basis of the root *ṣmd,* "to bind" (cf. Arabic *ḍamada*), that the weapon is double lightning. The lightning presages the appearance of the autumn rains. In the second section of the cycle, Asherah is glad for El's permission to build a palace for Baal so that Baal can produce the rains, evidently lacking up to this point (1.4 V 6-9). After the palace is built, Baal finally utters his thunder, literally "holy voice," through the rift in the clouds (1.4 VII 25-31). The completion of the palace, permitting the full manifestation of Baal's power in the storm, is after all the cosmic message that Baal had earlier intimated to Anat (1.3 III 13-31, IV 7-20). The third section of the Baal cycle, 1.5-1.6, expresses the issue of Baal's rain in a different way. In 1.5 VI 23-25 El laments the condition of humanity due to Baal's death, which means no rain (cf. 1.6 I 6-8). El's dream-vision indicates to him that the earth will flow with fertility produced by Baal's rains (1.6 III). The one season that fits the situation described in these passages is the autumn when the rains finally overtake the heat of late summer.

Like the biblical psalms used in the theory of the enthronement celebration, the Baal cycle has a manifestly royal theme. Just as the enthronement psalms proclaim the kingship of Yahweh, the Baal cycle asserts the kingship of Baal. The enthronement psalms and the Baal cycle express the political dimension of divine kingship. The Mari letter and Psalm 89 illustrate the connection between the human and divine levels of the West Semitic storm imagery, and it may be that the enthronement psalms and the Baal cycle likewise presupposed the human as well as the divine level of kingship. The two levels of kingship may have been celebrated in ancient Israel at the one time of year

131. For a full discussion of the following points, see Smith, "Interpreting the Baal Cycle," 313-39; cf. Gaster, *Thespis,* esp. 238; and de Moor, *Seasonal Pattern, ad loc.*

when the storm deity appeared most strongly, in the early fall. Moreover, the intertwined nature of divine and human kingship in compositions during the period of the monarchy suggest that the Tabernacles festival would have served as an appropriate occasion for communicating the relationship between the divine and human kings. In short, the storm imagery associated with Baal in Canaanite texts and Yahweh in Israelite tradition exhibited a political function. The martial imagery of the goddess Anat may have exercised a similar role.

4. Excursus: Yahweh and Anat

Although the Bible presents Baal, and, to a lesser extent, Asherah, as separate deities, there is no such depiction of Anat.[132] Except for personal names, Anat does not appear in the Bible.[133] The Jewish Aramaic papyri from Elephantine

132. On Anat, see Cooper, "Divine Names and Epithets in the Ugaritic Texts," 400-402; Oden, *Studies,* 81-82; M. Delcor, "Une allusion à Anat, déesse guerrière en Ex. 32:18?" *JJS* 33 (1982 = *Essays in Honour of Yigael Yadin*): 145-60; B. Z. Luria, "Who Was Shamgar ben Anat?" *Dor le Dor* 14 (1985-86): 105-7; Ahlström, *Who Were the Israelites?* 77; N. H. Walls, *The Goddess Anat in Ugaritic Myth,* SBLDS 135 (Atlanta: Scholars, 1992); P. L. Day, "Anat: Ugarit's 'Mistress of Animals,'" *JNES* 51 (1992): 181-90; "Anat," *DDD,* 36-43; idem, "Why Is Anat a Warrior and Hunter?" in *The Bible and the Politics of Exegesis: Essays in Honor of Norman K. Gottwald on His Sixty-Fifth Birthday,* ed. D. Jobling, P. L. Day, and G. T. Sheppard (Cleveland, OH: Pilgrim Press, 1991), 141-46, 329-32; and J. Day, *Yahweh and the Gods and Goddesses of Canaan* (JSOTSup 265; Sheffield: Sheffield Academic Press, 2000), 132-44. Day's assessment appears overly optimistic for the extent of Anat in pre-exilic Israelite religion. Anat appears in the Bible only in the form of proper names (see chapter 1, section 3), and no Phoenician inscription extant from the mainland attests to her. The goddess Antit is attested in an Egyptian stele from Beth-Shan (see A. Rowe, *The Four Canaanite Temples of Beth-Shan* [Philadelphia: Univ. of Pennsylvania Press, 1940], 34, pl. 65A; A. Kempinski, "Beth-shean," *EAEHL* 1:215). The vocalization of Ugaritic *ʿnt* as **ʿanatu* (hence the English spelling, Anat) is based on the occurrence of her name as [d]*a-na-tum* in RS 20.24.20 (*Ug V,* 44; see Knutson, "Divine Names and Epithets in the Akkadian Texts," 476-77) and Ugaritic personal names. For Anat in Phoenician and Punic, see A. Frendo, "A New Punic Inscription from Żejtun (Malta) and the Goddess Anat-Astarte," *PEQ* 131 (1991): 24-35. For the etymology of her name, see n. 135 below and chapter 3, section 3.

133. In addition to Shamgar son of ʿAnat *(ben ʿănāt),* see *bêt-ʿănāt* (Josh. 19:38) and *huion Anat,* "sons of Anat" (LXX Vaticanus Josh. 17:7) as well as *bnʿnt* in a seventh-century inscription from Ekron (see S. Gitin, T. Dothan, and J. Naveh, "A Royal Dedicatory Inscription from Ekron," *IEJ* 47 [1997]: 13-14). Cf. *ʿănātôt,* a place in Benjamin and the home of Jeremiah (Josh. 21:18; 1 Kings 2:26; Isa. 10:30; Jer. 1:1; 11:21, 23; 32:7-9; Ezra 2:23; Neh. 7:27; 11:32; 1 Chron. 8:45), possibly a place-name based on a divine name (cf. place-names ʿAshtarot, ʿAnat on the Euphrates, [URU]*Ba-'-li* in a Neo-Assyrian list; see Astour, "Yahweh," 33); cf. the Benjaminite with this name (1 Chron. 7:8). The personal name *ʿantōtiyyāh,* the name of a

contain the divine names, *ʿntbytʾl* (AP 22:125) and *ʿntyhw* (AP 44:3) and the personal name *ʿnty* (AP 22:108), which some scholars have interpreted as indirect evidence for a Jewish cult of Anat at Elephantine, a practice then inferred for ancient Israel. Attempts to mitigate this view by suggesting that **ʿnt* is a common noun that expresses a hypostasis of Yahweh[134] are problematic, since this derivation is controverted.[135] It appears rather that **ʿnt* in the Aramaic papyri from Elephantine derived from the name of the goddess Anat attested in other Egyptian Aramaic documents of the Persian period. The derivation of **ʿnt* from the name of the goddess may be viewed as due to either

---

Benjaminite (1 Chron. 8:24), could be related to the name of the goddess, but following the lead of Albright and Milik, Olyan ("Some Observations," 170 n. 56) takes this name as a sentence name meaning "Yahweh is my providence," connecting **ʿantôt-* with Aramaic *ʿantāʾ* and Akkadian *ittu,* "sign, omen" (cf. E. L. Curtis and A. A. Madsen, *A Critical and Exegetical Commentary on the Books of Chronicles,* ICC [New York: Charles Scribner's Sons, 1910], 163). See also the possibly related gentilic forms in 2 Sam. 23:27; Jer. 29:27; 1 Chron. 11:28; 12:3; 27:2. Concerning Anat as the theophoric element in proper names, in addition to the studies cited in the previous note, see A. G. Auld, "A Judaean Sanctuary of ʿAnat (Josh. 15:59)," *TA* 4 (1977): 85-86. Arguments that these names indicate cultic devotion to the goddess (e.g., Ahlström, *Who Were the Israelites?* 77) exceed the evidence, since the giving of personal names was subject to conventions other than those of cultic devotion (for further discussion, see Introduction). Furthermore, the place-names with the theophoric element *ʿnt* supply information pointing to the indigenous character of her cult, but the cult may predate the attestation of the names. For a proposal comparing the imagery of Anat and Deborah, see P. C. Craigie, "Three Ugaritic Notes on the Song of Deborah," *JSOT* 2 (1977): 33-49; idem, "Deborah and Anat: A Study of Poetic Imagery," *ZAW* 90 (1978): 374-81. See also R. M. Good, "Exodus 32:18," in *Love and Death in the Ancient Near East: Essays in Honor of Marvin H. Pope,* ed. J. H. Marks and R. M. Good (Guilford, CT: Four Quarters, 1987), 137-42.

134. For the elements *bytʾl, *ʾšm, *ʿnt,* and **ḥrm* as hypostases, see J. T. Milik, "Les papyrus araméens d'Hermoupolis et les cultes syro-phéniciens en Egypte perse," *Biblica* 48 (1967): 556-64; P. K. McCarter, "Aspects of the Religion of the Israelite Monarchy: Biblical and Epigraphic Data," in *Ancient Israelite Religion: Essays in Honor of Frank Moore Cross,* ed. P. D. Miller, Jr., P. D. Hanson, and S. D. McBride, 138-43; Olyan, "Some Observations," 170, and Burnett, *A Reassessment of Biblical Elohim,* Society of Biblical Literature, 90-92.

135. B. Porten discusses the two possibilities that these elements are either hypostases or survivals of old divinities (*Archives from Elephantine* [Berkeley and Los Angeles: Univ. of California Press, 1968], 154, 156, 165-70, 178-79, 317). J. P. Hyatt ("The Deity Bethel in the Old Testament," *JAOS* 59 [1939]: 81-98) and B. Levine (*In the Presence of the Lord: A Study of Cult and Some Cultic Terms in Ancient Israel,* Studies in Judaism in Late Antiquity 5 [Leiden: Brill, 1974], 131-32) see no impediment to the latter view. The name Bethel in Jer. 48:13 may point to a Phoenician source lying behind the evidence for Bethel as a divine name in both biblical and Jewish Egyptian sources. Such an explanation might account for the element **ʿnt* in the names from Elephantine. For various proposals for the etymology of Anat's name, see Pope, "ʿAnat," in Pope and Röllig, *Syrien,* 235-41. Lambert equates Anat's name with Hanat, an area populated by a group of Amorites with its capital at Terqa ("Old Testament Mythology," 132, esp. n. 6).

local Aramaean or Phoenician influence; the latter is viable, as the name Anat-Bethel belongs among the Tyrian deities mentioned in the treaty between Esarhaddon and Baal II of Tyre.[136] That her cult was known at Iron Age Bethel might be inferred from the mention of her in Papyrus Amherst 63 (column VII).[137] (Accordingly, *ʿntbytʾl* in *AP* 22:125 may be "Anat of Bethel.") While Anat was generally a goddess in some quarters of Egypt, including in a form combined with the names of other deities at Elephantine, there is little or no clear evidence that Anat was a goddess in Israel.

Although Anat was hardly a goddess in Israel, her savage battling in the Ugaritic Baal cycle (CTA 3.2 [KTU 1.3 II].3-30) has been often compared with numerous biblical passages. To illustrate the basis for comparison between Yahweh and Anat, first a translation of this Ugaritic text is provided:[138]

klʾat ṯǵrt bht ʿnt	The gates of Anat's house were closed;
wtqry ǵlmm bšt ǵr	And she met the youths at the foot of the mountain.
whln ʿnt tmtḫṣ bʿmq	And look! Anat fights in the valley,
tḫtṣb bn qrytm	She battles between the two cities.
tmḫṣ lʾim ḫpy[m]	She smites peoples of the wes[t],
tṣmt ʾadm ṣʾat š[p]š	Strikes the populace of the east.
tḥth kkdrt rʾi[š]	Under her, like balls, heads,

136. On Anat-Bethel of Tyre, see chapter 1, section 6.

137. See Steiner, "The Aramaic Text in Demotic Scripture," 314.

138. See Caquot, Sznycer, and Herdner, *Textes ougaritiques,* 1.157-61; Coogan, *Stories from Ancient Canaan,* 90-91; Gibson, *Canaanite Myths and Legends,* 47-48; del Olmo Lete, *Mitos y leyendas,* 181-82; see also the works cited in the following note. For *hln,* see M. L. Brown, "'Is It Not' or 'Indeed!': *HL* in Northwest Semitic," *Maarav* 4/2 (1987): 205. On *šbm//mdnt* as terms for enemies, see M. Held, "Studies in Comparative Semitic Lexicography," *in Studies in Honor of Benno Landsberger on His Seventy-Fifth Birthday,* Assyriological Studies 16 (Chicago: Univ. of Chicago Press, 1965), 404 n. 122; on *ksl qšth,* see Held, "Studies," 404. The verb *tǵll* has been usually rendered "wade." For the alternative interpretation of the verb as "glean," and for other examples of agricultural imagery used for descriptions of warfare, see R. M. Good, "Metaphorical Gleanings from Ugarit," *JJS* 33 (1982 = *Essays in Honour of Yigael Yadin*): 55-59. For *ḥlqm* as "neck(-deep)," see the contextual comparison with Rev. 14:14-20 suggested by D. Pardee, "The New Canaanite Myths and Legends," *BiOr* 37 (1980): 276; cf. Mehri and Harsusi *ḥelqemōt* and Jibbali *ḥalqūt,* meaning "Adam's apple" or "side of the throat" (so G. A. Rendsburg, "Modern South Arabian as a Source for Ugaritic Etymologies," *JAOS* 107 [1987]: 628). Due to similar martial language in both halves, most interpreters view the second half of the passage as a continuation of the fighting. The second half is not battle proper, but the goddess's feast on her captives. Concerning cannibalism following battle, see M. Harris, *The Sacred Cow and the Abominable Pig: Riddles of Food and Culture* (New York: Simon & Schuster, 1987), 216-22; see Harris's comments relating the decline of warfare cannibalism to state development.

ʿlh kʾirbym kp	Above her, like locusts, hand(s),
k qṣm ǵrmn kp mhr	Like hoppers, heaps of warrior-hands.
ʿtkt rʾišt lbmth	She fixed heads to her back,
šnst kpt bḥbšh	Fastened hands to her waist.
brkm tǵl[l] bdm ḏmr	Knee-deep she gleans in warrior-blood,
ḫlqm bmm[ʿ] mhrm	Neck-deep in the gor[e] of soldiers.
mṭm tgrš šbm	With darts she drives away captives,
bksl qšth mdnt	With her bow-string, foes.
whln ʿnt lbth tmǵyn	And look! Anat to her house goes,
tštql ʾilt lhklh	The goddess takes herself to her palace,
wl šbʿt tmtḫṣh bʿmq	For she is not sated with fighting in the valley,
tḫtṣb bn qrtm	With battling between the two cities.
tṯʿr ksʾat lmhr	She arranges chairs for the soldiery,
ṯʿr ṯlḥnt lṣbʾim	Arranges tables for the hosts,
hdmm lǵzrm	Footstools for the heroes.
mʾid tmtḫṣn wtʿn	Hard she fights and looks about,
tḫtṣb wtḥdy ʿnt	As she battles, Anat surveys.
tǵdd kbdh bṣḥq	Her innards swell with laughter,
ymlʾu lbh bšmḫt	Her heart fills with joy,
kbd ʿnt tšyt	The innards of Anat with triumph.
kbrkm tǵll bdm ḏmr	Knee-deep she gleans in warrior blood,
ḫlqm bmmʿ mhrm	Neck-deep in the gore of soldiers,
ʿd tšbʿ tmtḫṣ bbt	Until she is sated with fighting in the house,
tḫtṣb bn ṯlḥnm	With battling amidst the tables.

There are many parallels between this Ugaritic passage and a variety of biblical texts.[139] First, the divine battle takes place at the mountain of the deity, a motif found in Psalms 2:1-2; 48:5-8; 110; Joel 4:9-14; Zechariah 12:3-4; 14:2; and elsewhere. In Ugaritic, this motif is not restricted to Anat. Baal also fights his enemies on his mountain (KTU 1.6 VI 12-13; cf. 1.1 V 5, 18). Second, the battle is universal in scope; "peoples" are collectively the enemies of the deity. Many of the biblical passages just cited likewise contain this motif. Isaiah 59:15-19 describes the universal scope of Yahweh's warfare:

139. J. Gray, "The Wrath of God in Canaanite and Hebrew Literature," *Bulletin of the Manchester University Egyptian and Oriental Society* 25 (1947-53): 9-19; Pope, *Song of Songs,* 606-12; P. D. Hanson, "Zechariah 9 and the Recapitulation of an Ancient Ritual Pattern," *JBL* 92 (1973): 46-47 n. 25; J. Gray, "The Blood Bath of the Goddess Anat in the Ras Shamra Texts," *UF* 11 (1979): 315-24; Pardee, "The New Canaanite Myths and Legends," 276-77; V. Kubac, "Blut im Gurtel und in Sandalen," *VT* 31 (1981): 225-26.

wayyar' yhwh wayyēra' bĕ'ênāyw	Yahweh saw it, and it displeased him
kî-'ên mišpāṭ	that there was no justice.
wayyar' kî-'ên 'îš	He saw that there was no man,
wayyištômēm kî 'ên mapgîa'	and wondered that there was no one to intervene;
wattôša' lô zĕrō'ô	then his own arm brought him victory,
wĕṣidqātô hî' sĕmākātĕhû	and his righteousness upheld him.
wayyilbāš ṣĕdāqâ kašširyān	He put on righteousness as a breastplate,
wĕkôba' yĕšû'â bĕrō'šô	and a helmet of salvation upon his head;
wayyilbāš bigdê nāqām tilbōšet	he put on garments of vengeance for clothing,
wayya'aṭ kam'îl qin'â	and wrapped himself in fury as a mantle.
kĕ'al gĕmūlôt kĕ'al yĕšallēm	According to his deeds, so will he repay,
ḥēmâ lĕṣārāyw gĕmûl lĕ 'ōyĕbāyw	wrath to his adversaries, requital to his enemies . . .
wĕyîrĕ'û mimma'ărāb 'et-šēm yhwh	So they shall fear the name of Yahweh from the west,
ûmimmizraḥ-šemeš 'et-kĕbôdô	and his glory from the rising of the sun;
kî-yābô' kannāhār ṣār	for he will come like a rushing stream,
rûaḥ yhwh nōsĕsâ bô	which the wind of Yahweh drives.

Like Anat in KTU 1.3 II, here Yahweh is described as enraged *(qin'â)*, and the divine enemies are described according to the "west" *(ma'ărāb)* and the "east," literally "the rising of the sun" *(mizraḥ-šemeš)*.

Third, the battle produces heaps of corpses (Isa. 34:2) or skulls (Deut. 32:43; Ps. 110:6). The image of harvest appears in Anat's "gleaning" and in some biblical scenes of divine war (Joel 3:13; Rev. 14:14-20; cf. secular examples in Judg. 8:1-2; 20:44-46; Jer. 6:9; cf. Jer. 49:9; Obadiah 5). Fourth, like the second part of the Ugaritic passage given above, the aftermath of war is described as a feast, a feature attested in Isaiah 34:6-7, 49:26 and perhaps presupposed in the sacrificial language of Deuteronomy 32:43. This feast includes feeding on the flesh of captives (Deut. 32:42), drinking the blood of the victims (Isa. 49:26; LXX Zech. 9:15; cf. Num. 23:24), called "captives" in Deuteronomy 32:42 (as in KTU 1.3 II), and wading in the blood of the vanquished (Pss. 58:11; 68:24). Isaiah 49:26 alters the motif of feeding on the captives. In this verse, the enemies will cannibalize themselves: "I will make your oppressors eat their own flesh, and they shall be drunk with their own blood as with wine." The image of wading in the blood may be related to the theme of the battle as bloody harvest. Because of its blood red color, the image of the wine harvest appears in biblical descriptions of divine war (Deut. 32:42-43; Isa.

49:26; 63:3; Ezek. 39:19; Joel 4:13; Lam. 1:15; Rev. 19:15). Finally, the delight that Anat derives from her carnal destruction has biblical correspondences in the language of both divine laughter (Ps. 2:4; cf. Prov. 2:26) and drunkenness with battle (see Deut. 32:43; Isa. 34:2; 63:3-6; cf. Jer. 46:10).

The many parallels drawn between CTA 3.2 (KTU 1.3 II).3-30 and these biblical descriptions of divine war have generated theories concerning dependence of the biblical language on prior Canaanite tradition as represented by the Ugaritic material, much as divine storm language in the Bible is compared with the meteorological imagery of the Ugaritic god Baal. In the case of the war imagery associated with Anat, there are additional factors involved in assessing the relationship beween the Ugaritic and biblical evidence. Since Anat is not attested in the Bible excepting in a few personal names, the lack of contact between her cult and that of Yahweh forestalls any theory of direct dependence. The language in common between Anat and Yahweh could have derived from a third source. Or, possibly no source was involved, since the language of battle unfortunately belongs to general human experience. From ancient descriptions of human battle and carnage in New Kingdom Egyptian records, the Moabite stele (KAI 181:16-18), 2 Kings 10:10-27, and other texts, it might seem that no literary relationship needs to be imputed to the bloody rendering of Yahweh.

The bloody imagery of Yahweh seems to have reflected a complex dependence on imagery for Anat, nonetheless. There is indirect evidence for suspecting this dependence. The monarchy apparently had a role in transmitting the bloody martial imagery for Yahweh, and there are a few hints pointing to the royal role in the biblical passages. First, some biblical examples include references to Yahweh together with the human monarch (Ps. 2:1-2; cf. KAI 181:16-18). Second, the deity and the king in Psalms 2 and 110 are pitted against the nations. Third, some of the imagery used of divine battle appears in secular accounts of battle, both royal or otherwise (e.g., the severed heads, the harvest imagery, the drinking of blood). Like the solar imagery for Yahweh, the language of savage battle may have stemmed from attributing to divine kings the characteristics of their human royal counterparts according to indigenous models. Egyptian texts of the New Kingdom period used the names of Anat and Astarte to dramatize pharaonic prowess. One text describes Anat and Astarte as a shield to Ramses III.[140] By the biblical period, the savage, grisly descriptions of battle accorded Anat in the Late Bronze Age perhaps became one way to describe Yahweh, the divine warrior.

140. See Pritchard, *Palestinian Figurines,* 78-79; Stadelmann, *Syrisch-Palastinensische Gottheiten,* 91-96; *ANET,* 250.

Details in the biblical record provide a few indications as to how Israelite tradition incorporated the bloody type of martial depiction of Yahweh. Some passages, such as Deuteronomy 32:42-43 and Psalm 68:24, combine bloody martial imagery with storm language. These examples of conflation may suggest how the type of divine warrior language for Anat in Canaanite tradition was mediated to Israelite tradition for Yahweh. Both types of language describing the divine warrior — the storm language of Baal and the bloody imagery of Anat — appear in conflated form in Israelite tradition, much as various types of imagery associated with El and Baal in Canaanite texts are conflated in early biblical tradition.[141]

141. On the conflation of imagery of El and Baal in biblical tradition, see chapter 1, section 4.

CHAPTER 3

Yahweh and Asherah

1. Distribution in the Biblical Record

Narratives (Judg. 3:7; 6:25-30), legal prohibitions (Exod. 34:13; Deut. 7:5; 12:3; 16:21), and prophetic critiques (Isa. 17:8; 27:9; Jer. 17:2; Micah 5:13) indicate that the devotion to the cult symbol known as the asherah, a wooden pole of some sort, and the religious items collectively called the asherim was observed as early as the period of the Judges and as late as a few decades before the fall of the southern kingdom (2 Kings 23:4, 6, 7, 15).[1] As S. Olyan has

1. For a full treatment of the biblical evidence, see Olyan, *Asherah and the Cult of Yahweh,* 1-22; C. Frevel, *Aschera und der Ausschliesslichkeitsanspruch YHWHs,* Bonner biblische Beiträge 94 (Weinheim: Beltz Athenäum, 1995); O. Keel, *Goddesses and Trees, New Moon and Yahweh: Ancient Near Eastern Art and the Hebrew Bible,* JSOTSup 261 (Sheffield: Sheffield Academic Press, 1998), 15-57; P. Merlo, *La dea Ašratum — Aṯiratu — Ašera: Un contributo alla storia della religione semitica del Nord* (Mursia: Pontificia Universitè Lateranense, 1998); and J. M. Hadley, *The Cult of Asherah in Ancient Israel and Judah: Evidence for a Hebrew Goddess,* University of Cambridge Oriental Publications 57 (Cambridge: Cambridge Univ. Press, 2000). See also N. Wyatt, "Asherah," *DDD,* 99-105; J. Day, *Yahweh and the Gods and Goddesses of Canaan,* JSOTSup 265 (Sheffield: Sheffield Academic Press, 2000), 42-67; P. D. Miller, *The Religion of Ancient Israel* (London: SPCK; Louisville, KY: Westminster/John Knox, 2000), 29-40; and Z. Zevit, *The Religions of Ancient Israel: A Synthesis of Parallactic Approaches* (London/New York: Continuum, 2001), 472, 478, 537-38, 650-52, 677. For recent discussions of the interpretational problems pertaining to Asherah and her symbol, the asherah, see also Oden, *Studies,* 88-102; A. L. Perlman, "Asherah and Astarte in the Old Testament and Ugaritic Literature" (Ph.D. diss., Graduate Theological Union, 1978); A. Angerstorfer, "Asherah als — 'consort of Jahwe' oder Ašírtah?" *BN* 17 (1982): 7-16; Emerton, "New Light on Israelite Religion," 1-20; U. Winter, *Frau und Göttin: Exegetische und ikonographische Studien zum weiblichen Gottesbild im Alten Testament und in desen Umwelt,* OBO 53 (Fribourg: Universitätsverlag; Göttingen: Vandenhoeck & Ruprecht, 1983), 479-538, 551-60; J. Day, "Asherah in the Hebrew Bible and Northwest Semitic Literature," *JBL* 105 (1986): 385-408; Tigay, *You Shall Have No Other Gods,* 26-30; Smith, "God Male and Female," 333-40; R. Hestrin, "The Lachish Ewer and the Asherah," *IEJ* 37 (1987): 212-

shown, the asherah was acceptable in both northern and southern kingdoms, both outside (see 1 Kings 14:23; 2 Kings 17:10, 16; Jer. 17:2) and inside the royal cults of Samaria (1 Kings 16:33; 2 Kings 13:6) and Jerusalem (2 Kings 21:7; 23:6; 2 Chron. 24:18).[2] Besides Samaria and Jerusalem, devotion to the asherah is attested for Ophrah (Judges 6:25) and Bethel (2 Kings 23:15). From this information, it would appear that the symbol of the asherah was a general feature of Israelite religion.

Furthermore, there is no indication that devotion to the symbol was limited to a specific group or social stratum within Israel. Olyan has argued that criticism of the goddess Asherah and her symbol, the asherah, was restricted to a single quarter of Israelite society, namely, the Deuteronomistic tradition.[3] From this limited base of opposition, it might be inferred that many other quarters of Israelite society either accepted the asherah or at least did not oppose it. Neither Jehu nor Hosea opposed the asherah, although

---

23. For a survey of data pertaining to Asherah, including the South Arabic evidence, see Pritchard, *Palestinian Figurines,* 59-65. For further comments on the South Arabic evidence, see M. Hofner, *Sudarabien, Saba', Qataban und anderen,* Wörterbuch der Mythologie 1/6 (Stuttgart: Ernst Klett, 1965), 497. For the vocalization of Ugaritic *'aṯrt* as **'aṯiratu* but possibly **'aṯirtu,* see Huehnergard, *Ugaritic Vocabulary,* 111-12, 283. The goddess's name in the Canaanite myth of Elkunirsa (*ANET,* 519) is given either as [d]*A-še-er-du-uš* (with Hittite declensional endings) or the Akkadianized forms, [d]*A-še-er-tum* or *ŠA* [d]*A-še-er-ti* (H. A. Hoffner, "The Elkunirsa Myth Reconsidered," *Revue Hittite et Asianique* 23 [1965]: 6 n. 5).

2. Olyan, *Asherah and the Cult of Yahweh,* 6-9, 29, 34. Ahlström (*Aspects of Syncretism,* 51) and Olyan (*Asherah and the Cult of Yahweh,* 7) have noted that 2 Kings 13:6 indicates that the cults of Baal and the asherah were separate in Samaria. D. N. Freedman argues that behind 2 Kings 13:6 lies a different historical picture, that after the cult of Baal was removed from Samaria, the goddess Asherah was no longer paired with Baal but with Yahweh ("Yahweh of Samaria and His Asherah," *BA* 50 [1987]: 248). Olyan's demonstration that Baal and Asherah were not paired in the Late Bronze Age or the Iron Age vitiates Freedman's view of 2 Kings 13:6 (*Asherah and the Cult of Yahweh,* 38-61). Freedman also argues that *'ašmat šōmĕrôn* in Amos 8:14 alludes to the goddess. Other interpretations are feasible. The word *'ašmat* could be a negative reference to the "name" *(šēm)* of Yahweh; if so, *derek* in Amos 8:14 might be an aspect of Yahweh related to Ugaritic *drkt,* "power, dominion" (see Ringgren, *Israelite Religion,* 264 n. 54; n. 136 below). If so, *'ašmat* as a biform of the word *šēm* is anomalous for BH generally and for Amos specifically (cf. *šm* in Amos 2:7; 5:8; 6:10; 9:6, 12); nonetheless, it is possible (cf. Aramaic *'šmbt'l* in AP 22:124). For the view that *'ašmat* in Amos 8:14 might be an allusion, see the discussion in M. Cogan, "Ashima," *DDD,* 105-6. In any case, Freedman's proposal for *'ašmat* enjoys no more certitude than other proposals. Freedman's arguments for allusions to the goddess Asherah in Amos 2:17 and Ezek. 8:3 are ingenious, though unconvincing. The "Queen of Heaven" (Jer. 44:15-30) may not be Asherah, as Freedman suggests. She never bears this title in the extant texts, unlike Astarte, and to a lesser extext, Anat and Ishtar (so Olyan, "Some Observations," 161-74).

3. Olyan, *Asherah and the Cult of Yahweh,* 3-19.

they are depicted as outspoken in their criticism of Baal. In 1 Kings 18:19 the prophets of Asherah are referred to only once in the conflict on Mount Carmel between Elijah and the prophets of Baal, themselves mentioned five times in the story.[4] Some critics view the single reference as a secondary addition designed to cast aspersions on Asherah by connecting her with the cult of Baal.[5] Olyan observes that no prophet opposed the asherah until the eighth century, and the prophetic passages that criticize the asherah appear to be Deuteronomistic or derivative from Deuteronomistic passages. Even if not all the passages can be explained in this way, prophetic opposition to the asherah does not appear in any sources extant from before the eighth century. Analysis of the legal prohibitions is consistent with this conclusion. The laws pertaining to the asherah derive from the book of Deuteronomy, with the exception of Exodus 34:13, which some scholars, including Olyan, interpret as a Deuteronomistic addition,[6] although other commentators view it as representing an earlier critique of the asherah.[7] The biblical evidence pertaining to the asherah does not sustain a historical dichotomy between "normative Yahwism" over and against "Canaanite religion" or a "popular religion" tainted by Canaanite influence.[8] Rather, as biblical scholars have long noted, biblical criticism of the asherah points to its being an Israelite phenomenon.[9]

4. Olyan, *Asherah and the Cult of Yahweh,* 8.

5. Origen's Hexapla marks "the prophets of Asherah" with an asterisk indicating that these words are an addition in Origen's text of the Septuagint. For discussion, see J. A. Montgomery, *A Critical and Exegetical Commentary on the Books of Kings,* ed. H. S. Gehman, ICC (Edinburgh: T. & T. Clark, 1951), 310; Emerton, "New Light on Israelite Religion," 16; E. Lipiński, "The Goddess 'Aṯirat in Ancient Arabia, in Babylon and in Ugarit," *OLP* 3 (1972): 114; Olyan, *Asherah and the Cult of Yahweh,* 8. Against the view of D. N. Freedman ("Yahweh of Samaria," 248), recognizing that the reference to asherah in this verse is a secondary addition need not be resolved through emendation, only that the addition reflects a secondary stage in the development of the verse.

6. M. Noth, *Exodus; A Commentary,* trans. J. S. Bowden, OTL (London: SCM, 1962), 262; Childs, *The Book of Exodus,* 608; Ginsberg, *The Israelian Heritage,* 64; Olyan, *Asherah and the Cult of Yahweh,* 18. For similar analyses, see F. Langlamet, "Israël et 'l'inhabitant du pays'; Vocabulaires et formules d'Éx., xxxiv, 11-16," *RB* 76 (1969): 323-24.

7. See Langlamet, "Israël," 324-25, 483-90.

8. See Olyan, *Asherah and the Cult of Yahweh,* 4-5. For examples of this dichotomy used in discussion of the asherah, see J. C. de Moor, "*'ᵃshērāh,*" in *Theological Dictionary of the Old Testament,* vol. 1, ed. G. J. Botterweck and H. Ringgren, trans. J. T. Willis, rev. ed. (Grand Rapids: Eerdmans, 1977), 444; Tigay, *You Shall Have No Other Gods,* 26. On the further uses and abuses of the term "Canaanite religion," see also Hillers, "Analyzing the Abominable," 253-69. Further examples of the types of works that Hillers discusses include Oldenburg, *The Conflict,* 1; Mendenhall, *The Tenth Generation,* 226; cf. de Moor, "The Crisis of Polytheism in Late Bronze Ugarit," 1-20.

9. Ahlström, *Aspects of Syncretism,* 50-34.

There is the further matter of the distinction between the *asherah* and the *asherim*. Besides the difference in morphology, the first word being a feminine singular noun (with a feminine plural) and the latter a masculine plural noun, biblical passages suggest a functional difference. The asherah is erected next to the altar of a god (Deut. 16:21; Judg. 6:25-26). However, the asherim never appear next to an altar but beside or under a tree on high places (Jer. 17:2; 1 Kings 14:23; 2 Kings 17:10). Further distinctions offered are little more than educated guesses. J. R. Engle suggests that the female figurines found in abundance in Iron Age Israel are asherim, representing the goddess, as opposed to the wooden pole of the asherah.[10] R. Hestrin argues that the pillar figurines that she interprets as symbols of Asherah were household items designed to enhance fertility.[11] Yet scholars have long speculated that these figurines may represent Astarte, and given the maternal imagery for her in Phoenician, this is as plausible an identification as that with Asherah.[12] Moreover, these figurines may not represent any deity.[13]

2. The Symbol of the Asherah

The asherah was a wooden object symbolizing a tree. It was an item that was "made" (**śh,* 1 Kings 14:15; 16:33; 2 Kings 17:6; 21:3, 7; Isa. 17:7), "built" (**bnh,* 1 Kings 14:23), "set up" (**nṣb,* 2 Kings 17:10; **ʿmd* in the hiphil, 2 Chron. 33:19; cf. Isa. 27:9), and "planted" (**nṭʿ*, Deut. 16:21; cf. Gen. 21:33).[14]

10. J. R. Engle, "Pillar Figurines of Iron Age and Asherah/Asherim" (Ph.D. diss., University of Pittsburgh, 1979), 55, 62; cf. Hestrin, "The Lachish Ewer," 221-22; Ahlström, "An Archaeological Picture," 136; Pritchard, *Palestinian Figurines,* 86. See also T. A. Holland, "A Survey of Palestinian Iron Age Baked Clay Figurines, with Special Reference to Jerusalem: Cave I," *Levant* 9 (1977): 121-51. For considerations of Engle's view, with a survey of evidence, see also Hadley, *The Cult of Asherah in Ancient Israel and Judah,* 196-205. For further discussion, see R. Kletter, "Between Archaeology and Theology: The Pillar Figurines from Judah and the Asherah," in *Studies in the Archaeology of the Iron Age in Israel and Jordan,* ed. A. Mazar with the assistance of G. Mathias, JSOTSup 331 (Sheffield: Sheffield Academic Press, 2001), 179-216; and E. C. LaRocca-Pitts, *"Of Wood and Stone": The Significance of Israelite Cultic Items in the Bible and Its Early Interpreters,* HSM 61 (Winona Lake, IN: Eisenbrauns, 2001), 161-204.

11. R. Hestrin, "Israelite and Persian Periods," in *Highlights of Archaeology, The Israel Museum, Jerusalem* (Jerusalem: The Israel Museum, 1984), 172.

12. Albright, "Astarte Plaques and Figurines from Tell Beit Mirsim," in *Mélanges syriens offerts à M. René Dussaud,* vol. 1 (Paris: Geuthner, 1939), 102-20.

13. Pritchard, *Palestinian Figurines,* 87.

14. On the nature of the asherah, see W. L. Reed, *The Asherah in the Old Testament* (Fort Worth, TX: Texas Christian University, 1949); J. Barr, "Seeing the Wood for the Trees? An Enigmatic Ancient Translation," *JSS* 13 (1968): 11-20; J. B. Carter, "The Masks of Ortheia," *American*

According to the Mishnaic tractate *ʿAbodah Zarah* 3:5, the asherah is forbidden because "the hands of man have been concerned with" it.[15] In other words, the asherah involves human manufacture. *ʿAbodah Zarah* 3:7 is more detailed:

> Three kinds of asherah are to be distinguished: if a tree was planted from the first for idolatry, it is forbidden; if it was chopped and trimmed for idolatry and it sprouted afresh, one only need take away what has sprouted afresh; but if a gentile did but set up an idol beneath it and then desecrate it, the tree is permitted. What is an asherah? Any tree under which is an idol. Rabbi Simeon says: Any tree which is worshipped.[16]

Unlike the biblical data, this Mishnaic text includes both living and dead trees in its definition of the asherah, perhaps influenced by the phenomenon of sacred groves in Hellenistic religion. To date, no convincing examples of an asherah have been excavated, an understandable state of affairs since biblical accounts of the asherah describe it as made of wood. Y. Aharoni suggested, for example, that the burned tree trunk found next to a standing stone in an Israelite level (stratum V-III) at Lachish was perhaps an asherah.[17] The combination of stone and tree appears in some biblical texts, Jeremiah 2:27, for example.

Various pieces of iconography indicate that the tree was the Canaanite symbol of the goddess and represented her presence. K. Galling compared the asherah to a stylized tree on a clay model of a cultic scene from Cyprus.[18] O. Negbi has published drawings of several pieces of Canaanite female figures, often considered divine, with trees or branches etched between their navels and pubic triangle.[19] These pieces derive from Late Bronze Age levels at

---

Journal of Archaeology 91 (1987): 355-83; Hestrin, "The Lachish Ewer," 212-23; Olyan, *Asherah and the Cult of Yahweh,* 1-3. For scepticism about the "dendrical associations of Asherah," see S. A. Wiggins, "Of Asherahs and Trees: Some Methodological Questions," *Journal of Ancient Near Eastern Religions* 1/1 (2001): 158-86. E. Lipiński ("The Goddess 'Aṯirat," 101-19), A. Perlman ("Asherah and Astarte"), and P. K. McCarter ("Aspects of the Religion," 148-49) deny the relationship between the goddess Asherah and the symbol asherah.

15. H. Danby, *The Mishnah* (London: Oxford Univ. Press, 1933), 441.

16. Danby, *The Mishnah,* 441. For other discussions of the asherah in the Mishnah and Talmud, see C. E. Hayes, *Between the Babylonian and Palestinian Talmuds: Accounting for Halakhic Difference in Selected Sugyot from Tractate Avodah Zarah* (New York/Oxford: Oxford Univ. Press, 1997), 63-66, 102-4, 111-13, 115-16.

17. See Y. Aharoni, "Lachish," *EAEHL* 3:749.

18. K. Galling, *Biblisches Reallexikon,* HAT 1 (Tübingen: J. C. B. Mohr [Paul Siebeck], 1937), 35-36; Pritchard, *Palestinian Figurines,* 84; de Moor, "'ᵃ*shērāh,*" 443.

19. So Hestrin, "The Lachish Ewer," 215-17. See Negbi, *Canaanite Gods in Metal,* nos. 1661, 1664, 1680, 1685, 1688, 1691 (?), 1692.

Tell el-ʿAjjûl, Minet el-Bheida, and Ugarit. Another piece of iconography from Ugarit illustrates the development of the pole as the symbol of the goddess. A plaque from Ugarit depicts a female figure holding bundles of grain in either hand with animals feeding from each hand.[20] If this plaque were a depiction of the goddess Asherah, it would indicate that the tree found in comparable later iconography was a symbol of the goddess giving nourishment to the animals flanking her. Examples of the tree flanked by feeding twin animals appear in the Taanach stand, one pot belonging to the Kuntillet ʿAjrûd pottery known as pithos A, and on the Lachish ewer.[21] The ewer, found in a favissa, a cache of cultic items, in the Fosse Temple, is perhaps most pertinent. According to R. Hestrin,[22] the ewer links the tree and the goddess, since the goddess mentioned in the inscription appears directly above the depiction of the tree.[23] To illustrate the religious significance of the asherah, Hestrin compares two scenes from New Kingdom Egypt.[24] One shows the goddess Hathor as a tree giving nourishment to the king, and another renders Isis in the form of a tree giving suck to a noble and his wife. In these depictions, the tree stands for the fertile and nurturing goddess; the goddess is made present through the symbolism of the tree. This mode of representing Asherah in Canaan obtained in the Late Bronze Age. None of the iconographic depictions of the goddess derives from an Israelite stratum.

The asherah that Manasseh made in 2 Kings 21:7 was perhaps the same asherah that Josiah dragged out of the Jerusalem temple in 2 Kings 23:6-7; both were housed in the Jerusalem temple. The asherah of the temple may have been a more elaborate version of the symbol. It is perhaps for this reason that 2 Kings 21:7 calls it *pesel hāʾăšērāh,* "the graven image of the asherah."

20. Carter, "The Masks of Ortheia," 373-74. For discussion and pictures of the piece, see *Syria* 10 (1929): 292-93 and pl. 56; C. F. A. Schaeffer, *Ugaritica,* Mission de Ras Shamra 3 (Paris: Librairie Orientaliste Paul Geuthner, 1939), 32-33, frontpiece and pl. 11; *ANEP,* nos. 464, 303; A. Caquot and M. Sznycer, *Ugaritic Religion,* Iconography of Religions XV, 8 (Leiden: Brill, 1980), 22 and pls. 4, 5; R. W. Barnett, "Ancient Ivories in the Middle East," *Qedem* 14 (1982): 30 and pl. 124b. Carter identifies the cult of Ortheia in Sparta as Phoenician inspired. She argues that Ortheia may be the Greek name for Asherah/Tannit, and that her cult symbol, the upright wooden object, was the local realization of the asherah.

21. P. Beck, "The Drawings from Horvat Teiman (Kuntillet ʿAjrûd)," *TA* 9 (1982): 3-86, esp. 13-16; Hestrin, "The Lachish Ewer," 212-23.

22. Hestrin, "The Lachish Ewer," 221-22; idem, "Cult Stand from Taʿanach," 68-71. On the inscription on the Lachish ewer, see chapter 1, section 1.

23. Cf. W. Dever, "Asherah, Consort of Yahweh? New Evidence from Kuntillet ʿAjrûd," *BASOR* 255 (1984): 26-28.

24. Hestrin, "Cult Stand from Taʿanach," 68-71, fig. 6; idem, "The Lachish Ewer," 219; see also Keel, *The Symbolism of the Biblical World,* 186-87.

The asherah of 2 Kings 23:6-7 had *bāttîm,* often understood as "clothes" on the basis of both versional support (LXX *chettieim/n,* "tents"; Lucianic *stolās,* "garments"; and Targumic *mkwlyn,* "coverings")[25] and the Arabic cognate *batt,* "woven garments."[26] A number of scholars have compared the asherah with the nineteenth- and twentieth-century Palestinian custom of hanging clothes on holy trees,[27] including the *Spina christi lotus,* the Christ's thorn tree.[28] The hanging of clothes on the asherah might be compared also to clothes hung on cult statues in Mesopotamia and Ugarit attested in the second and first millennia and ridiculed in the Letter of Jeremiah 6:33.[29]

Although they are not specifically identified as such, some trees in sacred precincts were perhaps asherahs or the antecedents to asherahs. For example, Joshua 24:26-27 describes the placement of an altar next to a tree *('ēlāh)* in the sacred precincts of Yahweh at Shechem (cf. Gen. 35:4).[30] It was at a tree, *'ēlāh,* where an angel appeared to Gideon (Judg. 6:11), although the narrative assumes that the asherah was a different item (Judg. 6:25). Isaiah 1:29-30 condemns the oaks *('êlîm)* without providing any further information and states that the people shall be like an oak whose leaf withers. Isaiah 61:3 may transform this image in calling the people *'êlê haṣṣedeq,* "oaks of

25. For discussion, see B. Stade, *The Books of Kings: Critical Edition of the Hebrew Text,* trans. R. E. Brunnow and P. Haupt (Leipzig: J. C. Hinrichs'sche; Baltimore: Johns Hopkins Univ. Press; London: David Nutt, 1904), 293; and J. A. Montgomery, *A Critical and Exegetical Commentary,* 534.

26. E. Lane, *Arabic-English Lexicon,* Book 1, part 1 (London/Edinburgh: Williams & Norgate, 1863), 159; so, among many scholars, M. J. Lagrange, "Études sur les religions sémitiques," *RB* 10 (1901): 550 n. 2; J. Gray, *I and II Kings,* 2d ed., OTL (London: SCM, 1970), 734; A. Lemaire, "Les inscriptions de Khirbet el-Qôm et l'ashérah de Yhwh," *RB* 84 (1977): 606; M. Weinfeld, "Kuntillet ʿAjrûd Inscriptions and Their Significance," *SEL* 1 (1984): 129 nn. 21-22; Ahlström, "An Archaeological Picture," 135, 144 n. 108; McCarter, "Aspects of the Religion," 144; cf. H. Gressman, "Josia und das Deuteronomium," *ZAW* 1 (1924): 325-26. See also de Moor, "'*ᵃshērāh,*" 441. Weinfeld also compares clothing woven for Astarte and Athena ("The Kuntillet 'Ajrûd Inscriptions," 129 n. 22). Ahlström relates the textiles discovered at Kuntillet ʿAjrûd to BH *bāttîm.*

27. W. F. Baudissen, *Studien zur semitischen Religionsgeschichte* (Leipzig: F. W. Grunnow, 1876-70), 221-22; M. J. Lagrange, *Études sur les religions sémitiques* (Paris: V. Lecoffre, 1905), 175; Smith, *Religion of the Semites,* 186.

28. A. Abu-Rabia, *Folk Medicine Among the Bedouin Tribes in the Negev* (Beersheba: The Jacob Blaustein Institute for Desert Research, Ben-Gurion University of the Negev, 1983), 21; cf. T. Canaan, *Mohammedan Saints and Sanctuaries in Palestine* (Jerusalem: Ariel, 1927), 36-37.

29. L. Oppenheim, "The Golden Garments of the Gods," *JNES* 8 (1949): 172-93; D. B. Weisberg, "Wool and Linen Material in Texts from the Time of Nebuchadnezzar," *EI* 16 (1982 = H. Orlinsky Festschrift): 224*-225*; de Tarragon, *Le Culte à Ugarit,* 110.

30. See R. G. Boling and G. E. Wright, *Joshua,* AB 6 (Garden City, NY: Doubleday, 1982), 540.

righteousness." Hosea 4:13 condemns a variety of trees, including *'ēlāh,* as sites of improper sacrifice. Traditions contained in classical sources likewise point to the tree as a cultic symbol in Phoenician religion. Achilles Tatius describes the tree growing in a sacred precinct in Tyre.[31] Herodotus (*History* 2.56) mentions a Phoenician "holy woman," who before establishing the oracular cult of Dodona in Epirus, founded a temple to Zeus beneath an oak.[32] The biblical and classical witnesses may point to a common Canaanite tradition.

Was the tree originally the symbol of the goddess, and did the pole substituting for a tree secondarily come to be the symbol of the asherah?[33] In this case, the symbol developed originally from the cultic use of an actual tree. This interpretation underlies the proposal of Albright that BH *'ēlāh* may be derived from the epithet of Asherah, *'ilt,* "goddess."[34] Both Hebrew *'ēlāh* and Ugaritic *'ilt* are grammatically feminine singular nouns corresponding to the masculine forms *'ēl* in Hebrew and *'il* in Ugaritic. (Both BH *'ēl* and Ugaritic *'il* are generic words for "god" and designations for the god "El.") While the view of Albright might suggest that the usual LXX translation of asherah with *alsos,* "grove," and the less frequent *dendra,* "tree" (LXX Isa. 17:8; 27:9) and Mishnaic descriptions of the asherah as a living tree (*'Orlah* 1:7, 8; *Sukkah* 3:1-3; *'Abodah Zarah* 3:7, 9, 10; *Me'ilah* 3:8) could reflect a genuine recollection of the variety of forms that the asherah assumed in Israelite religion, it appears more likely that these texts reflect a later understanding of the asherah, perhaps influenced by the phenomenon of sacred groves in Hellenistic religion.[35]

Biblical texts provide a few indications for the cultic context of the asherah. According to two passages it was a wooden item erected next to the altar of a god. In Judges 6:25-26, Gideon is commanded to "pull down the altar of Baal which your father has, and cut down the asherah that is beside it."

31. Achilles Tatius, *The Adventures of Leucippe and Clitophon* 2:14. See S. Gaselee, *Achilles Tatius,* Loeb Classical Library (London: William Heinemann; New York: G. P. Putnam's Sons, 1917), 81-85. For further discussion, see M. Delcor, "The Selloi of the Oracle of Dodona and the Oracular Priests of the Semitic Religions," in *Religion d'Israël et Proche Orient Ancien: Des Phéniciens aux Esseniens* (Leiden: Brill, 1976), 116-23.

32. Herodotus, *History* 2:56 (Godley, *Herodotus,* vol. 1, 344-45).

33. See Emerton, "New Light on Israelite Religion," 15.

34. Albright, *Yahweh and the Gods of Canaan,* 189; Oden, *Studies,* 154. See also de Moor, "Diviners' Oak," *IDBSup,* 243-44; Ringgren, *Israelite Religion,* 25; Andersen and Freedman, *Hosea,* 158.

35. See J. A. Robinson, *The Mishna on Idolatry: 'Aboda Zara,* Texts and Studies, Contributions to Biblical and Patristic Literature, vol. 8, no. 2 (Cambridge: At the University Press, 1911; reprinted, Nendeln/Liechtenstein: Kraus, 1967), 60-61.

Deuteronomy 16:21 forbids the "planting" of "any tree — an asherah — besides the altar of the Lord your God which you shall make."[36] The asherah was a religious symbol within Yahwistic cult in both northern and southern capitals. It is indicated in 2 Kings 13:6 that the asherah belonged to the cult of Samaria. The Jerusalem temple was expunged of cultic objects considered unacceptable according to 2 Kings 23. The list includes the asherah, but there is no indication that the asherah was related to a cult of Baal. Rather, as Olyan has argued, the asherah was associated historically with Yahweh and not with Baal.[37]

The Late Bronze Age iconography of the asherah would suggest that it represented maternal and nurturing dimensions of the deity.[38] Jeremiah 2:27 may point to the maternal symbolism of the asherah in the waning days of the monarchy.[39] The verse refers to the house of Israel, with its priests, prophets, and kings "who say to a tree, 'You are my father,' and to a stone, 'You gave me birth'" (*'ōmĕrîm lā'ēṣ 'ābî 'attāh wĕlā'eben 'att yĕlidtānî* [Qere: *yĕlidtānû*]). Many scholars argue that the verse polemically reverses the roles of the maternal symbolism of the asherah with the paternal symbolism of the stone.[40]

Further cultic functions of the asherah may be queried, although data are sparse. De Moor suggests that the asherah perhaps involved divination.[41] Habakkuk 2:19 may allude to the "revelation," or "teaching," achieved through divination within the cult of the tree *('ēṣ)* and the stone *('eben):* The verse declares:

> Woe to him who says to a wooden thing *('ēṣ),* Awake;
> to a dumb stone *('eben),* Arise!
> Can this give revelation *(yôreh)?*
> Behold, it is overlaid with gold and silver,
> and there is no breath at all in it.

36. Olyan, *Asherah and the Cult of Yahweh,* 9.

37. Olyan, *Asherah and the Cult of Yahweh,* 38-61; cf. Day, "Asherah in the Hebrew Bible," 391. De Moor ("*'ashērāh,*" 441) argues that in Iron Age Israel Asherah was the consort of Baal because of the fusion of Baal's consort, Anat, with Asherah.

38. See Hestrin, "The Lachish Ewer," 212-23; idem, "Israelite and Persian Periods," 72; Weinfeld, "Kuntillet 'Ajrûd Inscriptions," 121-22; P. D. Miller, "The Absence of the Goddess in Israelite Religion," *Hebrew Annual Review* 10 (1986): 239-48; and *The Religion of Ancient Israel,* 29-40.

39. See J. A. Thompson, *The Book of Jeremiah* (Grand Rapids: Eerdmans, 1980), 180; Olyan, "The Cultic Confessions of Jer 2,27a," *ZAW* 99 (1987): 254-59. I thank Professor Olyan for bringing the biblical reference to my attention.

40. For further discussion of this verse, see section 4 below.

41. De Moor, "Diviners' Oak," 243-44.

The pairing of tree and stone might recall the asherah, since the tree is the goddess's symbol.[42] Indeed, this pairing occurs in Deuteronomy 29:16 and Jeremiah 2:27 (cf. Ezek. 20:32). This section of Habakkuk 2:18-19, however, may involve a description of making an idol from materials of wood and stone and may refer only to functions that deities may provide generally; therefore, it may not be a reference specifically to the asherah. Hosea 4:12 may also preserve a record of the role of divination through the asherah: "My people inquired of a thing of wood *(ʿēṣ)*, and their staff gives them oracles." While the parallellism has suggested to commentators that the wood constitutes a staff of some sort,[43] this verse may allude to divination by means of the asherah. Divination via the asherah might explain the grouping of asherim with diviners in Micah 5:11-13 (E 12-14). Furthermore, this approach to these passages would also provide further explanation for prophetic and Deuteronomistic criticisms of the asherah. In the popular religion of the high places and perhaps the royal religion of the capital cities, the asherah perhaps provided an access to divine information that competed with prophetic inquiry.

Another possible function of the asherah was healing. Like the bones of the prophet Elisha (2 Kings 13:21), the asherah perhaps was used for medicinal purposes. While no biblical texts hint at this feature of the asherah, a Talmudic passage, *Pesaḥim* 25a, mentions that any remedy, except the wood of the asherah, is acceptable:

> Rabbi Jacob said in Rabbi Johanan's name: We may cure ourselves with all things, save with the wood of the *asherah*. How is it meant? If we say that there is danger, even the wood of the *asherah* too [is permitted]; while if there is no danger, even all [other] forbidden things of the Torah too are not [permitted]. After all [it means] that there is danger, yet even so the wood of the *asherah* [must) not be used.[44]

42. Olyan, "Cultic Confessions of Jer 2,27a," 254-59; Andersen and Freedman, *Hosea*, 366. For further discussion of Jer. 2:27 and this pairing, see below in section 4.

43. See Freedman and Andersen, *Hosea*, 365-66. For criticisms of Hos. 4:12 as a reference to the asherah, see Olyan, *Asherah and the Cult of Yahweh*, 19-20.

44. I. Epstein, ed., *The Babylonian Talmud: Seder Moʿed* (London: Soncino, 1938), 114; I. Epstein, ed., *Hebrew English Edition of the Babylonian Talmud, Pesahim*, trans. H. Freedman, rev. ed. (London: Soncino, 1967), ad loc. My thanks go to W. Holladay, who brought to my attention the following description of the temple of Astarte standing at the grotto of the Afqa River at Khirbet Afqa in Syria about twenty-three miles northeast of Beirut, midway between Byblos and Baalbeq: "The river Adonis emerges from a huge grotto in the side of precipitous rock nearly 650 ft. high. . . . On the rock facing the grotto there is a platform where you will see the remains of a Roman temple. . . . The sacred character of the place has been strengthened by tradition. The inhabitants place oil-lamps beneath the vault which they light in honour of the 'lady' who haunts this region. There is

From this text it might be inferred that healing was an ancient aspect of the asherah that biblical sources do not mention. It is not possible to confirm further either the divinatory or healing aspects of the asherah, but the cultic features of the asherah were perhaps more far-reaching than the biblical and inscriptional sources indicate.

3. The Inscriptional Evidence

The evidence for the asherah in the Kuntillet ʿAjrûd inscriptions bears on the issue of whether Asherah was a goddess in ancient Israel and whether she was the consort of Yahweh. The inscriptions from Kuntillet ʿAjrûd in the eastern Sinai are dated on paleographic grounds to ca. 800.[45] The two following quotations typify the inscriptions containing the element **'šrth:*[46]

'mr X 'mr wlywʿśh w[l-Z] *brkt 'tkm lyhwh šmrn wlšrth*	X says: Say to Y and Yauʿaśah and [to Z]: I bless you to[47] Yahweh of Samaria, and to his/its asherah.
[']mr 'mryw l'dny [X] *brktk lyhwh [šmrn] wl'šrth*	Amaryaw [sa]ys: Say to my lord [X]: I bless you to Yahweh [of Samaria,] and to his/its asherah.

here a curious mixture of cults; both Shiites and Christians come to worship the *Zahra,* who, in Lebanon, was Venus' successor. The Christians affirm that the ruins of Afqa are those of a church dedicated to the Virgin. Nearby there is a fig tree on which pieces of the clothing of sick people are hung in order to bring about their recovery; this has the same function as the sacred tree in antiquity" (*The Guidebook, The Middle East — Lebanon, Syria, Jordan, Iraq, Iran,* Hachette World Guides [Paris: Hachette, 1966], 176; for more details of the site, see Pope, *El in the Ugaritic Texts,* 75-78).

45. For discussion of the dating, see Olyan, *Asherah and the Cult of Yahweh,* 23.

46. Z. Meshel, "Kuntillat ʿAjrûd — An Israelite Site from the Monarchial Period on the Sinai Border," *Qadmoniot* 9 (1976): 118-24; idem, "Kuntillet ʿAjrûd — An Israelite Religious Center in Northern Sinai," *Expedition* 20 (1978): 50-54; idem, "Did Yahweh Have a Consort?" *Biblical Archaeologist Review* 5/2 (1979): 24-34; J. Naveh, "Graffiti and Dedications," *BASOR* 235 (1979): 27-30; Weinfeld, "Kuntillet ʿAjrûd Inscriptions," 121-30; Lemaire, "Les inscriptions de Khirbet el-Qôm," 595-608; idem, "Date et origine des inscriptions paléo-hebraïques et phéniciennes de Kuntillet ʿAjrûd," *SEL* 1 (1984): 131-43; Dever, "Asherah, Consort of Yahweh?" 21-37. The bibliographical items listed in n. 1 also provide discussions of these inscriptions. The epigraphic evidence is summarized in W. A. Maier III, *'Ašerah: Extrabiblical Evidence,* HSM 37 (Atlanta, GA: Scholars, 1986); and Olyan, *Asherah and the Cult of Yahweh,* 23-37.

47. In the first edition of this book, I followed the standard translation, "to." S. Parker (*Hebrew Studies* 33 [1992]: 161) comments: "The expression means 'bless someone to a deity.' To say 'I bless you to Yahweh' is to report that in praying to Yahweh one says 'bless PN.' In other words it is tantamount to saying 'I am praying for you.'"

Since the initial publication of these inscriptions, scholars have noted that the pronominal suffix on **'šrth* indicates that the form is a common noun and not the personal name of the goddess Asherah.[48] This logic is not airtight. Indeed, although divine names do not appear in Hebrew with a pronominal suffix (i.e., an ending meaning "his"/"its"), many divine names are found in similarly "bound" syntactic constructions. Divine names appear in "bound" forms when they stand in genitive relationship with (or in "construct state" to) a noun or a pronominal suffix (nouns with the definite article belong to a closely related category).[49] For example, Yahweh stands in construct relationship with a number of place-names, a formula attested in "Yahweh of Teiman" in the inscriptions from Kuntillet ʿAjrûd; this construction warrants interpreting *šmrn* as a place-name, Samaria, rather than translating "our guardian."[50] As P. K. McCarter notes, this type of construction may be elliptical for deity X who dwells in Y place, as in BH *yhwh bĕṣiyyôn,* "Yahweh in Zion" (Ps. 99:2), *dāgôn bĕ'ašdôd,* "Dagon in Ashdod" (1 Sam. 5:5), Phoenician *tnt blbnn,* "Tannit in Lebanon" (KAI 81:1) and Ugaritic *mlk bʿṯtrt,* "Mlk in Ashtaroth" (KTU 1.100.41; cf. *mlk ʿṯtrt,* "Mlk of Ashtaroth" in RS 1986/2235.17).[51] Similarly, the form **'šrth* might be interpreted as the name of the goddess in a genitive relationship (or in construct state to) a pronominal suffix. From this evidence, it might be then argued that **'šrth* in the inscriptions represents a divine name. Although no Hebrew examples for a divine name with a pronominal suffix are attested, Ugaritic provides some examples, including *'aṯrty* (KTU 2.31.39) and *ʿnth* (KTU 1.43.13).[52] The bib-

48. See Emerton, "New Light on Israelite Religion," 14-19; Tigay, *You Shall Have No Other Gods,* 26-28; McCarter, "Aspects of the Religion," 143.

49. Emerton, "New Light on Israelite Religion," 14-19.

50. M. Gilula, "To Yahweh Shomron and His Asherah," *Shnaton* 3-4 (1978-79): 129-37 (Heb.; English summary 15-16); Emerton, "New Light on Israelite Religion," 3, 12-13; Weinfeld, "Kuntillet ʿAjrûd Inscriptions," 125; McCarter, "Aspects of the Religion," 139. "His" asherah would refer to Yahweh, whereas "its" asherah would refer to Samaria. The pottery discovered at Kuntillet ʿAjrûd includes "Samaria ware" (see J. Gunneweg, I. Perlman, and Z. Meshel, "The Origin of the Pottery of Kuntillet ʿAjrûd," *IEJ* 35 [1985]: 270-83), enhancing the interpretation of *yhwh šmrn* as referring to Samaria.

51. McCarter, "Aspects of the Religion," 140-41. On RS 1986/2235.17, see P. Bordreuil, "Découvertes épigraphiques récentes à Ras ibn Hani et à Ras Shamra," *CRAIBL* 1987, 298.

52. For discussion, see M. Dietrich, "Die Parhedra in Pantheon von Emar: Miscellanea Emariana (I)," *UF* 29 (1997): 115-22; Tigay, *You Shall Have No Other Gods,* 27, 34; Smith, *The Origins of Biblical Monotheism,* 72-73; A. P. Xella, "Le dieu et «sa» déesse: l'utilisation des Suffixes pronominaux avec des théonymes d'Ebla à Ugarit et à la Kuntillet ʿAjrud," *UF* 27 (1995): 599-610; and Zevit, *The Religions of Ancient Israel,* 403. *l'aṯrty* (KTU 2.31.39) occurs in a broken context. In RS 16.394:60, *PRU II* (9-10) reconstructs *[l]'aṯr[ty];* KTU 2.31.60 reads *l* aṯr[t]x.* Ugaritic *'il'ib,* "god, father" or divine ancestral father, occurs with pronominal suffixes (e.g.,

lical bound forms, *habbaʿal* ("the baal") and *ha'ăšērāh* ("the asherah") appear in a few cases to refer to a specific deity, but these instances may conform to their use as generic references to deities as in Judges 3:7 (cf. Judg. 2:13; 10:16; 1 Sam. 7:4; 12:10; Jer. 2:23; 9:14). Despite the possibility that the Ugaritic examples could point to taking **'šrth* as the name of the goddess, it appears better to follow the grammatical rule of seeing bound forms as common nouns rather than to discard the rule and thereby interpret **'šrth* as the goddess Asherah.[53] Z. Zevit has offered a different morphological interpretation of **'šrth* as the goddess's name.[54] Instead of viewing the ending *h* as a pronominal suffix, he considers it to be a second indicator of feminine gender. According to Tigay, most of the analogues Zevit marshalls as support do not contain two endings indicating feminine gender. Tigay denies the relevance of most of these examples because many are place-names with final *h* indicating direction ("heh-locale").[55] It might be argued that the object of the verb-preposition combination, **brk l-*, "to bless by X," denotes a deity in West Semitic votive offerings. As Tigay has observed,[56] this view is vitiated by a number of Phoenician inscriptions that have cultic objects following the preposition (KAI 12:3-4; 251; 256).

Apart from the grammatical problem, there are further semantic issues

---

KTU 1.17 I 27). On this figure, see chapter 1 n. 105. CTA 33 (KTU 1.43).13 may provide another Ugaritic example of divine name plus suffix, *lʿnth*, but the reading is uncertain (see CTA 116 n. 8; M. Dietrich, O. Loretz, and J. Sanmartin, "Die ugaritischen und hebräischen Gottesnamen," *UF* 7 [1975]: 553). KTU reads *lʿnth** without additional comment. Cf. AN.DA.MU-ia usually read as ᵈ*DA.MU-ia*, "my Damu," in EA 84:33 and *hattammûz* in Ezek. 8:14. For an alternative understanding of the deity in EA 84:33, see N. Na'aman, "On Gods and Scribal Traditions in the Amarna Letters," *UF* 22 (1990): 248-50, who believes the AN.DA.MU-ia is a title of the goddess known as "The Lady of Byblos" (cf. 132.53-55). This issue would affect the relevance of AN.DA.MU-ia for the category of divine names with pronominal suffixes.

53. Gilula, "To Yahweh Shomron," 134-37; Naveh, "Graffiti and Dedications," 28; Ahlström, "An Archaeological Picture," 20; idem, *Royal Administration,* 43; Dever, "Asherah, Consort of Yahweh?" 21-37; Hestrin, "The Lachish Ewer," 212-23; Olyan, *Asherah and the Cult of Yahweh,* 28. See the comments of Lambert, "Trees, Snakes, and Gods," 439-40. Before the discovery of the inscriptions, A. T. Olmstead, Ahlström, and other scholars anticipated this conclusion (see Ahlström, *Aspects of Syncretism,* 50-54; idem, "Some Remarks on Prophets and Cult," in *Transitions in Biblical Scholarship,* ed. J. C. Rylaarsdam (Chicago and London: Univ. of Chicago Press, 1968), 121. In previous discussions I held out for this possibility (Smith, "God Male and Female," 333-40; idem, "Divine Form and Size in Ugaritic and Pre-exilic Israelite Religion," *ZAW* 100 [1988]: 426).

54. Z. Zevit, "The Khirbet el-Qôm Inscription Mentioning a Goddess," *BASOR* 255 (1984): 39-47.

55. Tigay, *You Shall Have No Other Gods,* 30; see also Rainey, "The Toponyms," 4.

56. Tigay, *You Shall Have No Other Gods,* 28-29.

afflicting interpreting the noun as either the goddess's name or the symbol in its capacity of referring to the goddess. If *l'šrth* in the inscriptions from Kuntillet 'Ajrud refers to the goddess ("and to his Asherah"), then it is unclear what "his Asherah" means.[57] Only by assuming an ellipsis of "his consort, Asherah" or the like does this interpretation make reasonable sense. If *l'šrth* means "his asherah" referring to the symbol, then "his asherah" should denote something that is "his," and not hers. In short, it appears preferable to take "his asherah" as something that is "his," i.e., a symbol that once may have referred to the goddess by the same name, but functions in this context as part of Yahweh's symbolic repertoire, possibly with older connotations associated with the goddess. Some of these older connotations are explored below.

Attempts to interpret the name with a different semantic range are undermined by etymological fallacies of various kinds. For example, interpreting Hebrew **'šrth* on the basis of Ugaritic *'aṯr,* Akkadian *ašru,* and Phoenician *'šr,* "sanctuary,"[58] founders on the fact that such a meaning does not occur otherwise in Hebrew. Even greater difficulty attaches to meanings posited without any etymological basis in any Northwest Semitic language. This problem attends proposals such as "symbol,"[59] "consort,"[60] "goddess,"[61] and "trace."[62] The fourth translation, proffered by P. K. McCarter, offers an ingenious solution to interpreting **'šrth.* McCarter interprets the name to be a hypostasis of Yahweh and not a goddess as such; in this connection he compares other goddesses who bear titles expressing relationship of hypostasis with gods. The two main examples are the Ugaritic and Phoenician title for Astarte, who is called

57. As Zevit (*The Religions of Ancient Israel,* 403 n. 110) rightly asks: "What would it have meant to say that the goddess *belonged to* or was *possessed by* Yahweh?" (Zevit's italics).

58. Lipiński, "The Goddess 'Aṯirat," 101-19; idem, "The Syro-Palestinian Iconography of Woman and Goddess (Review Article)," *IEJ* 36 (1986): 87-96; cf. McCarter, "Aspects of the Religion," 145. For a Phoenician inscription from Akko with *'šrt* as "shrine(s)," see M. Dothan, "A Phoenician Inscription," 81-94. McCarter ("Aspects of the Religion," 145) relates the BH *'ăšērāh* to *'šrt* in a third-century Phoenician text from Ma'sub bearing the dedication "to Ashtart in the asherah of Baal Hamon," *l'štrt b'šrt b'l ḥmn* (KAI 19:4). Peckham ("Phoenicia and the Religion of Israel," 91 n. 24) compares Phoenician inscriptions from 'Umm el-'Amed and Pyrgi where an asherah is reserved for Astarte. In these instances, the Phoenician word means "shrine" or the like.

59. Meshel, "Did Yahweh Have a Consort?" 31.

60. M. H. Pope, "Response to Sasson on the Sublime Song," *Maarav* 2/2 (1980): 210-11; Engle, "Pillar Figurines," 84-85.

61. See the remarks of Pardee, "The New Canaanite Myths and Legends," 274; Cooper, "Divine Names and Epithets in the Ugaritic Texts," 342.

62. McCarter, "Aspects of the Religion," 137-55. McCarter is followed by J. S. Burnett, *A Reassessment of Biblical Elohim,* SBLDS 183 (Atlanta: Society of Biblical Literature, 2001), 91 n. 36.

"the name of Baal," *šm bʿl* (KTU 1.16 VI 56 [cf. 1.2 IV 28]; KAI 14:18),[63] and a title of Phoenician Tannit designated "the face of Baal," *pn bʿl* (KAI 78.2; 79:1, 10-11; 85:1; 86:1; 137:1; 175:2; 176:2-3; cf. 87:1) and *pʿn bʿl* (KAI 94:1; 97:1; 102:1; 105:1; cf. 164:1; cf. *ʾnpy-bʿl* twice in an incantation from Wadi Hammamat in Upper Egypt, written in Demotic script but Aramaic in language, and dated to the sixth or fifth century B.C.E.; cf. *phanebalos* on coins of the Roman period from Ashkelon; BH *pĕnûʾēl* [Gen. 32:32; Judg. 8:8, 9, 17; 1 Kings 12:25]/*pĕnîʾēl* [Gen. 32:31]; and the Greek place-name for a cape north of Byblos, *prosopon theou,* "face of God").[64] Following Albright, McCarter also

63. S. D. McBride, "The Deuteronomistic Name Theology" (Ph.D. diss., Harvard University, 1969), 135-37; Cross, *Canaanite Myth and Hebrew Epic,* 11, 30-31; T. N. D. Mettinger, *The Dethronement of Sabaoth; Studies in the Shem and Kabod Theologies,* ConBOT 18 (Lund: Gleerup, 1982), 38-79, 123-30; L. Laberge, "Le lieu que YHWH a choisi pour mettre son Nom," *Estudios Bíblicos* 43 (1985): 209-36; McCarter, "Aspects of the Religion," 155 n. 62. Examples of **šim/*šum* in Northwest Semitic personal names include Phoenician *šm,* "Name" (KAI 54:1), *šmzbl,* "Name is prince" (KAI 34:4), *šmʾdny,* "Name is lord" (see Gianto, "Some Notes on the Mulk Inscription from Nebi Yunis (RES 367)," *Biblica* 68 (1987): 397-400), Elephantine *ʾšmbytʾl,* "Name of Bethel" (AP 22:124; Oden, *Studies,* 126-27), and Shimil in Armenian Ahiqar 1:4 (*OTPs* 2:486 n. 50). See Cross, "Old Canaanite and Early Phoenician Scripts," 3; P. Bordreuil, "*Mizzĕbul lô:* à propos de Psaume 49:15," in *Ascribe to the Lord; Biblical and Other Studies in Memory of Peter C. Craigie,* ed. L. Eslinger and G. Taylor, JSOTSup 67 (Sheffield: JSOT, 1988), 93-98. In addition to the Akkadian examples cited by McBride, **šum* is also attested in Eblaite names (Pomponio, "I nomi divini," 152, 156) and one name from Emar (Emar 52:2). The longstanding view of the Deuteronomistic *šēm* theology has been questioned recently by Sandra Richter, *The Deuteronomistic History and the Place of the Name,* BZAW 318 (Berlin/New York: de Gruyter, 2002, in press). As a result, a serious reassessment of the extent of *šēm* in Deuteronomistic passages will be made. Passages such as 1 Kings 8 will likely hold up. Further consideration of non-Dtr passages with "the name" (e.g., Isa. 30:27, Ps. 29:2 [?]) needs to be included in the discussion. See further p. 142 below.

64. On *pānîm,* "face," as divine hypostasis in both Phoenician and Israelite religion, see Cross, *Canaanite Myth and Hebrew Epic,* 28. For the incantation from Egypt, see R. C. Steiner, "The Scorpion Spell from Wadi Ḥammamat: Another Aramaic Text in Demotic Script," *JNES* 60 (2001): 259-68. Secular usage of this term occurs in Gen. 33:10, Exod. 10:28-29 (cf. 2 Sam. 17:11; Rashi on Exod. 33:15), and the Late Bronze antecedents cited in chapter 4, section 1. RS 25.318 provides further background. The inscription, found on a lion rhyton, calls the rhyton *pn ʾarw,* "the face of the lion" (see M. Dietrich and O. Loretz, "Die keilalphabetische Krugausschrift RS 25.318," in *Ugaritica VI,* ed. C. F. A. Schaeffer, Mission de Ras Shamra 18 [Paris: P. Geuthner; Leiden: Brill, 1978]: 147-48; U. Zebulun, "A Canaanite Ram-Headed Cup," *IEJ* 37 [1987]: 96-99); cf. the name *pnsmlt,* "face of image" (KAI 57). These examples may illustrate in the secular realm what "Tannit, face of Baʿl," *tnt pn bʿl* (e.g., KAI 78:2; 79:1, 10-11; 85:1; 86:1; 137:1; cf. 87:1) and *tnt pʿn bʿl* (e.g., KAI 94:1; 97:1; 102:1; 105:1; cf. 164:1), attested in various Punic and neo-Punic sites from Tunisia and elsewhere, signified in the sacred realm, namely, that Tannit was the representation of Baal. On *phanebalos,* "face of Baal," on Roman coins from Ashkelon, see Albright, *Yahweh and the Gods of Canaan,* 129; Cross, *Canaanite Myth*

appeals to the uncertain hypostatic interpretation of the name Anat as meaning "sign" in the Aramaic divine names *ʿntyh* (AP 44:3) and *ʿntbtʾl* (AP 22:125).[65] The weakness of this suggestion for **ʾšrth* is not limited to the etymological difficulty identified above, namely, that the base ("root") **ʾṯr* does not mean "trace" in any Northwest Semitic language.[66] There is the more glaring problem that in the cases of Astarte and Tannit it is not the goddess's name but her title that is the term of hypostasis. These cases are therefore not true analogies for McCarter's proposals for Anat and Asherah, whose names he

---

and Hebrew Epic, 28; for the Greek place name for a cape north of Byblos, *prosopon theou,* "face of God," see Harden, *The Phoenicians,* 79. "The face of God" stands as a hypostasis for God in *Odes of Solomon* 25:4 (*OTPs* 2:758). Divine hypostases of the face and name may be one of several Israelite ways of referring to the divine military retinue of Yahweh. Given the attestation of such terms in Ugaritic and Phoenician, the origins of this usage predate biblical usage. Unlike the usages in the wider West Semitic world, the biblical usage is not associated with other deities. Another old way of describing the divine military retinue is to name other divinities as part of the retinue (Hab. 3:5). For these forms of the divine retinue, see Smith, *The Origins of Biblical Monotheism,* 47, 68, 74-76. A third way of referring to the retinue in its destructive function is as *mašḥîtîm* as in Gen. 19:3 (see p. 38 above). For *ʾĕlōhîm* as a possible fourth way, see Burnett, *A Reassessment of Biblical Elohim,* 79-119. This would comport with only divine pluralities (e.g., *bʿlm* and *ršpm)* which appear to be military in character (Smith, *The Origins of Biblical Monotheism,* 67-68). *PE* 1.10.20 which refers to *elohim* as the allies of Elos would constitute a good parallel for Burnett's proposal.

65. See chapter 2, section 4.

66. The Northwest Semitic attestations of the root **ʾṯr* suggest the base meaning of "to be/go after/to." Ugaritic *ʾaṯr,* Akkadian *ʾašru,* and Phoenician *ʾšr* mean "place" (see n. 58 above for references; cf. M. Dietrich and O. Loretz, "Ugaritisch *ʾṯr, aṯr, aṯryt* und *aṯrt,*" *UF* 16 [1984]: 57-62). The Ugaritic and Akkadian forms of the noun secondarily marked subordinate clauses denoting place (see A. Rainey, "Observations on Ugaritic Grammar," *UF* 3 [1971]: 162; D. Pardee, "A Further Note on *PRU V,* No. 60," *UF* 13 [1981]: 152, 156); this usage formed the basis for the development of BH *ʾăšer* and Moabite *ʾšr* as a marker for relative clauses (see Garr, *Dialect Geography,* 85, 87). The Ugaritic preposition *ʾaṯr* means "after" (for attestations in mythological texts, see del Olmo Lete, *Mitos y leyendas,* 519). Like later BH *ʾăšer* and Moabite *ʾšr,* the preposition apparently developed from accusative of place. In the Sefire inscription (KAI 222 B 3), the prep. *b-* plus the noun **ʾšr* means "in the place of" and refers to a successor (see J. A. Fitzmyer, *The Aramaic Inscriptions of Sefire,* Biblica et Orientalia 19 [Rome: Pontifical Biblical Institute, 1967], 18-19; cf. BA *ʾătar,* "place," in Dan. 2:35; 6:3, 5, 7; Ezra 5:15 and the preposition **bāʾtar,* "after," in Dan. 2:39; 7:6, 7). This sense of the root apparently underlies the Ugaritic noun *ʾuṯryn,* "successor" (cf. Huehnergard, *Ugaritic Vocabulary,* 112), referring to the heir apparent (Rainey, "Observations," 169). BH **ʾšr* (and perhaps Ugaritic **ʾṯr*) mean "to go, advance" (*BDB,* 80). Albright's (*Yahweh and the Gods of Canaan,* 105; *Archaeology and the Religion of Israel* [Garden City, NY: Doubleday, 1965], 76) interpretation of Asherah's name as a verbal sentence, i.e., *ʾaṯrt ym,* "she who treads on the sea [or, sea-dragon]," is more semantically consistent with the Northwest Semitic attestations of the root (see Oden, *Studies,* 72, 93). None of the proposed explanations for *ʾaṯrt ym* is satisfactory, however.

takes to be expressions of aspects of gods. Furthermore, the analogy with divine names *ʿntyh, ʿntbtʾl, ḥrmbtʾl* (AP 7:7), or *ʾšmbtʾl* (AP 22:124) is unsure. Some of these names may not be construct chains, "aspect X of god Y," but two divine names or divine name plus a place name.[67] The interpretation of these forms should not obscure the fact that different developments may lie behind them. In any case, the etymology "presence" or "sign," either for the element **ʿnt* in these names or the Ugaritic goddess Anat, is not secure. Finally, McCarter makes the problematic assumption that Asherah is historically disassociated from **ʾšrth* in the Kuntillet ʿAjrûd inscriptions, that the former was a Canaanite goddess and the latter an internal Israelite development. As both Asherah and **ʾšrth* are religious phenomena criticized in ancient Israel during the same period, McCarter's assumptions constitute dubious grounds upon which to build a further historical reconstruction.

Finally, an attempt to see these attestations as non-Israelite because the script may be non-Israelite appears unfounded.[68] McCarter and Olyan consider the Samaria ostraca as the inscriptions written in the nearest paleographic hand.[69] Ahlström groups Kuntillet ʿAjrûd with Arad and Beersheba as district administrative centers and military forts that had sanctuaries or cult places.[70] According to Ahlström, the royal character of Kuntillet ʿAjrûd lends credence to the view that the religious practices there represent official Judean religion. Furthermore, much of the pottery that served as the medium for the inscriptions and iconography derived from Judah.[71] The religious practices of Kuntillet ʿAjrûd probably do not constitute practices peripheral to Judean culture. Indeed, "Yahweh . . . and his asherah" are attested also in a Hebrew inscription from Khirbet el-Qôm (ca. 700) in the heartland of Judah.[72] Although problems attend the interpretation of this inscription, it supports the point that the asherah was an Israelite phenomenon. Yet, the precise importance of the infor-

67. For various proposals, see chapter 2, section 4.

68. See chapter 2, section 1.

69. McCarter, "Aspects of the Religion," 138; Olyan, *Asherah and the Cult of Yahweh,* 32.

70. Ahlström, *Royal Administration,* 40-43. J. M. Hadley ("Some Drawings and Inscriptions on Two Pithoi from Kuntillet ʿAjrûd," *VT* 37 [1987]: 180-213) argues that Kuntillet ʿAjrûd served as a caravanserei.

71. See Gunneweg, Perlman, and Meshel, "The Origin," 270-83.

72. See Zevit, "The Khirbet el-Qôm Inscription"; Tigay, *You Shall Have No Other Gods,* 29-30; J. M. Hadley, "The Khirbet el-Qôm Inscription," *VT* 37 (1987): 50-62; M. O'Connor, "The Poetic Inscription from Khirbet el-Qôm," *VT* 37 (1987): 224-30. A. Catastini ("Note di epigrafia ebraica I-II," *Henoch* 6 [1984]: 129-38) interprets *ʾšrt* as G passive participle meaning "cursed," derived from **ʾšr,* "blessed," an unlikely semantic development given what is known of the root (discussed above in n. 66). For the bench tomb where the inscription was found, see W. G. Dever, "El-Qôm, Khirbet," *EAEHL* 4:976-77.

mation attested at Kuntillet ʿAjrûd and Khirbet el-Qôm cannot be determined without recourse to the other textual source attesting to the asherah, the biblical record, itself a matter of controversy.

4. Asherah — An Israelite Goddess?

The question of Asherah as an Israelite goddess constitutes a major issue in understanding Israelite religion. Does the biblical and extrabiblical evidence support the view that Asherah was a goddess in pre-exilic Israel and that she was the consort of Yahweh? Or, alternatively, does the data point to the asherah as a symbol within the cult of Yahweh without signifying a goddess? The first position constitutes a majority view, represented by the older works of H. Ringgren, G. Fohrer, and G. W. Ahlström, and the studies in the 1980s by W. G. Dever, D. N. Freedman, R. Hestrin, A. Lemaire, and S. Olyan and more recent works by J. M. Hadley, J. Day, M. Dijkstra, O. Keel, and Z. Zevit.[73] A minority position, held earlier by B. Lang, P. D. Miller, J. Tigay, and U. Winter and recently by C. Frevel and M. C. A. Korpel, maintains on the paucity of evidence that *ʾăšērāh* neither referred to a goddess nor symbolized the goddess in Israel.[74]

The inscriptional evidence points to a cult symbol, the asherah. Demonstrating whether the symbol represented a goddess who was Yahweh's consort requires an appeal to the biblical evidence, since the inscriptional data does not resolve this issue. The discussion of Genesis 49:25 above indicated that Asherah may have been the consort of El, but not Yahweh, at some early point in Israelite religion.[75] Olyan's argument that Asherah became Yahweh's consort by virtue of the identification of Yahweh and El has pro-

73. See Introduction n. 6; and Dever, "Asherah, Consort of Yahweh?" 21-37; Lemaire, "Les inscriptions de Khirbet el-Qôm," 595-608; Freedman, "Yahweh of Samaria," 241-49; Hestrin, "The Lachish Ewer," 212-23; Olyan, "Cultic Confessions of Jer 2,27a," 255; idem, *Asherah and the Cult of Yahweh,* xiv, 1-22, 33, 35, 74; Hadley, *The Cult of Asherah in Ancient Israel and Judah;* Day, *Yahweh and the Gods and Goddesses of Canaan,* 42-67; Dijkstra, "'I Have Blessed You by YHWH of Samaria and His Asherah': Texts with Religious Elements from the Soil Archive of Ancient Israel," in B. Becking et al., eds., *Only One God?* 17-44; Keel, *Goddesses and Trees,* 16-57; and Zevit, 472, 478, 537-38, 650-52, 677.

74. B. Lang, *Monotheism and the Prophetic Minority: An Essay in Biblical History and Sociology,* The Social World of Biblical Antiquity Series 1 (Sheffield: Almond, 1983), 39-40; Miller, "Absence of the Goddess," 239-48; Tigay, *You Shall Have No Other Gods,* 26-30; Winter, *Frau und Göttin,* 551-60; Frevel, *Aschera und der Ausschliesslichkeitsanspruch YHWHs;* Korpel, "Asherah Outside Israel," in B. Becking et al., *Only One God?* 127-50.

75. See chapter 1, section 4.

vided a viable explanation for the development of the cult of Yahweh and his Asherah.[76] Indeed, a number of biblical passages have been cited in defense of the reconstruction that Asherah was a goddess in Israel. These texts, 1 Kings 18:19, 2 Kings 21:7, 2 Kings 23:4, Judges 3:7, and Jeremiah 2:27,[77] are addressed in turn to examine the strength of the reconstruction of Asherah as Yahweh's consort.

As many scholars have noted, the one Iron II (ca. 1000-587) passage that unambiguously mentions the goddess Asherah is 1 Kings 18:19. The prophets of Asherah are presented in chapter 18 as the prophets of the Tyrian Jezebel. Like the prophets of Baal in this chapter, the prophets of Asherah are presented as Tyrian functionaries. The historical difficulty with this depiction is that Asherah is not attested in any Tyrian text. It would appear that Asherah was not a Tyrian goddess; indeed, Asherah is not attested anywhere in coastal Phoenicia during the Iron Age. The reference to "the prophets of Asherah" apparently does not constitute a plausible historical witness to the cult of Asherah in ancient Israel. Indeed, the phrase "the prophets of Asherah" in 1 Kings 18:19 has been viewed as a secondary gloss to the story.[78]

The question is why the name of Asherah is used here. If Phoenician Astarte was the goddess lying behind this reference to Asherah, the reference to "the prophets of Asherah" in 1 Kings 18:19 might be explained in terms of the threat that Astarte may have posed. As the main Phoenician goddess during the Iron Age, Astarte could have represented an intrusion during the monarchy. The polemic against Asherah in 1 Kings 18:19 may have represented a reaction against the cult of Astarte either in the northern kingdom during the ninth century or in the Jerusalem cult at the end of the Iron Age. The references to "the asherah" in 2 Kings 21 and 23 might point to the late Judean monarchy as the time for the substitution of Asherah for Astarte in 1 Kings 18:19. It is precisely this period when Astarte had a cult in ancient Is-

76. Olyan, *Asherah and the Cult of Yahweh*, 38-61.

77. *BDB* (p. 81) lists the following passages as references to the goddess: 1 Kings 15:3; 18:19; 2 Kings 21:7; 23:4, 7. Reed ("Asherah," *IDB* 1:251) interprets 2 Kings 21:7 as the image of the goddess and 2 Kings 32:4 as a reference to the goddess. Dever ("Asherah, Consort of Yahweh?" 31) cites Judg. 3:7; 1 Kings 18:19; and 2 Kings 23:4 as references to the goddess. He takes 2 Kings 21:7 as a reference to the image or furnishing for Asherah. Olyan (*Asherah and the Cult of Yahweh*, 2 n. 7) asserts that 2 Kings 21:7 and 23:4 are references to the goddess. Olyan ("Cultic Confessions of Jer 2,27a," 254-59) adds Jer. 2:27 to the list. De Moor ("*'ashērāh*," 441) presents quite a different picture: "When one compares 2 K. 23:4-6 with 23:13 f., the cult object *'asherah* seems to be connected with both the Asherah cult (in v. 4 probably a proper name; cf. 21:7) and the Astarte cult." A comparable position is argued below with respect to 1 Kings 18:19 and Judg. 3:7.

78. See chapter 1, section 2; and chapter 2, section 1.

rael. There is no evidence for Astarte as a goddess in Israel prior to the second half of the monarchy. She does not appear to be an old Canaanite inheritance of Israel, as her name does not appear in the old Canaanite inscriptions of the Late Bronze or Iron I periods. Furthermore, biblical literature does not point to a historical witness for her in the period of the Judges. She makes her initial appearance in the Bible as a Philistine goddess (1 Sam. 31:10) during the reign of Saul and as the "goddess of the Sidonians" (1 Kings 11:5, 33; 2 Kings 23:13) in the reign of Solomon. She does not appear as an Israelite phenomenon explicitly except in the polemics of Judges 2:13; 10:6 and 1 Samuel 7:3, 4; 12:10. These references belong to the tradents of these biblical books; the references likely stem from the second half of the monarchy[79] and might reflect the Judean cult to Astarte in Jerusalem. The "Queen of Heaven" in the book of Jeremiah may refer either to Astarte, the only West Semitic goddess bearing this title during the Iron Age, or to Ishtar (or possibly some combination of the two).[80] Jeremiah 44 presents the cult of the "Queen of Heaven" as an old one in Israel. It included the cultic acts of burning incense and pouring libations in her name and the baking of cakes in her honor (Jer. 7:18; 44:15-28). It would appear dubious that either Asherah or Astarte was the threat in the northern kingdom that 1 Kings 18:19 implies. Rather, this reference has the appearance of being a retrojection onto the earlier history of the northern kingdom, perhaps inspired by the known Phoenician background of Baal. This god represented a threat not only in the north in the ninth century, but also in the south at the end of the Judean monarchy. In sum, 1 Kings 18:19 is a historically implausible reference to Asherah. The gloss may be the result of substitution and not historical report; it perhaps belongs to the seventh or sixth century.

Two other passages taken to refer to the goddess Asherah, namely, 2 Kings 21:7 and 23:4, also constitute questionable historical witnesses to the goddess. Both texts belong to the second half of the Judean monarchy. The

79. See chapter 1, section 3.

80. See Olyan, "Some Observations," 161-74; see also M. Held, "Studies in Biblical Lexicography in Light of Akkadian," *EI* 16 (1982): 76-85. Morton Smith, "The Veracity of Ezekiel, the Sins of Manasseh, and Jeremiah 44:18," *ZAW* 87 (1975): 11-16; cf. K. Koch, "Ashera als Himmelskönigin in Jerusalem," *UF* 20 (1988): 97-120. For iconographic evidence for Ishtar in Israel in the seventh and sixth centuries, see T. Ornan, "Ištar as Depicted on Finds from Israel," in *Studies in the Archaeology of the Iron Age in Israel and Jordan*, ed. A. Mazar with the assistance of G. Mathias, JSOTSup 331 (Sheffield: Sheffield Academic Press, 2001), 235-52. This evidence bolsters the case for Ishtar as the "Queen of Heaven." For further discussion with evidence from material culture and additional bibliography, see P. J. King and L. E. Stager, *Life in Biblical Israel*, Library of Ancient Israel (Louisville/London: Westminster/John Knox, 2001), 350.

first, 2 Kings 21:7, refers to "the image/idol of the asherah" *(pesel hā'ăšērāh).* The word "image" *(pesel)* here is elsewhere used for images of deities, and consequently this verse has been viewed as a reference to the image of the goddess Asherah. There is no question that the asherah in 2 Kings 21:7 was considered an idolatrous object by the writer. That it signified the image of the goddess cannot be determined. The item called *pesel hā'ăšērāh* here may not have been an image of the goddess; it may have been a more elaborate form of the asherah in the royal cult of Jerusalem.

After 1 Kings 18:19 and Genesis 49:25, the passage most strongly suggesting that Asherah was a goddess is the second, 2 Kings 23:4 (cf. vv. 6, 7, 15). This verse mentions the asherah in the phrase "the vessels made for the baal, the asherah, and all the host of heaven" *(hakkēlîm hā'ăśûyim labbaʿal wĕlā'ăšērāh ūlkōl ṣĕbā' haššāmāyim).* The terms "the baal" and "all the host of heaven" are deities, and the most natural reading of the placement of "the asherah" between these two terms is that it likewise refers to a deity, specifically Asherah. This reading is not compelling on a number of grounds. All three are recipients of cultic paraphernalia, but there is no reason not to suppose that the asherah and not a goddess was the object of cultic items. This is precisely the way the asherah of the Jerusalem temple is presented in the same chapter. According to verse 7, the asherah received "clothes" *(bāttîm).* Furthermore, it was dragged out of the Jerusalem temple, according to verse 6. In order to sustain the interpretation that the asherah in verse 4 refers to the goddess, it is necessary to separate the reference to the asherah in this verse from the asherah in verses 6-7. It may be that only the tree is involved in 2 Kings 21 and 23, however. It is further plausible that the same asherah is involved in 2 Kings 21:7 and 2 Kings 23:6. According to the first passage, the asherah was erected in the Jerusalem temple, and in the second passage, the asherah was removed from the temple.

The reference to "the asherahs" in Judges 3:7 has been used to establish the presence of Asherah in ancient Israel. The immediate difficulty with this view is that while "the asherahs" represent goddesses, they do not appear to refer to a specific goddess. Indeed, the term involved does not represent a single figure, but a collective group. The group is probably goddesses in general, as "the asherahs" are paired with "the baals" as a means of alluding to foreign gods and goddesses in general. The variation between "the baals and the asherahs" in Judges 3:7 and "the baals and the astartes" in Judges 2:13, 1 Samuel 7:4, 12:10 further reflects the fact that "the asherahs" in Judges 3:7 represents a generic usage. The question is how "the asherahs" came to be used in this way. One possibility is that these expressions reflect an interchange between Asherah and Astarte. The Hebrew names of Asherah *('ăšērāh)* and

Astarte *('aštōret)* are somewhat similar. Furthermore, Astarte shows some of the traits and roles earlier reckoned to Asherah. For example, in the Ugaritic texts, *rbt* is a standard title of Asherah (e.g., KTU 1.3 V 40; 1.4 I 13, 21; 1.4 IV 31, 40; 1.6 I 44, 45, 47, 53; cf. 1.16 I 36, 38; 1.23.54), but in inscriptions from Sidon, Tyre, Kition, and Egypt, this epithet belongs to Astarte (KAI 14:15; 17:1; 33:3; cf. 48:2; 277:1).[81] Similarly, Asherah is considered the mother figure in the Ugaritic texts (KTU 1.4 II 25-26, IV 51, V 1; 1.6 I 39-41, 46), but in Phoenician inscriptions it is Astarte who bears the title of "mother," *'m* (KAI 14:14).[82] The figure of Asherah did not continue by name in the Phoenician world, and Astarte may have been the bearer of some features earlier associated with Asherah. To be sure, some scholars[83] have argued that the goddess Tannit may have been the Phoenician-Punic descendant of Canaanite Asherah or included her features, including the titles "lady," *rbt* (e.g., KAI 78:2; 79:1; 81:1; 85:1; 86:1), and "mother," *'m* (cf. KAI 83:1).[84] Asherah was, apart from 1 Kings 18:19, nowhere called by her old Canaanite name in the first millennium. She is not once attested in Phoenician sources. The biblical authors characterizing the cult lying behind the symbol of the asherah perhaps telescoped the second-millennium goddess Asherah and the first-millennium goddess Astarte, just as the second-millennium storm-god Baal, part of Israel's old Canaanite inheritance, was conflated with the first-millennium storm-god Baal of Tyre.[85]

Jeremiah 2:27 has been understood as a reference to Asherah as the consort of Yahweh. According to a number of scholars, Jeremiah 2:27 reverses the role of the paternal symbol of the stone with the maternal role of the tree, symbols which refer to Asherah and Baal.[86] If so, Jeremiah 2:27 would provide a historical witness to Asherah as a goddess and the consort of Baal. In contrast, Olyan argues that Jeremiah 2:27 may refer not to Asherah and Baal,

81. Pritchard, *Palestinian Figurines,* 71, 91; Olyan, *Asherah and the Cult of Yahweh,* 57 n. 84.

82. See Pritchard, *Palestinian Figurines,* 91; Olyan, *Asherah and the Cult of Yahweh,* 58.

83. On Tannit, see references in Introduction n. 11.

84. See R. S. Tomback, *A Comparative Semitic Lexicon of the Phoenician and Punic Languages,* SBLDS 32 (Missoula, MT: Scholars, 1978), 23.

85. See chapter 2, section 1.

86. See Olyan, "Cultic Confessions of Jer 2,27a," 254-59. If Olyan's interpretation is correct, then Jer. 2:23-28 would include a polemic against both the cult of Yahweh and Asherah, on the one hand, and on the other hand, Baal (2:23 and LXX 2:28b). For the evidence on LXX 2:28b, see W. L. Holladay, *Jeremiah 1: A Commentary on the Book of the Prophet Jeremiah, Chapters 1–25,* Hermeneia (Philadelphia: Fortress, 1986), 54; W. McKane, *A Critical and Exegetical Commentary on Jeremiah,* vol. 1, *Introduction and Commentary on Jeremiah I–XXV,* ICC (Edinburgh: T. & T. Clark, 1986), 47.

but to Asherah and Yahweh, since paternal language is rarely, if ever, attributed to Baal, whereas Yahweh receives paternal language in a number of instances (e.g., Deut. 32:6; Isa. 63:16; 64:7 [E 8]; Jer. 3:4, 19; 31:9; Mal. 1:6; 2:10; Wisdom of Solomon 14:3; Ben Sira 23:1, 4; cf. Exod. 4:22; Hos. 11:1). According to Olyan's view, Jeremiah 2:27 may indicate that Asherah was a goddess in Israel and the consort of Yahweh during the waning decades of the Judean monarchy.[87] For all these scholars, the asherah was perceived as the goddess's symbol, not only by its critics, but also by Israelite worshipers. These views are historically problematic, however. The myth in Jeremiah 2:27 is not attributed to a goddess, as in Canaanite religion, but to a symbol in the cult of Yahweh. That such maternal language was appropriated to Yahweh is evident from Deuteronomy 32:18, discussed in the following section. It is possible, therefore, that the symbol named in this verse did not refer to Asherah. Yet there is a further difficulty for assuming that Asherah is described in Jeremiah 2:27. The larger context of this verse, Jeremiah 2:23-28, names Baal also as an object of opprobrium, and perhaps it is Baal and Asherah who are the objects of attack in this verse. Elsewhere in the Deuteronomistic History, especially in 1 Kings 18:19, the juxtaposition of Baal and Asherah may reflect the substitution of Asherah for Astarte. The same replacement may be involved in Jeremiah 2:27. Or, perhaps this verse reflects a historical connection made secondarily between Baal and Asherah in Jeremiah's own time. As a result of the complex problems that Jeremiah 2:27 presents, the precise divine referents of the symbols of tree and stone in this verse are difficult to establish; indeed, many scholars deny that there are any divine referents.[88]

To summarize the evidence for Asherah as the consort of Yahweh, there is no clear reference to the goddess in the Bible, apart from 1 Kings 18:19, possibly a polemic against Astarte. Genesis 49:25 may attest to Asherah as El's consort; it provides no support for the view that Asherah was Yahweh's consort. The other biblical references used to support this reconstruction are susceptible to other interpretations, which would vitiate the view of Asherah as a goddess. A further difficulty with positing Asherah as a goddess in monarchic Israel involves not only the biblical evidence, but the Phoenician evidence as well. Asherah was not a Phoenician or Punic goddess during the Iron Age. She apparently did not continue as a goddess in Phoenicia and therefore was not the Phoenician problem as 1 Kings 18:19 presents her. There is other negative evidence that might support the reconstruction that Asherah was not a

87. Olyan, "Cultic Confessions of Jer 2,27a," 254-59.

88. Besides the scholars cited by Olyan ("Cultic Confessions of Jer 2,27a," 255), see Day, "Asherah in the Hebrew Bible," 408; and Holladay, *Jeremiah 1,* 104.

goddess in Israel; this sort of evidence is, however, based on the argument from silence, and it has merit only in conjunction with the positive evidence presented above. It is to be noted that prophetic and legal condemnations never refer to the goddess, only to the symbol. There are no personal names formed with the theophoric element of the goddess's name.[89] Furthermore, unlike Yahweh, El, Baal, or even Anat, **'šrh* does not appear as the theophoric element in Israelite personal names. According to Tigay, this fact indicates a lack of religious cult devoted expressly to the goddess. The argument in itself would be unconvincing, because, as Emerton and Olyan have observed in the case of the name of Asherah,[90] onomastica do not always reflect accurately religious devotion. The cult of this goddess is attested at Ugarit, but her name does not appear as a theophoric element in Ugaritic names. However, the onomastic evidence comports with the other Iron Age evidence. Finally, there is the questionable argument that neither biblical nor inscriptional Hebrew has a word for "goddess" (*'ēlāh* notwithstanding). In conclusion, the evidence for Asherah as an Israelite goddess during the monarchy is minimal at best. In view of the difficulties raised about this historical reconstruction, the rejection of this position by B. Lang, P. D. Miller, J. Tigay, U. Winter, C. Frevel, and M. C. A. Korpel appears more compatible with the available evidence.[91]

If the symbol no longer represented the goddess, there are two historical questions. First, what was the historical development lying behind this situation? Second, why did the Deuteronomistic tradition, in so strongly opposing the symbol, suppose that the goddess Asherah was involved? In other words, if the symbol no longer represented the goddess, why was it condemned?

The first question is very difficult. On the basis of the biblical association between Baal and Asherah, some scholars argue that Baal replaced El as the husband of Asherah in the Iron I period (1200-1000), and that this is why biblical criticisms link Baal and Asherah.[92] This view suffers from the fundamental weakness that the evidence for Baal replacing El in Canaan is scant. To be sure, a weighty analogue could be based on various evidence, including the Elkunirsa narrative.[93] Despite the suggestive direction of this analogue, such a state of affairs perhaps never obtained in Iron Age Israel.

89. Tigay, *You Shall Have No Other Gods,* 13-14.

90. Emerton, "New Light on Israelite Religion," 16 n. 10; Olyan, *Asherah and the Cult of Yahweh,* 35-36.

91. See the references in n. 74 above.

92. See Olyan, *Asherah and the Cult of Yahweh,* 38-61.

93. See *ANET,* 519. For a critique of the use of this material in this way, see Olyan, *Asherah and the Cult of Yahweh,* 43.

Olyan has suggested that as a result of the Yahweh-El identification and the pairing of El and Asherah, Asherah was the consort of Yahweh and the asherah was her symbol.[94] At some point, however, perhaps as early as the period of the Judges, the symbol of the asherah, like the name and imagery of El, continued in the cult of Yahweh but did not refer to a separate deity. As seen in chapter 1, the evidence for Asherah as a goddess in Israel during the period of the Judges is minimal. The same difficulty afflicts the data for the period of the monarchy. Rather than supporting a theory of a goddess as the consort of Yahweh, it would indicate that the symbol outlived the cult of the goddess who gave her name to it and continued to hold a place in the cult of Yahweh. Other scholars such as Hadley would date this development generally to the post-exilic period. Yet she also allows for the development earlier: "By Manasseh's time, it is possible that the asherah statue had lost enough of its 'goddess background', and it was considered more as an aspect of (Yahweh's?) fertility."[95] Given the problematic references in the books of Kings to the goddess, the development may be earlier. In this connection, it is pertinent to note the number of Iron Age tree scenes which lack the female figure, as noted by Keel.[96] It is precisely this lack as well as the preponderance of biblical references to the asherah symbol compared to the putative number of references to Asherah the goddess that makes one think that the symbol outlasted the goddess's cult.

The second question is even more problematic. If the asherah was a Yahwistic symbol that no longer represented a separate goddess, why then did it fall under such weighty biblical criticism? Any answer is speculative, but some of the biblical criticisms of the asherah confined to Deuteronomistic influence observed by Olyan provide a starting point. Secondary association of the name of the asherah with the goddess Astarte, perhaps represented by the variation between "the baals and the asherahs" in Judges 3:7 and "the baals and the astartes" in Judges 2:13, 1 Samuel 7:4, and 12:10, may have provided a negative view of the asherah. Another reason for the condemnation of the asherah may be approached on the basis of its functions. Perhaps its roles in

94. See chapter 2, section 2. For the textual differences in the formulas of "the baals and the asherahs/astartes," see Oden, *Studies*, 97-98. Baal and Astarte are coupled together also in *PE* 1.10.31: "Greatest Astarte and Zeus, called both Demarous and Adodos, king of gods, were ruling over the land with the consent of Kronos," *Astartē de he megistē kai Zeus Dēmarous kai Adōdos basileus theōn ebasileuon tēs chorās Kronou gnōmē* (Attridge and Oden, *Philo of Byblos*, 54-55). For a cultic functionary who was both a prophet of Baal and a prophet of Astarte in the time of Akhenaten, see *ANET*, 250 n. 13.

95. Hadley, *The Cult of Asherah in Ancient Israel and Judah*, 80.

96. Keel, *Goddesses and Trees*, 39-46.

providing fertility or healing were offensive to its critics. Its function of divination may have competed with prophecy, which may have led to prophetic condemnations. In any case, its indictment belongs to a more sweeping rejection of a number of cultic practices.[97] From this survey of the biblical evidence, it would appear that the asherah continued with various functions in the cult of Yahweh without connection to the goddess who gave her name to the symbol.

5. The Assimilation of the Imagery of Asherah

The history of the Israelite asherah apparently ended with the Judean exile (587/6), but biblical passages that depict an independent divine figure might reflect at some level of the tradition the ongoing literary impact of the myth associated with the asherah. The female figure of Wisdom in Proverbs 1–9 is a possible candidate. G. Boström, H. Ringgren, W. F. Albright, and others compared the figure of Wisdom to the Canaanite goddess Asherah.[98] C. Camp's study on the figure of Wisdom, which otherwise minimizes the history of religion approach, also recognizes such an influence.[99] If the symbolic content of the asherah was in any sense a literary model for the figure of Wisdom (per-

97. See chapter 5.

98. See G. Boström, *Proverbiastudien: Die Weisheit und das fremde Weib in Spr. 1–9* (Lund: Gleerup, 1935), 12-14, 135f.; H. Ringgren, *Word and Wisdom: Studies in the Hypostatization of Divine Qualities and Functions in the Ancient Near East* (Lund: Håkan Ohlssons Boktryckeri, 1947), 132-34; L. A. Snidjers, "The Meaning of *zār* in the Old Testament: An Exegetical Study," *OTS* 10 (1954): 63; G. von Rad, *Wisdom in Israel*, trans. J. D. Martin (London: SCM, 1970), 167; R. J. Clifford, "Proverbs IX: A Suggested Ugaritic Parallel," *VT* 25 (1975): 305; B. Lang, *Wisdom and the Book of Proverbs: A Hebrew Goddess Redefined* (New York: Pilgrim Press, 1986). Concerning Ugaritic parallels to Proverbs 9, see Clifford, "Proverbs IX," 298-306; cf. M. Lichtenstein, "The Banquet Motifs in Keret and in Proverbs 9," *JANES* 1/1 (1968): 19-31; J. C. Greenfield, "The Seven Pillars of Wisdom (Prov. 9:1) — A Mistranslation," *JQR* 76 (1985 = Moshe Held Memorial Volume): 18 n. 25. For other opinions concerning the history of religion background to the figure of Wisdom, see H. Conzelmann, "The Mother of Wisdom," in *The Future of Our Religious Past: Essays in Honor of Rudolf Bultmann*, ed. J. M. Robinson, trans. C. Carlson and R. Scharlemann (New York: Harper & Row, 1971), 230-43; G. Fohrer, "Sophia," *Theological Dictionary of the New Testament*, vol. 7, ed. G. Friedrich, trans. G. W. Bromiley (Grand Rapids, MI: Eerdmans, 1971), 477-90; Winter, *Frau und Göttin*, 508-29; C. Camp, *Wisdom and the Feminine in the Book of Proverbs*, Bible and Literature Series 11 (Sheffield: JSOT, 1985), 23-68. See further S. Schroer, *Die Weisheit hat ihr Haus gebaut: Studien der Sophia in den biblischen Schriften* (Mainz: Matthias Grunewald Verlag, 1996).

99. Camp, *Wisdom and the Feminine*, 95, 103, 106, 115, 133, 187-90, 276, 283.

haps as a counter-advertisement, or *Kontrastbild* in von Rad's terms), it may have been due to the background of the indigenous cult of "Yahweh and his asherah."[100] The "tree of life," which recalls the asherah, appears in Israelite tradition as a metaphorical expression for Wisdom (Prov. 3:18; cf. Prov. 11:30; 15:4; Gen. 3:22; Rev. 2:7).[101] Like the symbol of the asherah, Wisdom is a female figure, providing life and nurturing. Proverbs 3:18 is especially pertinent: "She is a tree of life to those who lay hold of her; those who hold her fast are made happy" *(ʿēṣ-ḥayyîm hîʾ lammaḥăzîqîm bāh wĕtōmĕkêhā mĕʾuššār)*. This verse closes a small unit consisting of verses 13-18 and forms with verse 13 a conspicuous chiasm (a type of poetic structure connecting four terms). Verse 13 opens with "Happy the one who finds wisdom" *(ʾašrê ʾādām māṣāʾ ḥokmāh)*. The unit begins and ends with the same root, **ʾšr*, "to be happy," specifically with *ʾašrê*, "happy," in verse 13 and *mĕʾuššār*, "made happy," in verse 18. The inside terms of the chiasm are *ḥokmāh*, "wisdom," and *ʿēṣ-ḥayyîm*, "a tree of life." Finally, the terms, *ʾašrê* and *mĕʾuššār*, perhaps allude to the asherah, the tree symbolizing life and well-being.[102] Ben Sira (Ecclesiasticus) continues and amplifies the female personification of Wisdom. Ben Sira 1:20 draws on the image of Wisdom as a tree of life: "To fear the Lord is the root of wisdom, and

100. Coogan, "Canaanite Origins and Lineage," 119-20; Miller, "Absence of the Goddess," 246; Smith, "God Male and Female," 337; cf. Andersen and Freedman, *Hosea*, 326. Coogan links the descriptions of Sophia in Wisdom of Solomon 7–8 to the cult of Yahweh and the asherah as well (cf. G. Quispel, "Jewish Gnosis and Mandean Gnosticism," in *Nag Hammadi Studies VII*, ed. J. E. Menard [Leiden: Brill, 1975], 93).

101. Cf. Prov. 11:30; 15:4; Gen. 3:22; Rev. 2:7. The traditions lying behind the "tree of life" in Gen. 3:22 are complex. Besides the tradition of the goddess's tree and the snake evident in this story, further traditions of sanctuary and divine abode (cf. Ezek. 28:12-19) are present. For details, see F. Stulz, "Die Bäume des Gottesgartens auf dem Libanon," *ZAW* 82 (1972): 141-56; Lambert, "Trees, Snakes, and Gods," 435-51; and H. N. Wallace, *The Eden Narrative*, HSM 32 (Atlanta, GA: Scholars, 1985), 60-172. On the divine waters of Gen. 2:10, see also chapter 1, section 6. For Mesopotamian iconography of the sacred tree especially in the context of a sanctuary, see E. Dhorme, "L'arbre de verité et l'arbre de vie," *RB* 4 (1907): 271-74; van Buren, *Symbols of the Gods*, 3-4, 22-30. The snake of Genesis 2–3 need not be associated with a cosmic enemy of Baal (so Williams-Forte, "The Snake and the Tree," 18-43). Since the snake appears with the goddess (perhaps Asherah), in *ANEP*, nos. 470-474 (cf. no. 480), these depictions provide a better point of departure for addressing the biblical traditions. See also the serpent on a shrine model from Beth-Shan (*ANEP*, no. 590; A. Rowe, *The Four Canaanite Temples of Beth-shan*, fig. 10, no. 14; cf. *ANEP*, no. 585; E. Stern, *Excavations at Tel Mevorakh (1973-1976); Part Two: The Bronze Age*, Qedem 18 [Jerusalem: Magnes, 1984], 22-23).

102. I wish to thank Professor Anthony Ceresko for pointing out to me in a private communication the paronomasia evoking the asherah in the use of the root **ʾšr* in this passage. For criticism of this view, see Day, *Yahweh and the Gods and Goddesses of Canaan*, 66-67. Day's discussion ignores the argument that wisdom personified may be modelled on Asherah or her connotations associated with the tree as a foil or counteradvertisement.

her branches are long life."[103] Ben Sira 24:12-17 likewise describes Wisdom as different types of trees.[104] Ben Sira 4:13[105] and Baruch 4:1, echoing Proverbs 3:18, use the image of holding fast to Wisdom.

Other examples of the asherah's impact on biblical imagery are less convincing. J. Day perceives an instance of the asherah imagery in Hosea 14:9 (E 8).[106] Yahweh declares:

> O Ephraim, what have I do to with idols?
> It is I who answer *(ʿānîtî)* and look after him *(waʾăšûrennû).*
> I am like an evergreen cypress,
> from me comes your fruit.

Following J. Wellhausen,[107] Day sees in the second half of the verse an allusion to Anat and Asherah. He also reads **lô,* "him" (i.e., Ephraim), for *lî,* "me" (i.e., Yahweh).[108] An allusion is plausible for the asherah, but not in the case of Anat, since she appears only in proper names in Israelite sources.[109] Furthermore, the use of the root **ʿny,* "to answer," recalls rather the use of the same root in Hosea 2.[110] The reading **lô* for *lî* has little textual support and may misconstrue the nature of the religious problem under indictment. The idolatry is not merely a matter of Ephraim's sin; rather, the prophetic criticism may hint at the inclusion of the asherah with Yahweh. Finally, Hosea 14:10 (E 9) may be related to the theme of the preceding verse. While Hosea 14:10 is generally regarded as a secondary addition separate from the preceding section or the book as a whole, G. Yee treats the verse as part of the larger unit comprising

103. See G. T. Sheppard, *Wisdom as a Hermeneutical Construct: A Study in the Sapientalizing of the Old Testament,* BZAW 151 (Berlin/New York: Walter de Gruyter, 1980), 52-55. For text-critical issues, see P. W. Skehan and A. A. Di Lella, *The Wisdom of Ben Sira,* AB 39 (New York: Doubleday, 1987), 145.

104. Skehan and Di Lella, *The Wisdom of Ben Sira,* 334-35.

105. Skehan and Di Lella, *The Wisdom of Ben Sira,* 171. The medieval female personification of the Shekinah, the divine presence, has been connected with the personification of Wisdom (Pope, *Song of Songs,* 158-79).

106. Day, "Asherah in the Hebrew Bible," 404-6. Cf. Prov. 16:20; 29:18b. For a thorough critique of this interpretation, see Olyan, *Asherah and the Cult of Yahweh,* 20-21.

107. See Day, "Asherah in the Hebrew Bible," 404-5. See Cooper, "Divine Names and Epithets in the Ugaritic Texts," 401.

108. Day, "Asherah in the Hebrew Bible," 404 n. 59.

109. See above chapter 2, section 4.

110. See Yee, *Composition and Tradition,* 137, 139. For discussion of Hosea 2, see above, chapter 2, section 2. Given the possible appearance of asherah in the book of Hosea, Hosea's use of love language between Yahweh and Israel may represent a transformation of divine love language attested in Canaanite texts.

Hosea 14:2-10 and belonging to the final redactional level of the book.[111] If the verse is to be understood in the context of both the whole book[112] and the unit Hosea 14:2-10, then perhaps the subtext of this verse includes idolatry generally expressed throughout the book and specifically the object of opprobrium to which Hosea 14:9 alludes, the asherah. Read as part of the same unit, Hosea 14:9-10 is reminiscent of the imagery in Proverbs 3:13-18. Like Proverbs 3:13-18, Hosea 14:9 draws on the image of the tree, perhaps as a transformation of the asherah into the Yahwistic symbol of life. This transformation in both cases is perhaps disclosed by the use of the root *'*šr*, not as an explicit reference to the asherah, but as an allusion through paronomasia. Like Proverbs 3:13-18, Hosea 14:10 casts this motif into the mold of wisdom language. As Yee notes,[113] the image of the tree in Hosea 14:10 is unique in describing Yahweh as the tree. In this respect Hosea 14:2-10 differs in one significant way from Proverbs 3:13-18. In the latter passage it is the female personification of Wisdom being described metaphorically as a tree; in Hosea 14:9 this attribution falls to Yahweh. Perhaps paronomasia with the asherah is involved in this verse, although the evidence for this example is considerably weaker than the data supporting Proverbs 3:13-18. Another less than persuasive example of the imagery associated with the asherah may underlie Song of Songs 4:1-5 and 7:1-9. According to M. H. Pope,[114] the female protagonist of the Song of Songs 4 and 7 may have been modeled in part on a divine prototype; if so, the model may have been indigenous.[115]

The assimilation of language originally associated with the asherah may be illustrated by a comparison of Jeremiah 2:27 with Deuteronomy 32:18, which reads, "You were unmindful of the Rock who begot you, and you forgot the God who gave you birth" *(ṣûr yĕlādĕkā tešî wattiškaḥ 'ēl mĕḥōlĕlekā)*.[116] Whereas Jeremiah 2:27 reverses the role of the paternal symbol of the stone with the maternal role of the tree, Deuteronomy 32:18 forges from various cultic themes an image of Yahweh that transcends sexuality.[117] It has been argued that *mĕḥōlĕlekā* presents in this passage a female image of giving birth,[118] although this use of the word lacks specifically female connotations

111. Yee, *Composition and Tradition*, 131-42, 317.

112. See Sheppard, *Wisdom as a Hermeneutical Construct*, 129-36.

113. Yee, *Composition and Tradition*, 138.

114. Pope, *Song of Songs*, 465, 468; idem, "Sasson on the Sublime Song," 213.

115. Smith, "Divine Form and Size," 424-27.

116. The connection between the two texts has been noted also by W. L. Holladay (*Jeremiah 1*, 104).

117. For the date of Deuteronomy 32, see chapter 1, n. 39.

118. P. Trible, *God and the Rhetoric of Sexuality* (Philadelphia: Fortress, 1978), 63.

(Prov. 26:10). Deuteronomy 32:18 otherwise de-emphasizes the specifically sexual connotations of the stone and tree, first by omitting the specifically female image of the tree, and second, by using *ṣûr,* "rock," instead of *'eben,* "stone." The rock *('eben)* in Jeremiah 2:27 may represent the symbol of the god, hence the god himself (cf. Gen. 49:24), but in Deuteronomy 32:18 the image of the rock *(ṣûr)* functions very differently.

In its current context in Deuteronomy 32, the image of the rock is a leitmotif punctuating the poem (vv. 4, 13, 15, 18, 30, 31, 37). There are three further functions that the sevenfold repetition of *ṣûr,* "rock," exhibits in this poem. First, verses 4 and 15 use the image of the rock as an expression of divine strength. Second, verse 13 employs the image of the rock to recall the divine care in the wilderness, described in Exodus 17:1-7 and Numbers 20:2-13. In this way attention is diverted from rock as an image of the male deity, and rock is associated instead with the wilderness incident. Third, verses 18, 31, and 37 use the image of the rock in a polemical way. Verse 31a is most direct: "For their rock is not as our Rock" *(kî lō' kĕṣûrēnû ṣûrām).* Here the word *ṣûr* refers to both Yahweh ("our god") and other gods, a contrast at issue also in verses 12, 16, 21, 37-38, 39. The image in the poem, on the one hand, disarms the rock of its cultic associations with respect to Yahweh and places it in the context of Israel's wilderness traditions and, on the other hand, attacks the associations of this image with other gods. The image of the rock is a central one for this poem, expressing both Yahweh's parental care for Israel and Yahweh's negative posture toward other deities.

6. Excursus: Gender Language for Yahweh

Gender-specific language in the Bible that might be traced back to the asherah raises the issue concerning the background and significance of female metaphor occasionally used to describe either Yahweh or Yahweh's action. Reacting against the ideas of P. Trible, J. W. Miller argues that in Deuteronomy 32:18, Numbers 11:12, Psalm 22:9-10, and Isaiah 46:3; 66:9, 13, Yahweh was not considered female, either separately or in conjunction with male language for Yahweh. Rather, Yahweh was treated as a male deity to whom female imagery was occasionally attributed on a metaphorical level.[119] Miller claims that while paternal imagery is more attested and directly applied to Yahweh, female language for Yahweh is rarer, used indirectly to stress

119. J. W. Miller, "Depatriarchalizing God in Biblical Interpretation: A Critique," *CBQ* 48 (1986): 609-16.

qualities that Yahweh shares with female figures. Miller is therefore critical of Trible's attempts to maximize the female dimensions of Yahweh.[120] Finally, for the religious background for the personage of Yahweh, Miller appeals to the West Semitic antecedent of El as father, following a long-accepted scholarly tradition, as chapter 1 indicates.

There are both strengths and weaknesses in Miller's arguments. First, Miller correctly observes that paternal language is applied to Yahweh directly, although it is not very frequent (Deut. 32:6; Isa. 63:16; 64:7 [E 8]; Jer. 3:4, 19; 31:9; Mal. 1:6; 2:10; Wisdom of Solomon 14:3; Ben Sira 23:1, 4; cf. Exod. 4:22; Hos. 11:1). Other images of king, redeemer, warrior, and so on are considerably more widespread in the Hebrew Bible and deuterocanonical works.[121] Second, in support of Miller's argument, the claim that some passages, such as Deuteronomy 32:18 and Psalm 27:10 (cf. 2 Esdras 1:28), combine male and female imagery for Yahweh suffers from exegetical considerations. Deuteronomy 32:18 reads, "You were unmindful of the Rock who begot you, and you forgot God who brought you forth" *(ṣûr yĕlādĕka tešî wattiškaḥ 'ēl mĕḥōlĕlekā)*. The verbal forms in Deuteronomy 32:18 are both masculine, implying a masculine subject. Psalm 27:10 declares, "For my father and my mother have forsaken me, but Yahweh will take me up" *(kî-'ābî wĕ'immî 'ăzābûnî wayhwh ya'aspênî)*. This verse at best draws an indirect comparison between Yahweh and either a father or mother; indeed, Yahweh stands in contrast to either a mother or a father.

Third, the comparison between El and Yahweh is pertinent; yet it covers only part of the historical issue. Miller does not address the impact that the language of either the god Baal or the goddesses Asherah and Anat may have

120. Trible, "Depatriarchalizing in Biblical Interpretation," *Journal of the American Academy of Religion* 41 (1973): 30-48; idem, "God, Nature of, in the OT," *IDBSup*, 368-69; idem, *God and the Rhetoric of Sexuality*, 12-33. On the passages in Second and Third Isaiah, see also M. Gruber, "The Motherhood of Second Isaiah," *RB* 90 (1983): 351-59; idem, "'Will a Woman Forget Her Infant?' Isaiah 49:14 Reconsidered," *Tarbiz* 51/3 (1982): 491-92; J. J. Schmitt, "The Motherhood of God and Zion as Mother," *RB* 92 (1985): 557-69. For a critique against interpreting Isa. 42:10-17 as female imagery for Yahweh, see K. P. Darr, "Like Warrior, like Woman: Destruction and Deliverance in Isa. 42:10-17," *CBQ* 49 (1987): 560-71. According to Darr, the force of the activity that women exhibit in childbirth lies behind the comparison in Isa. 42:10-17, not an application of female imagery to Yahweh. Similar argumentation could be made for the other passages that Miller discusses. For the background of **rḥm*, see chapter 1, section 4. P. D. Miller ("Absence of the Goddess," 246) has independently argued that the language of the goddess has been assimilated into Yahweh and is reflected in female metaphors applied to Yahweh in various biblical passages.

121. See T. Mettinger, *In Search of God: The Meaning and Message of the Everlasting Names*, trans. F. H. Cryer (Philadelphia: Fortress, 1988).

made on characterizations of Yahweh. If El imagery was a constitutive component of Yahweh's nature, likewise it may be possible to identify in the nature of Yahweh elements of Asherah's character, specifically her maternal and nurturing character. The balance of the data in this chapter favors this reconstruction. The evidence may not be as widespread as the basis for comparing Yahweh with El or Baal, but it remains significant. While from the perspective of the ancient Near East, Yahweh constituted a male god, nonetheless some female features or traits, perhaps traceable to the assimilation of the goddess Asherah, were ascribed to him. In particular, Trible points to use of the root **rḥm* (Isa. 49:13; Jer. 31:20; Hos. 2:21 [E 19]; 2:25 [E 23]) and the image of mother for Yahweh in biblical texts,[122] and it is precisely these features that belong to Asherah in Canaanite literature and possibly underlie Genesis 49:25. Moreover, the description of Wisdom in Proverbs 3:13-18 illustrates another survival of language formerly associated with the asherah.

Finally, in defense of Trible's treatment of female metaphors for Yahweh, if Yahweh was considered essentially a male deity, then biblical passages with female imagery for Yahweh may have represented an expansion of the Israelite understanding of Yahweh. Such innovation may best explain the attestation of female images for the divine in Second Isaiah (Isa. 42:14; 46:3; 49:15; cf. 45:10-11; 66:9, 13). The innovative character of these passages would support the point that Miller attempts to discredit, namely, that Yahweh both encompasses the characteristics and values expressed through gendered metaphors and transcends the categories of sexuality (cf. Job 38:28-29).

Both Trible and Miller largely confine their perspective to the biblical material. The broader cultural setting of ancient Near Eastern literature provides further context for understanding female metaphors applied to Yahweh. The attribution of female roles to gods was by no means an Israelite innovation. Indeed, even specifically female roles for gods (and vice-versa) might be posited on the basis of proper names, such as Ugaritic *ʿṯtrʾum*, "Athtar is mother" (cf. *ʿṯtrʾab*, "Athtar is father"), *ʾilʿnt*, "Anat is (a) god," Akkadian *ummi-šamaš*, "Shamash is my mother," and *a-da-nu-um-mu*, "lord is mother."[123] Similarly, the combination of male and female roles for a single deity is not without parallel in the ancient Near East. Like the storm-gods Ningirsu and Marduk, Yahweh was represented with both storm and solar lan-

122. Trible, *God and the Rhetoric of Sexuality*, 31-71.

123. Gröndahl, *Die Personennamen*, 46, 83, 86, 90; Roberts, *The Earliest Semitic Pantheon*, 52. The most important study of this phenomenon is H. W. Jüngling, "'Was anders ist Gott für den Menschen, wenn nicht sein Vater and seine Mutter?' Zu einer Doppelmetapher der reliogiösen Sprache," in *Ein Gott allein?* ed. W. Dietrich and M. A. Klopfenstein, 365-86.

guage either separately or jointly, as in Hosea 6:3, indicating both power over and transcendence of these forces of nature (cf. 1 Kings 17–19).[124]

Yahweh was described in both male and female imagery, like deities in ancient Near Eastern prayers. Two examples suffice. In his prayer to Gatumdug, the city-goddess of Lagash, Gudea says:

> I have no mother — you are my mother,
> I have no father — you are my father,
> You implanted in the womb the germ of me,
> gave birth to me from out of the vulva (too),
> Sweet, O Gatumdug, is your holy name![125]

The poem combines parental imagery of mother and father. The same sentiment appears to underlie Psalm 27:10.[126] By implication compared to Gudea's prayer, this biblical verse suggests that Yahweh assumes the role of father and mother, thereby affirming divine care. A second-millennium Hittite prayer likewise attributes both parental roles to Istanu, the sun-god: "Thou, Istanu, art father and mother of the oppressed, the lonely [and the] bereaved person."[127] These examples illustrate the larger ancient Near Eastern background to the combination of parental roles for Yahweh. They also show that such combination was already ancient in Near Eastern literature. Ancient Near Eastern texts indicate that female metaphors do not imply a female status for a god. Rather, according to ancient Near Eastern categories, a god could be accorded female imagery without implying that he was considered both male and female. The inverse is true as well: a goddess could receive male metaphors without meaning that the goddess was thought to be both female and male. Yahweh could have been attributed female imagery without any influence from any goddess. Where specific signs of language for the asherah can be discerned (e.g., Prov. 3:13-18), however, the influence of the asherah on the cult of Yahweh and descriptions of Yahweh may be recognized.

The relative lack of gender language for Yahweh may be attributed in part to the avoidance of anthropomorphic imagery for Yahweh. Over the course of its history, Israelite religion reduced anthropomorphic depictions

124. See chapter 2, section 2 and chapter 4, section 1.

125. T. Jacobsen, *The Harps That Once . . . : Sumerian Poetry in Translation* (New Haven: Yale Univ. Press, 1987), 361.

126. W. W. Hallo, "Individual Prayers in Sumerian: The Continuity of a Tradition," *JAOS* 88 (1968 = *Essays in Memory of E. A. Speiser*, ed. W. W. Hallo, American Oriental Series 53), 78; S. M. Paul, "Psalm XXVII 10 and the Babylonian Theodicy," *VT* 32 (1982): 490.

127. H. Güterbock, "The Composition of Hittite Prayers to the Sun," *JAOS* 78 (1958): 240.

of Yahweh. This trend is perceptible in both specific, linguistic usages and general, thematic features. Five areas may be mentioned. First, the legal and prophetic requirement forbidding images reflects this trend at a relatively early point in Israel's history.[128] Second, some biblical sources, such as Psalm 50:12-14, play down the notion of Yahweh consuming sacrifices despite indications to the contrary.[129] Sacrifice is called a "pleasing odor to Yahweh" (Lev. 1:9, 13, 17; 2:2, etc.). Numbers 28:2 extends this imagery, calling sacrifices "my offerings, my food for my offerings by fire, a pleasing odor." Zephaniah 1:7 mentions the sacrifice to which Yahweh invites "his guests" (cf. 1 Sam. 9:12-13; 16:3-5). The related notion of the "bread of God" appears in Leviticus 21:6, 8, 17; 22:25. The background for these expressions seems to have been the view of sacrifice as a communal celebration where Yahweh and Israelites eat, although a depiction of divine and human participants eating jointly is unattested (cf. Exod. 24:9-11; Deut. 12:18). The biblical denial of the notion that Yahweh eats offerings in Psalm 50:12-14 suggests, however, that this was not an uncommon idea; the passage offers a less anthropomorphic rendering of the divine role in sacrificial celebrations. Third, A. Hurvitz has demonstrated how the book of Ezekiel avoided anthropomorphisms evident in parallel passages in Leviticus 26.[130] Leviticus 26:12 applies to Yahweh the verb *hithallaktî* (with *waw* consecutive), "I will walk," but the parallel passage in Ezekiel 37:26-27 omits the verb. Similarly, Leviticus 26:30 presents Yahweh's proclamation that "my soul will abhor you" *(wĕgā'ălāh napšî 'etkem).* Again the parallel passage in Ezekiel 6:5 omits the clause.

Fourth, entities personifying divine aspects, such as the divine "name" *(šēm),* "face" *(pānîm),* and "glory" *(kābôd),* sometimes describe the divine presence in priestly and Deuteronomistic traditions, attested in the Pentateuch as the priestly (P) and Deuteronomistic (D) traditions or "sources."[131] In Isa-

128. On the aniconic tradition in ancient Israel, see chapter 1, section 6. P. Amiet (*Art of the Ancient Near East,* trans. J. Shepley and C. Choquet (New York: Harry N. Abrams, 1980, 173) argues that depiction of the high deities in Mesopotamia diminishes beginning in the late second millennium. If such a view were historically viable, then Israel's aniconic requirement would belong to this larger Near Eastern development. See chapter 1, section 4.

129. Ringgren, *Israelite Religion,* 169, 171; Anderson, *Sacrifices and Offerings,* 14-19.

130. A. Hurvitz, *A Linguistic Study of the Relationship Between the Priestly Source and the Book of Ezekiel: A New Approach to an Old Problem,* CRB 20 (Paris: Gabalda, 1982), 102-7. For a similar argument regarding the priestly source's substitution of the verb **škn,* "to dwell, settle" (e.g., Exod. 24:16), for **yrd,* "to descend" (e.g., Exod. 19:11, 18, 20; 33:9; 34:5; Num. 11:17, 25; 12:5), to describe the motion of divine presence, see Mettinger, *The Dethronement of Sabaoth,* 81-97.

131. See section 3 above for discussion of Northwest Semitic *šm* and *pnm.* On *šēm* in biblical literature, see McBride, "Deuteronomistic Name Theology," 177-219; cf. the comments

iah 30:27, part of an oracle dated to the eighth or seventh century,[132] the divine name serves as the divine instrument of theophanic wrath: "Behold, the name of Yahweh comes from afar, burning with his anger, and in thick rising smoke, and his tongue is a devouring fire." In this instance, the divine name acts as warrior (cf. 1 Sam. 6:2), a depiction frequently applied to Yahweh in earlier material[133] and applied later to the divine *logos,* "word" (Wisd. of Sol. 18:15; Rev. 19:11-16). The substitution of the angel and the name for Yahweh is an issue in Exodus 32–33.[134] Exodus 32:34 and 33:2 declare that an angel will lead Israel. This leadership substitutes for Yahweh's guidance (Exod. 33:16b). In contrast, Exodus 33:14 states the divine "presence" *(pānîm)* will escort the people. Exodus 23:20-21 exhibits a third variation on this theme. This passage states that the divine name is in the angel leading Israel (cf. Isa. 63:9). The divine "glory" *(kābôd)* dwells in the temple according to priestly theology (Ps. 26:8; Isa. 4:5; Ezek. 43:3-5), like the divine "name" in Deuteronomistic tradition.[135] The "voice" *(qôl)* in Numbers 7:89 might be included in this group of personified terms (cf. Exod. 25:22).[136] Though otherwise devoid of any theo-

---

made in n. 63 above. On biblical *pānîm,* see J. D. Levenson, "The Jerusalem Temple in Devotional and Visionary Experience," *Jewish Spirituality: From the Bible through the Middle Ages,* ed. A. Green, World Spirituality: An Encyclopedic History of the Religious Quest 13 (New York: Crossroad, 1987), 43-44; M. S. Smith, "'Seeing God' in the Psalms: The Background to the Beatific Vision in the Hebrew Bible," *CBQ* 50 (1988): 171-83. On *kābôd,* see Cross, *Canaanite Myth and Hebrew Epic,* 165-67; Mendenhall, *The Tenth Generation,* 32-66, esp. 59; Mettinger, *The Dethronement of Sabaoth,* 80-115, 116-22. For discussion of how these divine traits relate to human features designated by these terms, see for face, R. A. Di Vito, "Old Testament Anthropology and the Construction of Personal Identity," *CBQ* 61 (1999): 217-38; for name, see p. 122 above and Smith, *The Origins of Biblical Monotheism,* 74-76; for glory, see Brettler, *God Is King,* 56-57.

132. See Clements, *Isaiah 1–39,* 252. The Name in this passage is reminiscent of descriptions of fiery divine messengers in Ugaritic, biblical tradition, and intertestamental literature, e.g., KTU 1.2 I 33; Num. 16:22; 27:16; Ps. 104:4; *1 Enoch* 14:11; the Songs of the Sabbath Sacrifice (4Q403, fragment 1, col. 2, line 9; and 4Q405, fragments 20-21-22, col. 2, line 10); and Rev. 4:5. For discussion, see P. D. Miller, "Fire in the Mythology of Canaan and Israel," *CBQ* 27 (1965): 256-61; idem, *Divine Warrior,* 31; R. Hendel, "'The Flaming of the Whirling Sword': A Note on Gen 3:24," *JBL* 104 (1985): 671-74; M. S. Smith, "Biblical and Canaanite Notes to the Songs of the Sabbath Sacrifice from Qumran," *Revue de Qumran* 48 (1987): 585-87.

133. See chapter 2, section 4.

134. Childs, *The Book of Exodus,* 584-97.

135. See McBride, "The Deuteronomistic Name Theology," 203; Cross, *Canaanite Myth and Hebrew Epic,* 30 n. 102. Exod. 12:23 and 2 Sam. 24:16 use *mašḥît* for a divine destroyer. The verbal form *(mašḥît)* refers to divine slaying in the form of a plague in Exod. 12:13 (Childs, *The Book of Exodus,* 183; see chapter 1, section 2). Cf. Gen. 3:24 (see n. 132 above).

136. BH *derek* in Exod. 33:13 may represent another form of divine manifestation. LXX Vaticanus reads *seauton,* "yourself," in this verse to translate *dĕrākekā,* not "way," as represented

phanic characteristics, this usage perhaps derives ultimately from old theophanic language of the storm (Ps. 29:3-9). These qualities of the divine seem to be one way to refer to the divine military retinue in its protection and help to devotees.[137] Some of these divine aspects could not be experienced directly, according to some biblical passages. Neither Yahweh, nor the divine "face," *pānîm* (Exodus 33–34), nor the divine "form," *tĕmûnāh* (Deut. 4:15-16; cf. Num. 12:8; Ps. 17:15; Wisd. of Sol. 18:1),[138] were supposed to be seen, despite indications to the contrary (Exod. 24:9-11; Pss. 11:7; 17:15; 27:4, 13; 42:3; 63:3; Job 33:26; 42:5; cf. Gen. 16:13; Judg. 6:22). In discussing those passages, R. S. Hendel comments: "The belief that one cannot see God and live is best understood as a motif of Israelite folklore, rooted in popular conceptions concerning purity and danger."[139] In these passages, some divine aspects are not to be directly present to the Israelites.

Fifth, the long tradition of describing the divine council exhibits a

by Vulgate *tuam viam* and Targum *'wrḥ ṭwbk* (see N. M. Waldman, "God's Ways — A Comparative Note," *JQR* 70 [1979-80]: 67-72). This interpretation of this word as "power" may be supported by appeal to Ugaritic *drkt,* "dominion" (e.g., KTU 1.2 IV 10, 13; 1.108.7; probably 1.4 VII 44), a connection made for BH *derek* in other passages (so Albright, "The North Canaanite Poems of Al'eyan Ba'al and the 'Gracious Gods,'" *JPOS* 14 [1934]: 130 n. 153; Dahood, "Ugaritic *DRKT* and Biblical *DEREK,*" *Theological Studies* 15 [1954]: 627-31; Cross, "A Recently Published Phoenician Inscription," 43-44; cf. Ginsberg, *The Israelian Heritage,* 21 n. 25). The interpretation also accords well with other terms in this dialogue, which all reflect some type of divine manifestation. I wish to thank John Strugnell for pointing out this interpretation to me.

137. For discussion, see above pp. 122-23 n. 64. Other instances of such a divine military retinue include *'ĕlōhîm* and *mašḥît(îm).*

138. Concerning BH *tĕmûnāh,* "form," applied to Yahweh, see Childs, *The Book of Exodus,* 343. The denial of seeing God's form in Deut. 4:12 plays off against the condemnations of (visible) images in Deut. 4:23, 25. The parallelism between *pāanêkā* and *tĕmûnāttekā* in Ps. 17:15 has been compared with the parallel term, *pnth* and *tmnh,* in KTU 1.2 IV 17, 26 (Cross, *Canaanite Myth and Hebrew Epic,* 33 n. 121). The meaning of Ugaritic **pnt* is, however, not "face." In KTU 1.2 IV 17 and 26, *pnt* refers to parts of Yamm's body that "shake" *(tnǵṣn).* In KTU 1.3 III 34-35 it is the sinews *(ksl)* of Anat's *pnt* that "shake" *(*nǵṣ).* Clearly her face is not under discussion (cf. KTU 1.4 II 19). Akkadian *panātu,* "front side," is closer to the meaning involved (*AHw,* 818). Perhaps Ugaritic *pnm* and *pnt* both underlie BH *pānîm;* in any case, the comparison between KTU 1.2 IV 17, 26 and Ps. 17:15 appears viable. For discussion, see M. Dietrich and O. Loretz, "Ug. *tmn,* 'Gestalt,'" *UF* 10 (1978): 432-33; J. C. de Moor, "The Anatomy of the Back," *UF* 12 (1981): 425-26; cf. M. Baldacci, "A Lexical Question Concerning the Ugaritic Anath's Texts," *UF* 10 (1978): 417-18.

139. Hendel, "Aniconism and Anthropomorphism in Ancient Israel," in *The Image and the Book: Iconic Cults, Aniconism and the Rise of Book Religion in Israel and the Ancient Near East,* ed. K. van der Toorn, Contributions to Biblical Exegesis and Theology 21 (Leuven: Uitgeverij Peeters, 1997), 221. See further chapter 4, section 1 below.

decreasingly anthropomorphic depiction of Yahweh in the works of Ezekiel and the priestly Pentateuchal "source" or tradition.[140] The earliest texts render Yahweh as a divine monarch enthroned among other heavenly beings. The divine status of the other members of the council is stressed by terms such as "sons of gods," *bĕnê 'ēlîm* (Pss. 29:1; 89:7) and "congregation of the holy ones," *qĕhal qĕdōšîm* (Ps. 89:6; cf. Hos. 12:1; Zech. 14:5). Similarly, *'ĕlōhîm* in Psalm 82:1b apparently means "gods," since it parallels the "divine council" *('ădat 'ēl)* in verse 1a. All these texts present Yahweh as the preeminent member of the divine assembly. In 1 Kings 22:19, Yahweh is surrounded by a heavenly army or "host" *(ṣĕbā')*. The prophetic vision of the divine assembly of Isaiah 6:1 renders Yahweh after the fashion of an enthroned human king. Ezekiel 1:26 minimizes the anthropomorphism of Isaiah 6:1. Ezekiel describes the "likeness" *(dĕmût)* of God as being "like *(kĕ-)* the appearance of a human." This vision lessens the anthropomorphism of the divine; it nonetheless renders Yahweh along essentially the same lines as Isaiah 6. Like Isaiah 6 and Ezekiel 1, Genesis 1:26-28 utilizes the traditional language of the divine council, as manifest, for example, in the use of the first common plural for divine speech in Genesis 1:26, a feature found also in Genesis 3:22; 11:7; and Isaiah 6:8.[141] The use of *dĕmût,* "likeness," and *ṣelem,* "image," in Genesis 1:26-28 presupposes the vision of the anthropormorphic god yet reduces the anthropomorphism radically compared to Ezekiel 1:26. In fact, Genesis 1 achieves the opposite effect of Ezekiel 1:26. While Ezekiel 1:26 conveys the prophet's vision of Yahweh in the likeness of the human person, Genesis 1 presents a vision of the human person in the likeness of the divine. Rather than reducing Yahweh to human terms through an anthropomorphic portrait, Genesis 1:26-28 magnifies the human person in divine terms. In this way, Genesis 1 draws on the older visionary tradition of the anthropomorphic deity but ultimately transcends it insofar as it omits any description of the divine.[142] In its

140. On the divine council, see chapter 1, section 2.

141. Cross, *Canaanite Myth and Hebrew Epic,* 187. For the "image" and "likeness" in the Tell Fakhariyeh Inscription and how it relates to Gen. 1:26, see the nuanced discussion of W. R. Garr, "'Image' and 'Likeness' in the Inscription from Tell Fakharijeh," *IEJ* 50 (2000): 227-34.

142. See Ringgren, *Israelite Religion,* 70, 124; A. Angerstorfer, "Hebräisch *dmwt* und aramäisch *dmwt:* Ein Sprachproblem der Imago-Dei-Lehre," *BN* 24 (1984): 30-43; Smith, "God Male and Female," 339. Part of the material in Gen. 1:26-28 discussed may predate the priestly or "P" source or tradition to which the entire chapter is frequently attributed. The poetic tricolon of v. 27 especially seems to predate its prose context. See U. Cassuto, *A Commentary on the Book of Genesis: Part I, From Adam to Noah, Genesis 1–VI 8,* trans. I. Abrahams (Jerusalem: Magnes, 1978), 56. For the dating of "P," see A. Hurvitz, *A Linguistic Study;* idem, "The Lan-

present context in Genesis 1:26, this anthropomorphic background is muted.[143]

The avoidance of anthropomorphic imagery was by no means a general feature of Israelite religion after the Exile. While the tendency away from anthropomorphism marks priestly and Deuteronomistic traditions belonging to the eighth through the fifth centuries, later works belonging to the priestly traditions continued to transmit anthropomorphic imagery. Postexilic priestly texts, such as Zechariah 3, attest to the divine council. Zechariah 3:7 includes the high priest in the ranks of the celestial courts (cf. Zech. 12:8). Postexilic apocalyptic circles also continued anthropomorphic renderings of Yahweh and the divine council (Daniel 7; cf. Zech. 14:4; 1 Enoch 14).[144] These and other biblical passages (such as Isa. 27:1) reflect the continuation of old mythic material in postexilic Israelite tradition.[145] Furthermore, nonbiblical Jewish

---

guage of the Priestly Source and Its Historical Setting — The Case for an Early Date," *Proceedings of the Eighth World Congress of Jewish Studies* (Jerusalem: World Union of Jewish Studies, 1983), 83-94; idem, "Dating the Priestly Source in Light of the Historical Study of Biblical Hebrew a Century After Wellhausen," *ZAW* 100 (1988): 88-100; B. A. Levine, "Late Language in the Priestly Source: Some Literary and Historical Observations," *Proceedings of the Eighth World Congress of Jewish Studies,* 69-82.

143. In Ugaritic scenes of divine council El proclaims such decrees. KTU 1.16 V may be the Ugaritic text most relevant to interpreting Gen. 1:26-27, as it describes El telling the divine council that he will create (causative stem of **kwm*) a being. Unfortunately, there is no Ugaritic text describing human creation. It might be inferred from El's epithet, *bny bnwt,* "Creator of creatures," and Athirat's title, *qnyt 'ilm,* that El and Athirat created humanity and deities in primordial time, although these titles do not bear on the creation of the cosmos (for discussion and references, see M. S. Smith, "Interpreting the Baal Cycle," *UF* 18 [1987]: 319-20). If so, it would furnish further Canaanite background, however distant, to the description of creating in Gen. 1:26-27 (so Ahlström, *Aspects of Syncretism,* 50; Smith, "God Male and Female," 339). Moreover, one instance of the topos of the divine council in both Ugaritic and biblical literature involves a dialogue of El and Athirat (KTU 1.6 I), including the use of the first person plural for this divine couple. However, this background appears to be so removed from Gen. 1:26-27 that it seems an unlikely parallel. A further possible example of decreased anthropomorphism involving the divine council may underlie MT Deut. 32:8. MT substitutes *bĕnê 'ādām,* "people," for Qumran *bny 'lhym,* "divine beings" (see chapter 1, section 2), which may reflect more than a text-critical variant; it also omits an anthropomorphic description of the divine council.

144. For a discussion of the circles that produced the book of Daniel, see R. R. Wilson, "From Prophecy to Apocalyptic: Reflections on the Shape of Israelite Religion," in *Anthropological Perspectives on Old Testament Prophecy,* ed. R. C. Culley and T. W. Overholt, Semeia 21 (Chico, CA: Scholars, 1982), 79-95. For 1 Enoch, see J. T. Milik, *The Books of Enoch* (Oxford: Clarendon, 1976); for discussion of 1 Enoch 14, see J. J. Collins, "The Place of Apocalypticism in the Religion of Israel," in *Ancient Israelite Religion: Essays in Honor of Frank Moore Cross,* ed. P. D. Miller, Jr., P. D. Hanson, and S. D. McBride, 545.

145. Cf. Cross, *Canaanite Myth and Hebrew Epic,* 135. For the distinctive biblical treat-

literature from the fourth to the second centuries, including 1 Enoch and the Book of Jubilees, represents an additional source of speculation.[146] The anthropomorphic language of Yahweh, other divine beings, and their heavenly realms never disappeared from Israel. The relative absence of this imagery from biblical texts during the second half of the monarchy reflects a religious reaction against Israel's old Canaanite heritage. Mythic imagery surfaced again in postexilic priestly traditions, though without the religious problems that it involved in the pre-exilic period. In the postexilic period, the old motifs associated with El, Baal, and Asherah in Canaanite tradition ceased to refer to the cults of deities other than Yahweh. With the death of the cults of the old Canaanite/Israelite deities, the imagery associated with them continued. Furthermore, the development of the apocalyptic genre provided fertile ground for mythic material.[147] This genre more than any other expressed mythic content in dramatic form. According to M. Stone,[148] widespread speculation in such areas as cosmology, astronomy, and the calendar represents one of the core interests in Jewish apocalypses (such as 1 Enoch) and a new development in Jewish religious literature. The postexilic interest in the old mythic content of Israel's Canaanite heritage was consistent with the new interest in cosmic speculation.

In sum, the picture of Yahweh, the male god without a consort, dominated religious discourse about the divine in ancient Israel from the Iron II period onward, at least as far as the sources indicate and assuming that these sources correspond with historical reality to a reasonable degree. At the same time, male language for Yahweh stood in tension both with less anthropomorphic descriptions for the deity and metaphors occasionally including fe-

---

ment of some mythic material, see B. S. Childs, *Myth and Reality in the Old Testament,* Studies in Biblical Theology (London: SCM, 1960), 30-93. While Childs rightly observes how the biblical record handles mythic material in manners differing from other ancient Near Eastern texts, various Near Eastern traditions also reflect distinctive treatments. Furthermore, the mythic material evident in other Near Eastern traditions, especially in Ugaritic literature, suffuses biblical texts more deeply than Childs's discussion indicates.

146. For intertestamental apocalyptic literature, see *OTPs* 1. For discussions of these texts, see J. J. Collins, *The Apocalyptic Imagination: An Introduction to the Jewish Matrix of Christianity* (New York: Crossroad, 1984); C. Rowlands, *The Open Heaven: A Study of Apocalyptic in Judaism and Early Christianity* (New York: Crossroad, 1982); M. E. Stone, ed., *Jewish Writings of the Second Temple Period,* Compendia rerum iudaicarum ad novum testamentum 2/II (Philadelphia: Fortress, 1984).

147. See I. Gruenwald, *Apocalyptic and Merkavah Mysticism* (Leiden: Brill, 1980); Collins, "The Place of Apocalypticism," 539-58.

148. M. E. Stone, *Scriptures, Sects and Visions: A Profile of Judaism from Ezra to the Jewish Revolts* (Philadelphia: Fortress, 1980), 42-43.

male imagery or combining it with male imagery. This state of affairs resembled neither a Greek philosophical notion of Deity as nonsexual Being nor some type of divine bisexuality. Rather, Israelite society perceived Yahweh primarily as a god, although Yahweh was viewed also as embodying traits or values expressed by various gendered metaphors and as transcending such particular renderings.

Just as some features of El and Baal can be perceived in the nature of Yahweh, it is possible to trace some female images for Yahweh to the goddess Asherah or at least her symbol, the asherah. Near Eastern examples invoking various gods in female and male language demonstrate how pliable language for a god or goddess could be, incorporating even language of the opposite sex. Female language for Yahweh could have stemmed from the flexibility of divine language. In those cases where the literary use of imagery specific to the asherah seems to function as the background for biblical divine language, as in Proverbs 3:13-18, the goddess, or at least her symbol, apparently made an impact, just as the gods El and Baal affected the shape of some male portrayals of Yahweh. Indeed, since the impact of the imagery of the asherah can be detected in some instances, it may be argued that its effects were more widespread than can be perceived at present.

CHAPTER 4

Yahweh and the Sun

1. The Biblical Record

The amount of solar language used for Yahweh is quite limited in the Bible. The classic example is Psalm 84:12: *kî šemeš ûmāgēn yhwh,* traditionally rendered, "for a sun and a shield is Yahweh." While this language is figurative (as noted in section 2 below), it assumes that the divine could be described in solar terms. Psalm 84 also reflects the larger context for the Bible's application of solar language to Yahweh. Psalm 84 displays the setting of a pilgrim longing for the experience of God in the temple in Jeruslaem. Verse 9b speaks of Yahweh as being "seen in Zion." The psalm presents a temple setting that explicitly draws on solar language for God to express the motif of "seeing God," in the psalms an expression for divine presence (Pss. 11:7; 17:15; 27:4, 13; 42:3; 63:3; cf. Judg. 14:20, 22; cf. 1 Sam. 1:22), later transformed into a motif of seeing God or the divine glory in the future (Isa. 35:2; 52:8; 66:5, 18).[1] Like Psalm 84, Psalms 42–43 exhibit the setting of a pilgrim longing for the temple in Jerusalem. Like Psalm 84:9b, Psalm 42:3 speaks of "seeing God." The solar

1. For the motif of "seeing God," see above, p. 143 and below, p. 154. For recent treatments of solar language applied to Yahweh, see H. P. Stähli, *Solare Elemente im Jahweglauben des Alten Testaments,* OBO 66 (Fribourg: Universitätsverlag; Göttingen: Vandenhoeck & Ruprecht, 1985); M. S. Smith, "'Seeing God' in the Psalms," 171-83; idem, *Psalms: The Divine Journey* (New York/Mahwah, NJ: Paulist, 1987), 52-61; idem, review of *Solare Elemente,* by H. P. Stähli, *JBL* 106 (1987): 513-15; J. G. Taylor, *Yahweh and the Sun: Biblical and Archaeological Evidence for Sun Worship in Ancient Israel,* JSOTSup 111 (Sheffield: JSOT Press, 1993); E. Lipiński, "Shemesh," *DDD,* 764-68; Day, *Yahweh and the Gods and Goddesses of Canaan,* 151-63. See also other works cited in n. 14 below. See also S. A. Wiggins, "Yahweh: The God of Sun?" *JSOT* 71 (1996): 89-106, with a retort by J. G. Taylor, "A Response to Steve A. Wiggins, "Yahweh: The God of Sun?" *JSOT* 71 (1996): 107-19, answered by S. A. Wiggins, "A Rejoinder to J. Glen Taylor," *JSOT* 73 (1997): 109-12. Both writers overargue an extreme view in my opinion, although Taylor's discussion better captures what may have been a "popular" view of Yahweh as solar in the Iron II period.

language in Psalm 84:12 would seem to constitute an expression for divine presence in the Jerusalem temple. Indeed, the setting of Psalm 84 and the explicit reference to the divine presence by the expression of "seeing God" in Psalm 84:9b supports this idea. The eastern orientation of the Jerusalem temple has led to speculative theories regarding the solarized character of Yahweh.[2] Psalms of vigil, such as Psalms 17, 27, and 63,[3] and Ezekiel 8:16[4] similarly suggest that the sun evoked at least the luminescent dimension of the divine presence, perhaps in keeping with a solar interpretation of Yahweh (cf. Zeph. 1:3; Ben Sira 49:7; Baruch 4:24). It might be argued that the simile for the appearance of the high priest in Ben Sira 50:7, "like the sun shining on the temple of the King" (NAB), derived from solar theophanic language in the context of the temple. Other passages, such as Josh. 10:12-13, suggest the sun (and the moon) as deities ultimately subservient to Yahweh.[5]

There are other instances of solar metaphor for Yahweh. These include describing Yahweh with the verbal root **zrḥ,* "rise," in Deuteronomy 33:2, Isaiah 60:1, Hosea 6:3, and once in the Kuntillet ʿAjrûd inscriptions.[6] This word is the normal verb for the rising of the sun (Judg. 9:33; 2 Sam. 23:4; Nah. 3:17; Jon. 4:8; Job 9:7; Ps. 104:4; Eccles. 1:5; cf. Judg. 5:31). Biblical and extrabiblical Yahwistic names with the elements **šḥr,* "dawn," *zrḥ,* "rise," and **n(w)r,* "light," may point to a solarized Yahwism.[7]

2. F. J. Hollis, "The Sun-Cult and the Temple in Jerusalem," in *Myth and Ritual,* ed. S. H. Hooke (Oxford: Oxford Univ. Press; London: Milford, 1933), 87-110; cf. J. Morgenstern, "Biblical Theophanies," *ZA* 25 (1911): 139-93, *ZA* 28 (1914): 15-60; idem, *The Fire upon the Altar* (Leiden: Brill, 1963); E. Lachman, "The Seraphim of Isaiah 6," *JQR* 59 (1968-69): 71-72. For further discussion, see Ahlström, *Psalm 89,* 85-88; idem, *Joel and the Temple Cult of Jerusalem,* VTSup 21 (Leiden: Brill, 1971), 84 n. 2; J. D. Levenson, "The Jerusalem Temple in Devotional and Visionary Experience," 43-44; Smith, "'Seeing God' in the Psalms," 171-83, esp. 175-76.

3. J. W. McKay, "Psalms of Vigil," *ZAW* 91 (1979): 229-47; A. R. Ceresko, "A Note on Psalm 63: A Psalm of Vigil," *ZAW* 92 (1980): 435-36. See n. 13 below.

4. On Ezek. 8:16, see Ahlström, *Royal Administration,* 70; M. Greenberg, *Ezekiel 1–20,* AB 22 (Garden City, NY: Doubleday, 1983), 172; Stähli, *Solare Elemente,* 9, 46-47. See also the references in n. 8.

5. See Taylor, *Yahweh and the Sun,* 114-18; H. A. J. Kruger, "Sun and Moon Grinding to a Halt: Exegetical Remarks on Joshua 10:9-14 and Related Texts in Judges," *Hervormde Teologiese Studies* 55 (1999): 1077-97; and note the discussion of astral bodies as divinities in Smith, *The Origins of Biblical Monotheism,* 61-66.

6. *BDB,* 280; C. L. Meyers, *The Tabernacle Menorah: A Synthetic Study of a Symbol from the Biblical Cult,* ASOR Dissertation Series 2 (Missoula, MT: Scholars, 1976), 145. On **zrḥ* used of Yahweh in the Kuntillet ʿAjrûd inscriptions, see Weinfeld, "Kuntillet ʿAjrûd Inscriptions," 126.

7. See Tigay, *You Shall Have No Other Gods,* 47, 58; Avigad, *Hebrew Bullae from the Time of Jeremiah,* 58 on **zrḥ,* 38-41, 72, 78, 79 on **šḥr,* and 26, 28, 35, 52, 83-87 on **nr.* Phoenician

Ezekiel 8:16 and 2 Kings 23:5, 11 criticize solar worship in the Jerusalem temple in the final decades of the Judean monarchy. Some scholars argue that these passages point to solar worship, either as an indigenous practice or as a result of Mesopotamian or Aramaean influence.[8] Ezekiel 8:16 belongs to a section detailing a number of cultic practices (including worship of idols and women weeping for Tammuz) conducted in the temple precincts:

> And he brought me into the inner court of the house of the Lord; and behold, at the door of the temple of the Lord, between the porch and the altar, were about twenty-five men, with their backs to the temple of the Lord, and their faces toward the east, worshiping the sun toward the east.

The verse interprets this cultic activity that takes place in the temple as worship of the sun. It is of further interest that the location of the practice points to priests as the culprits, unless this interpretation anachronistically assumes that only priests were permitted in this part of the temple.

In its denunciation of various temple practices, 2 Kings 23:11 includes "the chariots of the sun" *(markĕbôt haššemeš)*.[9] The picture is apparently one of chariots carrying the sun on its course, being pulled by horses. Archaeological findings may add to this picture. Horse figurines with a sun disk above their heads have been discovered at Iron Age levels at Lachish, Hazor, and Jerusalem.[10] The uppermost register of the tenth-century stand from Taanach

---

names with the element **n(w)r* are found with *b'l* as the theophoric element: *b'lnwr* and *b'lnr* (see K. Jongeling, review of *Vocabulario Fenicio,* by M. J. Fuentes Estañol, *BiOr* 42 [1985]: 361).

8. W. Eichrodt, *Ezekiel: A Commentary,* trans. C. Quin, OTL (Philadelphia: SCM, 1970), 127; N. Sarna, "Psalm XIX and the Near Eastern Sun-god Literature," *Fourth World Congress of Jewish Studies: Papers, vol. 1* (Jerusalem: World Union of Jewish Studies, 1967), 171-75; M. Cogan, *Imperialism and Religion: Assyria, Judah and Israel in the 8th and 7th Centuries B.C.E.,* SBLDS 19 (Missoula, MT: Scholars, 1974), 84-87; Greenberg, *Ezekiel 1–20,* 172; cf. W. Zimmerli, *Ezekiel 1,* trans. R. E. Clements, Hermeneia (Philadelphia: Fortress, 1979), 244. Cf. J. McKay, *Religion in Judah under the Assyrians,* Studies in Biblical Theology, 2d ser., no. 26 (London: SCM, 1973), 21, 32-35, 71, 99 n. 34. H. Schmidt and W. Eichrodt view Ezek. 8:16 as a description of devotion to Shamash (see Eichrodt, *Ezekiel,* 127). Greenberg (*Ezekiel 1–20,* 172) considers possible Aramaean influence. Zimmerli (*Ezekiel 1,* 244) categorizes the practice in Ezek. 8:16 as "solarized Yahwistic worship," although he allows for possible external influence. See further below n. 19.

9. J. W. McKay, "Further Light on the Horses and Chariots of the Sun in the Jerusalem Temple (2 Kings 23:11)," *PEQ* 105 (1973): 167-69; and references in n. 99; M. Weinfeld, "Queen of Heaven," *UF* 4 (1972): 150-52. A bilingual text from Boghazköi refers to horses of Shamash (see J. S. Cooper, "Bilinguals from Boghazköi. II," *ZA* 62 [1972]: 71, 76; I wish to thank Professor Victor Hurowitz for this reference).

10. See Holland, "A Survey," 149-50; Cogan, *Imperialism and Religion,* 87-88. Citing 2 Kings 23:11, K. Kenyon comments: "It is tempting to call this a sun-disk, and to think of those

likewise bears a sun disk above the body of a young bull.[11] At Ramat Rahel, two seals dating to the Persian period (ca. 587-333) depict bulls with solar disks between their horns.[12] Finally, the imagery of divine wings, as in Psalms 17:18, 36:7, 57:1, 61:4, and 63:7, invites comparison with the winged sun disk represented on pre-exilic seals (although the imagery could have coalesced with the iconography of the cherubim in the Judean temple). It would appear from Ezekiel 8:16 and 2 Kings 23:11 that either solar worship or worship of a solarized Yahweh took place in the temple during the waning years of the Judean monarchy.

Job 31:26-28 refers to an astral rite of some sort, although its precise setting is unclear:

> If I have looked at the light [i.e., sun] when it shone,
> or the moon moving in splendor,
> and my heart has been secretly enticed,
> and my mouth has kissed my hand;
> this also would have been an iniquity to be punished by the judges,
> for I should have been false to God above.[13]

Like 2 Kings 23:5, this passage connects solar worship with lunar devotion. Whether an indigenous development or a foreign import, these practices were allowed by the Judean dynasty at times to take place within the cult of its national god.

Several scholars situate solar or astral devotion in Iron II Judah within a larger context of the "astralization" of the chief god in a number of Levantine pantheons.[14] The criticism of solar cult in the Bible may be approached from

---

as miniatures of 'the horses that the kings of Judah had given to the sun,' which Josiah took away" (*Royal Cities of the Old Testament* [New York: Schocken Books, 1971], 120). Cf. n. 9. See also E. Mazar, "Archaeological Evidence for the 'Cows of Bashan Who Are in the Mountains of Samaria,'" in *Festschrift Reüben R. Hecht* (Jerusalem: Koren, 1979), 151-52. For further archaeological evidence of solar devotion, see Smith, "'Seeing God' in the Psalms," 178-79. For the Israelite or Canaanite provenience of the Taanach stand, see chapter 1, section four.

11. For a photograph of the stand with an archaeological summary, see A. E. Glock, "Taanach," in *EAEHL* 4:1142-43, 1147.

12. See the discussion in Smith, *Psalms,* 78 n. 65.

13. For textual support for *'ôr* as the sun, see LXX *helion,* Vulgate *solem,* and Targumic *'sthr* (E. Dhorme, *A Commentary on the Book of Job,* trans. H. Knight [Nashville/Camden/New York: Thomas Nelson, 1984], 461). The parallelism with moon also suggests this interpretation (cf. Job 37:21). On the motif of the hand to the mouth as a gesture of prayer, see Dhorme, *A Commentary,* 462; M. H. Pope, *Job,* 3d ed., AB 15 (Garden City, NY: Doubleday, 1973), 235; chap. 2 n. 67.

14. See Niehr, "The Rise of YHWH in Judahite and Israelite Religion," in *The Triumph of*

a further religious perspective. Following ancient Near Eastern tradition, the procession of divine "glory" *(kābôd)* described in Ezekiel 43:1-5 perhaps combines language from different realms of nature. The return of the warrior-god Ningirsu to his temple is rendered in both storm and solar language.[15] An enameled tile from the reign of the ninth-century Assyrian monarch Tukulti-Ninurta II[16] also provides an analogue to the description of the divine in Ezekiel 43:1-5. The tile depicts the god Assur[17] riding the winged sun disk with drawn bow aimed at the enemies of the king. On either side are storm clouds with rain falling. Enuma Elish 1:101-2, 157, and 11:128-29 apply solar qualities to Marduk, although storm language is more characteristic of him.[18] The combination of solar and storm imagery and iconography in Mesopotamian sources and biblical texts raises an important issue. By combining two types of natural phenomena, Psalm 50:1-3 and Ezekiel 43:1-5 suggest that the divine nature is beyond identification with a single natural phenomenon. In effect, Yahweh is equated metaphorically with natural phenomena, but also has power over and transcends these natural phenomena. Like Ningirsu and Marduk, Yahweh is "supernatural."

This perspective may help to explain criticism of the solar cult in the temple in Ezekiel 8:16. According to this passage, solar rendering of Yahweh reduced the divine to a form of natural idolatry, perhaps identified with the cult of a foreign deity. It may be argued, however, that the "idolatry" was an indigenous form of Yahwistic cult. Psalm 84 and other evidence for solar language predicated of Yahweh militates against interpreting solar worship in the temple as non-Yahwistic. There is no evidence for a separate sun cult, and the

---

Elohim: From Yahwisms to Judaisms, ed. D. V. Edelman, 67-71; O. Keel and C. Uehlinger, *Gods, Goddesses, and Images of God,* trans. T. Trapp (Minneapolis, MN: Fortress, 1998), 283-372; Keel, *Goddesses and Trees, New Moon and Yahweh: Ancient Near Eastern Art and the Hebrew Bible,* JSOTSup 261 (Sheffield: Sheffield Academic Press, 1998), 102-4; and J. Day, *Yahweh and the Gods and Goddesses of Canaan,* 151-84. For the issue of neo-Assyrian influence, see below, n. 19.

15. Gudea Cylinder B, V 109. See G. A. Barton, *The Royal Inscriptions of Sumer and Akkad* (New Haven: Yale Univ. Press; London: Humphrey Milford, Oxford University, 1929), 240-41; Jacobsen, *The Harps That Once . . . ,* 429. On Ningirsu in the inscription, see A. Falkenstein, *Die Inschriften Gudeas von Lagaš, I. Einleitung,* AnOr 30 (Rome: Pontificium Institutum Biblicum, 1966), 90-101.

16. Or possibly Assur-bel-kala of the mid-tenth century. See Mendenhall, *The Tenth Generation,* 44-45. For the god Assur with the winged solar disk, see van Buren, *Symbols of the Gods,* 89-90. On the motif of the "many waters" in Ezek. 43:2, see H. G. May, "Some Cosmic Connotations of *mayim rabbîm,* 'Many Waters,'" *JBL* 74 (1955): 17.

17. Cf. R. Mayer-Opificius, "Die geflügelte Sonne: Himmels und Regendarstellung im Alten Vorderasien," *UF* 16 (1984): 200, 233.

18. *ANET,* 62, 69-70.

explanation of foreign influence remains a matter of speculation. Indeed, the notion that neo-Assyrian rulers imposed their religious practices on their Levantine subjects has been discredited.[19] The theopolitical function of Yahwistic solar language may be further understood in the context of solar language predicated of the monarchy, both in Judah and elsewhere.

2. The Role of the Monarchy

Although the evidence is largely circumstantial, the application of solar language and imagery to Yahweh may have gained momentum under the impetus of the monarchy. The title of "the (divine) sun" goes back to royal titularies beginning in the second half of the third millennium. The Mesopotamian rulers, Ur-Nammu, Amar-Sin, Lipit-Ishtar, Hammurapi, and Zimri-Lim, are compared to the sun-god.[20] In international correspondence of the Late Bronze Age (1600-1200), solar language for monarchs is common. In this period, letters from El Amarna and Ugarit attest to the use of the title "the Sun" for the kings of Egypt, Hatti, and Ugarit.[21] For example, in KTU 2.16.6-10 Talmiyanu speaks to his mother, Thariyelli, concerning his audience before the Ugaritic king: *'umy td' ky 'rbt lpn špš wpn špš nr by m'id,* "My mother, you must know that I have entered before the Sun and the face of the Sun shone upon me greatly."[22] This text also furnishes background not only to Psalm 84:12's image of the divine king as the "Sun" and the shining of his face, but also to the biblical language of the shining of Yahweh's face elsewhere (e.g., Pss. 4:7; 31:17; 34:6; 67:2; 80:4, 8, 20; 89:16; 90:8; 119:25; Num. 6:24-26). Similarly, CTA 64 (KTU 3.1).24-25 reads: *'argmn nqmd mlk 'ugrt*

19. See McKay, *Religion in Judah;* Cogan, *Imperialism and Religion,* 42-61, and "Judah Under Assyrian Hegemony: A Re-examination of Imperialism and Religion," *JBL* 112 (1993): 403-14. The view is represented by H. Spieckermann, *Juda unter Assur in der Sargonidenzeit,* FRLANT 129 (Göttingen: Vandenhoeck & Ruprecht, 1982). See further Keel, *Goddesses and Trees,* 102-3; S. W. Holloway, "The Case for Assyrian Religious Influence in Israel and Judah," (Ph.D. diss., University of Chicago, 1992); and Smith, *The Origins of Biblical Monotheism,* 63.

20. R. Labat, *Le caractère réligieux de la royauté assyro-babylonienne,* Études d'Assyriologie 2 (Paris: Librairie d'Amerique et d'Orient, Adrien-Maissonneuve, 1939), 231-33; cf. Lambert, "Trees, Snakes, and Gods," 438-39 n. 25; G. Dossin, with A. Finet, *Correspondance Féminine,* Archives royales de Mari 10 (Paris: Geuthner, 1978), 150-51, text 99:5-6. My thanks to Mr. Gary Beckman for bringing these references to my attention.

21. See *ANET,* 483-90; McCarter, *II Samuel,* 484; Hess, "Divine Names," 158-59, 163.

22. On this letter, see D. Pardee, "Further Studies in Ugaritic Epistolography," *Archiv für Orientforschung* 31 (1984): 219-21; D. Pardee and R. M. Whiting, "Aspects of Epistolary Verbal Usage in Ugaritic and Akkadian," *BSOAS* 50 (1987): 8.

dybl lšpš mlk rb bʿlh, "The tribute of Niqmaddu king of Ugarit, which was brought to the Sun, the great king, his lord."[23] Finally, EA 147:59-60 records how the speaker has asked through a messenger when he will enter into the presence of the pharaoh. "Behold I have sent (a message) to the Sun, the father of the king, my lord (asking): 'When shall I see the face of the king, my lord?'" *(ma-ti-mi i-mur pa-ni šarri be-li-ya).*[24] This question bears a striking resemblance to the wording of Psalm 42:3c: "When shall I come and behold the face of God?"[25] The Ugaritic and Amarna letters would suggest that during the Late Bronze Age, New Kingdom Egypt was the source of this theology.[26] It spread to the rest of the Levant, leaving its imprint on biblical expressions for deity and king.

In the Iron Age, the Israelite king was described, as was Yahweh, in solar metaphor, sometimes in combination with rain imagery. Like Hosea 6:3 and perhaps Ezekiel 43:2, which compare Yahweh to both the sun and the

23. This Ugaritic passage illustrates the background of another divine title, namely, "great king," *melek rāb* in Ps. 48:3 and *melek gādôl* in 2 Kings 18:18, 29; Ps. 47:3; Eccles. 9:14; Isa. 36:4, 13; Mal. 1:14 (see J. J. M. Roberts, "Zion in the Theology of the Davidic-Solomonic Empire," in *Studies in the Period of David and Solomon and Other Essays,* ed. T. Ishida [Winona Lake, IN: Eisenbrauns, 1982], 94; and A. Malamat, "A Political Look at the Kingdom of David and Solomon and Its Relations with Egypt," in *Studies in the Period,* 197). On CTA 64 (KTU 3.1) and its parallels in Akkadian texts discovered at Ugarit, see M. Dietrich and O. Loretz, "Der Vertrag zwischen Šuppililuliuma und Niqmadu: Eine philologische und kulturhistorische Studie," *WO* 3/3 (1966): 206-45; D. J. McCarthy, *Treaty and Covenant: A Study in Form in the Ancient Near East and in the Old Testament,* rev. ed., AnBib 21A (Rome: Pontifical Biblical Institute, 1981), 68-69 n. 63.

24. *ANET,* 484; Moran, *Les Lettres d'El-Amarn,* trans. D. Collon and H. Cazelles, LAPO 13 (Paris: Les Éditions du Cerf, 1987), 379. See EA 266:12-15 and Num. 6:25.

25. On the "face" of God, see Smith, "'Seeing God' in the Psalms," 171-83. For the "hiding of the divine face," the opposite of "seeing the divine face," see R. E. Friedman, "The Biblical Expression *mastîr pānîm,*" *Hebrew Annual Review* 1 (1977): 139-47; S. E. Balentine, *The Hidden God: The Hiding of the Face of God in the Old Testament* (New York/Oxford: Oxford Univ. Press, 1983).

26. EA 155:6, 47 identifies the sun with the pharaoh: *šarru* ^{d}*šamaš dāritum,* "the king is the Eternal Sun." The latter phrase has equivalents in Ugaritic *špš ʿlm* attested in KTU 2.42 and 2.43.7 (see A. B. Knapp, "An Alishiyan Merchant at Ugarit," *TA* 10 [1983]: 39; D. Pardee, "Epigraphic and Philological Notes," *UF* 19 [1987]: 204-9) and Phoenician *šmš ʿlm* in KAI 26 A III 19. The Egyptian influence in KTU 2.42 and 2.43.9 is evident also from the presence of the name, *nmry,* referring to Nebmare Amenophis III (cf. KTU 2.23.21-24). See A. Cooper, "*MLK ʿLM:* 'Eternal King' or 'King of Eternity'?" in *Love & Death in the Ancient Near East: Essays in Honor of Marvin H. Pope,* ed. J. H. Marks and R. M. Good (Guilford, CT: Four Quarters, 1987), 3. For further Egyptian influence in the phraseology of the Amarna correspondence, see Albright, "The Egyptian Correspondence of Abimilki, Prince of Tyre," *Journal of Egyptian Antiquities* 23 (1937): 190-203.

rain,[27] 2 Samuel 23:3b-4 compares the king to the sun as it dawns and the rain as it causes grass to grow:[28]

> When one rules justly over people,
> ruling in the fear of God,
> he dawns *(yizraḥ)* on them like the morning light,
> like the sun bright upon a cloudless morning,
> like rain that makes grass to sprout from the earth.

Like 2 Samuel 23:3b-4, Psalm 72:5-6 first invokes the sun as an image of royal durability and then uses the lush rains as a metaphor for the well-being generated by the monarchy. The royal use of solar imagery extended to the winged sun disk on the royal *(lmlk)* stamp seals found on jar handles.[29] The inscription *nryhw bn hmlk*, "Neriyahu son of the king," may be mentioned in this connection. Here a solar attribution to Yahweh may lie behind the name of the king's son.[30] Given these bits of evidence for the royal background of divine solar language, P. K. McCarter suggests revocalizing MT *ûmagēn* in Psalm 84:12 to *ûmāgān*, understanding the half-verse to mean "for a sun and a sovereign is Yahweh."[31] Both titles render Yahweh as a divine suzerain. The royal context of this passage, exemplified by the reference to the "anointed" of Yahweh in verse 10, supports this interpretation.

27. On Hos. 6:3, see Andersen and Freedman, *Hosea*, 423-24; J. L. Mays, *Hosea: A Commentary*, OTL (London: SCM, 1969), 95-96; McCarter, *II Samuel*, 484. In connection with dawn imagery and psalms of vigil, the paronomasia between *yĕšaḥărūnĕnî*, "they will seek me" (Hos. 5:15), and *šaḥar*, "dawn" (Hos. 6:3), may be noted.

28. McCarter, *II Samuel*, 484; Stähli, *Solare Elemente*, 27-28. See also H. N. Richardson, "The Last Words of David: Some Notes on 2 Samuel 23:1-7," *JBL* 90 (1971): 259; D. N. Freedman, "II Samuel 23:4," *JBL* 90 (1971): 329-30; McCarter, *II Samuel*, 476-86. For a tenth-century dating of this poem, see Cross, *Canaanite Myth and Hebrew Epic*, 234-37; Freedman, *Pottery, Poetry, and Prophecy*, 95-97, 118; G. Rendsburg, "The Northern Origin of 'the Last Words of David' (2 Sam. 23, 1-7)," *Biblica* 69 (1988): 113-21.

29. For examples, see *ANEP*, 349 and 377, no. 809a-c; see McKay, *Religion in Judah*, 52-53, 102 n. 55. For the recent discussion of the *lmlk* stamps, see N. Na'aman, "Hezekiah's Fortified Cities and the *LMLK* Stamps," *BASOR* 261 (1986): 5-21; Y. Garfinkel, "The Distribution of Identical Seal Impressions and the Settlement Pattern in Judea Before Sennacherib's Campaign," *Cathedra* 32 (1984): 35-52; G. Barkay and A. G. Vaughan, "LMLK and Official Seal Impressions from Tel Lachish," *TA* 23 (1996): 61-74; and Vaughan, "Palaeographic Dating of Judaean Seals and Its Significance for Biblical Research," *BASOR* 313 (1999): 43-64, and *Theology, History, and Archaeology in the Chronicler's Account of Hezekiah*, Archaeology and Biblical Studies 4 (Atlanta, GA: Scholars, 1999), 81-167.

30. See N. Avigad, "Three Ancient Seals," *BA* 49 (1986): 51-53.

31. McCarter, *II Samuel*, 484. On *mgn* for suzerain, see M. O'Connor, "Yahweh, the Donor," *Aula Orientalis* 6 (1988): 47-60.

The use of solar imagery for the monarch continued into the postexilic period. Malachi 3:20[32] utilizes solar imagery to paint a picture of Israel's future savior and the effects that savior will have on Israel:

> But for you who fear my name the sun of righteousness shall rise *(zārĕḥāh)* with healing in its wings.

Similarly, Isaiah 58:8 uses solar language to describe the "theophany of the righteous," with the divine glory serving as the rearguard (cf. Judg. 5:31):

> Then shall your light *('ôrekā)* break forth like the dawn *(kaššaḥar)*,
> and your healing shall spring up *(tiṣmāḥ)* speedily;
> your righteousness shall go before you,
> the glory of Yahweh shall be your rearguard.

Like 2 Samuel 23:3-4 and Psalm 72:5-6, the first part of this verse employs solar imagery[33] and the second evokes imagery of natural growth. Isaiah 58:8 perhaps applies the royal theology expressed in 2 Samuel 23:3-4,[34] not to a royal group, but to Israel as a whole.[35] The royal background is perhaps echoed in the verb *tiṣmāḥ,* although Isaiah 58:8 in following 2 Samuel 23:4b employs this verb in its natural sense. Davidic kings were compared to a "shoot," *ṣemaḥ* (Jer. 23:5; 33:15; Zech. 3:8; cf. Zech. 6:12; KAI 43:10-11; Isa. 11:1, 4-5, 10; cf. 4:2; Ben Sira 47:22; 51:12 h).[36] Both Malachi 3:20 and Isaiah 58:8 mention healing, a blessing evidently rooted in the old royal idea that the monarch provides well-being for his subjects. Finally, the royal iconography of the winged sun disk compares well with the description of the royal scion in Malachi 3:20.

32. See Morton Smith, "Helios in Palestine," *EI* 16 (1982 = H. Orlinsky Festschrift): 205*; McCarter, *II Samuel,* 484; Stähli, *Solare Elemente,* 39. Cf. F. Vattioni, "Mal. 3,20 e un mese del calendario fenicio," *Biblica* 40 (1959): 1012-15.

33. On *'ôr* as the sun, see n. 13 above; cf. Gen. 1:14-16. For the image, cf. Ps. 97:11, LXX and Syriac.

34. M. S. Smith, review of Stähli, *Solare Elemente,* 514.

35. See O. Eissfeldt, "The Promises of Grace to David in Isaiah 55:1-5," in *Israel's Prophetic Heritage: Essays in Honor of James Muilenberg,* ed. B. W. Anderson and W. Harrelson (New York: Harper & Brothers, 1962), 201-6; M. S. Smith, "*Bĕrît 'ām/bĕrît 'ôlām:* A New Proposal for the Crux of Isa 42:6," *JBL* 100 (1981): 241-43.

36. See M. Fishbane, *Biblical Interpretation in Ancient Israel* (Oxford: Clarendon, 1985), 304-6, 471-72; C. L. and E. M. Meyers, *Haggai, Zechariah 1–8,* AB 25B (Garden City, NY: Doubleday, 1987), 202-3.

37. Van Buren, *Symbols of the Gods,* 89-90; Mendenhall, *The Tenth Generation,* 45; see also W. G. Lambert, "Trees, Snakes, and Gods," 439; *ANEP,* 215 and 328, no. 658.

While the evidence is meager, solar language for Yahweh apparently developed under the monarchy's influence. Stated differently, the application of solar language to Yahweh was a consequence of Yahweh's status as national god. Moreover, there are Late Bronze and Iron Age analogues for this development. In Assyria, the solar disk, originally the symbol of the sun-god, Shamash, was used for the national god, Assur.[37] Similarly, "Babylonian theologians" (to use W. G. Lambert's term) call their national god, Marduk, the "sun-god of the gods" in Enuma Elish 1:102 and 6:127.[38] A small god-list identifies various deities with specific functions of Marduk.[39] Shamash is the "Marduk of justice." Another text states that "Shamash is Marduk of the lawsuit."[40] On a stele from Ugarit, the winged sun disk belongs to a scene depicting the enthroned El.[41] The sun disk appears with *bʿl ḥmn* on an inscribed stone known as the Kilamuwa orthostat.[42] These analogues illustrate the assimilation of solar imagery to a chief deity. The solar imagery for the patron god in the royal setting served to enhance the power of the monarchy through identification with the power of the divine king. More specifically, the solar imagery, insofar as it was applied to both the king and the god, enhanced the divine aura of the human king.

To summarize, solar language for Yahweh apparently developed in two stages. First, it originated as part of the Canaanite, and more generally Near Eastern, heritage of divine language as an expression of general theophanic luminosity. Like Ningirsu, Assur, and Marduk, Yahweh could be rendered in either solar or storm terms or both together. Second, perhaps under the influence of the monarchy, in the first millennium the sun became one compo-

38. *ANET,* 62, 69; van Buren, *Symbols of the Gods,* 87-89; Lambert, "Trees, Snakes, and Gods," 439; Sommerfeld, *Der Aufstieg Marduk,* 174-81.

39. Lambert, "The Historical Development," 197-98; Lambert, "Trees, Snakes, and Gods," 439 n. 28; Sommerfeld, *Die Aufstieg Marduks,* 10.

40. Lambert, "Trees, Snakes, and Gods," 439 n. 28. For further evidence and discussion, see H. Frankfort, "Gods and Myths on Sargonid Seals," *Iraq* 1 (1934): 6, 21-29; and Sommerfeld, *Der Aufstieg Marduks,* 9-12.

41. See *ANEP,* 168, no. 493; A. Caquot and M. Sznycer, *Ugaritic Religion,* 23 and pl. 7. For speculation as to the meaning of the stele, see N. Wyatt, "The Stela of the Seated God from Ugarit," *UF* 15 (1983): 271-77. See also H. Niehr, "Ein umstrittenes Detail der El-Stele aus Ugarit," *UF* 24 (1992): 293-300. For a survey of the sun disk in Syro-Mesopotamia, see Mayer-Opificius, "Die geflügelte Sonne," 189-236. According to *PE* 1.10.36 (Attridge and Oden, *Philo of Byblos,* 56-57), Kronos had wings. For the identification of El with Kronos in Philo of Byblos' *Phoenician History,* see *PE* 1.10.16, 29; cf. 1.10.20 (Attridge and Oden, *Philo of Byblos,* 48-49, 50-51, 54-55).

42. *ANEP,* no. 281. See Cross, *Canaanite Myth and Hebrew Epic,* 24, 26. Cf. Y. Yadin, "Symbols of Deities at Zinjirli, Carthage and Hazor," in *Near Eastern Archaeology in the Twentieth Century: Essays in Honor of Nelson Glueck,* ed. J. A. Sanders (Garden City, NY: Doubleday, 1970), 208-12.

nent of the symbolic repertoire of the chief god in Israel just as it did in Assur, Babylon, and Ugarit.[43] In Israel it appears to have been a special feature of the southern monarchy, since the available evidence is restricted to Judah; it is not attested in the northern kingdom. Furthermore, it seems to have been a special expression of Judean royal theology. It expressed and reinforced dimensions of both divine and human kingship. This form of solarized Yahwism may have appeared to the authors of Ezekiel 8 and 2 Kings 23 as an idolatrous solar cult incompatible with their notions of Yahweh.[44]

3. The Assimilation of Solar Imagery

The solar descriptions of Yahweh during the monarchy perhaps furnish the background to descriptions of the sun in biblical cosmology. According to N. Sarna, Psalm 19 uses solar language as a polemic against solar worship in Israel, as reflected in Ezekiel 8:16 and 2 Kings 23.[45] The tone of Psalm 19 is, however, not polemical. In addition, the sun in Psalm 19:4-6 plays a role perhaps analogous to the Torah in verses 7-10: both attest to the glory of God. Similarly, the function of the sun as providing order in the cosmos in Genesis 1:14 and Psalm 104:19 has been related to this same theme by H. P. Stähli.[46] These religious expressions are not to be seen only as polemic, although this point is frequently made in the case of Genesis 1:14.[47] Rather, the sun serves

43. According to Hestrin ("Cult Stand from Ta'anach," 75), the winged sun disk "symbolized the supreme god in the Mesopotamian, Hittite and Canaanite pantheons." Her analysis includes a cult stand from Taanach (see n. 11 above); the top register of the stand depicts the solar disk above a four-legged animal that she argues signifies Baal. J. G. Taylor identifies the animal as an equid and connects it with the horses of the sun of 2 Kings 23:11 ("Yahweh and Asherah at Tenth Century Taanach," *Newsletter for Ugaritic Studies* 37/38 [1987]: 16-18; "Two Earliest Representations of Yahweh," 561-64). Questions about Taylor's interpretation of the stand have been raised (e.g., Miller, *The Religion of Ancient Israel,* 43-45; Zevit, *The Religions of Ancient Israel,* 321 n. 125, 323).

44. Ringgren, *Israelite Religion,* 62, 97-98.

45. Sarna, "Psalm XIX and the Near Eastern Sun-god Literature," 171-75.

46. Stähli, *Solare Elemente,* 17-23. For Egyptian influence on Psalm 104, see P. Auffret, *Hymnes d'Egypte et d'Israël: Études des structures littéraires,* OBO 34 (Fribourg: Éditions Universitaires; Göttingen: Vandenhoeck & Ruprecht, 1981), 279-302.

47. See G. von Rad, *Genesis: A Commentary,* rev. ed., trans. J. H. Marks, OTL (London: SCM, 1963), 54; C. Westermann, *Genesis I,* BKAT 1/1 (Neukirchen-Vluyn: Neukirchener Verlag des Erziehungsvereins GmbH, 1968), 179; B. Vawter, *On Genesis: A New Reading* (Garden City, NY: Doubleday, 1977), 48; Stähli, *Solare Elemente,* 17-19. It has been claimed (e.g., Vawter, *On Genesis,* 48) that Gen. 1:16 uses the title "great light" *(hammāʾôr haggādōl)* instead of "the sun" *(haššemeš)* in order to diminish the divine connotation of the solar deity. Nonetheless, the title

as a positive sign of order in Yahweh's creation. Reduced to a sign of divine order, solar imagery in these cases represents instances of "a harmless sun" (Wisd. of Sol. 18:3; cf. Letter of Jeremiah 6:60; Odes of Solomon 15:2).[48]

---

in Gen. 1:16 echoes common titles for the sun-goddess in Ugaritic literature where she is called "the great light," *nyr rbt* (KTU 1.16 I 37-38; 1.161.19), and "the light of the gods," *nrt 'ilm* (1.3 V 17; 1.4 VII 21; 1.6 I 8-9, 11, 13; 1.6 II 24).

48. For postbiblical use of solar imagery, see Morton Smith, "Helios in Palestine," 199*-214*.

CHAPTER 5

Yahwistic Cultic Practices

1. Yahwistic Cultic Symbols and Sites

As chapter 3 describes, the biblical record condemns the goddess Asherah much less frequently than the asherah. The symbol was initially an acceptable feature of Yahwistic cult, but later was treated as a non-Yahwistic aberration. In legal materials, the symbol of the asherah is not alone the object of opprobrium. Exodus 34:13 condemns not only the asherim of the other peoples previously in the land, but also "their altars" *(mizbĕḥōtām)* and "their pillars" *(maṣṣēbōtām)*. Pillars are denounced also in Deuteronomy 16:22 following a condemnation of the asherah in the previous verse. To this list of abominations Deuteronomy 7:5 and 12:3 add "their graven images" *(pesîlêhem)*. Prophetic condemnations of the asherah and asherim likewise include other cultic paraphernalia. Isaiah 17:8 and 27:9 denounce other deities' altars, asherim, and incense altars *(ḥammānîm)*. Jeremiah 17:2 includes not only altars and asherim in its criticism, but also the "high places" *(bāmôt)* where these objects were considered to have been used. The oracle of Micah 5:10-15 is more inclusive; sorceries, soothsayers, images, pillars, and asherim are all to be swept away by Yahweh.[1]

Some of these practices belonged to Yahwistic cult prior to and following the periods when legal and prophetic condemnations were raised against them. Like the asherah, the "high places" were acceptable both in the period of the Judges and during the monarchy.[2] In 1 Samuel 9–10 Samuel is described con-

1. Concerning the ancient Yahwistic background of these practices, see Fohrer, *History of Israelite Religion*, 57-58, 114; Ahlström, *Aspects of Syncretism*, 11, 50-51; Olyan, *Asherah and the Cult of Yahweh*, 17-18, 21-22, 73; Elizabeth C. LaRocca-Pitts, *"Of Wood and Stone": The Significance of Israelite Cultic Items in the Bible and Its Early Interpreters*, HSM 61 (Winona Lake, IN: Eisenbrauns, 2001); and Zevit, *The Religions of Ancient Israel*, esp. 256-63, 460-67.

2. On "high places" *(bāmôt)*, see in addition to references in the preceding note, Ringgren, *Israelite Religion*, 157-58, 177; W. B. Barrick, "The Funerary Character of 'High-Places' in An-

ducting worship at a high place, and in 1 Kings 3:4-5, Solomon goes to the high place of Gibeon, where Yahweh appears to him in a dream. A Deuteronomistic apology for Solomon's use of the high place (cf. Deut. 12:1-14), verse 2 reads: "The people were sacrificing at the high places, however, because no house had yet been built for the name of the Lord." Verse 3 relates how Solomon sacrificed and burned incense at the high places, indicating royal support for these traditional religious practices. The text of 2 Kings 23:8 (cf. 2 Chron. 14:4) suggests that high places functioned in Israel down to the reign of Josiah. Amos 7:9 refers to the high places in the northern kingdom. Like the royal religion of the central sanctuaries (Amos 7:13), the high places were staffed with priests (1 Kings 13:2, 33; 23:20; 2 Kings 23:8-9) who conducted sacrifice (2 Kings 18:22; 23:15; Ezek. 18:6, 15; 20:28; cf. 2 Kings 17:11; Ezek. 6:3-4). The geographical range of the high places likewise reflects widespread popular support for high places. High places were present in both rural (Ezek. 6:13; cf. Hos. 4:13) and urban settings (1 Kings 13:32; 2 Kings 23:8),[3] probably for clan religion, as opposed to sanctuaries and temples, which operated for higher levels of social complexity (tribes and nations), under "higher" authorities (traditional priestly lines at sanctuaries, some employed as monarchic functionaries).

Like the asherah, high places were not specific to Israelite society, but belonged to a broader cultural picture. The Mesha stele (KAI 181:3), Isaiah 15:2, 16:12, and Jeremiah 48:35 indicate that high places were a feature of

---

cient Palestine: A Reassessment," *VT* 25 (1975): 565-95; M. Haran, "Temples and Cultic Open Areas as Reflected in the Bible," in *Temples and High Places in Biblical Times: Proceedings of the Colloquium in Honor of the Centennial of Hebrew Union College — Jewish Institute of Religion, Jerusalem, 14-16 March 1977*, ed. A. Biran (Jerusalem: Nelson Glueck School of Biblical Archaeology of Hebrew Union College — Jewish Institute of Religion, 1981), 31-37; Ahlström, *Royal Administration*, 59-61; and J. A. Emerton, "The Biblical High Place in the Light of Recent Study," *PEQ* 129 (1997): 116-23. Emerton correctly questions whether "high place" is an accurate rendering for *bāmāh*. On *bāmôt* and especially the cultic installation at Tel Dan, see A. Biran, "Tel Dan," *BA* 37 (1974): 40-41; idem, "'To the God Who Is in Dan,'" in *Temples and High Places*, 142-51. G. Mendenhall (*The Tenth Generation*, 181) views the prohibitions against high places as a function of the political religious establishment of Jerusalem; in his own words, *bāmôt* "became increasingly incompatible with ancient Yahwism, especially after the political establishment of Yahwism under the Monarchy" (Mendenhall's italics). On the contrary, the monarchy conservatively retained many features of Israelite religion, including high places. On the conservatism of the monarchy especially under Manasseh, see Ahlström, *Royal Administration*, 75-81.

3. See T. H. Blomquist, *Gates and Gods: Cults in the City Gates of Iron Age Palestine; An Investigation of the Archaeological and Biblical Sources*, ConBOT 46 (Stockholm: Almqvist & Wiksell International, 1999), 151-63. For a dramatic illustration of a *bāmâ*, see A. Biran, "The High Places of Biblical Dan," in *Studies in the Archaeology of the Iron Age in Israel and Jordan*, ed. A. Mazar with the assistance of G. Mathias, JSOTSup 331 (Sheffield: Sheffield Academic Press, 2001), 148-55.

Moabite religion as well. Perhaps, like the asherah and high places, some of the other items mentioned in Micah 5:10-15 were initially acceptable in Yahwistic cult but later condemned. This was also the fate of some practices concerning the dead and child sacrifice, as the following sections illustrate.

2. Practices Associated with the Dead

The practices in the Bible concerning the dead belonged to Israel's Canaanite heritage. Feeding the dead (KTU 1.20-22; 1.142), consulting the dead (KTU 1.124; 1.161; cf. KAI 214), and mourning the dead (KTU 1.5 VI 11-22, 31–1.6 I 5) were all part of Canaanite religion. Ancient Israel continued most of these practices in juxtaposition with Yahwistic cult. A work by K. Spronk has sought to minimize the Canaanite/Israelite nature of Israelite customs pertaining to the dead by distinguishing between Yahwistic religion and popular religion.[4] The first is identified as Yahwistic and eschews practices associated

4. K. Spronk, *Beatific Afterlife in Ancient Israel and the Ancient Near East,* AOAT 219 (Kevelaer: Butzon & Bercker; Neukirchen-Vluyn: Neukirchener Verlag, 1986); cf. T. J. Lewis, *Cults of the Dead in Ancient Israel and Ugarit,* HSM 39 (Atlanta, GA: Scholars Press, 1989), 1-4. For further discussion, see M. S. Smith and E. Bloch-Smith, "Death and Afterlife at Ugarit and Ancient Israel," *JAOS* 108 (1988): 277-84. For a more fruitful treatment of the categories between "official" and "popular" religion in this area, see R. Albertz, *Persönliche Frömmigkeit und officielle Religion: Religionsinterner Pluralismus in Israel und Babylon,* Calwer Theologische Monographien, Reihe A, vol. 9 (Stuttgart: Calwer Verlag, 1979); W. Brueggemann, review of *Persönliche Frömmigkeit,* by Albertz, *CBQ* 42 (1980): 86-87; Halpern, "'Brisker Pipes Than Poetry,'" 83-84; J. S. Holladay, Jr., "Religion in Israel and Judah Under the Monarchy: An Explicitly Archaeological Approach," in *Ancient Israelite Religion: Essays in Honor of Frank Moore Cross,* ed. P. D. Miller, Jr., P. D. Hanson, and S. D. McBride (Philadelphia: Fortress, 1987), 249-99; Miller, "Israelite Religion," 215-18; Tigay, *You Shall Have No Other Gods,* 20 n. 64. To be sure, there was popular and official religion in Israel. Official religion during the period of the monarchy was not maintained, however, by the monarchy, priesthood, or prophets in the form suggested by Spronk. For the issue of religion and social segments, see S. Ackerman, *Under Every Green Tree: Popular Religion in Sixth Century Judah,* HSM 46 (Atlanta, GA: Scholars, 1992); J. Berlinerblau, "The 'Popular Religion' Paradigm in Old Testament Research: A Sociological Critique," *JSOT* 60 (1993): 3-26; idem, "Preliminary Remarks for the Sociological Study of Israelite 'Official Religion,'" in *Ki Baruch Hu: Ancient Near Eastern, Biblical, and Judaic Studies in Honor of Baruch A. Levine,* ed. R. Chazan, W. W. Hallo, and L. Schiffman (Winona Lake, IN: Eisenbrauns, 1995), 153-70; idem, *The Vow and the "Popular Religious Groups" of Ancient Israel: A Philological and Sociological Inquiry,* JSOTSup 210 (Sheffield: Sheffield Academic Press, 1996); K. van der Toorn, *Family Religion in Babylonia, Syria and Israel: Continuity and Change in the Forms of Religious Life,* Studies in the History and Culture of the Ancient Near East VII (Leiden/New York/Köln: Brill, 1996); Zevit, *The Religions of Ancient Israel,* 643-48. For some questions about Berlinerblau's approach, see my review of his book in *JSS* 43 (1998): 148-51.

with the Canaanites. The second is considered non-Yahwistic and embraces the Canaanite customs of the dead. Spronk defines neither the constitution and development of official Yahwistic religion, nor how this Yahwistic religion or the "mainstream of Yahwistic religion" functioned with official status in the nation, nor how it gave rise to the Hebrew Bible, assumed to be the official expression of "official Yahwistic religion." In short, the official religious policy of pre-exilic Israel does not conform to the societal bearers of the official religion defined by Spronk. To believe Isaiah (28:7; 30:10) and Jeremiah (2:26-28; 6:13), all sectors of Israelite society, including priests, prophets, and kings, participated in what was later condemned as non-Yahwistic religion. This problem is by no means restricted to practices pertaining to the dead but to deities and their cult symbols as well. Therefore, either the Law and the literary prophets do not represent the official religion of Israel, or a clear distinction between official and popular religion cannot be supported, at least for some deities and some cultic practices. As with the symbol of the asherah, some practices involving the dead, initially conducted without legal or prophetic criticism, were later regarded as non-Yahwistic.[5]

The only practice associated with the dead that was possibly forbidden prior to the seventh century was necromancy. Condemnation of necromancy is not recorded for any prophet before Isaiah (8:19; cf. 19:3; 29:4; cf. 57:6) or any legal code before the Holiness Code (Lev. 19:26-28; 20:6-7; cf. Deut. 18:10-11). The only passage perhaps suggesting that necromancy was viewed negatively before 750 is 1 Samuel 28, the story of the Necromancer of Endor. The chapter tells how by means of a female medium Saul inquired of the dead Samuel, whose appearance in verse 13 is called *'ĕlōhîm,* "a divine one." Verse 3 relates: "and Saul had put away the mediums and wizards of the land" *(wĕšā'ûl hēsîr hā'ōbôt wĕ'et-hayyidĕ'ōnîm mēhā'āreṣ).* This verse claims that Saul had banished necromancers. It may be noted in passing that 1 Samuel 28 does not address other practices involving the dead condemned in later legal and prophetic material. The material in 1 Samuel 28:3, as noted by commentators,[6] may have been an editorial addition. The narrator, perhaps a Deuteronomistic one, supplies background information, and indeed, some formulas in this verse are reminiscent of Deuteronomy 18:10-11. As in Deuteronomy 18:10-11, the issue in 1 Samuel 28:3 involves securing otherworldly

5. Ringgren, *Israelite Religion,* 219; B. Lang, "Life After Death in the Prophetic Promise," *Congress Volume; Jerusalem 1986,* ed. J. Emerton, VTSup 40 (Leiden: Brill, 1988), 144-56.

6. See J. Lust, "On Wizards and Prophets," in *Studies on Prophecy: A Collection of Twelve Papers,* VTSup 26 (Leiden: Brill, 1974), 133. Cf. H. R. Smith, *A Critical and Exegetical Commentary on the Books of Samuel,* ICC (Edinburgh: T. & T. Clark, 1899), 240; and McCarter, *I Samuel,* AB 14 (Garden City, NY: Doubleday, 1980), 422.

information from a source deemed unacceptable to the author.[7] The concern was not simply what was acceptable to so-called normative Yahwistic religion. Rather, the issue concerns a form of inquiry that competed with prophecy in ancient Israel. Like Isaiah 8:16-20 and Deuteronomy 18:9-22, 1 Samuel 28:3 frames the question of inquiry as a form of appropriating information from sources that some pre-exilic prophets and Deuteronomists considered wrong. Indeed, necromancy competed with prophecy (Isa. 8:19-20; 29:4; cf. Lev. 19:26). Later tradition understood the necromancy described in 1 Samuel 28 as an occasion of prophecy (Ben Sira 46:20). What is reflected in 1 Samuel 28:3 is either a later belief that Saul had banished necromancy or, less likely, a genuine pre-750 negative attitude toward necromancy.[8]

Like 1 Samuel 28:3, Psalm 106:28 and Numbers 25:2 have been taken as early criticisms of cult practices pertaining to the dead. Psalm 106:28 reads: "They yoked themselves to Baal Peor, and ate the sacrifices of the dead" *(zibḥê mētîm)*. This verse is dependent on Numbers 25:2,[9] which does not condemn practices associated with the dead; rather, it forbids "sacrifices of their gods" *(zibḥê 'ĕlōhêhen)*. Psalm 106:28 condemns the sacrifices intended for the dead. Elsewhere the dead are called *'ĕlōhîm*, "gods," as in 1 Samuel 28:3 and Isaiah 8:19. KTU 1.6 VI 45-49 illustrates this usage. In these four lines, *rp'im*, "rephaim," is parallel with *'ilnym*, "divinities," and *'ilm*, "gods," is parallel with *mtm*, "the dead." The second and third terms are etymologically related to Hebrew *'ĕlōhîm*, "gods." Similarly, Akkadian *ilu* and Phoenician *'ln* are used for the dead. Numbers 25:2 does not address the issue of sacrifices to the dead; only Psalm 106:28 does so. Psalm 106:40-47 refers to the Exile, indicating that this psalm was exilic or later.[10] To be sure, it could be argued that

7. For another apparent example of necromancy in Israel, 2 Sam. 12:16, see H. Niehr, "Ein unerkannter Text zur Nekromantie in Israel: Bermerkungen zum religionsgeschichtlichen Hintergrund von 2 Sam 12, 16a," *UF* 23 (1991): 301-6.

8. See Lust, "On Wizards and Prophets," 140-42; W. A. M. Beuken, "I Sam 28: The Prophet as 'Hammer of Witches,'" *JSOT* 6 (1978): 15.

9. M. Noth, *Numbers*, trans. J. D. Martin, OTL (London: SCM, 1968), 195-97; Cross, *Canaanite Myth and Hebrew Epic*, 202, 316. See also Spronk, *Beatific Afterlife*, 231-32. Unlike Ps. 106:28, Num. 25:2 does not explicitly describe devotion to the dead, although it could have presupposed it.

10. See F. C. Fensham, "Neh. 9 and Pss. 105, 106, 135 and 136: Post-Exilic Historical Traditions in Poetic Form," *Journal of Northwest Semitic Languages* 9 (1981): 35-51, esp. 35 n. 6. A. Weiser suggests the possibility that vv. 40-47 refer to the fall of the northern kingdom (*The Psalms*, OTL [London: SCM, 1962], 680, 682). In that case, Ps. 106:28 would provide information on "sacrifices of the dead" as it was perceived in the mid-eighth century or later. Ps. 16:3 may also refer to the honored dead, literally "the holy ones," *qĕdôšîm* (Pope in Cooper, "Divine Names and Epithets," 457; Spronk, *Beatific Afterlife*, 249, 334-38); the poem is often dated to the

verse 28 predates the Exile; nonetheless, it is unlikely that this verse is historically pertinent for examining practices with respect to the dead before the seventh century.

Prior to ca. 750, Israelites engaged not only in necromancy but probably in other practices pertaining to the dead. Early veneration for the dead probably included funerary mourning for the dead, feeding the dead, and invoking the dead as sources of divine information and perhaps aid. Negative criticism or negative depictions of customs concerning the dead first appeared around the middle of the eighth century, perhaps as a response to the competition that necromancy posed to prophecy. During the Iron Age, other practices associated with the dead were conducted without conflicting with the cult of Yahweh; not even later criticisms recorded in the Bible suggest otherwise.

Explicit objections to feeding the dead with the tithe of Yahweh appear in the seventh century (Deut. 26:14; cf. Psalm 16, and MT Ps. 22:30, which refers to the dead).[11] Following a late eighth-century criticism of necromancy in Isaiah 8:16-20a,[12] Isaiah 8:20b-21 possibly describes the dead who go about the land hungry:

> Surely for this word which they speak there is no dawn. He will pass through the land, greatly distressed and hungry; and when he is hungry, he will be enraged and will curse his king and God, and turn his face upward; and they will look to the earth, but behold, distress and darkness, the gloom of anguish; and they will be thrust into thick darkness.

This passage plays on the time of day when necromancy takes place, namely at night (1 Sam. 28:8; cf. Isa. 65:4). The "word" is not to be successful; it has no "dawn." The subject of the verbs is unclear. MT and 1QIsa^{a} read the verbs in the singular beginning in verse 21 with *ʿābar;* LXX renders the verbs in the plural. The one whose word has no dawn has no immediate antecedent; the closest antecedent is *hammētîm,* "the dead," in verse 19b, although this section is often regarded as a secondary addition, since it seems

sixth century or later (see C. A. and E. G. Briggs, *A Critical and Exegetical Commentary on the Book of Psalms,* vol. 1, 117-18; Weiser, *The Psalms,* 172-73). The practices to which v. 3 may allude, namely, the pouring out of libations for the dead and the naming of the dead, date back to the Late Bronze Age both at Ugarit and in Canaan proper (see Spronk, *Beatific Afterlife,* 334-38).

11. See Smith and Bloch-Smith, "Death and Afterlife," 283.

12. See Spronk, *Beatific Afterlife,* 40, 163, 252, 253, 255-56; Lewis, *Cults of the Dead,* 128-32. Neither work addresses vv. 20b-23. The following exegesis largely follows the lines drawn by J. G. Taylor, cited in G. C. Heider, *The Cult of Molek: A Reassessment,* JSOTSup 43 (Sheffield, England: JSOT, 1985), 329. For necromancy elsewhere condemned in Isaiah, see K. van der Toorn, "Echoes of Judaean Necromancy in Isaiah 28, 7-22," *ZAW* 100 (1988): 199-217.

unconnected to the preceding material.[13] The antecedents often proposed for these verbs are Jerusalem or the land.[14] Yet there is no comparable description of either Jerusalem or the land in biblical literature. The verbs perhaps characterize the dead, as found elsewhere. The interpretation of *ʿ*br* for the dead has been maintained for Ezekiel 39:11, 14.[15] This interpretation would clarify the images at the end of Isaiah 8:21b-22, that the dead will turn their faces upward to the earth and that they will be thrust into the darkness of the netherworld. The terms "king" and "god" are more difficult to understand, but elsewhere these terms both refer to the dead. Biblical and extrabiblical parallels to the use of "god" for the dead have been noted above. The term of king *(mlk)* may refer to the leader of the dead, like Ugaritic *mlk* in KTU 1.108.1 and perhaps surviving in a few biblical passages, such as Isaiah 57:9, a passage also dealing with necromancy (cf. Amos 5:26; Zeph. 1:5, 8; see below). In KTU 1.108.1, *rp'u* is called the "eternal king" *(mlk ʿlm)*, probably designating his leadership of the dead described in the following lines as "companions" or "divined ones" *(ḥbrm)*.[16] In Isaiah 8:21b the dead curse their leadership, their "king" and "god," and look upward to the land

13. Clements, *Isaiah 1–39,* 102.

14. See O. Kaiser, *Isaiah 1–12: A Commentary,* 2d ed., trans. J. Bowden, OTL (Philadelphia: Westminster, 1983), 200-202; Clements, *Isaiah 1–39,* 102. Kaiser argues for a Persian period date for these verses.

15. On *ʿ*br* for the dead, see J. Ratosh, "On *'ebr'* in Scripture or the Land of *hʿbrym,*" *Beth Mikra* 47 (1971): 549-68; B. Halevi, "Additional Notes on Ancestor Worship," *Beth Mikra* 64 (1975): 101-17; Pope, "Notes on the Rephaim Texts," 173; Spronk, *Beatific Afterlife,* 229-30.

16. For the suggestions that the *ḥbrm* in KTU 1.108.5 are the Rephaim and *rp'u* in 1.108.1 is their leader, see M. S. Smith, "The Magic of Kothar, the Ugaritic Craftsman God, in KTU 1.6 VI 49-50," *RB* 91 (1984): 377-80; idem, "Kothar wa-Hasis, the Ugaritic Craftsman God" (Ph.D. diss., Yale University, 1985), 444. On *mlk* and *rp'u* as terms for the dead in Ugaritic, see below in section 3. For a discussion of the identifications for *rp'u,* see Pope, "Notes on the Rephaim Texts," 170; idem, in Cooper, "Divine Names and Epithets," 446; Heider, *The Cult of Molek,* 90-91, 115-33; D. Pardee, "A New Datum for the Meaning of the Divine Name Milkashtart," in *Ascribe to the Lord: Biblical and Other Studies in Memory of Peter C. Craigie,* ed. L. Eslinger and G. Taylor, JSOTSup 67 (Sheffield: JSOT, 1988), 55-67. If *rp'u* is to be identified with any other deity, the available evidence would best support an identification with Ugaritic *mlk* who dwells in Ashtaroth *(ʿṯtrt),* although both *mlk* and *rp'u* could be epithets of one another or another deity. The title of ^{d}*NE.IRI*$_{11}$*.GAL be-el id-ri,* "Nergal, lord of Idri," attested at Emar (Emar 158:6) may be relevant. This epithet is found in a text describing a piece of land bound by a *ḫuḫinu* (a type of road or pathway) of "Nergal, lord of Idri." If Idri proves to be a toponym equated with Ugaritic *hdrʿy* and biblical Edrei, Cooper's identification of *rp'u* with Nergal/Resheph gains in force. I wish to thank Mr. Douglas Green for bringing this epithet to my attention. However, it is possible to read the more common Nergal name spelled syllabically *be-el ma-ḫī-ri,* "lord of the trade." My thanks go to Daniel Fleming for pointing out this possibility to me. See section 2 below for the Ugaritic evidence.

of the living for help. In any case, Isaiah 8:20b-22, although secondary in nature, may continue the criticism of Isaiah 8:16-20a against necromancy. Necromancy appears in prophetic condemnations dating to the seventh and sixth centuries (Jer. 27:9; Ezek. 13:17-23).

Legislation forbids the specific mourning customs of cutting hair or skin on account of the dead (Lev. 19:27-28; 21:5; Deut. 14:1). These texts appear to belong also to the second half of the monarchy, although the legal material of the Holiness Code is difficult to date.[17] These funerary customs passed uncriticized in the prophets of the eighth (Isa. 7:20; 15:3; 22:12; Hos. 7:14; Amos 8:10; Mic. 1:16; cf. Isa. 19:3) and sixth centuries (Jer. 7:29; 41:5). Only necromancy may have been viewed negatively prior to 750, if 1 Samuel 28:3 reflects historically reliable information. In 2 Kings 21:6 it is reported that Manasseh permitted necromancy, and 2 Kings 23:24 credits Josiah with eliminating *(bīʿēr)* necromancers and mediums. Down to this late point in the monarchy and perhaps beyond, necromancy flourished.

It would appear also that prior to the seventh century, feeding the dead and funerary practices of mourning and veneration for the dead flourished in various social strata and quarters of Israelite society. The ritual actions surrounding the dead perhaps formed a central feature of family life throughout Israel's history. A. Malamat has made the interesting suggestion that the feast mentioned in 1 Samuel 20:6 represented a family funerary celebration.[18] During the reigns of some monarchs, various funerary practices flourished under royal auspices. Royal tombs were presumably elaborate affairs (Isa. 22:15-17; Ezek. 32:11-32; cf. Isa. 28:16-20), although not different in type from the graves of nonroyalty (cf. Judith 16:23).[19] Israelite royalty participated in the common West Semitic custom of erecting funerary steles. According to 2 Samuel 18:18, Absalom erected a funerary stele in his own mem-

17. For various views as to the date of the Holiness Code, see G. von Rad, "Form-Criticism of the Holiness Code," in *Studies in Deuteronomy,* trans. D. Stalker, Studies in Biblical Theology 119 (Chicago: H. Regnery, 1953), 25-36; M. Haran, "Holiness Code," *EncJud* 8:820-25; I. Knohl, "The Priestly Torah Versus the Holiness School: Sabbath and the Festivals," *Hebrew Union College Annual* 58 (1987): 65-117; D. Patrick, *Old Testament Law* (Atlanta, GA: John Knox, 1985), 146-51. Cf. Hurvitz, *A Linguistic Study,* 102-7.

18. See A. Malamat, "King Lists of the Old Babylonian Period and Biblical Genealogies," *JAOS* 88 (1968): 173 n. 29.

19. See A. Mazar, "Iron Age Burial Caves North of Damascus Gate Jerusalem," *IEJ* 26 (1976): 1-8; G. Barkay and A. Kloner, "Jerusalem Tombs from the Days of the First Temple," *Biblical Archaeology Review* 12 (1986): 22-39; E. M. Bloch-Smith, "The Cult of the Dead in Judah: Interpreting the Material Remains," *JBL* 111 (1992): 213-24, esp. 217. For the meaning of "bed" in Isa. 28:16-20 as a reference to a cave bench tomb, see Halpern, "The Excremental Vision," 117.

ory, "for he thought, 'I have no son to invoke my name,'" *baʿăbûr hazkîr šĕmî* (cf. Isa. 56:5; 66:3).[20] A Persian-period inscription from Kition records a similar funerary inscription: *mṣbt lmbḥy . . . ʿl mškb nḥty lʿlm wlʾšty,* "a stele for among the living . . . on my eternal resting place and for my wife" (KAI 35:1-3). A Hellenistic-period Phoenician inscription from the environs of Athens (KAI 53) likewise attests to the practice of erecting a stele *(mṣbt)* as a "memorial," *skr,* a term apparently cognate with **zkr.* A third-century Phoenician inscription from Lapethos (KAI 43:6) records a commemoration for a father by a son (cf. KAI 34:1; CIS 44:1; 46:1-2; 57:1-2; 58:1; 59:1; 60:1; 61:1; RES 1208). This Phoenician funerary practice is also mentioned by Philo of Byblos (*PE* 1.10.10): "He says that when these men died, those who survived them dedicated staves to them. They worshipped the steles and conducted annual festivals for them."[21] The practice of erecting commemorative steles is also attested in the Ugaritic texts (KTU 1.17 I 28; 6.13; 6.14).[22]

Interacting with deceased ancestors was a practice that occurred among Aramaean and Israelite royalty. KAI 214:16, 21 records how the Aramaean king Panammu entreats his sons to invoke the name *(yzkr šm)* of the god Hadad and his own name after his death.[23] In 2 Chronicles 16:12 is recorded a tradition that Asa sought medical help from "doctors" *(rōpĕʾîm)* for his diseased feet. A contextual difficulty suggests that the correct reading may be not *rōpĕʾîm* but **rĕpāʾîm,* the dead ancestors. According to the verse Asa's feet contracted an unspecified disease. The verse continues: "yet even in his disease he [Asa] did not seek Yahweh, but sought help from physicians *(rōpĕʾîm).*" The contrast drawn between the help of Yahweh and the aid of physicians appears forced, as seeking help from doctors is not contrary to seeking help from Yahweh. However, if the reading of the word were not *rōpĕʾîm,* "physicians,"

20. Ringgren, *Israelite Religion,* 157.

21. For the text and translation of *PE* 1.10.10, see Attridge and Oden, *Philo of Byblos,* 42-43.

22. For the Akkadian evidence, see *šuma zakāru* (*CAD* E, 400a; Z, 18); Lewis, *Cults of the Dead,* 119. In CTA 17 (KTU 1.17 I 27f.), the son commemorates his deceased father. The stele that the son erects is apparently in honor of "his ancestral god," *ʾilʾibh.* Funerary steles are attested in KTU 6.13 and 6.14. Cf. Huehnergard, "The Vicinity of Emar," 13, 15 (text 1:8), 17, 19 (text 2:11-12), 27-28.

23. B. S. Childs, *Memory and Tradition in Israel,* Studies in Biblical Theology 37 (Naperville, IL: Allenson, 1962), 13; McBride, "The Deuteronomistic Name Theology," 101; J. C. Greenfield, "Un rite religieux araméen et ses parallèles," *RB* 80 (1973): 46-52. See also H. Tawil, "Some Literary Elements in the Opening Sections of the Hadad, Zakir, and the Nerab Inscriptions in Light of East and West Semitic Royal Inscriptions," *Orientalia* 43 (1974): 41 n. 3. See also KTU 1.161 (for studies of this text, see W. T. Pitard, "RS 34.126: Notes on the Text," *Maarav* 4/1 [1987]: 75-86; D. Pardee, "Epigraphic and Philological Notes," *UF* 19 [1987]: 211-16).

but *rĕpā'îm, "the dead," the objection would be clear.[24] Furthermore, the verb *drš, translated in this context as "seek help," is a regular term for divination. Seeking help from divinized dead ancestors runs counter to the prohibitions in Deuteronomy 18:10-11 and Isaiah 8:19-20 and the narrative of 1 Samuel 28:3. Though securing the favor of deceased ancestors was criticized in the eighth century and afterward in Israel, it was part of Israel's Canaanite heritage, paralleled in Ugaritic literature (KTU 1.161).

In 2 Kings 9:34-37 is apparently reflected the special concern for the proper burial of the royal dead. T. J. Lewis has proposed that the description of the disposal of Jezebel's corpse in this passage refers to traditional funerary custom. The command of Jehu to attend to Jezebel's corpse, *piqdû-nā'*, does not mean simply to "take care of" or "see to" in a general sense. Rather, this root has a cultic sense, tied to funerary ritual. It means to "act as a *pāqidu* on her behalf in fulfilling the customary funerary rites, including the essential services of the cult of the dead."[25] The command is motivated by Jezebel's royal lineage, "for she was a king's daughter" *(kî bat-melek hî')*. If this interpretation of this passage is correct, it would suggest that Jehu adhered to traditional funerary practices. With regard to practices involving the dead, royal and popular religion belonged to the same fabric.

Support for traditional practices pertaining to the dead extended beyond the lives of common people and royalty. At least some priests tolerated royal funerary traditions (Ezek. 43:7-9). The prophets in the early periods did not object to necromancy. Here comparing the criticisms against the marzeah feast conducted by the well-to-do in Amos 6:1-7 and Jeremiah 16:5-9 is illustrative.[26]

24. M. Jastrow, "*Rō'ēh* and Ḥôzeh in the Old Testament," *JBL* 28 (1909): 49-50 n. 23; Curtis and Madsen, *A Critical and Exegetical Commentary on the Books of Chronicles*, 391.

25. Lewis, *Cults of the Dead*, 120-22. See Finkelstein, "Genealogy of the Hammurapi Dynasty," 114-15.

26. On the marzeah in Northwest Semitic texts, including Amos 6 and Jeremiah 16, see M. H. Pope, "A Divine Banquet at Ugarit," in *The Use of the Old Testament in the New and Other Essays*, ed. J. M. Efird, W. F. Stinespring Festschrift (Durham, NC: Duke Univ. Press, 1972), 170-203; idem, "The Cult of the Dead at Ugarit," in *Ugarit in Retrospect: Fifty Years of Ugarit and Ugaritic*, ed. G. D. Young (Winona Lake, IN: Eisenbrauns, 1981), 176-79; N. Avigad and J. C. Greenfield, "A Bronze *phialē* with a Phoenician Dedicatory Inscription," *IEJ* 32 (1982): 118-28; B. Halpern, "A Landlord-Tenant Dispute at Ugarit?" *Maarav* 2/1 (1979-80): 121-40; R. E. Friedman, "The *MRZḤ* Tablet from Ugarit," *Maarav* 2/2 (1979-80): 187-206; Spronk, *Beatific Afterlife*, 169-70, 196-202, 232, 248; C. Maier and E. M. Dörrfuss, "'Um mit ihnen zu sitzen, zu essen und zu trinken' Am 6; 7; Jer 16,5 und die Bedeutung von *marzeaḥ*," *ZAW* 111 (1999): 45-57; J. L. McLaughlin, *The marzēaḥ in the Prophetic Literature: References and Allusions in the Light of the Extra-Biblical Evidence*, VTSup 86 (Leiden/Boston/Köln: Brill, 2001); and Zevit, *The Religions of Ancient Israel*, 547-49, 576-77.

The earlier prophet Amos deplores the marzeah not because of any funerary association, as the later Jeremiah does, but because of the exploitation of the poor symbolized in the lavish luxuries enjoyed in the feast. The story of Elisha's bones in 2 Kings 13:20-21 also shows that prophetic circles in the northern kingdom prior to its fall could treat the power of the dead in a positive manner (cf. Ben Sira 48:13).

Belief in the life of the dead continued for centuries. In the postexilic period, practices concerning the dead persisted. Isaiah 57:6-7 mocks the Israelite practice of feeding the dead: "with the dead of the wadi is your portion, they, they are your lot. Even to them have you poured out a drink offering, you have brought a cereal offering."[27] Verse 9 mocks necromancy: "You have journeyed to the king *(mlk)* with oil, and multiplied your perfumes; you sent your envoys far off and sent down even to Sheol." Isaiah 65:4 criticizes "those who sit among graves and lodge in vaults." Feeding the dead continued in the Hellenistic and Roman periods. While Ben Sira condones proper lamentation and burial for the dead (38:16-17), he takes a negative view of feeding the dead: "Good things poured out upon a mouth that is closed are like offerings of food placed upon a grave" (30:18).[28] Tobit 4:17 refers positively to either feeding the dead or the living mourners on the behalf of the dead: "Place your bread on the grave of the righteous, but give none to sinners."

Necromancy and prayer to the dead for help likewise continued for a long time in Jewish society. Necromancy is condemned in Isaiah 59:9. Communication with the dead is discussed also in a number of Talmudic passages and in intertestamental literature. According to Shabbat 152a-b, the dead hear what is said in their presence until decomposition begins; after that point the righteous dead cannot be reached through necromancy. According to *Berakot* 18b, a man visiting a cemetery received a message from a dead woman: "Tell my mother to send me my comb and my tube of eye-paint by so and so who is coming here tommorrow."[29] The same passage relates how a man heard two spirits in conversation. Praying to the dead is mentioned in 2 Baruch 85:12[30] and Pseudo-Philo 33:5.[31] According to *Sotah* 34b, Caleb

27. See W. H. Irwin, "'The Smooth Stones of the Wadi'? Isaiah 57,6," *CBQ* 29 (1967): 31-40; T. J. Lewis, "Death Cult Imagery in Isaiah 57," *Hebrew Annual Review* 11 (1987): 267-84.

28. Skehan and Di Lella, *The Wisdom of Ben Sira,* 379.

29. S. Lieberman, "Afterlife in Early Rabbinic Literature," in *Seper Ha-Yovel li-Kbod Tsevi Volfson* (Harry A. Wolfson Jubilee Volume), vol. 2 (New York: American Academy for Jewish Research, 1965), 511; E. Feldman, *Biblical and Post-Biblical Defilement and Mourning: Law as Theology* (New York: Yeshiva University/KTAV, 1977), 19.

30. *OTPs* 1:651.

31. *OTPs* 2:348.

went to Hebron to the grave of the patriarchs and prayed: "My fathers, ask mercy for me."

Later Jewish literature points to communication with the dead and belief in their powers. At the beginning of the tenth century A.D., the Karaite scholar Sahl ben Mazli'ah complained:[32]

> How can I remain silent when some Jews are behaving like idolators? They sit at the graves, sometimes sleeping there at night, and appeal to the dead: "Oh, Rabbi Yose ha-Gelih! Heal me! Grant me children!" They kindle lights there and offer incense. . . .

Concern for the dead and belief in the dead's powers derived from Israel's earliest Canaanite heritage, as reflected in the Ugaritic texts.[33]

3. The *mlk* Sacrifice

The divine recipients of the *mlk* sacrifice vary within the same cultures. In Israel *mlk* in Jeremiah 19:5 and 32:35 (cf. 2 Kings 17:16-17) is a term for a human sacrifice intended allegedly for Baal.[34] Psalm 106:34-38 attributes child sacrifice to Baal Peor. According to 2 Kings 17:31 the Sepharvites devoted child sacrifice to two gods, Adrammelek and Anammelek.[35] Jeremiah 7:31; 19:5, and 32:35 deny that *mlk* sacrifice was offered in Yahweh's name; these denials may suggest that offering this sacrifice in Yahweh's name occurred (cf. Lev. 18:21; 20:3; Genesis 22). Ezekiel 20:25-26 provides a theological rationale for Yahweh causing child sacrifice:

32. R. Posner, "Holy Places," *EncJud* 8:922.

33. On early twentieth-century Palestinian Christian and Islamic beliefs on feeding the dead, see Canaan, *Mohammedan Saints*, 188-93. Healing also occurs at tombs (Canaan, *Mohammedan Saints*, 114-15).

34. See P. G. Mosca, "Child Sacrifice in Canaanite and Israelite Religion: A Study in *Mulk* and מלך" (Ph.D. diss., Harvard University, 1975). The recent work of G. Heider, *The Cult of Molek*, presents a substantial collection of the pertinent material; cf. D. Edelman, "Biblical Molek Reassessed," *JAOS* 107 (1987): 730; J. D. Levenson, *The Death and Resurrection of the Beloved Son: The Transformation of Child Sacrifice in Judaism and Christianity* (New Haven/London: Yale Univ. Press, 1993), 3-52; K. Koch, "Molek astral," in *Mythos im Alten Testament und seiner Umwelt: Festschrift für Hans-Peter Müller zum 65. Geburstag*, ed. A. Lange, H. Lichtenberger, and D. Römheld, BZAW 278 (Berlin/New York: de Gruyter, 1999), 29-50; Zevit, *The Religions of Ancient Israel*, 469, 473, 476, 520-21, 530, 643, 653.

35. Olyan, *Asherah and the Cult of Yahweh*, 68.

> Moreover I gave them statutes that were not good and ordinances by which they could not have life; and I defiled them through their very gifts in making them offer by fire all their first-born, that I might horrify them; I did it that they might know that I am the Lord.

These passages indicate that in the seventh century child sacrifice was a Judean practice performed in the name of Yahweh.[36] Isaiah 30:27-33 appears as the best evidence for the early practice of child sacrifice in Israel. According to P. Mosca, the image of child sacrifice in this eighth- or seventh-century passage serves as a way to describe Yahweh's coming destruction of Israel.[37] In this text there is no offense taken at the tophet, the precinct of child sacrifice. It would appear that Jerusalemite cult included child sacrifice under Yahwistic patronage; it is this that Leviticus 20:2-5 deplores. Ezekiel 16:20, 21, 36 and 23:39 assume that child sacrifice was intended for a multiplicity of deities. The legal proscriptions against child sacrifice in the Holiness Code (Lev. 18:21; 20:2-5) and in Deuteronomy 12:31 and 18:10 are unclear regarding the divine recipients. Leviticus 20:2-5 suggests that this sacrifice is not to take place in Yahweh's temple, perhaps to avoid performance of it in his name.

Phoenician and Punic texts designate more than one recipient of the *mlk* sacrifice. A *mlk* offering is perhaps attested once for Eshmun in the only *mlk* text from the Phoenician mainland.[38] Evidence for a *mlk*-child sacrifice has also been reported for an unpublished Phoenician basalt stele discovered in 1993 in the southeastern Turkish village of Injirli.[39] Dated to the late eighth century, the inscription recounts two battles. Zuckerman and Kaufman comment: "Of particular importance . . . is the detailed discussion of the use of *mulk*-sacrifices of sheep, horses, and — if we read correctly — first-born humans in the process of war, and the gods' reactions to those sacrifices."

36. Greenberg, *Ezekiel 1–20,* 281, 369; Mosca, "Child Sacrifice," 216-20, 238-40; Heider, *The Cult of Molek,* 223-408; idem, "A Further Turn on Ezekiel's Baroque Twist in Ezek 20:25-26," *JBL* 107 (1988): 721-24.

37. Mosca, "Child Sacrifice," 195-223; Heider, *The Cult of Molek,* 319-26. Clements (*Isaiah 1–39,* 252) follows H. Barth in assigning this passage to a seventh-century Josianic redaction of Isaiah's oracles.

38. See B. Delavault and A. Lemaire, "Une stele 'molk' de Palestine dediée à Eshmoun? RES 367 reconsidéré," *RB* 83 (1976): 569-83; idem, "Les inscriptions phéniciennes de Palestine," *RSF* 7 (1979): 24-26; A. Gianto, "Some Notes on the Mulk Inscription from Nebi Yunis (RES 367)," *Biblica* 68 (1987): 397-400.

39. For now, see the report of E. Carter, "The Injirli Stela: A Preliminary Report on the Injirli Stela," at http://www.humnet.ucla.edu/humnet/nelc/stelasite/stelainfo.html; and "Recording the Stela: First Step on the Road to Decipherment," by B. Zuckerman and S. Kaufman, at http://www.humnet.ucla.edu/humnet/nelc/stelasite/stelainfo.html.

Zuckerman and Kaufman relate this discovery to the *mlk*-sacrifice known from around the Mediterranean. The *mlk* sacrifice in the western Mediterranean was offered to *bʿl ḥmn* and *tnt*.[40] According to Diodorus Siculus' *Library of History* XX, 14:4-7, Kronos was the recipient of child sacrifices at Carthage.[41] A tradition of some version of infant sacrifice introduced by the Phoenicians to Crete in the early Iron Age may lie behind a number of reports in classical sources.[42] The Cretans sent their firstborn to Delphi to be sacrificed (Plutarch, *Theseus* 16, citing Aristotle, *Constitution of Bottiaeans*).[43] According to *PE* 4.16.7 (citing Porphyrius), the Cretans used to sacrifice their children to Kronos. Clement of Alexandria (*Protreptikos pros Hellenas* III 42.5) cites Antikleides on the Lyktians in Crete who sacrifice men to Zeus.[44] The story of the Minotaur may partake of the same tradition. A semigod with the head of a bull, in Near Eastern fashion, the Minotaur demands that the Athenians send him seven youths and maidens every year, before Theseus slays him and ends the tribute.[45]

Punic sources provide some data regarding the site and mode of presentation for child sacrifice. Sacred precincts for child sacrifice are known from North Africa, Sicily, Sardinia, Spain, and possibly at Tyre.[46] The precinct at

40. For example, a *mlk* sacrifice is dedicated to *bʿl ḥmn* and *tnt* in Sousse (Hadrametum) in KAI 98:1-2 (cf. 99:1-2); to *bʿl ḥmn* in Constantine in 103:1-2; 107:1-4; 109:1-2; 110:1; to *bʿlmn* in Guelma (Algeria) in 167:1-2; and to *bʿl ḥmn* in Malta in 61A:3-4. For a full survey of evidence from the Western Mediterranean, see S. Brown, *Late Carthaginian Child Sacrifice and Sacrificial Monuments in Their Mediterraneann Context,* JSOT/ASOR Monograph Series 3 (Sheffield: Sheffield Academic Press, 1991). See also E. Lipiński, *Dieux et déesses de l'univers phénicien et punique,* Orientalia Lovaniensia Analecta 64, Studia Phoenicia XIV (Leuven: Uitgeverij Peeters & Departement Oosterse Studies, 1995), 481-83.

41. R. M. Geer, *Diodorus of Sicily,* vol. 10, *Books 14.66-100 and 20,* Loeb Classical Library (Cambridge, MA: Harvard Univ. Press; London: William Heinemann, 1957), 178-79. See Mosca, "Child Sacrifice," 4, 214; L. E. Stager, "Carthage: A View from the Tophet," in *Phönizier im Westen,* ed. H. G. Niemeyer, *Madrider Beiträge* 8 (1982), 158.

42. Sarah Morris, private communication. I wish to thank Professor Morris for providing me with the following classical references.

43. *Plutarch's Lives,* vol. 1, trans. B. Perrin, Loeb Classical Library 46 (Cambridge, MA: Harvard Univ. Press; London: William Heinemann, 1967), 30-31.

44. C. Alessandrino, *Protreptikos ai Greci,* Corona Patrum Salesiana, Series Graeca 3 (Turin: Societa Editrici Internazionale, 1940), 86-87.

45. On Theseus and the Minotaur, see Apollodorus, *The Epitome of the Library of Apollodorus* 1:7-9 (J. G. Frazer, *Apollodorus: The Library,* vol. 2, Loeb Classical Library [London: William Heinemann; New York: G. P. Putnam's Sons, 1921], 134-37). For further literary sources, see Lipiński, *Dieux et déesses,* 480-83.

46. Harden, *The Phoenicians,* 86-91; S. Moscati, "New Light on Punic Art," in *The Role of the Phoenicians in the Interaction of Mediterranean Civilizations: Papers Presented to the Archaeological Symposium at the American University of Beirut, March 1967,* ed. W. W. Ward (Beirut:

Carthage was an open-air enclosure surrounded by a wall.[47] The size of the precinct was, according to the excavator, L. E. Stager, at least 5,000-6,000 square meters during the fourth and third centuries. The number of urns estimated for the fourth and third centuries was placed at about 20,000. Both the size of the precinct and the number of urns indicate that the use of the precinct was not sporadic. Stager demonstrates on the basis of the excavated urns that the percentage of infant burials did not decrease over time; rather, they increased. In the seventh- and sixth-century sample of eighty urns, human-only burials constituted 62.5 percent of all burials (fifty), human plus animal 7.5 percent (six), and animal-only 30 percent (twenty-four). In the fourth-century sample of fifty urns, human-only burials increased to 88 percent (forty-four), animal decreased to 10 percent (five), and human plus animal decreased to 2 percent (one). Other scholars, such as M. Fantar and G. Picard, have argued against Stager's interpretation of the data.[48] H. Benichou-Safar further suggested that ancient witnesses to Carthaginian child-sacrifice represent anti-Carthaginian propaganda. She also noted irregularities in the rate of children's burials at Carthage and proposed that in fact, child sacrifice was rare, a point that would be in keeping with the literary evidence cited below, in particular Philo of Byblos (*PE* 1.10.44 = 4.6.11). Despite several issues raised and scholarly demurrals,[49] some level of child sacrifice evidently took place at Carthage. This is not to preclude the development of additional cultural understandings, such as "sacrifice" of children as a religious ritual to address infant and child mortality.

Possible information about the mode of presentation of child sacrifice comes from a tower discovered beneath a mid-fifth- to early-fourth-century Punic necropolis at Pozo Moro, a site near the Mediterranean coast approximately 125 kilometers southwest of Valencia.[50] Parts of a few panels to the

---

American Univ. of Beirut, 1968), 68-71; idem, "Découvertes phéniciennes à Tharros," *CRAIBL* 1987, 483-503; Lipiński, *Dieux et déesses,* 476-83. For a possible tophet in Tyre, see the discussion in Lipiński, *Dieux et déesses,* 439-40, with pertinent bibliography on p. 440 n. 127.

47. Stager, "Carthage: A View from the Tophet," 155-66; Stager and Wolff, "Child Sacrifice at Carthage — Religious Rite or Population Control?" *Biblical Archaeology Review* 10/1 (1984): 30-51, esp. 36-38; H. Benichou-Safar, "Sur l'incineration des enfants aux tophets de Carthage et de Sousse," *Revue de l'Histoire des Religions* 205 (1988): 57-67. For a history of discoveries at Carthage, see Brown, *Late Carthaginian Child Sacrifice,* 37-57.

48. This discussion is drawn from Brown, *Late Carthaginian Child Sacrifice,* 49-56, esp. 54-55.

49. See Lipiński, *Dieux et déesses,* 483.

50. See M. Almagro-Gorbea, "Los relieves mitológicos orientalizantes de Pozo Moro," *Trabajos de Prehistoria* 35 (1978): 251-78, 8 pls.; idem, "Les reliefs orientalisants de Pozo Moro (Albacete, Espagne)," in *Mythes et Personnification: Travaux et Memoires, Actes du Colloque du*

tower survive. One depicts the presentation of a small person or child in a bowl to a double-headed deity or monster seated on a throne. With the left hand, the monster holds the bowl bearing the child, whose head and feet are visible. With the right hand, the deity or monster holds the left hind leg of a pig, lying on its back on a table in front of the monster's throne. Behind the table stands a human figure wearing a long fringed tunic or robe. He raises a small bowl in a gesture of offering. Another figure across from the deity or monster appears to be standing, with right hand upraised holding a sword with a curved blade and with a head shaped like an animal, perhaps a horse or a bull. The human figure in the tunic or robe might be a priest, reminiscent of a priest carrying a child for sacrifice depicted on a stele excavated from the precinct for child sacrifice at Carthage.[51] The second human figure perhaps effects the cutting of the child. The animal shape of the head may represent a ritual mask, an item known from Carthage, other Punic sites, and on the Phoenician mainland.[52]

The function of some masks apparently was cultic. Cultic masks have been discovered in Late Bronze Age levels at ancient Emar and Hadidi in Syria and at Dan, Hazor, and Gezer in Israel.[53] The mask at Dan appears on the face of a cult musician, illustrating another cultic use of masks at this time. In the Iron Age Levant, masks are more common. Masks have been found at Tel Qasile (twelfth to tenth century), Tel Shera (tenth century), and

Grand Palais (Paris) 7-8 Mai 1977 (Paris: Société d'Édition "Les Belles Lettres," 1980), 123-36, 7 pls.; idem, "Pozo Moro y el influjo fenicio en el periodo orientalizante de la península Ibérica," *RSF* 10/2 (1982): 231-72. My thanks to Professor C. Kennedy for these references. For further discussion, see Brown, *Late Carthaginian Child Sacrifice,* 70-72, with a drawing of the relief on p. 288, figure 46a.

51. See *Viva Archaeologia* 1/2 (1968-69): 114 and 123, fig. 119.

52. C. G. Picard, "Sacra Punica, Étude sur les masques et rasoires de Carthage," *Karthago* 13 (1967): 49-115; Moscati, "New Light on Punic Art," 72; idem, *The World of the Phoenicians,* trans. A. Hamilton (London: Praeger, 1968), 163-65; E. Stern, "Phoenician Masks and Pendants," *PEQ* 108 (1976): 109-18; W. Cullican, "Some Phoenician Masks and Their Terracottas," *Berytus* 24 (1975-76): 47-87; R. Hestrin and M. Dayyagi-Mendels, "Two Phoenician Pottery Masks," *Israel Museum News* 16 (1980): 83-88; Carter, "The Masks of Ortheia," 355-74; A. Biran, "Tel Dan, 1981," *IEJ* 32 (1982): 138, pl. 16:B.

53. Y. Yadin et al., *Hazor II* (Jerusalem: Magnes, 1960), pls. 182-183; idem, "Symbols of Deities," 223; A. Ciasca, "Masks and Protomes," in *The Phoenicians,* ed. S. Moscati (Milan: Bompiani, 1988), 354-69. For the mask depicted on a dancer with a musical instrument on a Late Bronze Age clay plaque from Tel Dan, see A. Biran, "The Dancer from Dan, the Empty Tomb and the Altar Room," *IEJ* 36 (1986): 168-73. On masks in Israelite religion, see the speculations of Fohrer, *History of Israelite Religion,* 114. Note also the mask before the enthroned god, possibly Yahweh, depicted on a Persian period coin from Yehud (see chapter 1, section 1).

Hazor (eighth century). From the ninth century onward, masks along the Phoenician litoral are attested.[54] In view of these discoveries, L. E. Stager[55] has suggested following H. Gressman that BH *masweh* in Exodus 34:33-35, customarily regarded as a "veil," is a cultic mask; his suggestion deserves consideration. In the present form of the text, the *masweh* does not funtion as a cultic mask, since Moses removes the *masweh* when he communes with Yahweh. Indeed, the force of the text is to show Moses' experience of Yahweh's presence, since the *masweh* "horned" *(qāran)*, a theophanic expression like "horns," *qarnayim*, in Habakkuk 3:4.[56] Yet, the passage exhibits some internal tensions,[57] which might point to an earlier stage of the tradition representing a different view of the *masweh* compared to the present form of the text. Two possibilities may be suggested. Either the verb *qāran* referred originally to the horns of an animal mask, although they were understood in later tradition as theophanic language; or the description of the *masweh* drew on the imagery of the cult mask to form its theophanous description of the divine presence's impact on Moses.

Philo of Byblos (*PE* 1.10.44 = 4.6.11) describes the royal setting of child sacrifice: "Among ancient peoples in critically dangerous situations it was customary for the rulers of a city or nation, rather than lose everyone, to provide the dearest of children as a propitiatory sacrifice to the avenging deities. The children thus given up were slaughtered according to a secret ritual." This description is followed by Kronos' act of child sacrifice.[58] Before sacrificing his "only son," Kronos prepares him "in royal attire" *(tēn chōran basilikō)*, perhaps an echo of the sacrificial term *mlk*.[59] The motif of the "only son" to be sacrificed appears also in Genesis 22:2, and perhaps *yāḥîd*, "only one," in Zechariah 12:10b should be understood against this background. The expression of "only son" is not a literal one, but conveys the high value set on the child. Stager has suggested on the basis of double interment in urns of baby

54. See Childs, *The Book of Exodus*, 609-10; M. Haran, "The Shining of Moses' Face: A Case Study in Biblical and Ancient Near Eastern Iconography," in *The Shelter of Elyon: Essays in Honor of G. W. Ahlström*, ed. W. B. Barrick and J. R. Spenser, JSOTSup 31 (Sheffield: JSOT, 1984), 159-73; W. L. Propp, "The Skin of Moses' Face — Transfigured or Disfigured?" *CBQ* 49 (1987): 375-86.

55. L. E. Stager, private communication.

56. Childs, *The Book of Exodus*, 618-19.

57. Childs, *The Book of Exodus*, 604; cf. Rashi on Exod. 34:29 in *Pentateuch with Targum Onkelos, Haphtaroth, and Rashi's Commentary: Exodus*, trans. M. Rosenbaum and A. M. Silbermann (Jerusalem: The Silbermann Family, 1930), 196.

58. For text and translation, see Attridge and Oden, *Philo of Byblos*, 60-63. On the identification between Kronos and El in Philo of Byblos' *Phoenician History*, see chapter 4 n. 41.

59. M. H. Pope, "Moloch," in Pope and Röllig, *Syrien*, 300.

bones at Carthage that an "only child" was not literally involved.[60] *PE* 1.10.33 also relates: "At the occurrence of a fatal plague, Kronos immolated his only son to his father Ouranos."[61] Kronos had many other sons according to Philo of Byblos (*PE* 1.10.21, 24, 26).

A number of war reliefs dating to New Kingdom Egypt confirm the circumstances of child sacrifice in the Levant.[62] Scenes depicting the Egyptian siege of Canaanite cities include the sacrifice of children with various cultic personnel in attendance. The depiction of Ashkelon under siege by Merneptah's army is perhaps the most dramatic. Four men extend their hands to the sky, while three women kneel below them. The chief stands before them with a burning brazier in hand, and before him is a man with a young child. The child's arms and legs are limp, indicating that the child is dead. The same offering appears on the left hand side of the scene.

A battle relief of Ramses II at Medinet Habu likewise depicts the lowering of the limp bodies of two children over the wall. Here two braziers are alight as individuals raise their hands. Ramses II's battle against the Asiatic enemies at the city of Dapur, depicted at Abu Simbel, includes a child depicted on the citadel, next to a woman. To their right, the chief stands holding a brazier, this time flameless. The child is not dead, perhaps preserving an earlier part of the ritual prior to the child's demise.

The temple of Beit el-Wali in Nubia contains another depiction of child sacrifice in the midst of a battle conducted by Ramses II. It again shows a chief with brazier raised. This time, however, a woman lowers a child whose limbs are not flexed as in the scene from Medinet Habu, perhaps indicating that the child is not dead. This scene includes an inscription extolling Baal, probably as the recipient of the sacrifice. These scenes illustrate the indigenous Canaanite character of the rite and its specific context in battle.

Late Bronze Age remains from Amman included burned bones of infants, evidence of the cult of child sacrifice in Transjordan.[63] It is indicated in 2 Kings 3:27, 16:3 (//2 Chron. 28:3), 21:6 (//2 Chron. 33:6) and *PE* 1.10.44 (= 4.6.11) that in Moab, Judah, and Phoenicia, child sacrifice was a form of

60. Stager, "Carthage," 160-62. T. Canaan records that parents when praying to saints for help for their sick child call the child *wāḥîd*, "only one" (*Mohammedan Saints,* 106 n. 2).

61. Attridge and Oden, *Philo of Byblos,* 56-57.

62. A. Spalinger, "A Caananite Ritual Found in Egyptian Reliefs," *Journal of the Society for the Study of Egyptian Antiquities* 8 (1978): 47-60.

63. J. B. Hennessey, "Thirteenth Century B.C. Temple of Human Sacrifice," in *Phoenicia and Its Neighbors: Proceedings of the Colloquium Held 9-10 December 1983 at the Vrije Universiteit Brussels, in cooperation with the Centrum voor Myceense en archaische-Grieke Cultuur,* Studia Phoenicia 3 (Leuven: Uitgeverij Peeters, 1985), 85-104.

mlk sacrifice, performed primarily in times of national crisis.[64] The *mlk* sacrifices were not confined to royalty in Carthage, although it might be argued that *mlk bʿl* may preserve this distinctive royal background. According to P. Mosca, *mlk bʿl* (e.g., KAI 61A:1-2) represents the *mlk* sacrifice by nobles or families owning land, as opposed to *mlk ʾdm* (e.g., KAI 61B:1-2; 106:1-2; 109:1-2; 110:1), the *mlk* sacrifice of a commoner.[65] If one were to follow the etymology of *mlk,* it might be supposed that the *mlk* perhaps originated either as a Canaanite royal child sacrifice devoted to the main god of the locality or a sacrifice devoted to the deity considered in the locality as the king of the pantheon.[66] The *mlk ʾdm* might indicate that any hypothetical royal background had been lost by the time the Carthaginians practiced child sacrifice.

As support for connecting child sacrifice to a god *mlk,* M. H. Pope and G. C. Heider invoke Ugaritic attestations to *mlk* dwelling in Ashtaroth (*ʿṯtrt*).[67] As Pope, Heider, and Pardee have argued, Ugaritic *mlk* was the name of a god or an epithet of a god, perhaps to be identified with *rpʾu mlk ʿlm* in KTU 1.108.1 (Cf. *ᵈmilku* in Emar 472:62′; 473:15′).[68] Both *mlk* and *rpʾu* dwell in Ashtaroth, assuming that *ʿṯtrt* and *hdrʿy* in the following lines are place-names and not epithets.[69] The word *mlk* in these passages refers to a god or at

64. Ahlström, *Royal Administration,* 76 n. 2.

65. Mosca, "Child Sacrifice," 100. Cf. *mlk* and *ʾdm* in KAI 26 A III 12-13. For a different view, see Lipiński, *Dieux et déesses,* 428-29. For further discussion, see Brown, *Late Carthaginian Child Sacrifice,* 29-35.

66. Cf. the Ugaritic *dbḥ mlk,* "royal sacrifice," as in KTU 1.91.2. On this text, see Xella, "KTU 1.91," 833-38.

67. KTU 1.100.41; 1.107.17; and RS 1986/2235.17 (Bordreuil, "Découvertes épigraphiques," 298). See further H. Niehr, "Herkunft, Geschichte und Wirkungsgeschichte eines Unterweltgottes in Ugarit, Phönizien und Israel," *UF* 30 (1998): 569-85, esp. 570-74.

68. See n. 16.

69. Interpreters who view these two words as divine names include Virolleaud, *Ug V,* 553; Attridge and Oden, *Philo of Byblos,* 91 n. 127; Caquot, "La tablette RS 24.252 et la question des Rephaim ougaritiques," *Syria* 53 (1976): 299; Cross, *Canaanite Myth and Hebrew Epic,* 31; A. J. Ferrera and S. B. Parker, "Seating Arrangements at Divine Banquets," *UF* 4 (1972): 38; M. Görg, "Noch einmal: Edrei in Ugarit?" *UF* 6 (1974): 474-75; J. Gray, in *Ugaritica VII,* Mission de Ras Shamra 17 (Paris: Paul Geuthner; Leiden: Brill, 1978), 86; W. J. Horwitz, "The Significance of the Rephaim *rm. aby. btk rpʾim,*" *Journal of Northwest Semitic Languages* 7 (1979): 40 n. 12; C. E. L'Heureux, *Rank Among the Canaanite Gods: El, Baʿal, and the Rephaʾim,* HSM 21 (Missoula, MT: Scholars, 1979), 172; J. C. de Moor, "Studies in the New Alphabetic Texts from Ras Shamra," *UF* 1 (1969): 175; S. B. Parker, "The Feast of Rapiʾ*u,*" *UF* 2 (1970): 243. Increasingly, scholars favor interpreting *ʿṯtrt* and *hdrʿy* as place-names, originally suggested by B. Margalit ("A Ugaritic Psalm [RS 24.252]," *JBL* 89 [1970]: 292-304). See M. Dietrich and O. Loretz, "Baal *rpu* in KTU 1.108; 1.113 und nach 1.17 VI 25-33," *UF* 12 (1980): 174, 176 (reversing their earlier view of the two words as divine names in their article, "Der 'Neujahrspsalm' RS 24.252 Ug. 5,

least a divine epithet. Even so, this deity may not pertain to the cult of the dead at Ugarit. Indeed, Ugaritic *mlk* appears to be unrelated to either child sacrifice or the Phoenician sacrificial term *mlk*.[70] Although Phoenician *mlkʿštrt* may be related to the Ugaritic divine name or epithet, *mlk*, plus place-name Ashtaroth (*ʿṯtrt*),[71] neither Phoenician *mlkʿštrt* nor Ugaritic *mlk* occurs in the context of the *mlk* sacrifice or a child sacrifice described in any other way. Furthermore, Ugaritic does not attest to either child sacrifice or the sacrificial term, *mlk*. For these reasons, Heider's connection of Ugaritic *mlk*, the divine name or epithet, with Phoenician *mlk*, the sacrificial term, is conjectural.

Nonetheless, the Ugaritic references to *mlk* bear on the biblical evidence regarding *mlk* as a title for the leader of the dead. This name or epithet evi-

---

S. 551-557 Nr. 2," *UF* 7 [1975]: 115, 117); Heider, *Cult of Molek*, 118-23; Pardee, "The Preposition in Ugaritic," *UF* 7 (1975): 352 and *UF* 8 (1976): 245; Pope, "Notes on the Rephaim Texts," 170; M. H. Pope and J. Tigay, "A Description of Baal," *UF* 3 (1971): 120; Smith, "Kothar wa-Hasis," 385-88, 429-34; Spronk, *Beatific Afterlife*, 178; Olyan, *Asherah and the Cult of Yahweh*, 49; D. Pardee, *Les textes para-mythologiques de la 24ᵉ campagne (1961)*, Ras Shamra-Ougarit IX (Paris: Editions Recherche sur les Civilisations, 1988), 94-96; Niehr, "Herkunft, Geschichte und Wirkungsgeschichte," 570-74. Discussion of the subterranean complex discovered at Edrei (Deraa) appears in both Pardee's and Niehr's treatments. Interpreting *ʿṯtrt* and *hdrʿy* in KTU 1.108 as place-names is preferable to viewing them as divine titles on the following grammatical grounds: first, Ugaritic *yṯb b-* means to "sit, dwell in" a particular place and not "sit with" someone (D. Pardee, "The Preposition in Ugaritic," *UF* 8 [1976]: 245; idem, "More on the Preposition in Ugaritic," *UF* 11 [1979]: 686); second, Ugaritic *hd* occurs rarely, if ever, as an A-word; third, *ʾil* in KTU 1.108.1 need not refer to El, but it may mean "the god," referring to a separate figure, *rpʾu*, named in the following line. Furthermore, the biblical place-names Ashtaroth and Edrei are known in Josh. 12:4; 13:12, 31 (cf. Num. 21:33; Deut. 1:4; 3:1) as the home of the last of the Rephaim, just as *ʿṯtrt* and *hdrʿy* are the home of *rpʾu*, first noted by B. Margalit ("A Ugaritic Psalm [RS 24.252]," 193). It may be noted further that the place-name Edrei belongs to a pre-Israelite stratum of Hebrew, as **ḏ* underlying *d* in this place-name generally became /z/ in Hebrew, but *d* in Ugaritic and Aramaic (see Rainey, "The Toponyms," 4).

70. See Lipiński, *Dieux et déesses*, 477.

71. S. Ribichini and P. Xella, "Milkʿaštart, *mlk(m)* e la tradizione siropalestinese sui Refaim," *RSF* 7 (1979): 145-58. See also S. Ribichini, "In'ipotesi per Milk'aštart," *Rivista di Studi Orientalisti* 50 (1976): 43-55; A. Caquot, "Le dieu Milkʿashtart et les inscriptions de Umm el 'Amed," *Semitica* 15 (1965): 29-33. Gibson (*Textbook of Syrian Semitic Inscriptions*, vol. 3, 39) views *mlkʿštrt* as a combination of the names El and Astarte. Gibson's interpretation is based on the argument that *mlkʿštrt* is given the title *bʿl ḥmn* in an inscription from Umm el-ʿAmed (no. 13:1; see Cross, *Canaanite Myth and Hebrew Epic*, 24 n. 60; Gibson, *Textbook of Syrian Semitic Inscriptions*, vol. 3, 121), but Gibson interprets *bʿl ḥmn* in other inscriptions as a title of El (so also B. Landsberger, *Sam'al* [Ankara: Druckerei der Türkischen historischen Gesellschaft, 1948], 47 n. 117; Cross, *Canaanite Myth and Hebrew Epic*, 24-28; Olyan, *Asherah and the Cult of Yahweh*, 52-54).

dently survives in a handful of biblical passages. D. Edelman[72] cites Isaiah 8:21; 57:9; Zephaniah 1:5, 8; Amos 5:26 as possible examples. Pope notes the attestations in Acts 7:43 (citing Amos 5:26 after LXX) and Qur'an 43:77.[73] Like Acts 7:43, Testament of Solomon 26:6 (in manuscript P) refers to Moloch in connection with Rapha, probably to be traced to Ugaritic *rp'u* (KTU 1.108.1).[74] The connection between Ugaritic *mlk* and BH *mlk* as epithet is possible, but neither appears related to child sacrifice, to judge from the extant evidence. Indeed, the scholarly confusion between a god "Moloch" and the name of the sacrifice seems to have biblical roots. In 1 Kings 11:7 the god of the Ammonites is called "Moloch" instead of Milkom.[75]

BH *mlk,* whatever its precise background, seems to have been an acceptable practice, at least during the second half of the monarchy. Like the high places, child sacrifice was known in both Israel and Moab, and if Jeremiah 7:30-32 and 32:35 are any indication, child sacrifice was practiced at high places. Child sacrifice and veneration for the dead appear together in two polemics, Psalm 106:34-38 and Isaiah 57:3-13,[76] prompting the question of a possible historical relationship between the two practices.[77] Was child sacrifice or veneration for the dead conducted on a regular basis at high places during the period of the monarchy? In support of such a historical connection, Albright understood high places etymologically as "pagan graves" or funerary cairns.[78] While the philological part of this interpretation has not met with acceptance,[79] Albright drew attention to the relationship between high places and veneration for the dead, based on Ezekiel 43:7 and Job 27:15 (cf. 2 Sam. 18:17-18; Isa. 15:2).

Child sacrifice appears also in condemnations against high places. Was child sacrifice an element in the religion of the high places? The high places appear throughout the period of the Judges and monarchy as cultic sites, servicing not only the family and clan, but also the monarchy. The royal cult, at least in Jerusalem, as at Ugarit and probably Phoenicia, maintained some cult

72. Edelman, "Biblical Molek Reassessed," 730.

73. Pope, "Notes on the Rephaim Texts," 170, 172.

74. *OTPs* 1:987.

75. *BDB,* 574; Mosca, "Child Sacrifice," 121-22; E. Puech, "Milkom, le dieu ammonite, en Amos I 15," *VT* 27 (1977): 117-25; Heider, *Cult of Molek,* 302-4.

76. On Isa. 57:3-13, see Irwin, "The Smooth Stones," 31-40. Regarding Ps. 106:34-38, see Hackett, "Religious Traditions," 133. On both passages, see Spronk, *Beatific Afterlife,* 231-33.

77. Spronk, *Beatific Afterlife,* 231-33.

78. Albright, "The High Place in Ancient Palestine," in *Volume de Congrès, Strasbourg 1956,* VTSup 4 (Leiden: Brill, 1957), 242-58; Barrick, "The Funerary Character," 565-95. See also Ringgren, *Israelite Religion,* 157; Fohrer, *History of Israelite Religion,* 198.

79. Spronk, *Beatific Afterlife,* 44-48.

of veneration for the dead, and the bulk of the record assigns child sacrifice to royal practitioners. The religion of the clan likewise included veneration for the dead, and at least some of the religious practices involving the dead were celebrated at the local high places. Child sacrifice likewise belonged to the traditional religion of high places, assuming the historical veracity of biblical polemics. There is, however, no historical evidence outside biblical polemic for child sacrifice at the high places. Indeed, descriptions of child sacrifice in Canaan and Israel specify their largely royal character, as undertaken in moments of crisis. A city under siege seems to be the most characteristic setting; child sacrifice was designed to enlist the aid of a god to ward off a threatening army. If this does represent the customary setting for child sacrifice, then it belonged to urban, royal religion; it was reserved for special occasions and not part of regular cultic offerings. Given the available sources, the connection between child sacrifice and high places would not appear to be a general feature of Israelite religion.

To conclude this chapter's very brief consideration of Yahwistic cult practices, child sacrifice may not have been a common religious practice; the biblical and inscriptional records do not indicate how widespread the practice was. The religion of high places was generally Yahwistic in name and practice, allowing a wider variety of cultic activity than its critics in the second half of the monarchy. The religious practices of the high places were fundamentally conservative, preserving Israel's ancient religious heritage. Perhaps for this reason, many of these practices belonged also to the royal cult of Jerusalem. Yet, perhaps because some of these practices were maintained by Israel's neighbors, legal and prophetic condemnations rejected these traditional practices of Israel. In the name of the deity to whom the religion of high places was devoted, its legal and prophetic critics condemned this part of Israel's ancient religious inheritance.

CHAPTER 6

The Origins and Development of Israelite Monotheism

In reconstructing the history of Israelite religion, it is important to neither overemphasize the importance of deities other than Yahweh nor diminish their significance.[1] On the one hand, it would appear that each stage of Israelite religion knew relatively few deities. The deities attested in Israel appear limited, compared to the pantheons of Ugarit, Mesopotamia, and Egypt. The Phoenician city-states and the new nation-states of Moab, Ammon, and Edom perhaps reflect a lack of deities relatively comparable to early Israel.[2] In the Judges period, Israelite divinities may have included Yahweh, El, Baal, and perhaps Asherah as well as the sun, moon, and stars. During the monarchy, Yahweh, Baal, Astarte, and the sun, moon, and stars were considered deities in Israel.[3] Other candidates for Israelite deities are equated by some scholars with these deities; these are largely attested late in the Judean monarchy. The Queen of Heaven (Jer. 7:18; 44:18-19, 25) was the title of a goddess, perhaps Astarte, Ishtar (or, a syncretized Astarte-Ishtar) or less likely Anat.[4] Tạmmuz (Ezek. 8:14; cf. Isa. 17:10-11; Dan. 11:37) and Hadad-Rimmon (Zech. 12:11) are sometimes considered to be manifestations of Baal.[5] In the case of some

1. For some of the difficulties in assessing historical evidence, see Machinist, "The Question of Distinctiveness in Ancient Israel," in *Ah, Assyria . . . : Studies in Assyrian History and Ancient Near Eastern Historiography Presented to Hayim Tadmor,* ed. M. Cogan and I. Eph'al, Scripta Hierosolymitana 33 (Jerusalem: Magnes, 1991), 196-212.

2. On the deities of the states surrounding Israel, see chapter 1, section 4.

3. For minor deities in Iron Age Israel, see Tigay, *You Shall Have No Other Gods.*

4. See chapter 3, section 4.

5. On the biblical evidence for Tammuz, see E. M. Yamauchi, "Tammuz and the Bible," *JBL* 84 (1965): 283-90; McKay, *Religion in Judah,* 68-69. Regarding Dumuzi in Mesopotamian religion, see also T. Jacobsen, "Toward the Image of Tammuz," *History of Religions* 1 (1961): 189-213 = *Toward the Image of Tammuz and Other Essays on Mesopotamian History and Culture,* ed.

other deities identified in biblical sources, devotion appears to be restricted to a particular area or period. Deities in this category would include Bethel (Jer. 48:13), perhaps Chemosh (1 Kings 11:7; 2 Kings 23:17), and *mlk*, the name of a sacrifice except in Isaiah 8:21 and 57:9 (cf. Amos 5:26; Zeph. 1:5, 8).[6] It may be argued that some, if not all, of these deities appeared in Israelite religion during the last century of the Judean monarchy. In some cases, they may have been borrowed from another culture. Chemosh belongs to this category. The late appearance of Astarte and Bethel may reflect Phoenician influence. In Tyrian religion Bethel perhaps developed as an aspect of El into a god. This deity is attested in the treaty of Esarhaddon with Baal of Tyre, in double-names (AP 7:7; 22:124, 125) and proper names (AP 2:6-10; 12:9; 18:4, 5; 22:6; 42:8; 55:7) in the Jewish Aramaic papyri from Elephantine, the Aramaic version of Psalm 20 written in Demotic, and Jeremiah 48:13.[7] From these pieces of evidences, Bethel, like Astarte, may have been a specifically Phoenician import into Judean religion, an influence reflected in both Jeremiah 48:13 and the Jewish Egyptian evidence.[8]

On the other hand, the Israelite evidence should be neither minimized nor ignored. The data indicates a significant range of religious practice within ancient Israel. As the identification between El and Yahweh indicates, the cult of Yahweh could be monotheistic and "syncretistic," to use the polemical term customarily aimed at Baal worship. There was no opposition to "syncretism" with El. As the interaction of Baal worship and Yahwistic cult attests, Yahwism could vary from coexistence or identification with other deities to outright rejection of them. In this case, polytheistic Yahwism is indicated. The assimilation of El and the asherah symbol into the cult of Yahweh points to Yahwism's Canaanite heritage. At some early point, Israel perhaps knew a stage of ditheism in addition to its devotion to Yahweh (possibly reflected in Gen.

W. L. Moran, HSS 21 (Cambridge, MA: Harvard Univ. Press, 1970), 73-103; idem, "Religious Drama in Ancient Mesopotamia," 65-72; Livingstone, *Mystical and Mythological Explanatory Works*, 161-64. On the medieval evidence for the cult of Ta'uz (= Tammuz) among the Sabeans of Harran, see Livingstone, *Mystical and Mythological Explanatory Works*, 162. On Hadad-Rimmon, see J. C. Greenfield, "The Aramaean God *Rammān/Rimmōn*," *IEJ* 26 (1976): 197-98; J. Gray, "Baal," *IDB* 1:329. See the recent discussion of these figures by T. N. D. Mettinger, *The Riddle of Resurrection: "Dying and Rising Gods" in the Ancient Near East*, ConBOT 50 (Stockholm: Almqvist & Wiksell International, 2001), esp. 185-215. See also n. 27 below.

6. So Mosca, "Child Sacrifice," 117-272; Tigay, *You Shall Have No Other Gods*, esp. 11-12, 65-73. On "Molek," see chapter 5, section 3.

7. Cf. Smith, *Palestinian Parties and Politics*, 19.

8. See Hyatt, "The Deity Bethel," 81-98; Cross, *Canaanite Myth and Hebrew Epic*, 46-47 n. 14. For the attestation of El-Bethel in the Aramaic version of Psalm 20 written in Demotic, see Nims and Steiner, "A Paganized Version," 264.

49:25). That ditheism and polytheistic Yahwism were later condemned by monotheistic Yahwists does not indicate that nonmonotheistic Yahwism necessarily constituted "Canaanite syncretism" or "popular religion," tainted by Canaanite practices and therefore non-Yahwistic in character. Rather, the varied forms of Yahwistic cult reflected Israel's Canaanite background. Similarly, the asherah, high places, necromancy and other practices relating to the dead belonged to Israel's Canaanite heritage, enjoyed Yahwistic sanction in Israel, but were later condemned in Israel as non-Yahwistic.

The development of Israelite monotheism involved complex features in various periods. Convergence and differentiation occurred in conjunction with several societal factors that gave them their formative shape. Some of these factors can be isolated and placed within the context of four general periods: the period of the Judges (1200-1000); the first half of the monarchy (1000-800); the second half of the monarchy (800-587); and the Babylonian exile (587-538). Given the large-scale factors under review, it is difficult to specify their influence during more narrow time periods.

1. The Period of the Judges

The stage of convergence can be dated only along very broad lines, but it would appear to have belonged to the earliest stages of Israelite literature. This process of convergence continued down through the monarchy until the powers and imagery of Baal were fully assimilated by Yahweh, and it anticipates the later development of monolatry. The incorporation of divine attributes into Yahweh highlights the centrality of Yahweh in Israel's earliest attested literature. As warrior fighting on Israel's behalf, Yahweh exercises power in Judges 5 against powerful peoples and deities. In this poem Yahweh controls the cosmic bodies (Judg. 5:20), who fight for Israel. Judges 5 also asserts a distinction between Yahweh and "new gods" (5:8). The emergence of Israel as a people coincides with the appearance of Yahweh as its central deity.[9] Indeed, Yahweh was "the god of Israel" (Judg. 5:3, 5) who eventually was identified with El. It is difficult to add more to this picture of Yahweh's hegemony at this early stage, but inferences based on data from the period of the monarchy might be made. For example, older covenantal forms became prominent under the monarchy.[10] Since the monarchy tended to be conserva-

9. E. W. Nicholson, *God and His People: Covenant and Theology in the Old Testament* (Oxford: Clarendon, 1986), 202.

10. See McCarthy, *Treaty and Covenant*, 155-298; J. D. Levenson, review of *God and His*

tive in its modications of traditional religious forms, the royal Davidic covenant probably drew on an older Israelite concept of the covenantal relationship binding Israel to Yahweh as its main deity.

2. The First Half of the Monarchy

The monarchy was equally a political and religious institution, and under royal influence, religion combined powerful expressions of state and religious ideology. When the prestige of the national deity was increased, the prestige of the dynasty in turn was enhanced. The special relationship between Yahweh and the Davidic dynasty assumed the form of a formal covenantal relationship, called in 2 Samuel 23:5 an "eternal covenant" *(bĕrît ʿôlām).*[11] The binding of the deity and the king in formal relationship ensured divine well-being for the king and people as well as human devotion to the deity. More specifically, Yahweh ensured national well-being, justice, and fertility (Psalms 2; 72; 89; 110), while the king in turn guaranteed national cult to Yahweh (1 Kings 8; 2 Kings 12).[12] The covenantal relationship directly involved the land and the people of Yahweh. Through the king the people received the blessings provided by Yahweh. The people were also partners in the Davidic covenant. The partnership between Yahweh and the king and the people is described in 2 Kings 11:17: "And Jehoiada made a covenant between Yahweh and the king and people, that they should be Yahweh's people; and also between the king and the people."[13] The religious-political conceptualization of the covenant reached its fullest expression in the Davidic dynastic theology. The nationalization of the covenantal form exalted Yahweh as the national deity of the united monarchy. The national hegemony of Yahweh was thereby established for ancient Israel.

People, by E. W. Nicholson, *CBQ* 50 (1988): 307. Ahlström ("Travels of the Ark," 148 n. 34) notes that the cult of *'ēl bĕrît/baʿal bĕrît* in Judges 6–7 would point to covenant as a Canaanite feature. For the problems with this assumption, see R. E. Clements, "Baal-Berith of Shechem," *JSS* 13 (1968): 21-32. On Judges 6–7, see chapter 1, section 3. For an optimistic appraisal of the role of covenant in early Israel, see Sperling, "Israel's Religion in the Ancient Near East," 21-27.

11. Cross, *Canaanite Myth and Hebrew Epic,* 241-65; Smith, *"Bĕrît ʿām/bĕrît ʿôlām,"* 241-43; Nicholson, *God and His People,* 44-45.

12. In addition to the treatments of kingship noted in Introduction n. 16, see A. S. Kapelrud, "King and Fertility," *Norsk teologisk tidsskrift* 56 (1955): 113-22; and O. H. Steck, *Friedensvorstellungen in alten Jerusalem,* Theologische Studien 3 (Zurich: Theologischer Verlag, 1972), 19-35.

13. McCarthy, *Treaty and Covenant,* 215, 259-60, 284-85; idem, "Ebla, ὁρχαι τεμνειν, *ṭb, šlm:* Addenda to *Treaty and Covenant*²," *Biblica* 60 (1979): 250-51. See also K. L. Roberts, "God, Prophet, and King: Eating and Drinking on the Mountain in First Kings 18:41," *CBQ* 62 (2000): 632-44.

The continuing development of treaty language in covenantal literary forms may also be seen as part and parcel of royal influence. Born of political experience, treaty forms and expressions came to communicate the relationship between Yahweh and Israel in the law (Exod. 20:3; 22:19; 24:1-11).[14]

The innovative centralization of national worship was also part of the process leading to monotheistic Yahwism, as it encouraged a single national deity and devalued local manifestations of deity. The royal unification of national life — both political and religious — helped to achieve political and cultic centralization by concentrating and exhibiting power through the capital city and a relationship with the national deity residing in that city. This development was concomitant with the development of the monarchy itself. It began with the establishment of the capital city under David, continued in the religious importance that Jerusalem achieved under Solomon, and culminated in the religious programs of Hezekiah and Josiah. As P. K. McCarter comments on these two Davidic kings, "their policies, by unifying the worship of Yahweh, had the effect of unifying the way in which he was conceived by his worshippers, thus eliminating the earlier theology of local manifestations."[15] The religious function was but one dimension in the effects of cultic centralization. This religious policy held political and economic benefits as well.[16] The role of the monarchy was both innovative and conservative, react-

14. On the dating of Exod. 24:1-11, and the relationship between units, vv. 1-2, 3-8, 9-11, see Childs, *The Book of Exodus,* 499-507, esp. 501; Nicholson, *God and His People,* 122-33; Levenson, review of Nicholson, *God and His People,* 307; Roberts, "God, Prophet, and King," 638-40. On "E," see R. K. Gnuse, "Redefining the Elohist," *JBL* 119 (2000): 201-20. The general attribution of vv. 3-8 to the "Elohist" source or tradition would place this unit in the first half of the monarchy according to a traditional dating of the Pentateuchal sources or traditions.

15. McCarter, "Aspects of the Religion," 143. See also the comments of Y. Aharoni, "Israelite Temples in the Period of the Monarchy," in *Proceedings of the Fifth World Congress of Jewish Studies* 1, ed. P. Peli (Jerusalem: World Union of Jewish Studies, 1969), 73; and more recently, Z. Herzog, "The Date of the Temple at Arad: Reassessment of the Stratigraphy and the Implications for the History of Religion in Judah," in *Studies in the Archaeology of the Iron Age in Israel and Jordan,* ed. A. Mazar with the assistance of G. Mathias, JSOTSup 331 (Sheffield: Sheffield Academic Press, 2001), 156-78. The evidence from Arad suggests cultic activity through the late seventh century (see F. M. Cross, "Two Offering Dishes with Phoenician Inscriptions from the Sanctuary of ʿArad," *BASOR* 235 [1979]: 77; D. Ussishkin, "The Date of the Judaean Shrine at Arad," *IEJ* 37-38 [1987-88]: 142-57). The Korahites are known from the Arad inscriptions and in the Jerusalem temple, according to 1 Chron. 6:22; 9:19, the psalmic superscriptions bearing their name (see Psalms 42, 44-49, 84-85, 87-88), and the genealogy of Korah (1 Chron. 2:43; see J. M. Miller, "The Korahites of Southern Judah," *CBQ* 32 [1970]: 58-68). On the Korahites in 1 Chronicles, see also D. L. Petersen, *Late Israelite Prophecy: Studies in Deutero-Prophetic Literature and in Chronicles,* SBLMS 23 (Missoula, MT: Scholars, 1977), 55-87.

16. Smith, *Palestinian Parties and Politics,* 51.

ing to the needs of the developing state. And, as illustrated by the examples described in the previous chapters, like the monarchy Israelite monolatry developed out of both adherence to past religious traditions and departure from them, out of both conservatism and innovation.

As patron deity of the monarchy, Yahweh supported Israel in international conflicts. Divine power became international in scope, thereby promoting an early form of monolatrous faith. In a variety of ways, the Elijah-Elisha cycles communicate the scope of Yahweh's power against other deities, even outside of Israel. Through his prophets Elijah and Elisha, Yahweh works beyond Israel's borders (1 Kings 17:14; 19:15; 2 Kings 5:1; 8:13).[17] The story of Naaman in 2 Kings 5 sets the stage for an expression that the action and plan of Yahweh extends beyond Israel's national borders. Naaman is given victory, thanks to Yahweh, and in recognizing this fact, he declares "there is no God in all the earth but in Israel" (2 Kings 5:15). Political and religious conflict with other states during the pre-exilic period provided a political context for expressing the sovereignty of Yahweh over Israel's enemies and thereby "over all the earth" (Ps. 47:2; cf. Pss. 8:1; 24:1; 48:2; 95:4; 97:5; Isa. 6:3).[18] This notion of Yahweh's power over the nations continued into the prophets of the eighth century and reached full flower with the emergence of Israelite monotheism in the Exile.

Another historical factor of centralization during the period of the monarchy, significant for the development of Israelite monolatry, is the role of writing in Israelite society. J. Goody argues that the rise of writing helped to generate Israelite monolatry.[19] While Goody projects this development to the Mosaic period, his ideas regarding the influence of writing nonetheless merit consideration. He suggests that the process of writing gives the customs of oral law a more general application and a more authoritative status within

17. M. Cogan and H. Tadmor, *II Kings,* AB II (Garden City, NY: Doubleday, 1988), 67.

18. See J. J. M. Roberts, "The Religio-Political Setting of Psalm 47," *BASOR* 221 (1976): 129-32; cf. E. S. Gerstenberger, *Psalms: Part 1, With an Introduction to Cultic Poetry,* The Forms of the Old Testament Literature 14 (Grand Rapids, MI: Eerdmans, 1988), 198.

19. J. Goody, *The Logic of Writing and the Organization of Society* (Cambridge: Cambridge Univ. Press, 1986), 39-41; cf. Patrick, *Old Testament Law,* 189-218. For writing in Israel, see J. L. Crenshaw, "Education in Ancient Israel," *JBL* 104 (1985): 601-15, and *Education in Ancient Israel: Across the Deadening Silence,* Anchor Bible Reference Library (New York: Doubleday, 1998). A. Lemaire, *Les écoles et la formation de la Bible dans l'ancien Israël,* OBO 39 (Fribourg: Éditions Universitaires; Göttingen: Vandenhoeck & Ruprecht, 1981); idem, "Sagesses et Écoles," *VT* 34 (1984): 270-81. Note also the important cautions issued in S. Niditch, *Oral World and Written Word: Ancient Israelite Literature* (Louisville: Westminster/John Knox, 1996); and R. F. Person, Jr., "The Ancient Israelite Scribe as Performer," *JBL* 117 (1998): 601-9. See further pp. xxii-xxiv above.

a society. As a result, social norms in written form become authoritative for a wider audience. In Israel these norms included the notion of monolatry, which emerged in early legal and prophetic materials. The role of writing in the development of legal traditions is evident in the period of the monarchy (Jer. 8:7-8; 2 Kings 22:3; 23:24; cf. Hos. 8:12; 1 Chron. 17:7-9; 24:6) and appears explicitly in the postexilic period (Ezra 7:6, 11; Neh. 8:1). Like the monarchs of other ancient Near Eastern kingdoms, Israelite kings maintained written records of their reigns. Various biblical passages allude to written chronicles, such as "the annals of the kings of Judah" (1 Kings 14:29; 15:7, 23; 22:46), "the annals of the kings of Israel-Ephraim" (1 Kings 14:19; 15:31; 16:5, 14, etc.), and "the annals of the kings of Judah and Israel" (2 Chron. 16:11; 25:26; 27:7; 28:26, etc.). There were also "the records of David" (1 Chron. 29:29), "the book of the acts of Solomon" (1 Kings 11:41; 2 Chron. 9:29), "the records of the deeds of Rehoboam which had been written by Shemaiah the prophet and Iddo the seer" (2 Chron. 12:15; cf. 13:22), and a work of Jehu the son of Hanani that recounted the history of Jehoshaphat's reign and was incorporated into "the books of the kings of Israel" (2 Chron. 22:34). The written collections called "the book of the wars of Yahweh" (Num. 21:14) and "the book of Yashar" (Josh. 10:12; 2 Sam. 1:17) included material attributed to the premonarchic period and point to transmission of this material during the monarchy. Pentateuchal traditions attest to the importance of writing for storing legal material, a role attributed to Moses (Exod. 24:4, 7, 12; Deut. 30:10; 31:24-26) and the priesthood (Num. 5:23-24). Scribes were used to preserve records by the monarchy (2 Sam. 8:16; 1 Kings 4:3; Prov. 25:1; cf. Ps. 45:1), the army (2 Kings 25:19; Jer. 52:25; cf. Josh. 18:9; Judg. 8:13-17), and the judicial administration (Jer. 32:11-14). Similarly, the priesthood had scribes specializing in the storage of legal material through writing (Jer. 8:7-8; cf. KTU 1.6 VI 54-56; KAI 37 A 15).

The fostering of Baal language, the asherah, and other features served further political and ideological functions channeled and expressed by royal scribal activity (for example, in the records of kings, and presumably in their public monuments — though none of the latter are now extant). The inclusion of such a wide array of religious expressions during the monarchy may reflect functions of social and political integration. When David used the language of Baal for Yahweh, it may have served the function of extending divine dominion in order to confirm royal power. When Ahab and his line sought to promote Baal, it was perhaps to effect religious compatibility and perhaps to strengthen political ties with his royal relatives in Tyre. The inclusion of the asherah in the Jerusalem temple was perhaps no more than a conservative cultic preservation of Israel's ancient traditions; criticism of it was probably more the innovation.

Like the ark,[20] the asherah in the national temple cult tied the cult to Israel's ancient roots. Necromancy and prophecy competed as forms of inquiry for information from the divine realm, as the contrast of the two phenomena in Deuteronomy 18 and Isaiah 8 would suggest. The condemnation of high places was tied to the question of centralization of cult during the monarchy.

The monarchy played a significant role in encouraging the religious imagery of other deities within the cult of Yahweh. The examples of the asherah, solar language, necromancy, and feeding the dead would suggest that the monarchy accepted these traditional religious practices, and during the period of royal toleration and patronization of these practices, some prophets perhaps accepted initially a number of these practices. Furthermore, the monarchy was traditional in its preservation of the asherah, its appropriation of Baal and solar language for Yahweh, and possibly even its toleration for Baal worship. The issue then is not why the monarchy accepted such practices against the condemnations of prophetic critics, but why some of the prophets secondarily came to condemn these practices. For prophets and legal codes, the threat of Baal in the ninth century produced the initial precedent leading to later condemnation of some other religious features of Israel. In this struggle the status of Yahweh was seen to be crucially threatened. For this reason prophetic critics and legal codes opposed the monarchy on these issues and took innovative measures of attacking traditional devotion to the asherah and the traditional use of Baal and solar language for Yahweh. This conflict marked a turning point in the development of Israelite religion in creating a precedent for eliminating from the cult of Yahweh features associated with Baal or other deities. This process of differentiation reached full force in the next period.

3. The Second Half of the Monarchy

Some features from the preceding era continued even more strongly during the second half of the monarchy. The international scope of Yahweh's power expressed in the Elijah-Elisha cycles appeared as well in prophetic oracles against the nations. The condemnation of the foreign nations in Amos 1–2 and Isaiah 13–22 was premised on Yahweh's ability and choice to exercise power over the neighbors of Israel.[21] The differentiation of some religious

20. On the political function of the ark, see Ahlström, "The Travels of the Ark," 141-48.

21. Many commentators view the oracles against the nations in Amos 1:3–2:16 as secondary and late; nonetheless, some of these oracles may date to an eighth-century tradent. For the various positions, see H. W. Wolff, *Joel and Amos*, trans. W. Jansen, S. D. McBride, Jr., and

features from the cult of Yahweh, such as devotion to the cult of Baal and specific practices associated with the dead, signified a distinctive change from the previous period. Hosea's polemic against Israelite devotion to Baal reflects a strong witness to the differentiation of Yahweh from practices previously seen as compatible with Yahwism or at least tolerated by Israelites. Jeremiah's satire on idol making (Jeremiah 10) contrasts the falsity of other deities with Yahweh, the "true God," "the living God and the everlasting King" (v. 10), and anticipates the satires of idols by Second Isaiah during the Exile. Furthermore, priestly and Deuteronomistic avoidance of anthropomorphic depictions of Yahweh contributed to the uniqueness of the Israelite deity.

The appearance of some deities in late Judean religion may account for a further element in the development of monolatry. Some deities, such as Chemosh, patently reflect foreign influence. Other deities, such as Bethel (Jer. 48:13) and Astarte, seem to reflect late Phoenician influence. This late development may have laid the basis for further polemic against other deities, such as Baal, who belonged authentically to Israel's Canaanite heritage (in distinction to the Phoenician Baal of Jezebel). Chemosh, Bethel, and Astarte were known as religious imports, and Baal may have been understood along similar lines. It is precisely in this way that 1 Kings 17–19 presents Baal.

The covenant assumed a greater importance as an expression of Israel's exclusive relationship with Yahweh. By the second half of the monarchy, the law (Exodus 32–34) and the prophets (Hos. 6:7; 8:1) communicated the integral duties and blessings exercised by Israel and its deity with formulas found also in treaties between kings of differing status.[22] The development of writing perhaps went hand in hand with the evolution in the use of covenantal forms for expressing the human-divine relationship in ancient Israel. Writing became more important for Israelite legal traditions and prophecy during the second half of the monarchy. Legal material was shaped by its emergence in written forms, achieving a more authoritative status in Israel by addressing a wider audience. The two forms of the Ten Commandments in Exodus 20 and Deuteronomy 5, and the modeling of Deuteronomy 12–26 after the order and themes of the Ten Commandments,[23] indicate both the general form and au-

---

C. A. Muenchow, Hermeneia (Philadelphia: Fortress, 1977), 112, 139-42, 151-52; R. B. Coote, *Amos Among the Prophets* (Philadelphia: Fortress, 1981), 66-70.

22. See Nicholson, *God and His People*, 134-50, 179-88; cf. Levenson, review of Nicholson, *God and His People*, 307. On the dating of Hos. 6:7 and 8:1, see also Yee, *Composition and Tradition*, 279-81, 288-89.

23. S. Kaufman, "The Structure of Deuteronomic Law," *Maarav* 1/2 (1979): 105-58. See Miller, "Israelite Religion," 211-12; and the important book of B. M. Levinson, *Deuteronomy and the Hermeneutics of Legal Innovation* (New York/Oxford: Oxford Univ. Press, 1997).

thoritative status that they held in the circles that produced them and perhaps more widely in Israelite society. The Deuteronomistic narrative concerning the creation of the Ten Commandments presents them precisely as a written product penned by Yahweh, the divine scribe (Deut 9:10; 10:2, 4). Deuteronomy 12–26 illustrates how the Ten Commandments, although general in form, were made relevant for the changing circumstances of Israelite society, and how writing itself played a role in the growth of the parameters of covenant. Indeed, covenant and monolatry received elaboration and definition in written forms.

Writing eventually became the main mode of storing the prophetic cycles involving Elijah, Elisha, and their disciples, and this trend is reflected in prophets of the eighth and sixth centuries (Isa. 8:19-20; Jeremiah 36; Hab. 2:2). While oral transmission was the older mode of proclaiming the prophetic message (2 Kings 3:15), oral (Ezek. 33:2) and written forms of prophetic proclamation coexisted in the second half of the monarchy. Indeed, in the later half of the monarchy, the written form may have become the more common mode of communicating the prophetic word (Isa. 29:11-12; cf. 30:11; Jer. 25:13).[24] The rise of writing for both legal and prophetic proclamation and preservation evidently partook of a wider societal development (cf. Isa. 10:19). Similarly, while writing in the bureaucracy remained the domain of professionally trained scribes, other bureaucrats knew how to read (KAI 193:9-12). Wisdom texts also refer to writing (Job 31:35-37). It is difficult to gauge fully the effect that generating and preserving legal and prophetic texts through writing had on Israelite society. It would appear that legal and prophetic proclamation gained a wider audience through writing. In later times, writing was crucial in the efforts of legal and prophetic tradents to transmit, update, and proclaim the words they received. Therefore, the legal and prophetic criticisms of the monolatrous cult and proclamation of Yahweh's hegemony exercised further influence, in part thanks to writing.

4. The Exile

Texts dating to the Exile or shortly beforehand are the first to attest to unambiguous expressions of Israelite monotheism. Second Isaiah (Isa. 45:5-7) gave voice to the monotheistic ideal that Yahweh was the only deity in the cosmos.

24. See the essays in *Writings and Speech in Israelite and Ancient Near Eastern Prophecy*, ed. E. Ben-Zvi and M. H. Floyd, SBL Symposium 10 (Atlanta, GA: Society of Biblical Literature, 2000).

Not only are the other deities powerless; they are nonexistent.[25] Like Jeremiah 10, Second Isaiah (Isa. 40:18-20; 41:6-7; 44:9-20; 46:1-13; 48:3-8) stresses the uniqueness of Yahweh in marked contrast with the lifeless, empty idols who represent lifeless, nonexistent deities.[26] Israelite cult apparently came to grips with devotion rendered to other deities by Israelites. Down to the Babylonian captivity, Israelite religion tolerated some cults within the larger framework of the national cult of Yahweh. While some illicit practices persisted into the Persian period (Isa. 65:3; 66:17),[27] these religious phenomena do not appear to have been tolerated in the central cult of Yahweh.

As in previous periods, during the Babylonian captivity writing continued to play a formative role in the development of Yahwism. By the end of the monarchy writing became the dominant mode of generating prophetic texts. Ezekiel was perhaps generated largely as a written work.[28] There are a number of indications of the written composition of Ezekiel. First, its length betrays a written hand. Ezekiel's call narrative in chapters 1–3 covers sixty-five verses, whereas Isaiah's call in chapter 6 is a brief and succinct thirteen verses. Similarly, single oracles in Ezekiel are quite long. Ezekiel 16 has sixty-three verses, and both Ezekiel 20 and 23 have forty-nine verses. Second, the written character of the book is intimated in 2:9-10, where Ezekiel is commanded to eat the scroll bearing the divine word; it is the "words of lamentation and mourning" that constitute the remainder of the book (cf. 9:11). Third, as an indication of the written character of Ezekiel, R. R. Wilson observes that the book does not present the prophet orally delivering his

25. Barr, "The Problem of Israelite Monotheism," *Transactions of the Glasgow University Oriental Society* 17 (1957-58): 52-62.

26. R. J. Clifford, "The Function of Idol Passages in Second Isaiah," *CBQ* 42 (1980): 450-64; Smith, *The Origins of Biblical Monotheism*, 179-94.

27. See the essays in *The Crisis of Israelite Religion: Transformation of Religious Tradition in Exilic and Post-Exilic Times*, ed. B. Becking and M. C. A. Korpel, OTS XLII (Leiden/Boston/Köln: Brill, 1999). The gardens mentioned in Isa. 17:10-11, 65:3, and 66:17 may be related to the cult of Adonis. The practice of eating pig in Isaiah 65 and 66 could be suggestive of the cult of Osiris (Jonas Greenfield, private communication). For a general discussion, see de Vaux, *The Bible and the Ancient Near East*, 210-37.

28. See H. Gunkel, "The Prophets as Writers and Poets," in *Prophecy in Israel; Search for an Identity*, trans. J. L. Schaaf, ed. D. L. Petersen, Issues in Religion and Theology 10 (Philadelphia: Fortress; London: SPCK, 1987), 25, 28; A. Loisy, *The Religion of Israel*, trans. A. Galton (New York: G. P. Putnam's Sons, 1910), 196; L. Boadt, "Rhetorical Strategies in Ezekiel's Oracles of Judgement," in *Ezekiel and His Book: Textual and Literary Criticism and Their Interrelation*, ed. J. Lust, Bibliotheca Ephemeridum Theologicarum 74 (Louvain: Univ. Press/Uitgeverij Peeters, 1986), 187; R. R. Wilson, "Ezekiel," in *Harper's Bible Commentary*, ed. J. L. Mays (San Francisco: Harper & Row, 1988), 657-58; cf. Lang, *Monotheism and the Prophetic Minority: An Essay in Biblical History and Sociology*, The Social World of Biblical Antiquity (Sheffield, England: Almond, 1983), 138-56.

words.[29] Fourth, although the prose style generally found in Ezekiel does not prove that it was a written work from its inception, some features that do not appear regularly in oral speech[30] are common. The appearance of such features would further suggest that Ezekiel originally constituted a written work in the main. Fifth, the book of Ezekiel developed new forms, in part due to the written mode of producing prophecy. For instance, Wilson points to the first-person narrative extending throughout the book, a form that has continuity with eighth-century prophets. Other forms, including the vision of the divine chariot in chapter 1,[31] the tour given by a divine figure in chapters 8 and 40–48,[32] and the detailed plan in chapters 40–48, do not appear in prior prophetic tradition. Wilson attributes the rise of written prophecy reflected in Ezekiel to the geographical distances between Jewish communities of the sixth century. Between communities separated by great distances prophecy could be communicated more efficiently in written form.

A similar case might be made for Second Isaiah (Isaiah 40–55) as originally a written work[33] that imitates the poetic style of the prophet after whom

29. Wilson, "Ezekiel," 657-58. While the book of Ezekiel assumes of its audience the notion that some of the prophecies were orally delivered (e.g., 3:11; 6:2; 12:10, 23; 13:7; 14:4), the portrait of the silent prophet in Ezek. 3:26-27, 24:27, and 33:22 (Greenberg, *Ezekiel 1–20,* 120-21) would suit a reading audience better than a hearing audience. The extended portraits of Ezekiel and Jeremiah, in contrast to the descriptions of Isaiah, Hosea, or Amos, would also suggest a written work, although the observation of this contrast is not intended to imply that the stories of the eighth-century prophets were not possibly written in character.

30. J. MacDonald identifies some grammatical features common to both spoken speech and poetry; both are notably less marked than prose ("Some Distinctive Features of Israelite Spoken Hebrew," *BiOr* 33 [1975]: 162-75). Furthermore, inverted word order occurs proportionately more frequently in the prose of direct speech and poetry than in narrative prose. See also J. Blau, "Marginalia Semitica III," *IOS* 7 (1977): 23-27. For the problems involved in distinguishing between prose and poetry, see A. Cooper, "On Reading Biblical Poetry," *Maarav* 4/2 (1987): 221-41.

31. Greenberg, *Ezekiel 1–20,* 205-6.

32. See M. Himmelfarb, "From Prophecy to Apocalypse: *The Book of the Watchers* and Tours of Heaven," in *Jewish Spirituality: From the Bible Through the Middle Ages,* ed. A. Green, World Spirituality: An Encyclopedic History of the Religious Quest 13 (New York: Crossroad, 1987), 155.

33. O. Eissfeldt, *The Old Testament: An Introduction,* trans. P. R. Ackroyd (New York/Evanston: Harper & Row, 1965), 340. See also G. von Rad, *Old Testament Theology,* vol. 2, *The Theology of Israel's Prophetic Traditions,* trans. D. M. G. Stalker (New York: Harper & Row, 1965), 242; R. R. Wilson, "The Community of the Second Isaiah," in *Reading and Preaching the Book of Isaiah,* ed. C. R. Seitz (Philadelphia: Fortress, 1988), 60. See the strong literary arguments made for this view by B. D. Sommer, *A Prophet Reads Scripture: Allusion in Isaiah 40–66,* Contraversions. Jews and Other Differences (Stanford, CA: Stanford Univ. Press, 1998). While waw-consecutive forms are found in quoted speeches, they are considerably rarer in quoted speeches than in narrative (MacDonald, "Some Distinctive Features," 162-63, 175).

the book is named. That this is the purpose of the work may be inferred from the fact that the author(s) of Second Isaiah remains nameless; the authorship of Second Isaiah was sublimated into the identity of the original prophet. The verbal forms, known as the "*waw* consecutive," that is, the conjunction *waw* plus either doubling of initial consonant and imperfect, or the conjunction *waw* plus perfect, occur less frequently in direct discourse than in narrative,[34] suggesting that their frequency in Second Isaiah might point to a written composition.[35] The written works of Ezekiel and Second Isaiah permitted a sustained reflection on Israel's history and the nature of the Israelite deity. Out of the process of reflection and writing arose clear expressions of Israelite monotheism.

New reflections developed out of Israel's new social circumstances as well as its new political situation on the international stage from the seventh century on. The loss of family patrimonies due to economic stress and foreign incursions contribute to the demise of the model of the family for understanding divinity. With the rise of the individual along with the family as significant units of social identity (Deut. 24:16; Jer. 31:29-30; Ezekiel 18; cf. 33:12-20) came the corresponding notion on the divine level, namely of a single god responsible for the cosmos. Judah's reduced status on the world scene also required new thinking about divinity. Like Marduk, Yahweh became an "empire-god," the god of all the nations but in a way that no longer closely tied the political fortunes of Judah to the status of this god. With the old order of divine king and his human, royal representation on earth reversed, Yahweh stands alone in the divine realm, with all the other gods as nothing. In short, the old head-god of monarchic Israel became the Godhead of the universe.[36]

34. F. Blake, "Forms of Verbs After Waw in Hebrew," *JBL* 65 (1946): 57.

35. For cases of waw consecutive in Second Isaiah, see Isa. 40:4, 5, 14, 22, 24; 41:7, 9, 11; 42:15, 16, 25; 43:12, 14, 28; 44:4, 12, 13, 14, 15; 45:3, 4, 22; 46:4, 13; 47:6, 7, 10; 48:5, 15, 18, 19; 49:2, 3, 6, 7, 14, 21, 22, 23, 26; 50:6; 51:2, 3, 13, 15, 16, 23; 52:10; 53:2, 9; 54:12; 55:10, 11, 13 (cf. 42:6). MT *wĕʾāmar* in Isa. 40:6 is problematic. 1QIsa[a] reads *w'wmrh,* which has been understood as either a first person form with the final "cohortative" ending *-ah* (Cross, *Canaanite Myth and Hebrew Epic,* 188) or a feminine singular participle (Petersen, *Late Israelite Prophecy,* 20-21, 46-47 n. 15). The evidence favors the former view (see Barthélemy, *Critique Textuelle de l'Ancien Testament,* vol. 2, *Isaïe, Jérémie, Lamentations,* 278-79).

36. For these points, with further discussion, see Smith, *The Origins of Biblical Monotheism,* esp. 77-79, 163-66.

5. Israelite Monotheism in Historical Perspective

The historical reconstruction of Israel's religion that notes the variegated roles of state and popular religion, the mixture of indigenous and imported religious features, and the complex features of convergence and differentiation undermines some of the main scholarly views about Israelite religion in general and Israelite monotheism in particular. Some scholars argue for an early Israelite monotheism.[37] Albright speaks of a Mosaic age of monotheism deriving from the Sinai experience. H. Gottlieb, M. Smith, B. Lang, and P. K. McCarter note the role of the monarchy in the development of monotheism.[38] Morton Smith, followed by Lang, stresses the importance of the development of the "Yahweh-only party" in the ninth century and afterward. Lang especially emphasizes the "prophetic minority" that provided initial support for this religious posture in the northern kingdom before its fall and later in the southern kingdom. Many commentators attach great importance to the Exile[39] as the formative period for the emergence of Israelite mono-

37. For scholars who speak of monotheism in the "Mosaic age," see Albright, *From the Stone Age to Christianity: Monotheism and the Historical Process,* 2d ed. (Baltimore: Johns Hopkins Univ. Press, 1957), 257-72; Kaufmann, *The Religion of Israel,* 229-31; J. Milgrom, "Magic, Monotheism, and the Sin of Moses," in *The Quest for the Kingdom of God: Studies in Honor of George E. Mendenhall,* ed. H. B. Huffmon, F. A. Spina, and A. R. W. Green (Winona Lake, IN: Eisenbrauns, 1983), 251-65, esp. 263; I. M. Zeitlin, *Ancient Judaism: Biblical Criticism from Max Weber to the Present* (Cambridge, MA: Polity Press, 1984). For criticisms of this position, see T. J. Meek, "Monotheism and the Religion of Israel," *JBL* 61 (1942): 21-43; J. Barr, "Problem of Israelite Monotheism," 52-62; H. H. Rowley, "Moses and Monotheism," *From Moses to Qumran: Studies in the Old Testament* (London: Lutterworth, 1963), 35-63; Halpern, "'Brisker Pipes Than Poetry,'" 80-82; C. Schafer-Lichtenberger, review of *Ancient Judaism,* by I. Zeitlin, *JAOS* 108 (1988): 160-62.

38. Gottlieb, "El und Krt," 159-67; Smith, *Palestinian Parties and Politics,* 23; B. Lang, *Monotheism and the Prophetic Minority,* 13-59; McCarter, "Aspects of the Religion," 143. See also B. Hartmann, "Es gibt keinen Gott ausser Jahwe. Zur generellen Verneinung im Hebräischen," *ZDMG* 110 (1960): 229-35.

39. W. Eichrodt, *Theology of the Old Testament,* vol. 1, trans. J. A. Bakker, OTL (London: SCM, 1961), 220-27, 363-64; G. von Rad, *Old Testament Theology,* vol. 1, *The Theology of Israel's Historical Traditions,* trans. D. M. G. Stalker (New York/Evanston: Harper & Row, 1962), 210-12; Fohrer, *History of Israelite Religion,* 172; H. Wildberger, "Der Monotheismus Deuterojesajas," in *Beiträge zur alttestamentlichen Theologie: Festschrift für Walther Zimmerli zum 70. Geburtstag,* ed. H. Donner, R. Hanhart, and R. Smend (Göttingen: Vandenhoeck & Ruprecht, 1977), 506-30; Ahlström, *Royal Administration,* 69; H. Klein, "Der Beweis der Einzigkeit Jahwes bei Deuterojesaja," *VT* 35 (1985): 267-73; B. Lang, "Yahwé seul! Origine et figure du monothéisme biblique," *Concilium* 97 (1985): 55-64. For further surveys of the development of monotheism in Israel, see H. P. Müller, "Gott und die Götter in den Anfängen der biblischer Religion: Zur Vorgeschichte des Monotheismus," in *Monotheismus im Alten Testament und seiner*

theism.[40] Israel's position in a foreign land threatened the validity of its religious heritage and the centrality of Yahweh; the Exile changed the circumstances of national life and therefore altered the definition of Yahweh's centrality. The radical circumstances of the Exile issued in a radical redefinition of Yahweh.

All these views require at least minor modification in view of the evidence presented in the previous chapters. Monotheism was hardly a feature of Israel's earliest history. By the same token, convergence was an early development that anticipates the later emergence of monolatry and monotheism. The monarchy was one of many formative influences on the development of monolatry. Furthermore, convergence appeared by the time of the monarchy and continued well into the monarchy. The "Yahweh-only party" represented a modification of the cult of the national deity and an important step in the development of monolatry. By the same token, other factors gave definition and impetus to this religious position. Differentiation gave shape to the form that the religion of the "Yahweh-only party" assumed in the second half of the monarchy. Furthermore, it is not clear that this "Yahweh-only party" originated as "a prophetic minority," to paraphrase the words of B. Lang. Rather, although prophetic works provide the best witness to the "Yahweh-only" position, Israelite prophecy was largely dependent on other quarters of society. In other words, the "Yahweh-only party" may not have developed as a purely prophetic position (cf. Exod. 20:3; 22:19; 2 Sam. 22 [Ps. 18]: 32).[41] Finally, the literary expression of monotheism at a relatively late point in Israel's history, either in the late monarchy or the Exile, "overwrites" and obscures the long development involving the earlier phenomenon of monolatry as well as the important roles of convergence and differentiation.

Some scholars have stressed early Israelite religion as the quintessential period of pure Yahwism. Following in the footsteps of Albright, G. Mendenhall and J. Bright posit an early pure Yahwism that was polluted secondarily in the land by the cult of Baal and other idolatry.[42] In their schemes, the mon-

---

Umwelt (Fribourg: Verlag Schweizerisches Katholisches Bibelwerk, 1980), 99-142; F. Stolz, "Monotheismus in Israel," in *Monotheismus im Alten Testament,* 143-89; Halpern, "'Brisker Pipes Than Poetry,'" 77-115; Petersen, "Israel and Monotheism," 92-107.

40. See Introduction.

41. R. R. Wilson, *Prophecy and Society in Ancient Israel* (Philadelphia: Fortress, 1980), 192-212.

42. G. Mendenhall, "The Monarchy," *Interpretation* 29 (1975): 155-70; idem, *The Tenth Generation,* 21-31, 114, 181, 196; cf. J. Bright, *A History of Israel,* 2d ed. (Philadelphia: Westminster, 1972), 141, 221-24, 281-82. For criticisms of these negative views of the mon-

archy was largely a negative influence. There are three major problems with this characterization of Israelite religion. First, some of the features that Mendenhall and Bright view as secondary idolatry belonged to Israel's Canaanite heritage. The cult of Baal, the symbol of the asherah, the high places, and the cultic practices involving the dead all belonged to Israel's ancient past, its Canaanite past. Second, the "purest form of Yahwism" belonged not to an early stage of Israel's history but to the late monarchy. Differentiation of the cult of Yahweh did not begin until the ninth century and appeared in full flower only in the eighth century and afterward. Even this stage of reform was marked by other religious developments considered idolatrous by later generations; the cults of the "Queen of Heaven" and "the Tammuz" undermine any idealization of the late monarchy. The temple idolatry denounced in Ezekiel 8–11 probably constituted the norm rather than the exception for the final decades of the monarchy. The religious programs of Hezekiah and Josiah have been claimed as moments of religious purity in Judah, although even these policies had their political reasons.[43] The pure form of Yahwism that Mendenhall and Bright envision was perhaps an ideal achieved rarely, if ever, before the Exile — if even then. Third, the monarchy was not the villain of Israelite religion that Mendenhall and Bright make it out to be. Indeed, the monarchy made several religious contributions crucial to the development of monolatry. In short, Mendenhall and Bright stand much of Israel's religious development on its head.

In the analysis presented in the preceding chapters, the classic problem of monotheism is pushed back in time. The issue is not one of identifying the earliest instances of monolatry; rather, the old question of explaining monotheism becomes a new issue of accounting for the phenomenon of convergence, a stage in Israelite religion older than the appearance of monolatry. Three levels of development in early Israel bear on convergence. The first reflects Israel's Canaanite heritage; features in this category include El, Baal, Asherah, and their imagery and titles, and the cultic practices of the asherah, high places, and devotion to the dead. The second level involves features that Israel shared with its first-millennium neighbors: the

archy and a positive assessment of the monarchy, see J. J. M. Roberts, "In Defense of the Monarchy: The Contribution of Israelite Kingship to Biblical Theology," in *Ancient Israelite Religion: Essays in Honor of Frank Moore Cross,* ed. P. D. Miller, Jr., P. D. Hanson, and S. D. McBride, 377-96.

43. L. K. Handy ("Hezekiah's Unlikely Reform," *ZAW* 100 [1988]: 111-15) disputes the religious motives attached to Hezekiah's reform in 2 Chronicles 31 and attributes Hezekiah's changes in religious policies to the political vicissitudes of Sennacherib's advances into Judah.

rise of the new national deity, the presence of a consort goddess, and the small number of attested deities compared with second-millennium West Semitic cultures. Third, there are characteristics specific to Israelite culture, such as the new god, Yahweh, the traditions of separate origins and the southern sanctuary, the aniconic requirement, and decreased anthropomorphism. Any of the features in this third category might be invoked to help explain convergence. Biblical tradition concerning Israel's separate religious development includes aspects of all the items in the third category; it especially stresses the origins of Israel outside the land, the giving of Law (Torah), and the creation of the covenantal relationship at Mount Sinai. The features belonging to the third category are the most promising "explanations" currently known.

Yet appeal to them would be premised on the assumption that these religious elements were causes, and convergence and monotheism were the effects. The historical relationship lying behind these items (or others that might be mentioned) is unknown, and how to explain the emergence of any one of these items is historically problematic for the Iron I period. Significant cultural continuities and discontinuities of Israel with its Canaanite past and its Iron Age neighbors are identifiable, but historical causes cannot be clarified further at this stage of investigation. The development lying behind Israelite monotheism becomes impossible to trace back to the point of ancient Israel's historical appearance ca. 1200.

Though the reasons for Israelite "convergence" are not clear, the complex paths from convergence to monolatry and monotheism can be followed. The development of Israelite monolatry and monotheism involved both an "evolution" and a "revolution" in religious conceptualization, to use D. L. Petersen's categories.[44] It was an "evolution" in two respects. Monolatry grew out of an early, limited Israelite polytheism that was not strictly discontinuous with that of its Iron Age neighbors. Furthermore, adherence to one deity was a changing reality within the periods of the Judges and the monarchy in Israel. While evolutionary in character, Israelite monolatry was also "revolutionary" in a number of respects. The process of differentiation and the eventual displacement of Baal from Israel's national cult distinguished Israel's religion from the religions of its neighbors. Furthermore, as P. Machinist has observed,[45] one feature clearly distinguishing Israel from its neighbors was its

44. Petersen, "Israel and Monotheism," 92-107. Mendenhall (*The Tenth Generation,* 21, 194) and de Moor ("Crisis of Polytheism," 1-20) argue for a revolutionary schema.

45. P. Machinist, "The Question of Distinctiveness in Ancient Israel: An Essay." See also E. L. Greenstein, "The God of Israel and the Gods of Canaan: How Different Were They?" *Proceedings of the World Congress of Jewish Studies, Jerusalem, July 29–August 5, 1997, Division A,*

apologetic claim of religious difference. Israelite insistence on a single deity eventually distinguished Israel from the surrounding cultures, as far as textual data indicate.

The Bible and Its World, ed. R. Margolin (Jerusalem: World Union of Jewish Studies, 1999), 47-58; S. A. Geller, "The God of the Covenant," in *One God or Many? Concepts of Divinity in the Ancient World,* ed. B. N. Porter, Transactions of the Casco Bay Assyriological Institute (Bethesda, MD: CDL Press, 2000), 273-319; Zevit, *The Religions of Ancient Israel,* 687-90.

CHAPTER 7

Postscript: Portraits of Yahweh

1. Processes Leading to Divine Portraiture in Israel

The development toward monotheism in Israel involved complex processes of convergence and differentiation of deities. The convergence of other deities, or at least their characteristics, toward Yahweh involved no single pattern. Polemic, for example, was directed against Baal, and to a lesser extent, asherah and the sun. Polemic was not only a negative factor in these cases, but involved a positive process at work as well, namely, the attribution of the positive characteristics of other deities to Yahweh. In some instances, polemic involved direct criticism of other deities, such as Baal, or cultic items, such as the asherah (2 Kings 21:7; 23:4), the asherim (2 Kings 23:14), and "the horses . . . dedicated to the sun" and "the chariots of the sun" (2 Kings 23:11). Sometimes polemic assumed the form of negative depiction, as in the description of the priests bowing down before the sun in Ezekiel 8:16. Identification of Yahweh and another deity occasionally escaped polemic. Since El was no longer a religious threat in the first millennium, the positive identification of Yahweh-El was made without later accusations of idolatry.

This discussion has emphasized the process of addition of other deities or their traits to Yahweh. Yahweh is given the titles *'ēl* or *baʿal,* or is called "the Sun," or is attributed their features. The word addition may also be applied to the incorporation of distinctly different attributes within Yahweh. Both solar and storm language are attributed to Yahweh in different passages and even within the same units. Similarly, Yahweh embodies both male and female, both El and Asherah. Addition is not infrequently accompanied by the feature of paradox. For example, 1 Kings 17–19 dramatizes how Yahweh, while controlling the natural power associated with Baal, transcends it as well. Yahweh is known in some way in both sun and storm, but at the same time transcends such manifestations. Where explicit criticism of another deity is involved, as in this case, paradox functions as a form of polemic. Another use of paradox again involves the application of gender. While Yahweh embodies the characteristics of mother and father, for example in the parental experience they convey, Yahweh also transcends the human finiteness inherent in both of them (Ps. 27:10). The paradox of natural manifestation is posed also by the biblical language of "seeing God," an experience that was denied at times (Exod. 33:20, 23) and at other times affirmed (Num. 12:8; Isa. 6:1; Job 42:5; cf. Deut. 34:11; Pss. 11:7; 17:15; 27:4, 13; 42:3; 63:3).

A further process underlying the development of convergence and differentiation was the creation of new contexts for metaphorical expressions that functioned originally in polytheistic settings. Yahweh is called a "sun" (Ps. 84:12) and described as "rising" like the sun (Deut. 33:2). Although this solar attribution was thought to have been taken too literally (at least according to Ezek. 8:16), solar language functioned to convey aspects of Yahweh without reducing Yahweh to being the sun. In Genesis 1:14, the absorption of solar language works in another direction. In this passage, the sun is not a deity, but functions as the great light that God *(ʾĕlōhîm)* created and set in the firmament. Some originally polytheistic motifs were changed into forms deemed compatible with monotheistic Yahwism. One dramatic example of this alteration is the female figure of Wisdom in Proverbs 1–9. In addition to her other components, she perhaps included some features of Asherah. The representation of the divine presence as "glory" *(kābôd)* or "name" *(šēm)* constituted alternate strategies for expressing divine presence.[1] The background to the divine "name" and "face" of God is to be found precisely in the Canaanite milieu of the other deities. While these terms in both Canaanite-Phoenician and Israelite contexts expressed divine qualities, in Israel these terms lessened the anthropomorphism that characterized older descriptions of the deity more in continuity with Israel's Canaanite heritage.

Finally, the biblical record involves a shift in temporal perspective regarding Yahweh and other deities. Although features of El and Baal have been convincingly recognized in Yahweh, some biblical passages regard other deities as originally alien to Israel and Yahweh (Exod. 34:11-16; Deut. 32:12, 39; Ezekiel 28). Ezekiel 20:25-26 provides a different type of explanation for the otherwise forbidden practice of child sacrifice. In this passage Yahweh describes child sacrifice as divine punishment: "Moreover, I gave them statutes that were not good and ordinances by which they could not have life; and I defiled them through their very gifts in making them offer by fire all their first-born, that I might horrify them; I did it that they might know that I am

1. See chapter 3, section 5.

Yahweh." Similarly, Jeremiah 7:21-22 dismisses the divine authority for child sacrifice by denying that Yahweh ever commanded it. For the biblical record, the order of history is not theologically tantamount to the order of reality. Hence, understanding Yahweh involves a theological interpretation of history that, according to the biblical perspective, permits the nature of Yahweh to be disclosed more fully. While drawing on older tradition and claiming basis in Israel's earliest history, later prophetic and legal materials reflect a sustained reflection concerning Yahweh, supplementing and correcting older incomplete renderings of the divine.

These processes represent various aspects of convergence and differentiation. Convergence and differentiation influenced the depictions of the divine found in the Hebrew Bible. The inclusion of solar language for Yahweh, the acceptance of the symbol of the asherah and the cultic sites of the high places, and numerous practices pertaining or relating to the dead, long escaped priestly, Deuteronomistic, and prophetic criticism. The old body of Israelite literature assigns solar language to Yahweh. From the reconstruction offered in chapter 3, the symbol of the asherah was assimilated into the Yahwistic cult. Convergence apparently accounts for the numerous descriptions of Yahweh with imagery associated in Canaanite tradition with El, Baal, and other deities. Differentiation of Yahweh from some descriptions traditional for these deities is also evident. Some traditional religious features were eventually condemned as non-Yahwistic and ultimately passed from the national cult of Yahweh. Some aspects, including the Yahweh-El identification and the attribution of Baal's characteristics to Yahweh, continued to be acceptable. Within monotheistic Yahwism the figure of Yahweh absorbed some features of other deities without acceptance of their separate reality.

2. The Absence of Some Canaanite Divine Roles in the Biblical Record

The traits of Canaanite deities are attested in biblical tradition in widely varying degrees. Some roles were applied frequently to Yahweh, others less so, and some not at all.[2] A number of descriptions of El and Baal are highly conspicuous in some biblical depictions of Yahweh. Other features describing the di-

2. See the important compilation of M. C. A. Korpel, *A Rift in the Clouds: Ugaritic and Hebrew Descriptions of the Divine* (Münster: Ugarit-Verlag, 1990). See also the suggestive study of J. D. Fowler, *Theophoric Personal Names in Ancient Hebrew: A Comparative Study*, JSOTSup 49 (Sheffield: JSOT Press, 1988).

vine play a lesser role. For example, the divine council in biblical texts shows little sign of the magnificent feasting of the Ugaritic pantheon, although traces of divine feasting survive in the biblical record (Exod. 24:11).[3] Descriptions of the heavenly temple barely materialize in biblical tradition (Exod. 24:10; Ezek. 1:26), although 1 Enoch 14 and the Songs of the Sabbath Sacrifice from Qumran indicate the availability of this material in Israelite tradition.[4] Indeed, intertestamental apocalypses and the book of Revelation attest strongly to the persistence of mythic material. Various biblical books, especially Ezekiel, provide glimpses of this material and indicate knowledge of these traditions.

Other divine roles known from the Ugaritic literature are conspicuously absent from both the biblical record and extrabiblical Jewish literature. Yahweh does not appear like El, the drunken carouser (KTU 1.114) and sexual partner of goddesses (KTU 1.23.30-51; cf. 1.4 V 38-39), or Baal, the dying god (KTU 1.5 V–1.6 V) and voracious sexual partner of animals (KTU 1.5 V 18-22) and perhaps of his sister, Anat (KTU 1.11.1-5). Yahweh is unlike Anat, who feasts on the flesh of her military victims (KTU 1.3 II), or the sun-goddess in her netherworldly role (KTU 1.6 I 10-18, VI 42-53; cf. 1.161.8f.).[5] Of these images, only the language of feasting on the enemies is attested in biblical literature, and even this imagery appears indirectly with respect to Yahweh. Moreover, the feature of divine feasting in biblical tradition hardly conveys the rich and vivid character of divine imagery expressed in the Ugaritic narratives. The Canaanite descriptions render divine behavior in human or natural terms differing from biblical renderings of Yahweh in primarily two areas, sex and death. El, Baal, and perhaps Anat engage in sexual activity, and Baal, Anat, and the sun-deity are intimately involved in the processes of death and return to life. In Ugaritic texts, sexual relations belong to the di-

3. On divine feasting in Ugaritic, see especially KTU 1.3 I; 1.4 VI; 1.15 III; 1.20-22. The sequence of feasting and sexual relations underlie 1.4 IV 27-39 and 1.23.37-52. On this section of 1.23, see del Olmo Lete, *Mitos y leyendas,* 434-35, 444-45; and R. M. Good, "Hebrew and Ugaritic *nḥt,*" *UF* 19 (1987): 155-56.

4. On the topos of the heavenly temple in Ugaritic, biblical, and intertestamental literature, see Himmelfarb, "From Prophecy to Apocalypse," 145-65; Smith, "Biblical and Canaanite Notes," 585-87.

5. On KTU 1.114, see Spronk, *Beatific Afterlife,* 198-201. On El's sexual exploits in KTU 1.23, see Pope, *El in the Ugaritic Texts,* 37-41; idem, "Ups and Downs in El's Amours," *UF* 11 (1979 = Festschrift für C. F. A. Schaeffer): 701-8; cf. Cross, *Canaanite Myth and Hebrew Epic,* 22-24; Olyan, *Asherah and the Cult of Yahweh,* 42 n. 13. Regarding KTU 1.5 V and the site of Baal's mating, see M. S. Smith, "Baal in the Land of Death," *UF* 17 (1986): 311-14. Biblical literature generally renders the power of death as demonic and not a full-fledged deity (see chapter 2, section 2, and Smith, *The Origins of Biblical Monotheism,* 130-31).

vine life. Death, both in its manifestation in the figure of Mot and in descriptions of its effects, is part of the natural and divine realm, on par with Baal, the source of life and well-being in the cosmos. Although some of this mythic material appears in biblical tradition in various settings and in fractured forms, the language of death applied to Yahweh is rare and largely metaphorical. Yahweh does not die, even figuratively. Yahweh does not have a consort according to any biblical source; nor does he engage in divine sex.

Establishing reasons for the selection and distribution of divine roles in biblical texts is exceptionally difficult.[6] A few suggestions may be offered, but only most tentatively; this exploration bears the character of the possible but not verifiable. First, numerous critics of Israelite cult during the latter half of the monarchy, including the priestly and Deuteronomistic quarters, rejected the religious practices of Israel's neighbors that both Israel and its neighbors shared as a result of their common Canaanite heritage. High places constitute an especially pertinent example, since criticisms of foreign peoples sometimes include mockery of this religious practice.

Second, as noted in chapter 3, depiction of Yahweh became decreasingly anthropomorphic to some extent, especially in priestly and Deuteronomistic traditions.[7] These same traditions dominated the production and transmis-

6. One problem in comparing conceptions of deity in Ugaritic and Israelite literatures is the way in which scholars use different genres to serve as the basis for comparison. For example, depictions of deities in the Ugaritic Baal cycle, Aqhat, or Keret are commonly compared with descriptions of Yahweh in the Psalms. While there is certainly common material between these two groups, the relative anthropomorphism might be gauged better by comparing descriptions of deity in the Psalms and Ugaritic prayers (e.g., KTU 1.119.26-38). On these problems, see Cassuto, *Biblical and Oriental Studies,* vol. 2, *Bible and Ancient Oriental Texts,* 69-109; C. Conroy, "Hebrew Epic: Historical Notes and Critical Reflections," *Biblica* 61 (1980): 1-30; Cross, *Canaanite Myth and Hebrew Epic,* esp. viii-ix; Greenfield, "Hebrew Bible and Canaanite Literature," 545-60; Hallo, "Individual Prayers," 71-75; S. Parker, "Some Methodological Principles in Ugaritic Philology," *Maarav* 2/1 (1979): 7-41; S. Talmon, "Did There Exist a Biblical National Epic?" in *Proceedings of the Seventh World Congress of Jewish Studies: Studies in the Bible and the Ancient Near East* (Jerusalem: World Union of Jewish Studies, 1981), 41-61. It might be argued that Israel's lack of mythic material compared to its Canaanite neighbors is a further sign of its distinctive religious character. However, the strong mythic character in some apocalyptic material indicates that Israel continued to employ highly anthropomorphic renderings of Yahweh (see chapter 3, section 5, for discussion). For discussion of some of these problems in a theological framework, see Childs, *Myth and Reality,* 94-105. For the question of mythic material in the Deuteronomistic History, see Halpern, *The First Historians,* 266-71.

7. The labels "priestly" and "Deuteronomistic" are not intended to imply that proponents of Deuteronomistic theology did not participate in Israel's priesthood. Some members belonged to the Levitical priesthood in the northern kingdom down to the time of its fall and probably afterward, given the biblical indications of later religious activity (2 Kings 23:19; cf. 2 Chron. 30:1-

sion of biblical texts from the late eighth century to the sixth century. The phase of differentiation in the second half of the monarchy and the Exile coincided with the period of greatest literary production in ancient Israel, and it is precisely this phase of Israelite literary production where the priestly and Deuteronomistic traditions have so strongly left their mark. In contrast, textual material dating to the Iron I period is sparse, and the full range of religious phenomena from this period is lacking in the extant record.[8] Indeed, biblical tradition alludes in passing to now-lost textual sources of the Iron I period (Num. 21:14; 21:27; Josh. 10:12; 2 Sam. 1:17). It would appear that the priestly and Deuteronomistic traditions heavily influenced the divine roles exhibited in the Bible, at least for those roles that survive into postexilic Jewish literature, including the divine council (Zechariah 3; Daniel 7) and the heavenly temple (1 Enoch 14; the Songs of the Sabbath Sacrifice).

Third, a further process seems to underlie the omission of some roles. Divine language of sex and death did not survive at all, although polytheism in a Yahwistic context sporadically persisted. These omissions might be explained by appeal to the influence of the priestly and Deuteronomistic traditions. Given the priestly insistence on the impurity of death and sexual relations, it is difficult to resist the suggestion that the presentation of Yahweh generally as sexless and unrelated to the realm of death was produced precisely by a priesthood whose central notions of holiness involved separation from the realms of impurity, specifically sexual relations and death. For the priesthood there were several levels of cultic purity, and the deity represented the epitome of this hierarchy. Priests are restricted in their selection of spouses and also in their contact with the dead (Lev. 21:7), compared to non-priests (Num. 11–19; 31:19).

12; 31:1; 34:9; 35:18; Jer. 41:5). (To be sure, the reform of the cult of Bethel following the fall of the northern kingdom mentioned in 2 Kings 23:15 does not point to southern influence generally in the north, as Bethel belonged to the tribe of Benjamin. Due to its geographical proximity to the south, Benjamin became a virtual part of the southern kingdom, as Jer. 16:26 illustrates. For the northern border of Judah, see Cross, *Canaanite Myth and Hebrew Epic,* 109 n. 57) Some members of the northern Levitical priesthood came to Jerusalem in the wake of the north's fall. At this time Deuteronomistic views became influential in the southern capital (see Wilson, *Prophecy and Society in Ancient Israel,* 156-57, 298-306). The Levitical background of Deuteronomistic theology illustrates how much the Pentateuch and the historical and prophetic books were shaped by members of Israel's priesthood. Indeed, the development of the Hebrew Bible is due largely to the history of conflict and compromise between Israel's various priestly lines. For an analysis of the history of Israelite religion along these lines, see P. D. Hanson, *The People Called: The Growth of Community in the Bible* (San Francisco: Harper & Row, 1986); cf. S. D. McBride, Jr., "Biblical Literature in Its Historical Context: The Old Testament," *Harper's Bible Commentary,* ed. J. L. Mays (San Francisco: Harper & Row, 1988), 14-26.

8. Smith, *Palestinian Parties and Politics,* 19.

The chief priest is even more restricted than the priesthood in general (Lev. 21:11-13). Unlike other priests, the chief priest is associated with the holiness of the divine sanctuary. Holier than the holy of holies, the deity constituted the fullest manifestation of holiness, one totally removed from the realms of sexuality and death. Given the development of this concept within priestly circles, it might be understood as an inner-Israelite development and not necessarily an original feature of Yahweh. This rendering of Yahweh may have been aimed not only against other views of Yahweh or other deities in ancient Israel to whom sexual relations and death were attributed, but perhaps specifically against family religious practices and life, which included contact with the deceased ancestors and belief in a household religion headed by a divine couple (as modelled in their own family life).[9]

The absence of divine sex and death from the biblical record may belong to a reaction that predates the priestly and Deuteronomistic production of biblical texts. Given the historical viability of Baal language down to the ninth century and the virulent opposition to Baal from the ninth century and afterward, the divine roles involving sex and death and polytheism perhaps ceased early in some priestly and Deuteronomistic quarters. Perhaps in the areas of divine sex and death, reduced anthroporphism constituted a significant factor. Reduced anthropomorphism apparently belonged to an earlier stage of Israelite religion and continued through the Exile. It may therefore help to explain the general reduction of the goddess in Israelite religion and the omission of the roles of sex and death for Yahweh. In any case, thanks to the evidence that Genesis 49 provides, it may be surmised that polytheism was part of the religion of Israel prior to the tenth century, and in the case of the "Queen of Heaven" and perhaps other minor deities, afterward as well. Similarly, divine roles in sex and death could have belonged to the repertoire of descriptions for Yahweh or other deities worshiped by Israelites prior to the tenth century, and possibly afterward, although no evidence known at present supports this reconstruction.

In conclusion, the cults of the major deities developed differently in Israel and its neighbors. Religious developments specific to Israel played a role in the processes underlying the selection and shaping of the main divine roles and images for Yahweh from Israel's Near Eastern heritage, especially manifest in Canaanite and Mesopotamian texts and traditions.[10] Like other Near

9. For these points, see M. S. Smith, "Yahweh and Other Deities in Ancient Israel," in *Ein Gott allein?* ed. W. Dietrich and M. A. Klopfenstein, 222-23.

10. T. Jacobsen, *The Treasures of Darkness: A History of Mesopotamian Religion* (New Haven: Yale Univ. Press, 1976), esp. 164; Petersen, "Israel and Monotheism," 92-107.

Eastern deities, Yahweh provided fertility in the cosmos, acted as ruler of the world, and showed the care of a divine parent. Yet, unlike other deities who combined these functions (such as Marduk), Yahweh exercised a variety of roles, even sometimes conflicting ones, to the detriment of the cults of other deities. Yahweh sometimes embodied apparently contradictory capacities. Yahweh was seen as manifest in nature and beyond nature; Yahweh was sometimes anthropomorphic and yet beyond humanity. Imaged in the human person (Gen. 1:26-28) yet only partially imaginable (Isa. 55:8-9), Yahweh was a deity sufficiently powerful both to protect (Psalm 48; Isa. 31:4) and punish Israel (Jer. 9:8-9). Yahweh was equally a personal deity (Deut. 4:7), whose pain matched Israel's pain (MT Jer. 9:9 [E 10]; cf. 12:7-13). Yahweh consoled Israel (Isa. 40:2), answered Israel (Exod. 3:7; Ps. 99:8; Hos. 2:23-25 [E 21-23]), and loved Israel (Hos. 2:16 [E 14]; Job 37:13). Yahweh's qualities were often expressed in terms largely shaped by the characteristics of other deities belonging to ancient Israel's heritage that Israel rejected in the course of time.

Indexes of Texts

BIBLICAL CITATIONS

Genesis

Exodus

OTHER NEAR EASTERN INSCRIPTIONS

CLASSICAL

Index of Authors

General Index